PRELUDE TO TERROR
The Rise of Hitler 1919-1923

PRELUDE
TO TERROR

The Rise of Hitler 1919-1923

Richard Hanser

Rupert Hart-Davis London

Granada Publishing Limited
First Published in Great Britain 1971 by Rupert Hart-Davis Ltd
3 Upper James Street London W1R 4BP

Copyright © 1970 by Richard Hanser

ISBN 0 246 64049 9
Printed in Great Britain by Fletcher & Son Ltd,
Norwich

FOR ANNE

"The foundations are shaking . . . something is creeping up that threatens to destroy us . . . Listen, and you will hear the new pulse-beat of our time."

Kurt Tucholsky, 1920

CONTENTS

Prelude To Terror

BIRTH OF A MYTH

"THE.RE IS A STERN TIME COMING. I SHALL SEE TO THAT."
—ADOLF HITLER

THE CHURCH BELLS of Berlin were striking noon on January 30, 1933, when the official announcement came that Adolf Hitler was the new Chancellor of Germany. The city promptly erupted. People poured from their homes and shops and taverns, and embraced each other in the streets. Impromptu parades and spontaneous demonstrations turned the Monday afternoon into a sudden festival, and by nightfall the Government Quarter was teeming with jubilant thousands who were sure that, in a troubled time, the savior of the nation had at last appeared.

Through the Brandenburg Gate came unending columns of singing and shouting Storm Troopers with torches that flared weirdly against the darkness. They surged along the broad avenue of Unter den Linden and flooded into the Wilhelm Strasse toward the gray stone mass of the Chancellery. There they chanted their hoarse and exultant chorus of *"Sieg Heil!"* and *"Heil Hitler!"* all through the night.

Adolf Hitler stood at a second-story window with arm upraised in acknowledgment and salute as the flaming procession streamed by below him hour after hour. The way was now open before him. Soon far mightier legions than these would march out at his command and make him absolute ruler of an empire stretching from Africa to the Arctic, and the time was nearing when he would astound and appall the world as no Alexander or

Napoleon had done before him. But now it was sufficiently incredible that he should be standing in the Chancellery window at all.

Once, years before, when his fortunes were at their lowest, with his National Socialist movement in collapse and himself in jail, he had boldly predicted that one day he would come into power "with mathematical certainty." Nobody had believed it; there seemed no reason to. But now power was his, and there was reason enough for his brown battalions to shout *"Sieg Heil!"* —"Hail victory!"—all through this January night.

The scene of his triumph was necessarily Berlin, but Berlin was a place he never liked. Not long after the last torch had guttered out in the rising dawn, the new master of Germany arranged to leave his capital and board a plane for Munich.

Munich was his city.

Nobody was more awed by Adolf Hitler's rise out of nowhere and nothing to unparalleled world significance than Adolf Hitler. All his life he harped on the wonder of it in public speeches and private conversations. Even at the pinnacle of his power, while the world shook to the tread of his invading armies, he paused in the midst of a major address for a personal reminiscence on the subject: "When I set out on my course in 1919 as an unknown, nameless soldier, I built my hopes for the future upon a most vivid imagination. Yet all has come true." Over and over the theme recurred: "When we let the years pass before our eyes in memory, it is a marvelous story that unfolds itself." He called the growth of this movement "a miracle . . . an absolute miracle," and he said:

"To posterity it will appear like a fairy tale."

This obsession with his own career as something fabulous, almost supernatural, was what brought him to Munich almost immediately upon his assumption of power. For here had occurred one of the most curious and significant events not only in his personal history but in the history of his time. He was bent on transmuting this event from the bloody fiasco it had originally been into a Wagnerian epic of overpowering proportions. Out of it he would create the central fable of his own legend, and to it he would build a shrine at which the entire German nation might worship.

The site of his myth-making was the Odeon Platz, a spacious and attractive square in the heart of Munich. Across its south end extends an Italianate pavilion called the *Feldherrnhalle,* the Hall of the Field Marshals, which houses the quite commonplace statues of two not very distinguished generals. On this spot, ten years before, Adolf Hitler's first bid for power had collapsed in the gunfire of the Bavarian State Police, and sixteen of his followers died at and around the *Feldherrnhalle.* He himself had run away, only to be arrested a few days later and brought to trial for high treason.

It was this abortive insurrection, this *Putsch,* which he now hastened to Munich to commemorate, though the wiser course might well have seemed to relegate it forever to the past and forget it. In Germany the march of Hitler and his Storm Troopers to the *Feldherrnhalle* had been scoffed at and dismissed as a "Wild West stunt," and a "piece of melodramatic buffoonery." Outside Germany the incident was derisively labeled "the beer-hall *Putsch,"* since the futile uprising had first been proclaimed in a tavern to the clatter of beer steins.

But time, and a supreme irony of history, had transformed Hitler's rash and bungled venture of 1923 into one of the major milestones on his road to power, and he knew what he owed to it.

So now, with a few close followers, he reverently approached the *Feldherrnhalle* and laid a huge wreath on the steps. Across it was a wide ribbon with the inscription:

"UND IHR HABT DOCH GESIEGT!"

The words were addressed to the sixteen men who had died there—"And you were victorious after all!"

The saying became a kind of incantation for an elaborate and idolatrous *Putsch*-cult that grew from the initial ceremony. "We are determined," Hitler said, "to make this a Holy Day for the German nation in the future and for all time." Rite, ritual

and liturgy were evolved until the annual wreath-laying acquired
heavy layers of religious solemnity and Teutonic mysticism.

The sixteen were enshrined as "the first blood witnesses of
the movement," and it was written in the Party scriptures that
"from their blood grew the seeds of a new time in all the lands of
Germany." Regularly each year, on the anniversary date, all the
survivors of the march assembled at the beer hall, formed up in
their original order, and paced off the same route to the *Feldherrnhalle* with measured tread and to the sound of muffled
drums. Along the way, smoking funeral urns lined the streets,
and hidden loudspeakers intoned the names of the dead at set intervals between passages of majestic music.

Later, twin Romanesque temples were built near the center
of the city, and the bones of the martyrs were ceremoniously
reinterred in two enormous bronze coffins, one in each temple.
Over them black-uniformed *SS* sentries kept guard day and night
in what was called "The Eternal Watch." Pedestrians were required to raise their arms in salute as they passed, and school-
children were made to memorize the orthodox version of the
Putsch as part of their elementary education. A Party poetaster
composed a dithyramb that said:

> *"Let others erect cathedrals.*
> *"Our altar is the steps of the Feldherrnhalle."*

As creator, idol and High Priest of his own myth, Adolf
Hitler particularly fostered the cult of the *Putsch,* and especially
favored Munich as the Holy City of National Socialism. He officially designated it the "Capital of the Movement," kept his residence there, and returned to it as often as circumstance allowed.
Only in Munich, perhaps, could he have launched his revolution,
and only there could the special conditions have arisen which
made his emergence certain and his ultimate success possible. It
is not surprising that in his first formal speech in Munich as
Chancellor he said, "For me this is more than a city. I am devoted to it in boundless love."

He was not the only one to speak extravagantly of the

place. In *The Web and the Rock* Thomas Wolfe asked, "How can one speak of Munich but to say it is a kind of German heaven?" and he called it "a great Germanic dream translated into life." Thomas Mann wrote warmly of his "lovely and leisurely city" where he produced some of the greatest novels of his time. Munich was the first to hear *Tristan und Isolde, Die Meistersinger* and *Das Rheingold,* which were composed and magnificently presented there, and there Richard Strauss was born and developed his genius. The most profound innovation in twentieth-century art occurred in a Munich studio where Vassily Kandinsky conceived the first abstract painting, and there the pathfinding works of Paul Klee were first shown to the world. The two greatest German poets of modern times, Stefan George and Rainer Maria Rilke, were contemporaries there, and the first revolutionary dramas of Bertolt Brecht were written for Munich stages.

"Athens on the Isar" it was called, after the river flowing through it, and everything enlightened and liberated flourished in Munich as nowhere else in Germany. And there was, besides, the ambrosial beer, the superb sausages and the untranslatable *Gemütlichkeit*—the congeniality and coziness—of its restaurants, wine rooms and beer cellars. All in all, the inhabitants might be excused for considering their town the most attractive in Germany, one of the most inviting in Europe, one of the most civilized in the world.

But by a great paradox of history, this became the focal point from which the infection spread that poisoned all Germany and required the surgery of mankind's worst war to remedy.

Lion Feuchtwanger pondered this terrible transformation of his birthplace in one of his books, *Erfolg.* Writing of what happened there in the early 1920's, he said: "Formerly the beautiful, easygoing city drew to itself all the best talents of the Reich. How was it that they were gone now, and in their place everything that was rotten and evil in the Reich, and could not maintain itself elsewhere, fled as if magically attracted to Munich?"

The causes that changed Munich from the city of Thomas Mann and the poets to the domain of Adolf Hitler and his Storm Troopers were many and complex, and they involved war, defeat and revolution. But the decisive factor was the presence, in that place and at that time, of Adolf Hitler himself.

He began by talking in the dingy back rooms of the beer halls, and his talk had incalculable consequences. Shabby little groups of bitter and rancorous men listened to him, and what he said was what they wanted to hear. He said that the German army had never been defeated in the World War just ended, but had been foully done to death by sinister forces behind the lines. He said that the Versailles Peace Treaty was a murderous outrage on a broken and humiliated people. He said that Germany's new democracy was a deliberate fraud designed by Jews and traitors to complete the destruction of the nation. He said that Germany must gird itself for a day of vengeance and reckoning.

In the social and political turmoil of postwar Munich, a hundred other speakers were saying the same things in a hundred dingy meeting places. But no one spoke as this one did. Some strange and disturbing power, which even today cannot be completely described or explained, went out from him with his words. Something primitive and compelling in his voice, like the thump of tom-toms, arrested and electrified his listeners. His speeches were calls to violence, and the time was sodden with the hates and resentments that hear such calls gladly.

"It is our mission to cause unrest," he said. *"Jawohl,* we want to stir up a storm! The people must not be allowed to sleep. They must know that a tempest is coming!" Over and over, at first to only twenty and thirty at a time and then to thousands, he repeated his summons to upheaval and revolt. They called him the *Trommler,* the drummer, for never in modern times had Germany heard anything like the insistent, hypnotic beat of his oratory.

But centuries before there had been another like him, and he, too, was called the *Trommler*—the Drummer of Niklashausen. He, too, emerged from nowhere, from out of the anonymous mass, and spoke with an astonishing eloquence that stirred a wild excitement among the people.

He was a shepherd who suddenly began haranguing the

peasants and artisans in taverns and market places, attacking first the local lords and princes and then the whole social system of his day. As his fame spread he addressed thousands at once, sometimes from the top of a tub, sometimes from an upper window or from a tree. He represented himself as one sent by God, and his message was always revolutionary and violent against the constituted authorities. "The Emperor is a scoundrel and the Pope is useless," he told the people. "Alas, poor devils that you are!" The oppressed and impoverished and resentful in all the towns and villages along the Valley of the Tauber flocked to hear him. He seemed to be speaking out of their own souls, but with flaming words which they themselves could not command. He seemed to know with uncanny instinct what was in their hearts, and to echo it in a way that seemed to the simple peasants nothing less than supernatural. He made all their deepest aspirations sound like his own, and they saw in him a *Führer,* a leader and protector, sent by providence in a dark hour. He created a mass hysteria whenever he spoke, and his followers swarmed around him in such numbers and with such fervor that guards were needed to save him from being crushed to death. People snatched pieces of his clothing and treasured them like sacred relics. His town of Niklashausen became another Holy City, and his following grew and spread from the Valley of the Tauber throughout the land.

The time came when the uproar and unrest that the Drummer of Niklashausen was causing could no longer be tolerated, and the Prince-Bishop determined to put an end to his inflammatory talk and re-establish the authority of the Town Council. The Drummer's followers rose up to protect him, and there were bloody riots and fatal clashes. The Drummer was tried by an ecclesiastical court and found guilty of sorcery and heresy. When he was burned at the stake, his ashes were thrown into the river lest they be gathered up and worshiped by his followers . . .

That happened in Germany in 1476, at a time when the social order seemed to be disintegrating, when civil discord was rampant, when nameless fears of the future gripped the populace. In such times the people look for prophets and saviors with mysterious powers to appear and somehow set things right. In a similar time, and in a like way, Germany's new *Trommler* appeared, but no prince-bishop or town council was able to step across his path and stop him before it was too late.

He went on to cause more death and destruction than any man in history. He became the architect and instigator of what Winston Churchill called "the horrors and miseries of this ferocious epoch," which history will know as the Hitler Era. At the high tide of his career, 400,000,000 people were under his yoke; and when the combined might of the three greatest powers on earth at last succeeded in bringing him down, more than 30,-000,000 human beings were dead by battle, bombing, torture, hunger, disease and execution.

It is a record so monstrous that one of his own closest followers, repentant in a death cell at Nuremberg, could only liken him to a cataclysm of nature. "Around his name," wrote Dr. Hans Frank, who was Hitler's Governor-General of Poland, "is the reek of millions of corpses, of ruins, starvation, despair, decay and horror.

"He was the greatest and most dynamic factor of destruction that humanity so far has had to endure. One has to think of catastrophic upheavals of nature, of revolutions, of plagues and pestilence, in order to find an example to compare him to."

And yet, when he first raised his voice in the pleasant city on the Isar, he was often laughed at as a comical little figure with a Charlie Chaplin mustache, or ignored entirely. When he started on his way, nothing seemed more probable than that he was merely another ranting malcontent destined to pass quickly from the scene and be soon forgotten. "I would have jeered at anyone who prophesied that this was the beginning of a new epoch in world history," said Konrad Heiden who was a student at the University of Munich in the early '20's, watched the first ragged demonstrations of the Nazis, and scuffled with them on the streets. Only later would Heiden, one of the pioneer chroniclers of Hitler's rise, write of him: "As a human figure, lamentable; as a political mind, one of the most tremendous phenomena in all history."

The *Putsch* that made Hitler was also blindly misjudged when it happened, and misinterpreted for years thereafter. By many it was classed with the comic-opera riots of the previous century caused by Lola Montez, the Irish mistress of the Bavarian King, who stirred up the Munich citizenry by combining an extravagant fondness for jewelry with an unwelcome passion for social reform. The Hitler *Putsch* was dismissed as just another such manifestation of the native tendency to erupt into theatrical violence from time to time, usually for no good reason and with no lasting effect.

But what happened at the *Feldherrnhalle* on November 9, 1923, came, with the perspective of time, to be called "that most momentous farce in all history" and to be recognized as the "prologue to a world drama of frightful and frightening dimensions."

In only ten years the march that began at a Munich beer hall ended with the torchlight parade in Berlin that hailed Adolf Hitler as master of Germany.

1 THE OUTCAST

"TO THAT PERIOD I OWE IT THAT I GREW HARD . . ."

—ADOLF HITLER

AUGUST KUBIZEK, an upholsterer's helper in the town of Linz on the Danube, had a favorite spot in the standing-room section of the local opera house where he never missed a performance. After a day of coping with burst sofas and decrepit wing chairs in his father's shop, he would rush to buy one of the earliest tickets and hurry inside to the two wooden pillars that supported the Royal Box. The advantage of the pillars was twofold, since the position afforded an unobstructed view of the stage and also provided something to rest against during the long performances. Freshly washed and hoping that he didn't still smell of glue, August Kubizek could lean back and give himself up to the enjoyment of the opera.

In later years he didn't remember the date precisely, but sometime around All Saints' Day in the year of 1904, Kubizek began to notice a particular rival in the standing-room section. A strikingly pale and intense youth of about August's own age, sixteen, appeared at the coveted pillars, often arriving first. A rather forbidding air of superiority about the newcomer, who followed the opera "with glistening eyes," prevented quick familiarity, and it was some time before any words were exchanged. Even then the first conversations were confined to brief comment between the acts on the quality of the performances. Kubizek, who was studying the viola in his spare time, noticed that, while

12

his pillar-mate seemed to have little technical knowledge of music, his opinions were always sharp and assured.

August Kubizek was impressed.

The shared enthusiasm of the two boys for the opera gradually closed the distance between them, and one evening they walked together to the home of the newcomer in the Humboldt Strasse. On parting, Kubizek learned the name of his companion for the first time: Adolf Hitler.

Thereafter they were together frequently, on walks through the town, along the banks of the Danube, and on excursions into the countryside. Before long, August Kubizek regarded his chance acquaintance of the opera house as his best friend. In the course of the ensuing four years they were to become roommates, and the young upholsterer's helper of Linz learned to know Adolf Hitler more intimately as a private personality, and came into closer human contact with him, than anyone else ever did throughout his life.

It was an odd and lopsided relationship that developed between them, never an easy friendship. From the first it was Hitler who dominated, though he was the younger by nine months at a time when such age differences count heavily with boys. Kubizek's role remained that of the acknowledged inferior, the admiring adherent, the receptive audience, and he accepted his status with hardly a reservation or protest. Forty years later he was still disturbed and awed at the memory of his early involvement with a personality that, strange and unsettling enough at the time, turned out to be "a scourge and mystery to the world."

What impressed Kubizek particularly at the start was that his friend was a poet and artist. On their walks together, Hitler would sometimes stop, take a black notebook from his pocket, and read out a poem he had written. He frequently showed Kubizek drawings, sketches and designs of his own, and his talk was mostly of art and of the great artist he intended to be—"my beautiful dream of the future," as he called it. Young Hitler was also something of a dandy, meticulous about his clothes, and stiffly insistent on good manners and correct behavior.

Promenading along the main street of an evening, as was

the custom in Linz, he wore black kid gloves, twirled a small ebony cane with an ivory head and sported the faint beginning of a mustache. But there was never anything frivolous or light-hearted about him. He was abnormally serious, reserved and tense for his years.

Apart from Kubizek, whom he called "Gustl," he had no friends, and he seldom spoke of his family or background. When he did, he seemed to be carrying on a protracted dispute with his dead father, who had violently opposed his ambition to become an artist.

Alois Hitler, the father, had been a Senior Collector in the Imperial Austrian Customs. He was determined that his son Adolf should also become a civil servant, the calling that had raised the father from impoverished peasant beginnings to comparative affluence and to respectability. He was, Adolf recalled long afterward, "struck speechless" at the idea of his son's becoming a painter. "Never! As long as I live, no!" But his stubbornness was matched by his son's, and a bitterness grew between them that lasted until the father's death, and on the son's part it did not end even then.

Adolf was living off his mother's pension, and resisting the repeated suggestions of relatives and family friends that he stop dabbling in poetry and painting, and go to work. But the idea of settling into the same mold as his provincial schoolmates, and so grant his father a posthumous victory, infuriated him. It was one of the many subjects that could set off the kind of outburst that so often stunned his friend Gustl. Some inner pressure seemed constantly to demand release, and it came, not from his poems and paintings, but only in repeated explosions of words. "These speeches, usually delivered somewhere in the open," Kubizek recalled, "seemed like a volcano erupting. It was as though something quite apart from him was bursting out of him." At first Gustl hardly knew how to respond, but he soon learned. "All he wanted from me was one thing—agreement." Gustl Kubizek gave it unstintingly. He was the first to succumb to the peculiar power of Adolf Hitler's oratory; it began by dazzling a single boy in Austrian Linz and would, not many years later, overwhelm thousands in German Munich, and millions more thereafter.

In some way that defies analysis, the young Hitler appears to have had an intimation of what was coming, an early conviction that destiny had marked him. Kubizek caught a disquieting glimpse of this one November evening after the opera. On the program was Wagner's *Rienzi,* which neither of the boys had seen before. They were both enthralled at the musical drama based on the life of the Roman tavern-keeper's son whose tempestuous career raised him to glorious heights as tribune of the people, but whose violent and dictatorial rule led to his downfall and assassination.

When it was over, young Hitler left the theater in what seemed to his companion a kind of trance. His usual gush of comment on the performance was not forthcoming, and he did not allow Kubizek to speak, either. He silently led the way through the dark and sleeping town to the Feinberg, a hill on the outskirts. "As if propelled by an invisible force," he climbed to the top.

There he gripped Kubizek by both hands, a thing he had never done before, and began to talk feverishly, almost incoherently. He appeared to his companion to be "in a state of complete ecstasy" in which he applied the story of Rienzi's rise to himself and his own future. Someday, he said, he, too, would receive a mandate from the people, and lead them to new heights of glory.

Kubizek was shaken. "It was an unknown youth who spoke to me in that strange hour," not the cane-twirling dandy of their usual promenades. "Many years had to pass before I realized the significance of this enraptured hour."

More than thirty years did pass before the incident was mentioned again between them, and by that time Adolf Hitler was the *Führer* of Germany and on the verge of unleashing the Second World War. He and Kubizek met, for the first time after many years, in Bayreuth at the home of Wagner's son, Siegfried. Hitler had not forgotten the *Rienzi* night on the mountain when he was seventeen. He described the whole episode to Frau Wagner, just as Kubizek remembered it, and he ended his story with the statement: *"In jener Stunde began es"*—

"In that hour it began."

During the years in Linz, however, it was not apparent that anything was beginning. He was aimless and self-indulgent, with a gaunt, unhealthy look and eccentric habits. While others attended school, or learned a trade, or found jobs, he holed up in his room and scribbled poetry, painted pictures and devoted days to grandiose designs for rebuilding the city of Linz. His ailing mother bought him a piano she could barely afford, and he took lessons from a Prof. Prevratski for a time, but was incapable of applying himself to the exercises, and gave it up. Though he was accomplishing nothing and getting nowhere, he carried himself with an invincible air of superiority, and furiously resented any suggestion of advice or reproof.

A passing lung ailment gave him an excuse to break off his schooling, which he never resumed. He had started out as an unusually bright pupil, but his grades steadily deteriorated through a laziness and indifference that he afterward attributed to his quarrel with his father. It was his indirect way of defying what he called the "ruthless authority" of his parent. He began to get report cards studded with "Below Standard," and he failed one grade completely. In the end he left secondary school for good without a certificate.

In view of subsequent events, his class reports show two curious notations. His last report card cited him as "Very Satisfactory" in Moral Conduct, and he regularly got bad marks in German. He never mastered the grammar and spelling of the language he was destined to use with more power and effect than any German before him.

He himself recalled only one teacher with admiration. This was Dr. Leopold Pötsch, his history professor at the Linz Technical School, whose influence, according to Hitler, was "perhaps a determining factor for my entire later life." Dr. Pötsch inflamed him with the virulent German nationalism that was to remain an obsession, a mania, all his life. Using colored pictures of the life of the ancient Teutons, and what the pupil remembered as "dazzling eloquence," Dr. Pötsch fired his imagination with visions of Germanic grandeur that never left him. "How could anyone study German history under such a teacher," Hitler later wrote, "without becoming an enemy of the state . . . ?"

He meant the state of his birth, the Austro-Hungarian Empire, with its mixture of contending nationalities, languages and dialects, which he learned to despise from childhood. From his earliest school days, in various towns, like Lambach, Hafeld and Leonding where his restless family lived, he constantly heard slogans like: "German boy, always remember that you are *German*," and "Little girl, never forget that you are to be a *German* mother." He came to feel himself superior to the conglomeration of peoples that comprised his native land, and a member of a greater and more exalted racial community, the German.

With other budding Pan-German fanatics among his schoolmates, he wore a cornflower as a symbol of loyalty to the Prussian House of Hohenzollern. He defiantly sang *Deutschland, Deutschland über alles* rather than the prescribed Hapsburg anthem. He used the Germanic greeting *Heil!* rather than the Austrian *Grüss Gott*. "The greatest inner experience" of his childhood, he said, was the reading of an illustrated book on the triumphs of the German Army in the Franco-Prussian War of 1870. "From then on I became more and more enthusiastic about everything connected in any way with war and soldiering," he remarked. He played at war tirelessly, often recruiting younger boys to continue with him when companions of his own age grew bored with the game.

Another kind of make-believe in which he steeped himself was inspired by tales of the American West written by Karl May, whose novels he devoured as a boy and continued to read long after his boyhood was past.

Karl May was a phenomenon of German literature, a convicted thief and swindler who, in jail and out, wrote a series of adventure stories that won him the biggest audience any German author ever enjoyed. Without ever having seen America, he produced dozens of wild and woolly romances about trappers, hunters and Indians. Somehow these tales so gripped the imagination of his readers that it was said he "exerted more influence on the German people than Shakespeare did on the English."

A generation of German boys adored such May heroes as "Old Shatterhand," the intrepid frontiersman, and Winnetou, the noble chief of the Apaches. Old Shatterhand was a kind of Tom Swift of the Wild West, a dead shot at impossible ranges with his trusty rifle that could repeat forty-eight times and wipe out an entire herd of buffalo. The Westerners in the May books spoke a peculiar language of his own invention, bursting forth in moments of tension with such expletives as *"Zounds!"* and *"'s death!"* or, in their lighter moods, *"Heigh-day!"* Footnotes were sprinkled liberally through the books to explain the fabricated Western lingo May continually used. The German reader learned that *Leggins* were Indian pants, that a "braggart" was a *Grossmaul,* and that when a *Westmann* said, "Hang it all!" what he meant was *"zum Henker!"* Karl May's Indians did not say "How!"; they said "Howgh!" His stories were bloody and violent, shot through with a kind of cold cruelty that was only intensified by the accompanying pious declamations and mystical overtones. The heroism of May's protagonists was equated with animal cunning and savage trickery, always described with relish as being worthy of applause and admiration. But May had a primitive story-telling gift that riveted millions to his pages.

Men like Albert Einstein and Albert Schweitzer were also enthusiastic Karl May fans in their youth. Like many others they read him as an innocent pastime of boyhood. To Adolf Hitler the stories meant far more. When he became Chancellor of Germany, a seven-foot expanse of his bookshelf was taken up with the works of Karl May. In the first years of his regime he read them all through again. And he was not alone in sensing something more than juvenile fantasy and penny-dreadful adventure in the tales. For him Old Shatterhand was a Siegfried in buckskin, a symbol of the Teutonic superman who by guile, craft or brute force strikes down every enemy in his way. The heroes of Karl May, though they performed their fabulous deeds in a mythical American West, were basically idealized Prussians, exemplars of a master race that conquered wherever it went and invariably showed itself superior to lesser breeds.

It was indicative of the quality of Adolf Hitler's mind that the sleazy romances of Karl May made so deep and lasting impression upon him. How deep the impression was may be gauged by the assertion of a brilliant German intellectual that Hitler's later actions and attitudes were strongly influenced by his reading of Karl May, and that many of Old Shatterhand's deceptions and stratagems were reflected in the reckless policies of the Third Reich. "It is hardly an exaggeration to say," Klaus Mann wrote in 1940, "that Karl May's childish and criminal fantasia has actually—though obliquely—influenced the history of the world."

It is tempting to speculate on how different the history of the world might have been if the young Hitler had been able to find fulfillment as an artist, if his gift for drawing and design had been great enough to absorb his energies and divert him from becoming the Shatterhand of European politics. Instead, his early artistic bent led to the most decisive rejection of his life, and to that furious rebellion against society that "closes up the channels of the soul and shuts out the airs of heaven."

In the fall of 1907, when he was eighteen, he decided that he had outgrown Linz and was ready for the world beyond. Perhaps the repeated urgings of his guardian and relatives that he finally start doing something constructive with himself prompted him to action. He had just come into a small inheritance from his father, about $150, enough for a year's study at the Academy of Fine Arts in Vienna, where he now intended to embark seriously on his career as a painter. With a thick pack of drawings under his arm, and a satchel that the faithful Gustl lugged to the station for him, he set out for the Imperial City.

He was certain that he would pass the entrance examination for the Academy of Fine Arts *"spielend leicht"*—it would be child's play for him. After all, he noted, he had been by far the best at drawing in his class at the Technical High School, and since then, he thought, his talent had developed greatly.

"My own satisfaction caused me to take a happy pride in hoping for the best."

He rented a room on the third floor of 29 Stumper Alley, a rundown building near the West Railway Station in a lower-middle-class section. The room was tiny and dingy, and stank of kerosene from the lamp. Here he prepared for the Academy tests, which required candidates first to submit sample drawings on given subjects. If these were found to indicate sufficient talent, a further examination was required.

Adolf Hitler took the tests twice, and failed completely both times. The files of the Academy preserved his record:

Composition exercises in drawing. First day: Expulsion from Paradise, etc. Second Day: Episode from the Deluge, etc. . . . The following took the test with insufficient results, or were not admitted: . . . Adolf Hitler, born Braunau-on-the-Inn, April 20, 1889, German, Catholic. Father civil servant. 4 classes Technical School. Few heads. Test drawing unsatisfactory.

The second judgment repeated the fatal phrases: ". . . *insufficient results . . . Not admitted to the test.*"

He was staggered. "I was so confident of my success," he wrote, "that the announcement of my rejection struck me like a thunderbolt from a clear sky." He demanded an explanation from the Rector of the Academy, believing that some mistake must have been made. Afterward he reported that the Rector advised him to apply for admission to the School of Architecture, since his drawings showed his real talent to lie in that direction. Whether it did or not, the School of Architecture was no solution; a high school certificate was required before entrance, and this Hitler had failed to receive because of his poor work and indifference at the Technical School.

"For the first time in my young life," he wrote, "I was at odds with myself." His deep-seated confidence, the inborn conviction that he was destined for greatness, was shaken. His cherished image of himself as an artistic genius—hadn't he already brilliantly redesigned the entire city of Linz?—was cracked. He could not bear to tell anyone of his defeat, neither his mother

nor his friend Gustl. He went back to his reeking cubbyhole in
the Stumper Alley and resumed littering the place with sketches
and designs, refusing to acknowledge the judgment of the Academy. In the periodic registrations required by the Vienna police,
he continued to describe himself defiantly as "art student" and
"painter." But with his failure at the Academy of Fine Arts, a
hidden turning point in his career, and in the history of his time,
had been reached. He would never become a painter. He would
never become an architect. He would become something else.

In December of 1907 his mother died of cancer—Klara
Pölzl Hitler, whose fourth child he was. Her first son, Gustav,
had died in his second year. Her second child, Ida, had died at
the same age. Her third, Otto, was dead within a few days of his
birth. But her fourth, Adolf—he had lived.

Klara had been a peasant girl from a dreary and barren district known as the Waldviertel, in Lower Austria, where she spent
an unhappy girlhood with her impoverished family. At fifteen
she was a servant in the home of Alois Hitler, by whom she was
pregnant when she became his third wife ten years later. She was
remembered by neighbors as a neat and submissive housekeeper
who had "nothing to smile about" in her life with her husband,
who was twenty-three years older than she. The boy Adolf resembled her, and for a while she had hoped he would become a
priest. He showed some signs of doing so when they were living
in Lambach and he was singing in the cloister choir there. As he
grew older she understood him less and less, and could not help
believing that his father was right in insisting on a solid civil-
service career for him. She was bewildered and distressed by
Adolf's desire to be an artist, but she pampered him and supported him, and defended him against the attacks of her relations, saying: "He is different from us."

She made him, as he said himself, a mama's boy—a
"Muttersöhnchen"—and she went to her grave believing that her
Adolf was a student at the Academy of Fine Arts who would
make himself famous in the world as a painter. Klara Pölzl Hitler never knew that she had mothered a monster.

Adolf came home for the funeral, and took her picture

back with him to Vienna. "Adolf really loved his mother . . . ," Kubizek wrote, and then added a curious reinforcement that would seem quite unnecessary in the case of anyone else—"I swear to it before God and man." With Klara Hitler's death, the only living link that held Adolf to his roots was broken. From then on he was emotionally isolated in the world, with none of the normal ties and affections that warm and humanize most of mankind. After his mother, he never again had a satisfying love relationship with anyone at all.

Early in 1908 August Kubizek escaped from the upholstery shop, his skill on the viola having developed so satisfactorily that he felt justified in making music his career. He came to Vienna to study at the Academy of Music, and moved into No. 29 Stumper Alley with Adolf Hitler. They occupied a slightly larger room than the one Adolf had been using, but it had the same reek, was just as dingy, and was still so small that Gustl had to climb on a bed to make room when Adolf paced up and down during his interminable tirades and declamations.

"He was at odds with the world," Gustl discovered. "I had the impression that Adolf had become unbalanced." He was continually erupting in fury against society, against a system that was not granting him the opportunity he deserved to exercise his talents, against the decadent and misbegotten city of Vienna. Kubizek was dismayed as he listened to his roommate "choking on his catalogue of hates," the face livid and tense, the eyes with the peculiarly penetrating stare that would transfix so many others.

And, like millions to come, young Kubizek felt drawn and fascinated by the speaker in spite of himself. When the raving was over, he could hardly remember what it had been about, but certain phrases, often repeated, would lodge in his mind. "The less they actually meant, the more they impressed me," he said, and he often found himself agreeing even when his own convictions were basically the opposite. He afterward attributed this phenomenon to his friend Adolf's "overwhelming gift of persuasion," but it puzzled him all his life.

Kubizek had been accepted by the Conservatory after the

usual tests, and he was still under the delusion that Adolf was formally enrolled at the Fine Arts Academy. Every morning Kubizek arose promptly, and set off for his classes. His roommate was seldom up when he left, and seemed to have no schedule. When Adolf spoke of the Academy at all, it was only with contempt and derision. The place was run by a miserable pack of outright incompetents. It was governed by brainless bureaucrats who knew nothing about art. And so on. But once, when Gustl ventured to defend the Academy as a place where, after all, Adolf must be learning something useful about drawing and painting, the truth came out.

Adolf went white to the lips, as he did in his sudden seizures of fury. "They rejected me!" he finally admitted. "They threw me out! They turned me down!"

Gustl was appalled for his friend. "Nothing more terrible could have happened to him," he felt.

Thwarted as a painter, unacceptable as an architect, Hitler attempted to retain his vision of himself as an artistic genius by turning to writing. In erratic bursts of energy, he outlined plays and conceived elaborate dramas based on his favorite reading at the time, a volume called *Legends of Gods and Heroes: the Treasures of Germanic Mythology.* His conceptions were always super-Wagnerian in scale and, as even young Kubizek could see, impossible to produce. Though he had no technical musical training, and could play no instrument, he plunged into the composition of an opera about *Wieland the Smith,* full of Nordic violence, family murders and incest. This, like all his early attempts at authorship, remained fragmentary and was soon discarded. He spent much of his time on a stone bench in the Schönbrunn Park, avoiding contact with people and feeding the birds and squirrels. Kubizek's diffident suggestion that he would do well to find a part-time job met with no response, and he continued to drift and fume, spending his days posing as an artist without doing anything to justify the title.

In the summer of 1908, Gustl Kubizek went home to Linz to spend his vacation from the Conservatory with his parents. He and Adolf agreed to resume their arrangement in the Stumper

Alley in the fall. When Kubizek returned, however, the landlady told him that Hitler had moved out. He left no forwarding address, and no message. Without a word to his friend, he had simply disappeared. Kubizek did not see him again for thirty years. When, in the intervening time, August Kubizek first heard reports of a rising politician in Munich called Adolf Hitler, he thought it must be somebody else of the same name. To Kubizek it had always seemed certain that his friend Adolf would become great in architecture or art. The idea that the companion of his youth was destined to be Chancellor of Germany, to say nothing of a latter-day Genghis Khan, would have seemed too fantastic. Even at the end, when it was all over and his former roommate had inflicted unsurpassed agony and ruin on the world, August Kubizek could hardly bring himself to believe it. He could only, in a sincere but bewildered memoir on his boyhood friend, pose the unanswerable question: "What were God's intentions when He created this man?"

Adolf Hitler's disappearance from the Stumper Alley opened a phase of his career so decisive for the future that he was able to write of it afterward: "During this period there formed within me a picture of the world, and a view of life, which became the granite foundation of all my activity. Afterward I needed to add but little to the philosophy I created for myself then. And I needed to change nothing."

He had vanished because he had no choice. His small patrimony gone, and still without work, he could no longer afford a room of his own. He became one of Vienna's thousands of floaters and vagabonds, roofless at night and with neither fixed base nor goal to give stability to the day. For many months he drifted through the slums of the metropolis, sinking deeper and deeper into the netherworld of the uprooted and discarded. He slept on benches or the grass of the parks when the weather was mild, and went creeping into charity hostels for the homeless when it turned cold.

Flophouses became his habitat, and soup kitchens supplied his sustenance. He was seen in the shuffling queues that lined up daily for a handout at the Sisters of Mercy Convent in the Gumpendorf Strasse. An old-clothes dealer, a Hungarian Jew named Neumann, took pity on him and gave him a tattered overcoat, and he was grateful. One night he begged a rich drunk for money, and was almost beaten for it with the man's cane. He ate horse sausage when he could get it, and in such dismal sections of the city as working-class Brigittenau he encountered a kind of degradation he had never known before.

Years afterward he still "shuddered in horror," he said, at what he saw and experienced there—"those miserable holes where people lived, the lodgings and tenements, those repulsive expanses of garbage, disgusting filth and worse." He was gripped by an intense revulsion against his environment, an unquenchable sense of outrage that this should be happening to *him*. He became convinced that nothing less than "the most extreme and brutal measures" would avail against "this world of misery and poverty" into which fate had cast him. "Brutal" and "extreme" were words that remained permanently embedded in his vocabulary.

"To that period," he wrote, "I owe it that I grew hard."

He spoke afterward of earning his bread as a day laborer on construction jobs, and this allowed him to address meetings of working men with matey "I-was-one-of-you" phrases. But in reality he worked only sporadically. He lived in terror of forfeiting his status as a member of the middle class, and slipping permanently back to the lower level from which his father had only just managed to climb. He did not want steady work as a laborer, and nothing short of the threat of starvation could compel him to do any manual work at all. According to one of his own stories of his Vienna time, he so stoutly resisted the demand of his fellow workers on a construction job to join their union that they threatened to throw him off the scaffold. He left the job rather than join, but he took with him another lesson for the future. The method that had been used against him with such effect, he noted, was the one "which most easily overcomes reason —terror and violence."

His subsequent hatred of trade unionism, and of the Social

Democracy that was its traditional political expression, was rooted in his Vienna experience, and never left him. But in Vienna, too, he became indelibly impressed by the immense power latent in the labor movement. He watched the mass demonstrations of Viennese workers, the long columns marching four abreast,—that "monstrous human dragon," he called it—and he never forgot the overpowering effect of those disciplined ranks. They were marching, he thought, in a contemptible cause. But what if they could be made to fall in step to another tune?

Even in the loose and undemanding camaraderie of the social underworld, among his fellow bums and rejects, he was considered an eccentric and could find no human contact. Even among outcasts, he was an outcast. "I drank my bottle of milk and ate my piece of bread somewhere off to one side," he wrote, "and covertly studied my new surroundings or pondered my wretched situation." He felt himself infinitely above the men he worked with, when he did work. He gave himself airs—"my speech was cultured and my manner reserved"—that must have infuriated his more earthy fellows and won him many a contemptuous cursing, if not physical blows.

He came to see existence as a jungle where the strong and secure prevail ruthlessly over the weak and exposed, and· he came to regard jungle law as the proper and inevitable order of nature. He himself had always been in conflict with his environment, first in the collision of wills with his father when he had had to submit to a higher authority that could not be altered or broken, but only circumvented by craft and guile. (One had to be both wolf and fox to survive.) He had clashed with the Academy of Art, and again authority had prevailed, unjustly but decisively. Now his adversary was the whole city of Vienna. It had also rejected him and was attempting to crush him completely. And Vienna was the world.

There was no possible way to win except, somehow, to obtain sufficient power and authority of one's own to be able to dominate, prevail, and strike back ruthlessly in turn. This was the way of the world, and it was foreordained. "If the strong get the better of the weak, it is an inexorable law of life," wrote the much-admired German historian Heinrich von Treitschke, whose books became part of Hitler's library. From his own experience in Vienna—which, he said, "I could feel on my skin and taste with my soul"—Hitler developed his own version of the world as jungle: "The fundamental motif through all the centuries has been the principle that force and power are the determining factors. All development is struggle. Only force rules. Force is the first law." It was the law he lived by ever afterward.

But even the most ferocious Darwinist is seldom above accepting outside assistance to assure that the fittest—*i.e.,* himself —will indeed survive. Hitler, in his desperation, turned to a relative for financial help. His maternal Aunt Johanna, a humpback who was said to be not quite normal, sent him some money and rescued him from complete degradation. Early in 1910 *Tante* Johanna's charity enabled him to move into a halfway respectable Home for Men, which became his residence for his three remaining years in Vienna. It happened none too soon. A fellow drifter who saw him in the home on his first day there described him as follows:

"There was a man sitting on the bed next to mine who wore nothing but a pair of torn pants. It was Hitler. His clothes were being deloused. He had been without shelter for days, running around in a terribly tattered and rundown condition."

The home was designed for men alone in the world who were making only meager or uncertain incomes, and it accommodated about 550 persons. Besides an iron bed with a mattress, double blanket and horsehair bolster, it provided bath facilities and recreation rooms where the men could read and play chess or dominoes. It also provided temporary salvation of a sort for Adolf Hitler.

He went into partnership with a fellow inmate of the home, a Bohemian tramp named Reinhold Hanisch, who was enterprising enough to see commercial possibilities in Hitler's knack for drawing. Using the recreation room as his studio, Hitler turned out a series of cramped, unimaginative copies of Vienna sights —the Burg Theater, the Schönbrunn Park, the Parliament House—which Hanisch then peddled on the street and in taverns

for a few pennies apiece. Hanisch was essential to the arrangement, since Hitler was unable to approach strangers and strike
up even the most passing contact with them. He was, a witness
says, "terribly shy" about his drawings, throwing his arm across
the paper to hide them when anybody chanced to look over his
shoulder while he worked. He never mastered perspective, and
his few attempts to draw a human head or figure turned out la-
mentably.

The partnership broke up when Hitler suspected that he
had been cheated out of his 50 percent share of the proceeds of
one of his pictures, and hauled Hanisch into police court for
fraud. Thereafter Hitler continued to make a scanty living with
other middlemen. Some of his work survived his rise to eminence, notably an advertisement for "Teddy's Perspiration Powder," signed "A. Hitler," and a poster featuring the spire of St.
Stefan's rising majestically out of a mountain of soap. This was
what his dream of being an artist had come to.

He did not, in fact, spend much time at his drawing, having
no fundamental feeling for it. Whenever he contrived to gather in
a few Kronen, he promptly abandoned his art work and spent
his time haunting the cafés and coffee houses where his true interests and inclinations could unfold.

He was an insatiable newspaper reader, consuming three
and four at a sitting, and what stirred him to passionate outbursts and arguments was never art or literature or music, but
only politics. In the cheap cafés and coffee houses of Vienna,
and largely from its gutter press, Adolf Hitler gradually accumulated the store of ideas, convictions and beliefs that became his
ideological arsenal for the future. Not one of the ideas was original with him. They were all rife in the atmosphere of the time
and place, circulating freely and available to anyone. Like thousands of others, he merely sopped up and retained whatever answered to his nature and conformed to his prejudices and pre-
conceptions, blindly rejecting everything else. The difference was
that the shabby, neurotic Adolf Hitler—white-faced at a corner
table, devouring his copies of the anti-Semitic *Deutsches Volks-
blatt* and the racist *Ostara,* day after day—possessed something

the others did not, something that has since been recognized as a "hideous genius," peculiar to himself. In his hands the meanest ideas were capable of becoming political and psychological explosions that could rock a world.

This was the time, he wrote later, when he experienced "the greatest inner upheaval" he ever knew. He lived in an almost constant state of agitation, and his own account of the period is studded with phrases like ". . . the blood rose to my head," ". . . a cold shudder ran over me," ". . . my revulsion became boundless," and "I was outraged . . ." Everywhere he looked, in a city that others thought incomparable for its charm and light-heartedness, he saw something to arouse his fury and trigger one of the sudden harangues with which he often startled the inmates of the home and the habitués of his favorite cafés.

He was outraged that lesser races like the Czechs, Serbs, Hungarians, Croats and Slovenes should dare to contend for precedence with the German element that so obviously deserved unquestioned supremacy within the framework of the twelve-nation Empire. The mingling of the races in society and government, the parliamentary system that attempted to give each nationality a reasonable representation, the intermarriage of Magyars and Czechs with Germans, of Jews with Christians— all this appalled him. It affronted his belief, cultivated by Prof. Pötsch and the slogans of his boyhood, that German blood in itself was a warrant of unassailable superiority, and must be kept undefiled at any cost. Vienna's widespread disregard of these sacred principles was intolerable to him. "To me," he wrote, "the giant city seemed the embodiment of racial desecration."

It was a curious obsession for a man of Adolf Hitler's background. His own origins were so clouded that when he was born in the little town of Braunau, on the border between Austria and Bavaria, the identity of his paternal grandfather was unknown, and it remains unknown to this day. The Waldviertel district of his ancestors was notorious for inbreeding and even incest, and any idea of his own racial "purity" becomes absurd in view of the murkiness surrounding his antecedents. His mother may have been of Bohemian extraction; his name quite possibly derived from "Hidlar," which could be Czech (Hidlarček). At any rate, it was spelled in a variety of ways in his native district—Hytler, Hietler, Hütler, Hüedler, and so on. His father Alois was born out of wedlock to a peasant woman named Maria Anna Schickl-gruber who, five years afterward, married a penniless stray named Georg Hiedler. Alois bore the surname Schicklgruber all through the first forty years of his life, and even his ultimate legitimization as Alois Hitler occurred under extremely dubious circumstances. It took place only twelve years before the birth of his son Adolf, the future fanatic of racial purity, who was in all likelihood part Bohemian, part Czech, part German, and part whatever his unknown grandfather may have been—to say nothing of other vagrant strains that may well have been introduced by generations of tangled couplings in the Waldviertel.

But Adolf Hitler never let objective fact change or dilute his passions and prejudices. He was a corrupt dreamer who saw the world in a vision of his own, which reality could not seriously affect. To Schopenhauer's "The world is my idea" he added "*I* am my idea." Those who passed him on the Vienna streets saw an unprepossessing figure of medium height, with pasty face, receding forehead and distinctly un-Nordic hair of nondescript brown. He saw himself as a shining paragon of all the Teutonic virtues, physical and spiritual—a human Holy Grail filled with the precious blood of an exalted and unsullied lineage.

Though in his autobiography he made much of the agonizing soul-struggle that converted him to anti-Semitism, calling it "certainly the most difficult transformation of all for me," Hitler was in fact ready-ripe for it when he arrived in Vienna, where it was rampant. Large numbers of impoverished and unassimilated Jews from the eastern provinces crowded the district where Hitler lived, and they provided ready targets on which to discharge his hatred and contempt. "Once when I was sauntering through the inner city," he wrote, "I suddenly came upon an apparition in a black caftan and black earlocks." He was appalled. "Is this a German?" he asked himself. His answer was, of course, no; and not to be a German was itself heinous. The anti-Semitic press, which became his favorite reading matter, confirmed him in his suspicion that the specter in caftan and earlocks was not only no German, but hardly human. In the economic and political deterioration of a creaking empire, the Jews were cast in their immemorial role of scapegoats, and freely blamed for everything from the decline of agriculture to the rise of prostitution. Heinrich von Treitschke's saying that "the Jews are our misfortune" was a handy formula, applicable at all times to all situations, and repeated with a thousand variations.

The most dynamic public figure in the Vienna of the time was Dr. Karl Lueger, the mayor, who used anti-Semitism as a political weapon, although one of his own ancestors was Jewish. "Handsome Karl" the mayor was called, a vigorous and gifted man who could dominate crowds and generate mass reaction with his inflammatory speeches. Hitler admired him greatly, calling him "the most powerful German mayor of all times." He noted and filed away for future use Dr. Lueger's technique of playing on the fears of the economically threatened middle class, and his employment of "all existing instruments of power" to gain his ends.

But Lueger's anti-Semitism did not satisfy Adolf Hitler. It was modified by humane considerations, and was political and social in content, not racial. This was not nearly extreme enough for the seething outsider who simultaneously ached to strike back at an environment he hated and burned to find a place in it. He needed stronger meat, and Vienna provided it.

In a tobacco kiosk Hitler chanced upon a series of pamphlets and brochures, published at irregular intervals under the title of *Ostara*. They featured headlines such as: ARE YOU A BLOND? THEN YOU ARE A CULTURE-CREATOR AND A CULTURE-RETAINER! and: ARE YOU BLOND? IF SO, DANGERS THREATEN YOU! READ "OSTARA"!

Subtitles promised revelations on subjects such as "Race and Nobility," "Race and Foreign Affairs," and "The Metaphysics of Race." The editorial policy was explained as "the practical application of anthropological research for the purpose of . . . preserving the European master race from destruction by the maintenance of racial purity."

The editor, who wrote most of the pamphlets himself, was a

renegade Cistercian monk who called himself Dr. Jörg Lanz von Liebenfels. On leaving his monastery he founded a cult that he named "The Temple of the New Order." Only men who were blond and blue-eyed, and who pledged themselves to marry only blond and blue-eyed women, could belong. Anyone at all, however, could buy *Ostara* by paying thirty-five pfennig at a kiosk. Adolf Hitler became such an enthusiastic reader that he took the trouble to seek out Lanz von Liebenfels for a personal interview, and to request some back numbers he had missed. Lanz not only gave him a batch of free copies, but, taking pity on his scruffy appearance, also gave him two kronen. Years later, when Hitler was well on his way to domination of Germany, Lanz was able to write proudly to another of his followers: "Do you know that Hitler is one of our students?"

He was indeed. Almost every phase and aspect of the racial doctrines that ultimately led to Auschwitz and Buchenwald, and the murder of millions, can be found in the preposterous pages of *Ostara,* which Hitler read during his Vienna years. Passage after passage in *Mein Kampf,* which became Hitler's own blueprint for atrocity, read like paraphrases of *Ostara* articles. Dr. Wilfried Daim, a Viennese psychologist who wrote a book on Lanz von Liebenfels, called it *Der Mann, der Hitler die Ideen gab*—"The Man Who Gave Hitler His Ideas."

The ideas themselves were of such incredible foolishness that, reading them, one pauses in amazement at the realization that they could have had such staggering consequences. But Adolf Hitler took them seriously, and what he did with them became appalling proof of the saying of the Indian philosopher Sarvepalli Radhakrishnan: "If we believe absurdities, we shall commit atrocities."

Writing in a turgid, pseudo-scientific style, Lanz divided mankind through the ages into two classifications. For the first group he used a number of names with heroic and mythical connotations—*Asinge, Arioheroiker, Heldlinge*. These were the white, blond, blue-eyed members of the species, and in them resided, by virtue of blood and breeding, all that was great, cultured, admirable, exalted and superior in the human race. On the other hand, there were the *Äfflinge, Waninge, Schrättlinge, Tschandale*—all names with implications of ape-like inferiority, baseness and subhuman worthlessness. In them resided everything vicious, mean, contemptible and disgusting in man's physical and spiritual nature.

All history and all culture was a mortal contest between these two breeds—a contest that the lesser was threatening to win by defiling the blood of the superior through intermarriage and bastardization. No greater catastrophe could be imagined for the world than this progressive pollution of the bloodstream of the master race by the insidious encroachments of the dark subhuman, the *Tschandale*.

Lanz was tormented by a recurrent vision of the blond, blue-eyed women of the higher breed succumbing to the erotic advances of dark seducers. His quasi-profundities about race and blood purity were sodden with sexual fear and envy, and shot through with a morbid hatred of the female. He repeatedly stressed the lust of blond women for dark men as the main source of the corruption that was threatening to destroy the God-given superiority of his *Heldlinge*. "Through woman, sin came into the world, and it is so over and over again because woman is especially susceptible to the love artifices of her animal-like inferiors." Therefore the blond male must ever and always be a Siegfried, slaying dragons and giants as his Teutonic forebears did, and thus, by his heroism and virility, winning and dominating the blond female and keeping her from the clutches of the dark seducer.

On this contest between the light and the dark, Lanz taught, hung the future of mankind, the fate of the world. The issue was of such transcendent importance that no method was too stern or extreme to maintain the supremacy of the master race. A holy crusade was called for: "Blonds, arm yourselves for the reconquest of the world!" Subdue the *Tschandale* and make them your servants, for the enslavement of inferior races is ethically justified by the divine right inherent in superiority of blood. If necessary, kill and exterminate to keep the race pure—and here Lanz proposed measures that would read like a bill of particulars from the Nuremberg War Crimes Trials thirty-five years later. Lanz advocated forced labor as a way of exploiting the *Tschandale*. He urged mass deportations: ". . . out into the jungle with them where the apes and baboons will greet them as 'comrades' and racial relatives." He anticipated the "final solution" of the Nazis in all its phases and aspects: castration, sterilization and complete extermination (". . . *Zertretung und Ausrottung des Ur- und Untermenschen*").

"The day will come," said *Ostara,* "when the hybrid breed will have to be eradicated from the face of the earth."

Of the 100,000 circulation that *Ostara* sometimes reached in Austria and Germany, no reader was more receptive to its teachings than the part vagabond and part-time artist, Adolf Hitler. In a café called *zur Goldenen Kugel* he hotly defended Lanz's theories against scoffers and skeptics, and he discussed them by the hour with whoever would listen to him in the Home for Men. He counted himself a member of the master race as a matter of course, though he was distinctly not blond and his eyes were a dullish gray-blue at best. The doctrine allowed for that, however, by stating that racial superiority was indicated by the sum total of physical attributes involving the size and shape of nose, hands, feet, skull and even buttocks. Blue-gray eyes were awarded twelve plus points on the superiority scale; black eyes meant twelve minus points. Adolf Hitler would never be mistaken for a Nordic demigod, but he had no difficulty ranking himself among the *Asinge* and *Arioheroiker*. It made him feel part of something grander than his mean surroundings. It made him one of the elect according to what he called "the aristocratic principle of Nature," which for him was unassailable and unalterable. And if the immutable laws of creation ordained all history to be a death struggle between the racially elect and the *Untermensch,* the subhuman, he thus acquired a higher sanction for his instinctive cruelty and self-aggrandizement. "I believe that I act in conformity with the will of the Almighty Creator," he wrote later. *"In defending myself against the Jew, I am fighting for the work of the Lord."* The italics were his.

Lanz took pains to cultivate this aura of religiosity and

mysticism around his movement. Ritual and language that derived from his monastic background embellished the ceremonies of the cult, and the pages of *Ostara* were decorated with runes and symbols taken from mythology and legend. One of the symbols used repeatedly was the swastika, whose origin is unknown but which occurs mysteriously in every major civilization from the earliest onward. It has been variously interpreted as standing for good fortune, the cycle of life, sex, and even (when its upper arm points to the left instead of to the right) death. Lanz emblazoned a swastika—in red—on the flag of his cult, and hoisted it as early as 1907. It may have been the first of all swastika banners.

He survived to see one like it, but with the symbol in black, flying from the spire of St. Stefan's Cathedral in 1938 when the scruffy vagabond who was his disciple returned to Vienna in triumph to take over the city, and the country, where he once begged in the streets. Lanz von Liebenfels lived long enough, in fact, to see the swastika banner hauled down again, and trampled underfoot, and his theories with it. The exact degree of responsibility he bears for what happened to the world between the rise and fall of the swastika can never be accurately assessed. But this scribbling psychopath with his insane *Ostara* remains one of history's most disturbing examples of the unforeseen consequences that can flow from even the basest and most preposterous ideas.

As for his disciple, Adolf Hitler, "a long, internal struggle of the soul had reached its conclusion," as he put it later. During his time in Vienna he had, he felt, read, studied and meditated so profoundly on what he called the "inner conditions" of human society that he had found the basic truth he'd been searching for. "The racial question," he decided, "supplies the key not only to world history, but to the culture of mankind in general."

This profundity, by which he lived thereafter, was, of course, another of his borrowings. Sixty years earlier, in a many-volumed essay called *On the Inequality of the Races,* the Comte Joseph Arthur de Gobineau had said the same thing in almost identical words. So had, among others, Houston Stewart Chamberlain, and Guido von List, and a man named William Marr who, in 1873, coined the phrases "anti-Semitism" and "anti-Semite." But they had merely put their beliefs on paper. Adolf Hitler was equipped to put them into effect.

Now he was ready to move on. Looking back at that time, he wrote: "Vienna was and remained the harshest, if also the most fundamental, school of my life. I first entered this city still half a boy, and I left it a man grown calm and serious. Here I acquired the basis of a world philosophy in general, and a political outlook in particular, which later on I only had to supplement in detail, but which never left me."

But, by every outward sign, Vienna had been a complete failure for him. He had accomplished nothing, advanced himself not at all, and was in fact worse off financially and socially after five years than when he arrived. He hated the city, and now there was nothing to hold him there.

"A yearning grew stronger and stronger within me," he wrote, "to go at last to the place to which my secret wishes and secret love had drawn me since early youth."

He meant Germany, the German Reich.

He left for Munich.

2 MUNICH

". . . IT IS AND REMAINS INSEPARABLY BOUND UP WITH THE DEVELOPMENT OF MY OWN LIFE."

—ADOLF HITLER

THE EXACT DAY of Adolf Hitler's arrival in the city he was to make his own is not known for certain. It remains one of those hidden dates in history that go unnoticed at the time but in retrospect mark the faint beginnings of world-changing events to come.

Some time toward the end of May in 1913, perhaps on the 25th, he came to Munich and rented an attic room in the home of a tailor named Popp, on the Schleissheimer Strasse in the district called Schwabing. He was then twenty-four years old, still virtually penniless, without work or income, and with no better prospects than Vienna had offered him. But from the first he felt he had arrived where he wanted to be and where he would stay.

"A *German* city!!" he wrote of it, using italics and double exclamation points to express his elation at being there. Of all German cities, he had chosen this one because he still thought of himself as an artist, and Munich was incomparably the city of German art. Munich's strange misfortune was that precisely its finest and most civilized aspect became the lure that attracted the advocate of a new barbarism that would taint its name forever.

In 1913 the city was something of a vast art gallery, an *al fresco* panorama of styles and periods where Gothic and baroque, classic and rococo, mingled generously without clash or dissonance. From its center the twin domes of the Cathedral of

Our Lady, the *Frauenkirche,* reared 300 feet into the air like two enormous eyes keeping a constant but indulgent watch over a well-ordered spread of squares and avenues, fountains and parks, museums and monuments, beer halls and gardens, and innumerable lesser churches. The cathedral's powerful Gothic dominated the scene without imposing its tone upon it. Everywhere the native German solidity was relieved by an exotic lightness expressed in airy and antic façades that revealed the touch of Latin hands.

Situated nearly midway between Paris to the west and Vienna to the east, with the Alps juśt on the south and the Danube to the north, the city sat at a cultural crossroads of the continent and responded to the play of aesthetic movements from all four directions. As the residence of the reigning house of Bavaria, it was additionally favored by the resolve of the Wittelsbach kings to make their seat as beautiful and impressive as possible. When Ferdinand Maria, Elector of Bavaria, married into the House of Savoy in the seventeenth century, his bride brought her entire court, including a retinue of artists and artisans, across the Alps with her. Masters of Italian baroque gave the face of Munich a capricious southern look. From Paris another Wittelsbach monarch summoned the genius-dwarf Francois Cuvilliés, who contributed yet another bright cadenza to the rich orchestration of Munich's architecture with rococo masterpieces like the Residenz Theater, where early Mozart operas were first performed.

The place seemed almost as much a setting as a city, a stage designed for gaudy and implausible events. The people, though, often appeared to have been miscast and were somehow inappropriate to their *mise en scène,* like characters from another play who had blundered into the wrong theater. Deliberate and heavy in look and manner, they were in pronounced contrast to the picturesqueness of their surroundings. Amid the sophisticated baroque and fanciful rococo, they exhibited an incongruously rustic mien that seemed more suited to the city's agricultural outskirts and the nearby mountains. Many of them looked more at home in the *Viktualienmarkt,* the open-air market in the heart of the town, than anywhere else. If there was a storybook atmosphere about the buildings of Munich, there was an unmistakable earthiness about its people.

"In the Bavarian," a native novelist wrote, "you won't find a delicate, cultivated, lovable character. Rather, you find quiet speech and a composed outward appearance, but with them a tendency toward roughness and violence, as well as to coarse pleasures, great reserve, and suspicion of strangers."

The seedy stranger Adolf Hitler seemed among the least significant of Munich's 600,000 inhabitants. The poverty and defeat of Vienna still clung to him, and he added to his rootless and vagabond air by registering with the police as "stateless." This was, perhaps, a gesture of contempt and renunciation toward his homeland, since his move across the border had in no way invalidated his Austrian citizenship; but if he could not yet officially call himself a German, he would call himself nothing else.

The home of Popp the tailor was in a poor quarter of the town near an army barracks. Though Hitler had now escaped from the slums of Briggitinau and the Home for Men, his new situation was not much of an improvement socially or financially. Still chronically impoverished, he was often forced to take any odd job that came his way to avoid actual hunger. It was from this period of hand-to-mouth scrabbling that the later contemptuous references to him as a former house painter and paper hanger stem—references that never failed to infuriate him; but whether he ever painted a house or hung a strip of paper is not reliably recorded. Years afterward a neighborhood priest recalled that Hitler now and then earned a few pfennig by running out for beer when a card game was going at tailor Popp's of an afternoon or evening, hardly an exalted mission for a twenty-four-year-old man.

Still, the sorry reality of menial errands and a cubbyhole under the eaves had no effect on his conception of himself as a burgeoning genius of the arts. Having failed in Vienna to make even a start as either painter or architect, he now represented himself as an "architectural painter." The title was sufficiently grandiose to invigorate his ego, always in need of artificial stimu-

lus, and to provide him with the sense of superiority to his surroundings that his fantasy of himself demanded.

"I had the conviction," he wrote of this period, "that one
day I would achieve the artistic goal I had set for myself in spite
of everything. And this made it possible for me to face the minor
difficulties of everyday existence easily and without concern."

He took to selling his sketches and water colors again, making postcard and souvenir paintings of the local sights, as he had
done in Vienna. Necessity sometimes forced him to overcome his
aversion to direct human contact and peddle them himself on
Munich's broad Leopold Strasse, where tourists might be encountered. He sometimes designed commercial posters, and was
not above using his brush to paint news of the day's bargains on
the windows of grocery and butcher shops.

"My earnings were extremely meager," he wrote, "but, after
all, I was not living in order to paint, but painting to earn a living, or rather to secure the means of continuing my studies."

Had he actually possessed the artist's gift and temperament
—if his talent had been in fact what he fancied it to be—the
time and place could not have been more propitious for him.
Munich in the years before the First World War was not only the
"metropolis of German art" that Hitler called it but also a center
of creative ferment and innovation whose impact was felt far beyond the borders of Germany. As an art student, Adolf Hitler
had undoubtedly come to the right place.

The district of Schwabing where he lived was a preserve of
artists, writers and intellectuals unmatched anywhere except perhaps on the Left Bank of the Seine. It was the combined Latin
Quarter and Montmartre of Central Europe, with overtones of
Greenwich Village and Bloomsbury. Sprawled over the northeast
area of the city, it glittered with studio skylights and was lavishly
sprinkled with art shops, book stalls, cafés and coffee houses. The
University and the spacious park called the English Garden, with
its five-story Chinese Pagoda, were on its fringes, though the
boundaries of the district were never strictly defined. *"Schwabing,"* the saying went, *"ist kein Ort, sondern ein Zustand"*—it
wasn't so much a place as a condition.

42

Hitler's home at Nr. 34 Schleissheimer Strasse was on the farthest permissible edge of Schwabing in a neighborhood more colorless-shabby than colorful-Bohemian, and there was no skylight in the roof of his attic room. He was, nevertheless, officially registered as an artist, and as such was automatically numbered among Munich's *Schlawiner,* which was the mildly derisive nickname applied locally to the out-at-elbows gypsy types who swarmed through the district with canvases under their arms, manuscripts in their pockets, or merely uncut hair and loose cravats to advertise their genius.

In a self-pitying letter that Hitler wrote to the authorities, he complained of the difficulty of maintaining himself as a freelance in competition with the "nearly three thousand artists" who, as he put it, "live or at least try to live here." But Munich of that time, and particularly Schwabing, was as stimulating and inviting for an artist as any other place in the world. It was a town where a new and genuine talent could send a thrill of excitement through the streets, and where a fresh and daring stroke of technique brought crowds clustering around the window of the art shop where it was displayed.

In the Munich of this period a pivotal incident so profoundly changed the direction of painting that its effects are still reverberating. It occurred in 1910 in the Schwabing studio of Vasily Kandinsky, a Russian who had abandoned professorships in law and economics to study art under the Munich masters.

"One day as dusk was falling I came home with my paintbox, still dreamy and bemused by the work I had been doing," he wrote afterward. "Suddenly, there in my studio, I saw an indescribably beautiful picture that glowed with an inner radiance. I was dumfounded at first, and then hurried toward this puzzling painting on which I could see nothing but forms and colors, and whose subject was incomprehensible . . ."

He discovered the mysterious picture to be one of his own that had been left leaning against the wall on its side. The overwhelming impression made by the lines and colors alone, when emptied of their objective meaning, confirmed Vasily Kandinsky in a radically new philosophy of art toward which he had long

been groping—"pure" painting devoid of representational content. Shortly afterward he created the first abstract water color,
and thus launched the nonobjective movement that critics have
since called "the most decisive breakthrough in twentieth-century
art."

Amid this sunburst of artistic activity, Adolf Hitler continued to hawk his little sight-seeing sketches on the streets, unaffected by the expanding horizons of the special world of Schwabing.

His obsession with art stayed with him all his life, but it
remained stubbornly narrow, stilted and sterile. He never heard
"the whispering of colors" as Kandinsky did, and there could be
no place for him within the circle of the elect because he could
paint only the surface of what he saw, contributing no dimension
or depth from any vision of his own. As an unregarded drifter
on the lower level of a community that offered him no acceptance, he only added to his mounting store of hatreds and resentments by conceiving a boiling animosity against those who were
succeeding where he was so obviously failing. To him the experiments of modern art were nothing but the "symptoms of the
decay of a slowly rotting world." The inner necessity that drove
him was not to create new worlds through art, but to destroy the
one that continued to reject him.

The delusion that he was a painter had brought him to
Munich, but for his as yet unsuspected development into a political force he seemed to have chosen the least likely spot in all
Germany. The city, when he first came to it, was famous
throughout the continent as a "happy island" of tolerance and
freedom, generously disposed toward all the liberal values and
attitudes that he was subconsciously preparing himself to attack
and destroy. On the surface, nothing could have seemed more
implausible than that the solid and comfortable social structure
of the time and place would, within a few years, be rocked to its
roots by revolution, and then dominated and corrupted by this
obscure alien.

Though second to Prussia in size and influence in the German federation of 26 states, Bavaria regarded itself as easily su-

perior in all ways that really mattered. In comparison with its beautiful lakes and cloud-capped mountains, the north seemed barren and unalluring. In contrast with the more sunny and easy-going mode of life below the Danube, the harsh efficiency of industrial Prussia seemed positively repellent.

In their cozy inns and taverns, at the unpainted wooden tables scrubbed white with sand and water, rural Bavarians had reason to lift capacious mugs brimming with Bavarian beer and toast themselves in Bavarian dialect: *"Mir san gsund!"*—we're healthy, here's to us, we're all right. The toast echoed in the flourishing cities, in Regensburg and Augsburg and Nuremberg, and especially in the capital, Munich.

A Schwabing humorist who signed himself Roda Roda once began a satirical sketch on the city by calling Munich "the capital of the world," and then going on to give its longitude (48°10′) and latitude (11°35′), as if all three statements were equally accurate and equally beyond dispute. As a parody of city pride and local chauvinism, it was hardly more extreme than the reality. A guidebook that lapsed into momentary candor by admitting that "the high elevation of 520 meters results in a rather severe climate" immediately made amends by adding that "over it all gleams a sky more Italianate in its radiance than that of any other German city." Heaven itself reserved its special favor for Munich.

It was, after all, still the seat of kings. Ludwig III, who came to the throne in 1913 after a long regency, was not a very striking figure, being small and looking rather like a provincial professor of church history, a subject on which he was, in fact, learned. But as a Wittelsbach he represented the oldest princely house in Germany, and the citizenry regarded him fondly as he went for his daily stroll accompanied only by a lackey and cordially returning the greetings of his subjects as they passed by.

The citizenry lived mainly from brewing, the town's major industry, whose boast of producing the best beer in the world was not seriously challenged anywhere this side of Pilsen. Trading in vegetables, fruit and wood, along with banking and the art business, contributed further jobs and profits to the general prosperity.

But, while social conditions seemed uncommonly placid along the Isar, there was an intellectual ferment in the city that brought to the surface symptoms of uneasiness and discontent to clash with the prevailing *Gemütlichkeit.* The radical experiments of the abstractionist artists were only one manifestation of a spreading dissent from tradition and convention. The satirical weekly *Simplicissimus,* published in Schwabing and read all over Germany, constantly derided the standards and personalities of the day in slashing caricatures and recklessly impertinent prose and verse. Its editors, cartoonists and writers were jailed from time to time, and the magazine was now and then suppressed, but enough leeway remained for a drumfire of mockery and ridicule against the established order, its idols and ideals. The weapon here was humor, which the authorities were inclined to grant a certain indulgence, but deeper and darker tones were also being sounded.

Today a Munich square is named for Frank Wedekind, and charming little essays are written about him as one of the colorful eccentrics of Schwabing's greatest years, but when he was alive he seemed an improbable candidate for municipal honors. He sang in the disreputable cabarets of the quarter, delivering his own songs with a nasal vigor and accompanying himself on the guitar. He was notorious for his *Henkershumor,* his hangman's humor, and in a nightclub called The Eleven Executioners he gave performances that were called "astounding and insulting." Sardonic and saturnine, with an aggressively beaked nose, he viewed the world with a scalding contempt for morality and convention that made his listeners gasp.

As a dramatist he stunned and appalled audiences all over Germany with plays like *Pandora's Box* and *Earth Spirit.* They centered on sex and depravity with such uninhibited candor that a critic wrote, "In German literature today there is nothing as vile as the art of Frank Wedekind." He filled his stage with violence and abominations committed by a repellent array of scoundrels, degenerates and murderers—characters so crude and grotesque that they sometimes seemed laughably improbable. But Wedekind's plays reflected a latent ferocity in the society around him, and his characters exhibited the indelible mark of the beast in human nature.

When war came, his admirers retroactively endowed his plays with prophetic virtues; they were regarded as portents. But even while the milieu in which Wedekind worked still seemed outwardly serene and safe, his plays were seen as revelations of something dire and submerged in his surroundings. The American author and journalist Percival Pollard, enthusing in 1910 about the happy state of the arts in Munich, was brought up short by Frank Wedekind. "What he has dared to do," Pollard reported, "is to lay bare all the brute in normal, as well as abnormal, mankind." And he added that upon the German theater Wedekind had "gashed the irremediable savagery of our time."

It was an acute comment. When it was made, the slaughter of Flanders and Verdun was in the offing; and the Munich of which Pollard wrote would, not long after, add immeasurably to the savagery of the age by launching Adolf Hitler upon the world.

Another German author then living in Munich was also writing of social disintegration and moral decay, and in works far more subtle and profound than the lumbering histrionics of *Pandora's Box* and *Earth Spirit*. He was a genius, and was already deep in the body of work that would win him a Nobel Prize. By a symbolic coincidence of history, the artist colony of Schwabing was harboring, side by side, the two men who most completely personified the uttermost extremes of German culture and the German character: Thomas Mann and Adolf Hitler.

Though they never met, the worlds they represented were to clash catastrophically; and years later, in exile, Thomas Mann admitted a kind of personal relationship between himself and his onetime neighbor. In a strange essay called *Bruder Hitler*— "Brother Hitler"—he discerned the lineaments of the eternal artist and dreamer, however perverted and diseased, in the chaos of Hitler's personality, and acknowledged him to be a genius of a special kind. For the phenomenon of the shiftless *Schlawiner* who rose to the mastery of Europe Mann admitted "a certain shuddering admiration," and in it he saw an event of almost mythological dimensions.

"There are traits of the legendary about it all—distorted, of course . . . ," he would write. "The motif of the poor, wool-gathering simpleton who wins the princess and the kingdom; the ugly duckling who becomes a swan; the Sleeping Beauty surrounded by a rose-hedge instead of Brunnhilde's circling flames and smiling as her Siegfried hero wakes her with a kiss. . . . It is ghastly, but it all fits in, as well as many another folk-tradition, mingled with debased and pathological elements. The whole thing is a distorted phase of Wagnerism . . ."

In his art and in his person, Thomas Mann himself reflected the ominous ambiguity of his time and place. A model of the cultivated middle-class German, he was fastidiously correct in manner and demeanor, aloof and apart from the raffish elements of the Bohemian community in which he lived.

But what he wrote of was disorder and decay, and his theme was disease and death. Where others could see only stability and health and permanence in the system under which they lived, Thomas Mann "spotted the canker, scented decay." In 1912, not long before Hitler's arrival in Munich, he published the novella called *Der Tod in Venedig*—"Death in Venice." Again the theme was deterioration, this time mirrored in the dissolution of a single personality. Though told with cool precision, and deep with philosophical insights, *Der Tod in Venedig* leaves upon the reader the effect of "a nightmare of horror."

Brooding in the isolation of his Munich attic a few miles away, Adolf Hitler was already accumulating within himself the demonic impulses that would one day loose an assault upon reason and dignity whose extent not even Thomas Mann could imagine.

It is possible, though difficult, to live in Munich without drinking beer, but it is not possible to live there and ignore it.

Life revolves around the beer mug, economically and socially, and always has. City records show that before Munich had twenty-five streets, it already had 321 "dispensaries of malted beverages." The brewing began 800 years ago with the Benedictine monks who gave the place its name (*"zu den Munichen"*—"at the monks"). The town's official symbol is a little girl in a monk's cowl, and she is usually shown with a beer stein in her hand.

From the vast breweries it gushes in amber oceans—the Löwenbräu and the Bürgerbräu and the Spatenbräu and the Hackerbräu and the Pschorrbräu and dozens more, almost all with names ending in *bräu,* denoting "brew," the most conspicuous syllable in Munich's municipal lexicon. Flooding inexhaustibly into the taverns, halls and cellars, beer conditions the social life of the city, gives it its coloration and character, lubricates it. The biggest pub in the world, the Hofbräuhaus, is run by the city, but Munich itself could be regarded as one enormous *Bierstube,* or taproom.

The atmosphere was particularly lax and free in the taverns and cafés of Schwabing, where a Bohemian contempt for convention was mingled with the general amiability that accompanied the dispensing of beer. Nobody's social status, background, belief or abberation was held against him. The place teemed with odd and rootless characters, a resort of misfits and rebels of all gradations from the authentic artist and intellectual to the freak and the floater. Schwabing rejected no one.

There Adolf Hitler found, for the first time, a kind of social acceptance. For a few pfennig he could take his place at any tavern table and become part of the loose fraternity that admitted anyone with a beer mug in his hand. He became a frequent figure in cheaper beer halls of the district like the Mathäser and the Schwabinger Brauerei. Neither his appearance nor his opinions caused undue notice in surroundings where shabbiness was commonplace and outlandish ideas taken for granted.

What caused attention, when any was paid him, was the vehemence with which he talked about politics, his favorite theme. Then his face, which struck people as *"schwammig,"* or spongy, lost its nondescript look and was lit by the glow of his eyes, always his most arresting feature. Their dullish gray-blue came alive with an intensity that made some of his listeners uneasy. He tended to sweat and raise his voice when launched upon one of his tirades, but he was often listened to with respect by the laborers, clerks and drifters who populated the pubs he usually favored. To them he was, after all, a registered artist, and he had an impressive vocabulary derived from years of voracious newspaper reading. He was looked upon as *ein Studierter,* an educated man.

It was in the saloons of Schwabing that Hitler came to feel most assured and least isolated. They provided him with his first audiences, and for the first time gave him the feeling of imposing himself and his ideas on his surroundings. In them, as nowhere else, he could break temporarily from the prison of his aloneness without that direct involvement with another human being of which he knew himself to be incapable. In a taproom the man at his elbow or across the table could be freely harangued or disputed; code and custom allowed it and encouraged it. But he was not required to make any personal commitment that might breach the barriers behind which he lived. When the mugs were empty and the gathering broke up, he could always withdraw again into the safety of his inner self without having revealed anything of the emptiness and uncertainty that existed there.

He did not particularly like beer, but it became a determining factor in his career. It washed away the constraints that otherwise kept him from making any kind of human contact at all. Only where it was liberally served and consumed could he become something more than a faceless nonentity, a human fragment. In the *Bierstuben* of Munich he had found the one setting where he could function in the only way open to him, and out of the *Bierstuben* would eventually arise the movement that brought him to power. Adolf Hitler's career was launched on beer.

The ideas he brought with him from Vienna, the ideological baggage he was to carry to his grave, were no novelties in his new environment. His racist and nationalist notions were already

50

widely current, having been spread for years by various *völkisch* groups that permeated the middle class of Munich and Bavaria, especially on its lower levels. The word *völkisch* is untranslatable, and has no clear definition even in German. It derives from *Volk*—the people, the race—and denotes an extreme nationalism shot through with mystical implications of the racial glory of Germanism, of being a German.* Anti-Semitism is inherent in it, inseparable from it. In its atmosphere Hitler felt at home, in his element. Among its advocates he first found listeners, and would later find followers.

But the primitive nationalism of Hitler's circle was not the dominant note of Schwabing. It was receptive to all shades of radicalism. There was in "this little nation of artists" at least one *Bierstube* to accommodate every persuasion from the extreme right to the farthest left. A favorite saying was: "The Schwabinger is always clear-cut in his political attitude. He is always against." The typical personalities of the quarter were not *völkisch* fanatics but Marxist dreamers, and what they were against was the entire bourgeois world. What they dreamed of was not merely a greater Germany but a better world, to which they were sure they alone possessed the key.

The prototype of the Schwabing revolutionary was Erich Mühsam, a twitchy little man with a pointed red beard whom nobody took seriously but the police. It turned out afterward that the police were right.

He was less of a Marxist than an outright anarchist, though the precise doctrine he adhered to was never clearly defined, least of all by himself. His basic conviction was that things as they were needed drastic changing, and that if the world were only run his way everybody would be much happier. Since he was a gay and good-hearted man, there was some reason to be-

* The word is sometimes translated as "folkic" or "folkish." I have rejected this as meaningless and misleading. There are, in the first place, no such words in our language. *Völkisch* has no useful connection with "folk" as we commonly use it—*e.g.*, in "folklore," "folk song," and "the old folks," all of which have a quaint and agreeable flavor. I have chosen to use *völkisch* itself, untranslated, wherever necessary, hoping to retain its peculiarly Germanic and racial implications.—R.H.

lieve him until the time came when he was given the chance to put his ideas into practice. The results, it then developed, were not notably utopian.

The son of a well-to-do druggist, and trained as one himself, he preferred the Bohemian life and expressed his rebellion in articles and books, some of which got him arrested. His fellow anarchists, deadly serious all, were frequently disconcerted by Mühsam's whimsical notions of how to bring about the revolution. In proselytizing the downtrodden to throw off their chains, he concentrated on outcasts who tended to embarrass even the wildest Jacobins—pimps, pederasts, whores, sneak thieves and hopeless derelicts. To Mühsam they seemed just the people who needed unchaining most; there was much more of the social worker than the bomb-thrower about him. Some called him Christlike, and some called him childlike.

He spent a good deal of his time playing chess in the Café Stefanie, a comfortable Schwabing den furnished with red plush benches and redolent of musty upholstery and stale cigarette smoke. He also wrote charming light verse, which he recited to unfailing applause in the cabarets. He was one of the rare species of radical who earnestly wishes to destroy society, but does not hate anybody, does not want to hurt anybody, and believes it can be done without hating or hurting.

Almost as unlikely as Mühsam for the role of world-shaker was another habitué of the Café Stefanie named Kurt Eisner. He was the theater critic for the local socialist newspaper, the Munich *Post,* and he looked like every Philistine's idea of every Bohemian. His unruly grayish-blond beard obscured most of his face except for the short-sighted eyes that peered over glasses worn well down on his nose. Another overplus of tangled hair behind matted his collar, and he looked perpetually unwashed and unpressed.

He was, however, a university graduate, a student of philosophy and a brilliant writer whose studies of Nietzsche and Kant were read with respect by scholars. His political writings were read with attention by the police, for Eisner, too, was an enemy of society and the ringleader of the Schwabing circle that was planning to overthrow the government sometime between chess games. He was Marxist in outlook, but his radicalism had a vague and cloudy quality. His mind was clearer and more disciplined than Mühsam's, and his articles and speeches reached beyond his coterie into working-class and union areas, but his character was incorrigibly bookish and benign. He lacked almost entirely the true fire and fanaticism of the born revolutionary. To those solid citizens of Munich who knew of his existence at all, Kurt Eisner seemed just another of the harmless *Kaffeehausliteraten,* or coffee house high-brows, of which every artist colony always has a sufficient supply. He and his circle alarmed nobody.

The contempt of the solid citizen for the café intellectual usually endures right up to the moment when the world begins to collapse around the citizen's ears under the impact of the intellectual's ideas . . .

A group of men meets quietly in a corner of the Schwabinger Café on the Leopold Strasse, Nr. 41, in the year 1900. They are speaking Russian.

Their leader is obviously the small man of about thirty, round-shouldered, intense, with a slight Mongolian cast to his features. For all his intensity he has a shy, suspicious air, but he is listened to, and what he says is law to the others. He has three names. He was born Vladimir Ulianov. Here in Munich he has taken the cover name of Meyer. In the Russian revolutionary underground he is known as Lenin.

What he and his fellow exiles are discussing with their German co-conspirators is the launching of Citizen Meyer's subversive publication called *Iskra,* "The Spark." It will be printed in small type on onion-skin paper, suitable for smuggling into Russia. It will be secretly stored in the basement of the Social Democratic newspaper *Vorwärts* in Berlin and there painstakingly folded into small packets by trusted collaborators. The little parcels will be tucked into packing cases containing other goods, which are then shipped to frontier towns and turned over to practiced smugglers who get them across the border.

Inside Russia, agents pick up the packets and distribute *Iskra* to party cells throughout the country. It is pasted on factory walls and scattered in the streets by night. It is passed from hand to hand until every copy has been read so many times that the paper hardly holds together and the type is illegible. Hundreds of readers, thousands, receive instructions, indoctrination, guidance. The faithful are supported. The wavering are steadied. New converts are won. The movement grows and spreads, nourished by Citizen Meyer at his faraway café table.

The café is not his favorite milieu. He has none of the Bohemian's gift for letting time slip easily by in trifling pleasures. He is too obsessed with the enormity and urgency of his mission. A cold passion that no Mühsam or Eisner could know possesses him, though even he succumbs momentarily to the charms of Munich, and he writes home to his mother of his pleasure in the famous local Mardi Gras, called *Fasching*—". . . a procession of masked paraders on the streets; wholesale tomfoolery; clouds of confetti thrown in the faces of passersby; little paper kites. Here they know how to make merry in the streets!"

He seldom makes merry. He sits in a barren workingman's flat in Schwabing and writes steadily, complaining now and then of the poor quality of the German pen points. He writes "What's To Be Done?" It contains, in embryo or fully outlined, nearly all the basic ideas on politics and party organization that were to become known as "Leninist" and have a decisive effect on the growth and structure of world communism.

Lenin spends a year and a half of his exile in Munich, and part of the time he lives in the home of a cabinet-maker at Nr. 106 Schleissheimer Strasse, only a few blocks from Popp the tailor's at Nr. 34 where Hitler later lived. By another arresting coincidence, the two greatest fanatics of the age, the one on the left and the other on the right, found the same street in Schwabing in their times of preparation.

For the masthead of *Iskra* Lenin chose words of Pushkin that, in the light of what was to come, applied equally to himself and to Adolf Hitler: *"Out of the spark shall spring the flame."*

There were many sparks, and some found tinder that produced a sickly, phosphorescent glow hinting at conflagrations to come.

"Strange regions there are," Thomas Mann wrote in *At the Prophet's*, "strange minds, strange realms of the spirit. . . . At the edge of large cities, where street lamps are scarce and policemen walk by twos, are houses where you mount till you can mount no further, up and up into attics under the roof, where pale young geniuses, criminals of the dream, sit with folded arms and brood . . . ."

Adolf Hitler was not the only such criminal of the dream at that time and place. There were others, brooding in other attics, who were unconsciously preparing his way for him. There were, for instance, Ludwig Klages and Friedrich Gundolf and Karl Wolfskehl and Alfred Schuler, who called themselves the "Cosmics." Pale young geniuses all, they were ridden by wild visions of a coming *Blutleuchte*—a great purification-by-blood that would heal the world under the mystic symbol of the swastika. They were advocates of a "holy madness" that alone could purge the degenerate contemporary society they despised, and rejuvenate it. They longed and looked for the coming of a Great Man, a leader dazzling and exalted, who would create a new society, a new world.

Their own leader was the poet Stefan George. Around him they formed a circle, a cult, so worshipful that it was said his followers came to resemble him not only in dress, walk and manner, but even facially. They called him The Master and felt themselves to be part of a secular priesthood, a closed sect, a monkish order. It had branches, or chapels, around the country, in Heidelberg, Kiel, Berlin. The Master moved from place to place imparting his teaching, and reading from his works to small groups in private homes. Always unapproachable, he would appear unexpectedly and leave with almost mysterious abruptness. To many he became a living myth. He had no fixed residence, but his favorite city was Munich, where his most influential disciples, themselves poets and writers, lived.

George himself looked somewhat like Dante, and consciously fostered the resemblance. His smoldering eyes were set deep between high cheekbones and strong, protruding brows. He was graceful and slim, and affected black clothes of severe clerical cut. A visiting Englishman, a young composer named Cyril Scott who became fascinated by the cult, wrote that Stefan George "represented in his person what a place like Siena represents in towns; to look at him and hear him talk was to be wafted back several centuries into the romantic atmosphere of the Renaissance." His German adorers were more unrestrained. One of them described George's ears as being "of especially beautiful construction." Friedrich Gundolf once drew a series of portraits of his heroes from history—Caesar, Dante, Shakespeare, Goethe and others. He made all of them look like Stefan George. When The Master walked the streets, another disciple wrote, "a breath from a higher world" emanated from him and made passersby stop in their tracks.

In all this there was something silly, and even morbid. The George cult, in its most intimate circle, had a hothouse atmosphere, and about it there was a faint stench of rotting lilies. The homosexual taint was unmistakable. (The Master himself idolized a Munich boy of unusual beauty whom he called "Maximin" and described in adoring verses as a god come to earth). Two factors, however, made of Stefan George and his movement much more than passing literary curiosities.

He was a poet of genuine power whose marble and magisterial lines deeply affected many discriminating readers. Works like *The Seventh Ring* and *The Star of the Covenant,* published in 1914 on the eve of the war, evoked critical comment that ranked him as "the greatest German poet of the age." He was master of a spare and sculptured style with an austere beauty distinctly his own. His poems reflected an aristocratic disdain for the rank materialism of his time, a vision of a loftier plane of living, which spoke to the young and the spiritually discontented.

The other factor was less literary and more ominous. George had adopted much of the philosophy of Nietzsche and infused it deeply into his poetry and teachings. The haunting image of the superman; the contempt for middle-class morality;

the hostility toward reason and rationality; the dream of power, ruthless and unlimited—these Nietzschean themes recurred in a score of variations in the literature of the George circle. In their revulsion against the modern world, the cultists immersed themselves in ancient Germanic lore and pagan mysteries. They wallowed in a feverish anti-intellectualism, and glorified instinct and feeling. They saw themselves as latter-day Dionysians, reviving the elemental spirit of ancient and more untrammeled times. Along with this emotional churning, and deeply embedded in it, went a virulent nationalism centered on the concept of a coming hero who would lead Germany to the rejuvenation of Europe and the world:

"He bursts the chains, refurbishes order on the ruins, whips the decadents home to eternal justice where greatness is once more greatness, master once more master, discipline once more discipline. He fastens the true symbol on the *völkisch* banner. Through storm and terrible signals of dawn he leads the troop of his followers to the task of the bright day and plants the new Reich."

The symbol for the *völkisch* banner that was still to come was already emblazoned on the publications of the George circle: the swastika. It was brought to the attention of The Master by one of his disciples, Alfred Schuler, who had discovered it while delving into the myths and rites of antiquity. Schuler believed that the sign—called *Hakenkreuz,* or hooked cross, in German—had come down through the ages from prehistoric man, whose central emblem it was. He read all manner of occult meanings into it, and was the first to promote it in Germany as symbol of major significance. His own life revolved around it.

Schuler was a dumpy little man with moist blue eyes who scurried through the streets of Schwabing with hurried little steps by day, often arrayed in a long monkish cloak with a cowl. By night he spoke to small gatherings where a silver platter was conspicuously placed to receive contributions from his devotees. He could lose himself in a trancelike intoxication as he celebrated what The Master himself called "language orgies," and many listeners were infected by his delirium.

He preached that civilization had been poisoned at the roots by the dogmas of the Hebrew god Jehovah, which stifled and corrupted the spirit. Only an apocalyptic purging of all Jewish elements from the world could purify it, and take mankind back to the unpolluted wellsprings of heathen antiquity, which alone held the possibility of spiritual rebirth. He imbued his anti-Semitism with a metaphysical import that went far beyond the social and political prejudices of the day. Carried to the cloudy heights Schuler advocated, hostility and hatred for Jews acquired a cosmic nimbus by which any measures, however appalling, could be justified, as in the teachings of Lanz von Liebenfels. The seeds of the coming death camps were in the teachings of Alfred Schuler, whose lectures the Schwabing postcard peddler named Adolf Hitler is known to have attended.

Stefan George broke with Schuler over his extreme anti-Semitism, but retained to the last his ideal of hero-worship and his anti-democratic outlook. His poetry and its teachings spread in academic circles, taken up by professors, who passed them to their students, who spread them further. The influence of George and his circle penetrated all the areas where opinions are made and convictions formed, seeding ground far beyond the back streets of Schwabing.

The shape of coming things was also being forecast, sometimes with startling accuracy, by another Munich writer who had not yet acquired a cult or even a reputation. Almost penniless, solitary in his slum lodgings, Oswald Spengler was writing *The Decline of the West*. In it he was predicting a time of terrible upheaval, of wars and aggressions, an age of tyrants. He began work on the first volume of *The Decline* in 1912, while the world was still at peace.

He saw all history as a kind of biological process, with successive cultures passing through the same stages as living organisms. Born mysteriously, each culture grows, flourishes and dies, following a set and predictable life cycle like that of insects, animals and men. History was not an ordered and continuing process leading to steady advance and improvement in mankind, but an inexorable round of growth and decay. Using what he called his "morphological" method, he examined eight major cultures of the past and demonstrated that they all proved his theory. By applying what was known of the pathology of cultures that had sickened and died, he argued that the historian could, like a doctor, detect the same fatal symptoms in contemporary civilization and predict *its* dissolution with scientific certainty.

The West, he said, was in its "late" period. There would be violent death throes in the form of colossal conflicts in which "whole continents will be staked." The masses of mankind in their desperation would turn to new Caesars and follow them blindly, while the Caesars, leading huge armies, fought each other over the ruins of civilization. The age of Caesarism was at hand.

Much of what Spengler said would happen, did happen. But for all his air of scholarly profundity and cold analysis, he was hagridden by many of the same nationalistic concepts and clichés that had been running through German thinking for generations. The son of a minor post-office official, he revered caste and hierarchy, and spoke of "race" and "blood" like any *völkisch* fanatic. Unfit for military service because of a weak heart and myopia, he glorified war and saluted the barbaric strain in the German, "the beast-of-prey man" who was entitled to seize the world. A doctor of philosophy and former school-teacher, he scorned reason and espoused an outright irrationalism, like the hysterics of the Cosmic group, relying on "feel" and "intuition," as they did. His book was riddled with inconsistencies and contradictions, and turgid with reactionary dogmatism. But its influence was to be enormous, and it helped to spread and deepen the attitudes and prejudices that made possible the appearance of the Caesar whose coming Spengler predicted with such assurance.

The coming Caesar and his herald may well have passed each other repeatedly on the streets of Munich, or sat at a table in the same beer cellar at the same time. But it is not likely that the ponderous and imposing Spengler would have deigned to pay any attention to Hitler then, even if he had encountered him. Much of what Oswald Spengler foresaw Adolf Hitler would make come true, but at the time the coming Caesar was undergoing one of the most humiliating experiences of his life. He was being sought by the police as a draft dodger.

In the town of Linz an examination of the municipal records in August of 1913 had revealed that a certain Adolf Hietler (*sic*) failed to register for military service at the times prescribed by Austrian law for his age classification. A further check disclosed that this Hietler had gone abroad, thereby committing a double offense for which the penalty was a year's close confinement and a fine up to 2,000 kronen.

The delinquent having left no forwarding address, an investigation was begun to find and arrest him. Through his sisters, neither of whom had heard from him for four years, the police eventually traced him to Vienna and learned of his residence at the Home for Men. There the report was that the fugitive was believed to have left for Munich.

The investigation took months, involving the Linz, Vienna and Munich police departments. Hitler was unaware that he was being sought, and it must have been a considerable shock when he answered the door on the afternoon of January 18th, a Sunday, and found himself being arrested by a uniformed officer of the Criminal Police.

His predicament was grave. He was in imminent danger of being sentenced and sent to jail as a draft dodger, with all the attendant ugliness of implied cowardice and lasting stigma. It was another of those minor crossroads where history wavers momentarily before resuming its fated course. It is hardly thinkable that the Germans, of all people, would ever have followed a jailbird with a conviction for evading military service on his record.

But, as was to happen repeatedly in the career of Adolf Hitler, an accidental circumstance came to his rescue, and he made the most of it. Through a bureaucratic delay, the summons had been delivered too late to allow him to appear in Linz on the date set for a hearing of the charges. This gave him a few days' grace while other arrangements were being made. He used the time to compose a long letter of self-justification, which helped him evade prison and disgrace.

The letter covers three and a half large pages, and is one of the very few communications of any length extant in his own handwriting. He was a man who talked incessantly; but he seldom wrote anything, and was always uncertain with grammar, and even spelling. The letter to the draft board is pock-marked with the same blunders he made in elementary school. He confuses *das* with *dass,* writes *den* for *denn,* uses *lies* when he means *liess,* and has no idea where to put a comma. But as an unconscious revelation of character, and an insight into how he saw himself at this period of his life, the letter is a unique document.

His basic answer to the charge of not registering for the draft was that he had actually done so in February of 1910 when he lived in Vienna. He gave convincing details of this registration, and said that he had duly filled out all the necessary forms. Since then, he said, he had heard nothing. Admitting an oversight in not reporting in the fall of 1909 as he should have, he argued that his subsequent registration remedied this and put him on the rolls, thus making him available to the authorities as the law required. "It could never occur to me to evade the call-up," he wrote.

This much of the letter was to the point and may have been true, but it occupied only a fraction of the document. The rest was an abject plea for leniency and special favor that mingled a cringing submission to authority with a muted note of protest that so worthy and deserving a character as himself should be put upon so unjustly. He stressed his difficult situation as a free-lance artist, enclosing his tax certificate to show that he was making only 1,200 marks a year (about $300) and noting that he was the son of a civil servant and without private means. He brought up a version of his favorite art-student gambit: "I can devote only a fraction of my time to breadwinning, as I am still preparing myself to be an architectural painter." As such, he did not fail to point out, his expenses were "considerably greater than that of a workman in a similar position."

What all this had to do with the issue was obscure, but he left no chord unstruck that might evoke an answering tremolo of pity for his plight. And, as he later did on many equally inappro-

priate occasions, he seized the opportunity to indulge his obsession with his own past. Even before he had accomplished anything or gave any promise of doing so, he was already an
autobiographer infatuated with his subject. Recalling, unasked,
his years in Vienna, he wrote:

"And as to my sin of omission in the fall of 1909, that was
for me an infinitely bitter time. I was young and inexperienced,
without financial aid of any kind and too proud to accept it from
anyone, let alone ask for it . . . For two long years I had no
other friends but care and want, no companion but eternally unsatisfied hunger. I was never acquainted with that lovely word:
youth. Today, even after five years, the souvenirs of those days
are still with me in the form of chilblains on hands and feet."

All but overcome by the memory of how splendidly he had
conducted himself in his time of tribulations, he continued:

"And yet I cannot think back on that period without a certain joy, now that I have risen above the worst of it. Despite the
utmost distress, often in the midst of more than dubious surroundings, I kept a decent name, I am unblemished before the
law, and I have a clean conscience with the single exception of
omitting to report to the military authorities, an obligation I was
not then even aware of . . ."

It was a curious performance for a coming advocate of
ruthlessness who derided "so-called humaneness" as a "mixture
of stupidity and cowardice," and who believed it a "mockery" to
interfere with "the natural struggle for existence" that quite
rightly "leaves only the strongest and healthiest alive."

At the time there was nothing at all of the Spenglerian
beast of prey or the Nietzschean superman about him. When he
delivered his letter to the Austrian Consulate-General he reinforced its plea for pity with a verbal statement that he was suffering from an ailment, unspecified, which made him unfit for
military service. His appearance was such that he was readily believed. Between the letter and his sickly appearance, the forbear-
ance he begged for was granted him. No fine or other penalty
was imposed. On February 5, 1914, Adolf Hitler appeared for
examination as a recruit in the armed forces of His Imperial

Majesty Franz Joseph. The verdict on the future war lord of Europe was:

> *"Unfit for combat or auxiliary duty.*
> *Too weak. Incapable of bearing arms."*

It was another rejection, but with the sting of this one must have come a sense of relief. Not only had he escaped jailing, but he was also freed of the necessity of serving the Austro-Hungarian Empire. Much of his orating in the Munich pubs had been devoted to denunciations of the Hapsburg monarchy and the folly of Germany's alliance with it. His hatred of the Empire's slavic components, and what he called its progressive "de-Germanization," was obsessive. His flight from Vienna may, in fact, have been partly motivated by the hope of avoiding his military duty to a state he believed to be "moving closer to dissolution hour by hour." There was no element of physical cowardice in this, as subsequent evidence showed. "I did not want to fight for the Hapsburg state," he wrote, "but I was ready to die at any time for my people and the Reich that embraced them."

He had always, from boyhood on, dreamed of being a soldier and was inordinately fascinated by violence, in books and in reality. The Boer War, which broke out when he was ten years old, was "like summer lightning" to him, he said, and he had followed it in the newspapers with the avidity other boys devoted to sports. He used to lament that he had been born a century too late when "the waves of historical events seemed to have subsided, so that niches in the Halls of Fame are reserved only for shopkeepers and bureaucrats." He worried that he might live and die without ever being given the chance to prove himself in battle. He hungered for war.

And when, on August 3, 1914, the German Reich declared war on France, he volunteered for combat before the day was out.

His health had improved since the preceding winter, and so this time he was accepted.

Six months after being pronounced unfit to bear arms, Adolf Hitler was in uniform and on his way to the front.

3 THE CHOSEN

"WE ARE THE SALT OF THE EARTH . . ."
—WILHELM II

OTTO VON BISMARCK-SCHÖNHAUSEN made a prediction in 1897, the year before he died. "The great European war," he told a friend, "will come out of some damned fool thing in the Balkans."

He knew about wars, having waged three highly successful ones against Denmark, Austria and France, and founded the German Reich in the process. He also understood his era. In one of his first official appearances, before a committee of the Prussian House of Delegates, he declared: "The great questions of the time will be decided not by speeches and the resolutions of majorities . . . but by iron and blood." The phrase was taken up, and became historical, in reverse: "blood and iron."

When Bismarck began the career that was to make him dominant in European diplomacy for almost thirty years as the "Iron Chancellor," his country was a loose collection of far from homogeneous states held together mainly by a common language. With his war against Denmark he added the duchies of Schleswig-Holstein to German territory. With his war against Austria, he freed Germany from the Hapsburg influence that had endured for generations. And by swiftly defeating France in 1871, he humbled the hereditary enemy and made possible the crowning of King Wilhelm I of Prussia as Kaiser of a German Empire in the Hall of Mirrors at Versailles. He also annexed the provinces of Alsace and Lorraine, and collected an indemnity of one billion dollars, a colossal sum at the time.

With his trio of tidy wars and his great sagacity in diplomatic maneuver, Otto von Bismarck forged his country into a state more unified and powerful than it had ever been before, and created a new European balance of power within which the new Germany was predominant.

The great impetus that Bismarck gave his nation in war and diplomacy maintained itself in peacetime, outlasting his chancellorship and continuing unabated into the new century. In 1910 an exhaustive survey of German economic advance by a British expert concluded:

"The statistics [covering the previous thirty years] prove that in all productive industries, in mining, manufacture, agriculture and commerce, Germany's progress is stupendous, that Germany has overtaken Great Britain in industrial production, although England is still supreme in cotton and shipping; and it stands to reason that the German people must have fully participated in this enormous expansion of national wealth production and consequent prosperity . . ."

Prosperity was, in fact, spread wider than in most other countries, and was accompanied by social legislation so progressive that the rest of the world would not reach the standards it set until decades later. Bismarck, for all his authoritarian bent, had wooed the support of the German masses by inaugurating a program for what he called the "positive advancement of the working classes." It included compulsory sickness and accident insurance; old-age insurance; free medical and hospital services; limitation of the work week; and provisions for adequate light and ventilation in factories, as well as sanitary toilets for the workers—legislation of the sort that caused an uproar of debate and opposition when presented as the "New Deal" in the United States almost a half-century later.

Despite continuing political and legal hindrances, the oldest, largest and most influential socialist party in the world, the German Social Democrats, flourished during this period. Theoretically founded on Marxist principles and dedicated to the liquidation of capitalism, the party and its membership shared so satisfactorily in the general affluence that its outlook tended to be moderate to the point of mildness. Its leaders kept their radicalism within comfortable bounds, and its members seldom betrayed any impulse to mount barricades and hurl paving stones. They were by temperament more inclined to heed the admonition "Keep Off the Grass" than the rallying cry "Workers of the World, Unite!" The party did, however, control a powerful trade-union movement with which the reactionary industrialists and the land-owning Junkers of Prussia had to reckon.

As the First World War approached, Germany gave many outward signs of a nation poised for further social and political progress, and possibly for enlightened leadership of the western world. Culturally its achievements compared favorably with those of any neighbor or rival, and in some significant categories it was without peer. Germans won almost twice as many Nobel Prizes as any other people, and from all over the world students came to attend German universities and sit at the feet of German professors whose scholarship was proverbial in academic circles everywhere. The Germans boasted that they were the best-educated people on earth, a claim that may well have been technically true. They had the fewest illiterates and the highest college attendance of any country. Their attitude toward higher education bordered on outright awe. Respect for a university professor was second only to that accorded an army officer—a capsule summary, perhaps, of the notorious ambiguity of the German character. It was said that a German confronted with two doors, one marked "Paradise" and the other "Lecture on Paradise," would invariably enter the second.

At a time when scientific thought was breaching the barriers of the physical world as never before, two of the most profound penetrations were achieved in Germany, and they radically changed man's view of the universe. Max Planck, professor of physics at Kiel and Berlin, announced his Quantum Theory that revolutionized all accepted concepts of light and radiant energy. Not long after, in 1905, Albert Einstein, who grew up in Munich and studied there, first published the formula $E = mc^2$ to express the principle of mass-energy equivalence upon which

modern nuclear physics is based and from which the atomic
bomb evolved.

The intellectual life of the nation was diverse and active
enough to encourage those who wished to regard Germany as
das Land der Dichter und Denker—the land of poets and
thinkers—and who preferred Weimar, where Goethe and Schiller
were enshrined, to Potsdam. In 1910 Heinrich Mann, the au-
thor-brother of Thomas, issued a manifesto called "Mind and
Deed," in which he summoned writers and artists to oppose,
freely and openly, the traditional polarity of *Obrigkeit* (authority) and *Untertan* (subject) which most Germans were still taking for granted as the best possible social arrangement, if not
the only one. A good deal of opposition was, in fact, already
being expressed, some of it extremely spirited.

Munich's *Simplicissimus* was available at every German
railway station, barber shop and café, and week after week it
made savage sport of the established order. Skillful caricaturists
like Th.(Thomas) Th.(Theodor) Heine and Olaf Gulbransson
and Eduard Thöny cruelly lampooned their society with a sure
eye for its most vulnerable aspects. *Simpl's* artists, writers and
versifiers spit and slashed in all directions—at the officious bureaucrat, a particularly numerous and offensive breed in Germany; at the braying patriot and the pompous politico; at the
moralizing pastor and the intriguing priest; at the arrogant Prussian *Junker* and the money-blind industrialist; at the German as
a species, with his beer-soaked complacency and his inbred ser-
vility.

Not even the House of Hohenzollern and the sacrosanct
military escaped the arrows of the satirists who made *Simpl* one
of the most forthright journals of social and political criticism in
the world. Even foreigners were sometimes startled at the daring
of its cartoons and text, and many Germans were appalled, denouncing it as *ein Volksgift,* a poison for the people. It was not
alone. Other influential papers and magazines, like the *Berliner
Tageblatt* and the weekly *Schaubühne,* also spoke out against a
society that, for all its surface glitter and apparent well-being,
was dangerously distorted at its base.

For it was not the *Simplicissimus* attitude and outlook that reflected the real nature of prewar Germany, nor the achievements in art and science, nor the 4,000,000 votes cast by Social Democrats. Its essential symbols were not Nobel Prizes but the sword and the goose step.

How matters actually stood in the German Reich of 1913–14, in the twenty-fifth year of the reign of Kaiser Wilhelm II, was demonstrated for the world, and particularly for Germany itself, by an episode that became known as the Zabern Affair.

Zabern was a town in Alsace garrisoned by Infantry Regiment No. 99, in which a certain Baron von Forstner, a twenty-year-old Junker, served as lieutenant. His command included a number of native Alsatians, whom he repeatedly referred to as *Wackes,* an offensive slang term hotly resented by the local recruits. In one of his outbursts of arrogance, the young lieutenant-baron offered a reward of ten marks for the shooting or stabbing of any *Wackes* who failed to conform to proper Prussian style. An N.C.O. volunteered to contribute three more marks to the reward.

A report of the incident in the local paper infuriated the citizenry, and Lieutenant von Forstner became the target of jeers from gangs of small boys whenever he appeared on the street. His colonel, another Junker, assigned a bodyguard of troops with fixed bayonets to accompany him, and announced that if there were any further demonstrations, blood might flow, and he hoped it would.

This naturally inflamed the situation further. When protests took the form of stone-throwing crowds at the barracks, a state of siege was declared. Women and children were beaten with rifle butts, and scores of indiscriminate arrests were made. The prisoners, including two local officials, were locked up in the coal cellar of the barracks overnight and subjected to drumhead trials the next day. In one melee on the street Lieutenant von Forstner, ever in the thick of things, drew his sword and cut open the head of a crippled shoemaker.

News of the outrages in Zabern spread throughout Germany, and caused widespread indignation. The military establishment responded with the insolence it regarded as the only possible attitude toward civilians.

In the Germany of Wilhelm II there was a saying, only half-jocular, that went: "The human race begins with the lieutenant." Army officers were not only a corps, a class and a caste, but a cult. To don the *Kaiserrock,* the Kaiser's coat, was to become, instantly and forever, a being apart from and superior to *das Civil,* civilians.

At a time when the United States Congress found it necessary to pass a kind of public-accommodations statute to prohibit hotels and restaurants from discriminating against soldiers, and when the English were being scolded in verse by Rudyard Kipling for neglecting and mistreating their soldiers between wars, the German reverence for the uniform bordered on the idolatrous. No public or social function was considered official or complete without the presence of officers in uniform, whether it was a private dance or the cornerstone-laying for a church. "Indeed," a British visitor noted, "if the supreme fetish of German exteriors, the uniform, is not before their eyes, they feel like the ancient Jews in the absence of the Ark of the Covenant." The same visitor recorded that "a dazzling lieutenant is of greater importance than the burgomaster of a great city. The latter may walk through the streets unrecognized, but every policeman, tram-conductor, post or railway official salutes an officer."

From the Army's viewpoint, the Zabern demonstrations were an intolerable affront to the *Kaiserrock* and hence to the national dignity. The prestige of a "dazzling lieutenant" was at stake, and with it the authority of the Army itself. The demonstrators, after all, were mere civilians, and only Alsatians at that, and could be treated any way the local garrison saw fit. Lieutenant von Forstner, his colonel and all the German troops involved were supported by the chain of command up to the Kaiser himself. The Crown Prince sent telegrams of personal congratulation to the area commanders, reputedly using the phrase *"Immer feste druff!"*—barracks slang for "Keep it up!" or "Let 'em have it!"

But the Zabern affair ballooned into a national issue, and

rallied opposition to the military on a scale never before known in Germany. Intellectuals, liberals, leftists and Social Democratic factions seized the opportunity to form a united front and seriously challenge the age-old domination of the Army in German society. To the defense that the Army had merely defended itself against attack in what was "practically enemy territory," the *Schaubühne* wrote:

"Germany itself has virtually become enemy territory for civilization and for every kind of human progress. . . . Doesn't anyone realize that Zabern is the battle cry in a struggle that, on the whole earth, is still being fought only in Prussia-Germany: the struggle for equal rights (and who isn't seized with fury at that idea—equal rights!) for civilian and military?"

The uproar reached such proportions that the current Chancellor, Theobald von Bethmann-Hollweg, was forced to go before the Reichstag with a lengthy report defending the Army's actions in Alsace. For the first time in German history a vote of no confidence was passed against the Chancellor and the Minister of War.

It made no difference.

Under the German system of the time, the Reichstag had no ultimate control of policy; it was determined by the Chancellor, the Kaiser and the General Staff of the Army, where the real power lay. The united liberal and enlightened elements in the best-educated country in the world counted for nothing in collision with Prussian militarism, just as they would not suffice in a later and larger confrontation with a greater evil. The Zabern officers were cleared by courts-martial, and that ended the matter.

The events in Alsace did not unduly surprise a world accustomed to hearing the martial trumpetings of the German emperor. Kaiser Wilhelm II was an uninhibited spokesman for the policy of what he called "the mailed fist." His phrases, which came readily and were often arresting, almost always had the clang of steel in them. He could not discuss a new educational bill without working in an expression like "war to the knife," and when he sat for a picture in full military panoply, which he frequently did, his ferocious up-thrusting mustachios and imperious glare made him look as if he were about to command the entire world to do squads right. An especially bellicose painting of him was reported to have caused a foreign diplomat to remark, "That is not a portrait. It is a declaration of war."

He spoke almost exclusively in exclamation points. "Whoever opposes me I shall smash!" In sending a body of troops to China during the Boxer Rebellion, he ordered them to take no prisoners, give no quarter, and ravage the land "like the Huns of Atilla." The phrase provided Germany's enemies with an epithet for German soldiers throughout the World War, and afterward: Huns.

On another occasion, when addressing a unit taking the military oath at Potsdam, he said: "A soldier must have no will of his own. You must all be animated by one will, and that is my will. . . . Perhaps during the present socialistic agitation, I may have to order you to shoot down your own relatives, your brothers, nay, your own parents—which I hope to God may never be. But even so, you are obliged to carry out my orders without protest."

With the rhetoric and saber-rattling went a heady sense of mission, the conviction that conquest by Germany could only be a benefaction to the conquered. It would spread *Kultur,* by which was meant the incomparable German way of doing things —everything from creating music to running tram lines, from educating children to preparing cabbage soup. Germany's emergence as a nation came late and was incomplete, and its recent rush onto the world stage had given it all the characteristics of the upstart—the bluster and overcompensation of the *nouveau riche.* The Kaiser was a singularly appropriate figurehead for such a state. His left arm, damaged at birth, was withered and shorter than his right. Special tailoring of the sleeve was needed to disguise the deformity. Like his nation, he felt that strutting and shouting were the best methods of diverting attention from a basic defect. Surrounded by older, sounder and more stable nations, Germany found it necessary to proclaim through its Kaiser that "God has created us so that we should civilize the world."

There were many Germans to whom this sort of rodomontade was an embarrassment. They hoped that the rest of Europe was not taking it seriously. But there were Germans who objected to the Kaiser on other grounds. They felt he did not go far enough.

In 1912 Dr. Heinrich Class, a respected jurist, published a book called *If I Were Kaiser* in which he laid down a program for German nationalism such as Wilhelm himself would have hesitated to defend. Dr. Class was president of the *Alldeutscher Verband,* or Pan-German League, which advocated "an actively vigorous German power policy in Europe and overseas." The League's propaganda took the form of an extreme nationalism, including the usual delusions of racial superiority as expressed in the semi-mystical *völkisch* concept, a word that the League brought into general use.

Dr. Class's work was widely read and approved in influential sections of the intelligentsia, including professors, teachers and publicists, many of whom were themselves members of the League and spread its teachings far beyond its 20,000 members. The recurrent Pan-German thesis was bluntly and briefly expressed by one of its professor members in 1905 when he wrote: "Our race, with its culture, is superior to all other nations and races of the earth . . . our civilization has reached a height where it incomparably excels and dominates that of all other nations and races of the earth." An earlier Pan-German pronouncement was more specific: "We are without a doubt the best warrior-race on earth, we are the most accomplished people in all fields of science and the arts. We are the best colonizers, the best sailors, yes, even the best businessmen. . . . God, who has breathed his living breath into mankind, thinks through us."

Even before the League was founded, its theme was succinctly expressed in a much-repeated rhyme composed by Emmanuel Geibel, a professor of aesthetics at Munich in the nineteenth century:

> ". . . *es mag am deutschen Wesen*
> *Einmal noch die Welt genesen."*

["One day the spirit of the German nation may bring the world regeneration."]

A systematic anti-Semitism, beyond anything modern Germany had known until then, was advocated in Dr. Class's book, and accepted as part of the Pan-German program. Jews who had not obtained German citizenship would be expelled from the country, "ruthlessly and to the last man." But this, he said, was not nearly enough. Jews who remained would be treated under law as foreigners. They would be barred from all public offices and honorary posts in the nation, the states and local communities. They would be prohibited from voting, from serving in the Army or Navy, and from owning real estate. They would be compelled to pay double taxes. These and similar measures, Dr. Class asserted, would have to be undertaken "for the health of our national life" even if "the innocent have to suffer with the guilty."

This nearly verbatim forecast of the Nuremberg Laws of the Third Reich, a generation before they were put into effect at the cost of 6,000,000 Jewish lives, was coupled with the dream of an omnipotent leader that had haunted the minds of Germans since the time of Friedrich Barbarossa. "Today the best of our people feel the need to follow a strong, competent *Führer*," Dr. Class wrote. "All who have not been seduced by the teachings of un-German democracy yearn for such a leader, not because they are servile or weak in character but because they know that greatness can only be achieved by the concentration of individual strengths which, in turn, becomes possible only through subjugation to a single *Führer*."

A world war would be needed, and a catastrophic defeat, and a revolution, and a failed *Putsch,* before the long-sought leader could begin his march to absolute power. But all the essential elements and attitudes he would require for his purposes were already present in the Germany of Wilhelm II and Dr. Heinrich Class. Fifty years later, in 1964, a German historian would take the witness stand in Frankfort, at the trial of war criminals connected with the Auschwitz extermination camp, and describe the Nazi atrocities as "a natural, evolutionary development of German history." The emergence of Adolf Hitler, said Dr. Helmut Krausnick of the Institute of Contemporary History, "was not an accident . . ."

The war that delivered the first of the seismic shocks to German society began, as Bismarck had predicted it would, with a "damned fool thing in the Balkans." On the sunny Sunday of June 28, 1914, the Archduke Franz Ferdinand of Austria and his wife Sophie were being driven through the streets of Sarajevo, in Bosnia, a hotbed of Serbian nationalism. On their official tour they had already survived one bombing attempt and ridden safely past several other would-be assassins. Then their chauffeur, confused over directions, turned down the wrong street. He braked to correct the error and, by one of the most freakish and fateful chances in history, stopped the car directly in front of a young terrorist named Gavrilo Princip. The two point-blank shots Princip fired from his pistol caused the death of the Archduke and his wife on the spot, and ten million more in their aftermath.

All through the preceding forty-four years of peace among the major powers, the continent's national rivalries, military and commercial, had been mounting and intensifying. In an atmosphere grown sultry with increasing tensions, the patchwork of treaties and alliances designed to hold hostilities in check had worn dangerously thin. "Unsatisfied by material prosperity," Winston Churchill has written, "the nations turned restlessly towards strife. . . . National passions, unduly exalted in the decline of religion, burned beneath the surface of nearly every land with fierce if shrouded fires. Almost one might think the world wished to suffer. Certainly men were everywhere eager to dare. On all sides the military preparations, precautions and counter precautions had reached their height." Europe was "a powder magazine from end to end" needing only "one single hellish spark" to set off the explosion.

Within weeks of the spark at Sarajevo, Austria had marched across the Archduke's grave against Serbia, and Russia had mobilized in Serbia's support, and Germany had fallen in step with Austria, and declared war on France, and England had declared war on Germany. As the German armies crossed the Belgian border on August 4, 1914, Chancellor Theobald von Bethmann-Hollweg began his speech in the Reichstag with the words: "A stupendous fate is breaking over Europe . . ."

4 PRIVATE FIRST CLASS

"THE WAR ENTERED INTO US LIKE WINE . . ."
—ERNST JÜNGER

4 PRIVATE FIRST CLASS

IN MUNICH the declaration of war was read to the public from the steps of the Hall of the Field Marshals, the *Feldherrnhalle,* on the Odeon Platz. Well down in front among the cheering and singing thousands was the postcard artist Adolf Hitler. "For me, as for every German," he said afterward, "there now began the greatest and most unforgettable time of my earthly existence."

His elation at the coming of war glowed plainly on his face. Unsuspected by himself or anyone else at the time, a camera recorded him in his moment of open and unfeigned emotion amid the dense pack of humanity that jammed the spacious square that day. This became known years later when he chanced to tell the photographer who had snapped the scene, "I was in that crowd." A face-by-face scrutiny of the photograph was immediately undertaken to find him. After many hours of microscopic search, he was finally discovered standing almost under the mane of one of the stone lions that look out across the square from either side of the pavilion. Blown up and lifted out from the surrounding blur of undistinguishable faces, his picture turned out to be one of the most revealing of all the thousands ever taken of him.

The enlargement shows him not merely excited but enraptured, the mouth half-open and the eyes upraised and fixed. All around him men have their hats on, but his head is bare. The hair is uncut and unkempt, adding to his look of intense agitation. The whole attitude is that of a man transported. Nearby another member of the crowd appears to be staring at him curiously, suggesting that Hitler's fervor attracted attention even in so emotional a crowd as this.

The accidental photograph is an historical rarity, perhaps the most completely candid and unposed ever taken of him. Seldom has a man, still utterly unknown and undistinguished, been caught by the camera at a moment so significant for his future, and for the world's. In a sense, the picture freezes forever the precise instant at which the career of Adolf Hitler became possible. The war that was being proclaimed as the photo was taken would produce the social chaos indispensable to his rise. The Army he was now about to join would adopt him as its own, opening the way for his escape from obscurity and ultimately setting him on his path to power. And the Odeon Platz, the scene of this moment that changed everything for him thereafter, became his particular arena. The stone lions of the *Feldherrnhalle* that stared into the square when he was still an anonymous fragment of the crowd would see him in the same place as protagonist of the fantastic *Putsch* that made his name known throughout Germany and became the second great milestone in his career. And they would, in due course, witness his return to the square in a triumph no one could possibly have imagined on that August day in 1914, the beginning of the First World War.

"I am not going to talk about our war," wrote the German publicist Heinrich Hauser years after it was over. "Its only significance is that of a turning point toward the roaring plunge into barbarism."

That was not how most Germans felt about it at the time. The war was welcomed, with a jubilation that bordered on hysteria, as a release. Some vast, smothering oppression, undefined but long felt by millions, seemed to have been suddenly and miraculously lifted. "It was as if a nightmare had vanished," another German who lived through it has said. "As if a door had opened, and an old yearning been satisfied." Germany plunged into the war as into "a bath of steel" that would somehow cleanse and purge. "May it purify our public life as a thunderstorm does the atmosphere," said another commentator shortly after the war's outbreak. "May it allow us to live again, and make us eager to risk our lives in deeds such as this hour commands. Peace had become insupportable."

A mass intoxication, a national delirium, swept over the German people. They were not alone in it. There were also scenes of tumultuous enthusiasm in Paris, London, Vienna and St. Petersburg. But Germany greeted the war with a passion that deepened the natural response of patriotism into something more ominous. For generations their poets and professors had preached the "moral sublimity" of war and spoken of its "civilizing majesty," endowing it with an aura of awe and reverence unknown in other countries. "Quietly and deeply must the joy of war and the longing for it live in the German heart. . . . Yes, war is beautiful," a German youth publication had written in January of 1913. Now, at last, war had come, and it was welcome.

Adolf Hitler, who believed that "in eternal peace mankind perishes," welcomed it with an ardor of his own. "Overpowered by a rapturous enthusiasm," he said, "I fell upon my knees and thanked Heaven from an overflowing heart for granting me the good fortune of being allowed to live in these times."

For no one did the war come as more of a release, an escape, than for Hitler. At twenty-five his life had become an oppressive futility, offering him nothing of what he sought from the present and promising nothing for the future. Since coming to Munich, he had made no advance, professionally or personally. His drawing had brought neither reward nor recognition. Socially he remained a cipher. No woman had entered his life. In a teeming city known for its social warmth and easygoing ways, where the customary greeting even between strangers was *Herr Nachbar,* Mr. Neighbor, he remained wholly isolated, imprisoned within a personality so tense and wary that it would neither let him escape its confinement nor allow anyone in. He himself spoke of the war as a kind of deliverance—"a deliverance from the vexatious feelings of youth," he called it. His enlistment, when the chance came, was a form of flight.

As an alien, Hitler was required to petition the King for permission to join the Bavarian Army. With most of Germany's young manhood moving to the fronts, his petition was promptly granted. "My joy and gratitude knew no bounds," he said. "Within a few days I was wearing the tunic that I would not take off until almost six years later."

He was immediately mustered into the 7th Reserve Company of the 16th Infantry Regiment. The Bavarian Army's training and discipline were hardly less severe than the Prussian, and Hitler underwent weeks of rigorous field training, which only left him eager for battle and fretful that the war might end before he faced the enemy. In October he caught his first glimpse of the Rhine from the troop train that was taking him to Flanders. The soldiers began singing *Die Wacht am Rhein*—"The Watch on the Rhine"—and "I felt as if my heart would burst from my chest," said Adolf Hitler.

He need not have worried about getting his chance to fight. The 16th Bavarian, called the List Regiment after its first commander, was plunged almost at once into a furious engagement with the British, who were holding a line athwart the German drive to the Channel ports, one of the most crucial offensives of the war. This was the first Battle of Ypres, and the Bavarians suffered appalling casualties. Hitler's first taste of war was enough to surfeit a normal soldier for a lifetime, but it did not abate his ardor for the slaughter.

He wrote about it with almost juvenile relish in a letter to the tailor Popp. Hitler had just gone through the most shattering experience a man can know, but he had no one to communicate his feelings to except a former landlord whom he addressed not by his first name, or even "Dear Popp," but as "Honored Sir." It was a long and gushing letter, sprinkled with clichés derived from his lifelong reading of war stories, and it betrayed again his curious ineptitude with the language unless he was speaking it. The letter, for all its color and narrative detail, might have been written by a boy fresh from high school, rather than by a mature man of intellectual pretensions. There was not a hint of depth or insight in it.

"Like a giant snake our column twined its way forward . . . ," he wrote. "We could hardly see into the foggy, seething witches' cauldron before us. At last the command rang out: 'Forward!'

"We swarmed out . . . I was out in front, ahead of our squad. . . . We crawled on our bellies to the edge of the woods. Over us the shells were howling and whistling, splintered tree trunks and branches flew around us. . . . We ran into the fields like lightning, and after bloody hand-to-hand fighting in different places, we threw them out of one trench after the other . . .

"Day after day we are under the heaviest artillery fire from eight in the morning until five in the afternoon. In time, that shatters even the strongest nerves. I often think of Munich . . .

"We want an all-out fight, at any cost, and we hope that those of us who have the good fortune to see their homeland again will find it purer and more purified of foreignism . . . that through the stream of blood that flows here day after day against an international world of enemies, not only Germany's enemies abroad will be crushed, but that our internal internationalism will also be broken. That would be worth more than any territorial gains. With Austria it will come as I have always said . . ."

In Hitler's letter there was only a pale and shallow suggestion of the enormous impact of the front on the thousands of Germans for whom the war would remain the decisive experience, haunting and indelible. As with Hitler himself, it would color and condition their thoughts and attitudes for the rest of their lives so that in a sense they would never be civilians again. Their combat trenches would run through the postwar years like wounds across the nation's life, open and unhealed. From the battlefields of the First World War, carried undiminished into a turbulent peace, would come the fatal emotional and psychological thrusts that propelled Germany into the second.

What Hitler experienced of the mystique of combat, but could express only clumsily in writing, was vividly stated by another German soldier on the Western Front, a young lieutenant named Ernst Jünger. He was only nineteen when he took command of a platoon of the 73rd Hanoverian Fusiliers in a sector of the Champagne in 1915. Before the war was over he was wounded twenty times and awarded the *Pour le Mérite,* the highest German decoration for valor. In the prolonged slaughter of No Man's Land he did not see a reversion to barbarism, a return to savagery. Instead, the land that no man possessed became a sacred *Heimat,* a homeland, for which he, and thousands with him, would yearn forever after. There he experienced unforgettably what Rainer Maria Rilke called "the identity of terribleness and bliss." For Jünger, war was, in truth, majestic and sublime, just as his favorite poets and professors had told his generation. In it he found what Moltke and the mystics of militarism had promised, "the noblest virtues of man" manifested to a degree that made civil life seem pallid and contemptible in comparison.

Ernst Jünger became a writer of stature after the war, preaching "the Reich of the future" to yet another generation, and the youth listened, infected by his terrible vision of total conflict in a total state. For Jünger, and for many of his comrades, the front was "an incomparable schooling of the heart." The front schooled the German heart for much that was to come after.

"We had left lecture room, classroom and bench behind us," he wrote in *Storm of Steel.* "We had been welded by a few weeks' training into one corporate mass inspired by the enthusiasm of one thought—to carry forward the German ideals of 1870. We had grown up in a material age, and in each of us there was the yearning for great experience such as we had never known. The war had entered into us like wine. We had set out in a rain of flowers to seek the death of heroes. The war was our dream of greatness, power and glory. It was a man's work, a duel on fields whose flowers would be stained with blood. There is no lovelier death in the world . . ."

That was how it began, but even after many months of the most violent combat he still "looked forward to the battle with a certain joy"—for what, he asked, could be "more sublime than to face death at the head of a hundred men?"

In the war's "carnival of carnage," in the "orgy of destruction" was contained a "logical gospel of force." And in the presence of violent death one was transported into realms of feeling where the "godlike and the bestial are inextricably mingled."

And it transcended sanity, obliterating normal consciousness and creating new states of being:

"The nerves could register fear no longer. Everyone was mad and beyond reckoning; we had gone over the edge of the world into superhuman perspectives. Death had lost its meaning . . ."

But the war had not. Out of it was growing a blind, unreasoning nationalism that thousands of Germans on all the fronts embraced as the only possible justification for what they were enduring. "I was gripped by the sad and proud feeling of being more closely bound to my country because of the blood shed for her greatness . . . ," Jünger wrote. "The idea of the Fatherland had been distilled from all these afflictions in a clearer and brighter essence. That was the final winnings in a game on which so often all had been staked . . ."

For Hitler also, undergoing what he called "the most tremendous impressions of my life," the front was distilling and deepening the beliefs and prejudices he had brought to it and would carry away from it. He would take away something else as well. In a series of battles much like those Jünger described, Hitler discovered that he could control his fear under fire. He had been uncertain about his reactions. With the knowledge that he could make his will prevail over his weakness in extreme situations, his character hardened, his confidence in himself increased, he matured. "Now I was calm and determined," he wrote of his 1915–1916 period. "And this endured. Now fate could apply the ultimate tests without my nerves breaking or my reason failing."

It was, unfortunately, true.

If in the future there would often be an abnormal, even hysterical, element in his courage—if his nerves did, in fact, sometimes fail him—what he learned of himself as a soldier under fire sustained him afterward in many another battle critical for his career.

He was a good soldier from the start, but in many ways a peculiar one. After the first battles of the List Regiment in which he fought with the assault troops, his assignment was changed. He was made a *Meldegänger,* or dispatch runner, charged with carrying orders from the Regimental Staff to the advanced units in the trenches. This was his function through the rest of the war.

The work was lonely, which perhaps suited him, and it was dangerous. The dispatch runner, making his way forward under frequent sniper and artillery fire, was on his own. The backs of men who stood shoulder-to-shoulder in the trenches were stiffened by the presence of witnesses: their comrades. The dispatch carrier usually had no eyes upon him. Much depended on his getting through, for the orders he carried were often crucial. The worse the situation in the lines, the more urgent the mission, the heavier became the burden for the lone runner, obligated to deliver his pouch regardless of obstacles in the way. It was a job that required a high degree of resourcefulness and devotion to duty.

On the other hand, it entailed privileges denied the men in the trenches, and they regarded it as a soft touch. The dispatch runners were billeted at Staff Headquarters, which was always some distance behind the front lines. Between assignments they lived in comparative comfort, were less frequently under fire, and they ate better. They were not required to go over the top and storm into enemy positions, or fight hand-to-hand except in extraordinary circumstances. In his speeches after the war, Hitler constantly referred to his days in the trenches where, in fact, he did not spend much time. Nevertheless, he did distinguish himself sufficiently at Ypres, at Chemin des Dames, on the Somme and the Aisne, to be decorated early and often. He was awarded the Iron Cross Second Class in December of 1914, one of the first of his unit to get it, and won the Military Merit Cross later on. More remarkable, he also won the Iron Cross First Class, an uncommon decoration for an enlisted man in the German Army of that time.

There is thus no doubt about his bravery. Once, after the war when he had entered politics, a Hamburg newspaper accused him of cowardice as a soldier. He brought suit and was able to produce evidence from eyewitnesses who testified to his courage. One affidavit was from a Lieutenant Colonel Engelhardt, who commanded the List Regiment in bloody fighting around Wytschaete in Flanders. He described how Private Hitler and another runner protected him from machine-gun fire with their bodies when he stepped out of a woods into the open to survey the situation.

But the feat for which he won the coveted Iron Cross I, awarded on August 4, 1918, remains unclear. Various accounts of it were afterward given, but no official document describing it has ever been produced. The List regimental history does not mention it, and the citation that must have accompanied the medal has never been traced. Even the year in which the exploit is said to have taken place is not certain, and details differ widely in various accounts. One version says that Hitler, armed with a pistol, singlehandedly captured fifteen Englishmen, including an officer and a sergeant. In other versions his captives are ten, eleven, twelve, or even twenty Frenchmen whom he persuaded to surrender at rifle-point after talking to them in French, a language he couldn't speak. Another account says Hitler won the decoration for taking a message through heavy fire to an artillery command post and thereby saved German troops from being bombarded by German cannon.

For whatever reason it was awarded, the Iron Cross I proved to be an invaluable acquisition. It went far to legitimatize him as a German. Though it did not legally make him a citizen, it turned out to be a credential far more effective than any naturalization papers could have been. Possession of the Iron Cross I proved a shield against future slurs against him as an alien unqualified by birth for prominence in the German community. It went far toward canceling the handicap of being born in Austria, a foreigner. The men who first became his followers, and made his emergence as a political leader possible, would hardly have given their support and allegiance to an Austrian outsider, however gifted a demagogue, without some added factor to make him one of their own kind. But as a veteran of the German Army, a front-fighter wearing the accepted symbol of German valor, he could be listened to. In winning the Iron Cross, Adolf Hitler won more than he knew at the time. His military record was an indispensable pre-condition to his political ascent.

His record as a soldier having been so good in some respects, the question arises why it was not better in others. Promotion was not rapid in the Imperial German Army, advancement in the ranks was not easy. But in four years of staggering losses it did happen with some frequency. In the course of the war 100,000 men became lieutenants. Hitler served at the front almost continuously throughout the war, was repeatedly decorated and, as will be seen, twice wounded. His superior officer, Lieutenant Colonel Engelhardt, pronounced him "an exceedingly brave, effective and conscientious soldier." Yet the highest rank he was able to achieve was that of *Gefreiter*.

The term is usually translated as "corporal," but a corporal is a noncommissioned officer, which Hitler never was.* The rating of *Gefreiter* was closer to that of an American private first class or a British lance-corporal. For all his decorations and devotion to duty, the man who would one day be the absolute ruler of 70,000,000 people, and command the mightiest war machine the world had ever seen, was not considered fit to take charge of so much as a squad during his own days in the Army. His defects as a person evidently outweighed his virtues as a soldier.

His comrades found him odd—"a white crow," one of them called him. Though he afterward made much of the *Kameradschaft*, the comradeship, of the Army, even there he kept within his self-drawn circle, unable to step wholly outside it or allow anyone to cross into it. His continual tenseness and apart-

* Hitler is frequently called the "Bohemian corporal," which is wrong on both counts. He was not Bohemian, either. The epithet originated in a confusion over his birthplace, Braunau, on the Austrian-German border. He was mistakenly thought by some to have come from another town of the same name in the Sudetenland.

ness, which made him seem peculiar anywhere, was especially strange in the front lines, where men facing death together normally feel very close to one another. In his inability to mingle freely with his comrades, or win their confidence and affection, his officers may have found sufficient reason to deny him promotion. He seemed too eccentric for command.

There was something manic in the intensity of his soldiering. During a night barrage he would leap from his bed in the couriers' quarters, seize his rifle, and pace restlessly up and down until, one witness said, "his comrades felt like throwing a boot at him." He constantly infuriated the others by an unflagging zeal for duty that seemed to them well beyond what the situation required. When the regiment was relieved and came out of the line after a particularly harrowing engagement at Neuve Chapelle, the troops threw themselves gratefully on the ground, went to sleep on their knapsacks, or began writing letters home. Not Pfc. Hitler. He made no pause in getting on with the war. While the others looked on incredulously, he began grooming his equipment, cleaning his rifle and polishing his bayonet. "The Austrian never relaxes," a soldier remarked of him. "He always acts as if we'd lose the war if he weren't on the job every minute." When the runners disputed among themselves over whose turn it was to carry the next dispatch to the front, Pfc. Hitler would volunteer. Reproached for letting him do all the dirty work, one runner said: "If Hitler's that stupid—well, we're not."

One Christmas at Massines, a comrade recalled, the men were talking longingly of home. "Some wouldn't have objected to a light Christmas wound to get them to their families for the holidays." Pfc. Hitler stood aside, taking no part in the conversation. "He had no use for that sort of yearning." He had no home to go to.

When Christmas packages were distributed, there was none for him, and no greetings. A fellow runner named Hans Mend, who afterward wrote a book about Hitler at the front, remembered how some of the soldiers, moved to sympathy by the holiday mood, offered to share their packages with their empty-handed comrade. Hitler refused with a curt thanks, and sat in a corner brooding by himself while the others made merry. "I almost wept for him," Mend said. "I thought: 'The poor devil is going through plenty and doesn't even know for whom in Germany he's risking his life and sacrificing his health.' " His life and health seemed to mean nothing to him. "The trenches around Formelles were his world, and what lay behind them didn't exist for him." It was incomprehensible to his comrades that he repeatedly refused furloughs from the front.

He did not want to leave the front. There, for the first time, he had found a place where he could belong, a role to play that linked him as a participant to the mighty events for which he felt himself destined. He would always need outward upheaval and violence in which his own inner turmoil could be released and assert itself. He sensed that in a settled, orderly world he would be lost, remaining a cipher. He did not want peace to come. He did not want the war to end.

The fanatical soldier did not, however, cut a very soldierly figure. His build was dumpy and shapeless, and his uniform sat sloppily on it. He was awkward, as if loosely put together, and one of his officers recalled him as *"reichlich unmilitärisch"*— rather unmilitary—in appearance. He then wore a full mustache whose drooping ends added to his generally dolorous look. He was seldom known to smile or joke, and Mend remarked that he usually wore "a face that made it seem as if he went down to the cellar to laugh." A picture of him in a dugout survives. The men with him are either hatless or wearing cloth caps, relaxing. Pfc. Hitler is standing upright staring intently into the camera from under a spiked helmet with the chin strap in place.

Toward civilians behind the lines, and in his contact with enemy wounded and prisoners of war, he behaved correctly as army regulations and his war books had told him a good soldier should. But he set himself further apart from his fellows by refusing to have anything to do with the women of the rear areas. While the others bantered and flirted with the French girls as opportunity offered, Pfc. Hitler remained disapprovingly aloof. He became known in the regiment as *"der Weiberfeind,"* the woman-hater, and it added to his reputation for oddity among the men.

To Hans Mend, whose liaison with a certain Marie, a gravedigger's daughter, was the talk and envy of the outfit, he tried to justify his attitude as patriotic—it was unseemly for a German soldier to fraternize with enemy women in enemy territory. In reality, his behavior in this respect had little relation to the war.

From adolescence on, his life was abnormally void of contact with women. Since the death of his mother he had known no feminine affection or influence. He had reached full manhood without ever experiencing a normal relationship with a woman. The trap of his personality did not permit any escape from himself into the emotional giving and receiving of romantic love or even, apparently, the momentary involvement of sheerly sexual contact. In the Home for Men in Vienna, in the beer halls of Munich, and now in the Army, his associations, such as they were, consisted exclusively of men. Not really at home anywhere or with anyone, he was less uncertain and isolated among males. He felt safer there, where his personality was less in danger of penetration, and perhaps exposure, than in the presence of women. The Army, being free of the female element, was his ideal milieu. He did not want its wall of unadulterated maleness breached. The girls behind the lines were doubly enemies; they were both French and female.

His one self-indulgence was singularly juvenile for a frontline warrior. He had an uncontrollable passion for sweets. It showed itself early and stayed with him all his life. Gustl Kubizek had noticed it. Once, in Vienna, he took Hitler to a canteen whose menu included a kind of nutcake. The place was a favorite of Jewish college students, and this had posed an acute dilemma for Hitler. He could scarcely bring himself to eat with Jews, but he was mad for the cakes. Time and again nutcake had triumphed over anti-Semitism. At the front his choice of sweets was limited, but he devoured whatever came his way. It was a joke in the unit. "If he found a tin of artificial honey," Mend recalled, "nothing could get him away from it, shells or no shells." After one of the most furious British attacks the regiment ever sustained, Pfc. Hitler, exhausted and lucky to be alive, was seen soothing his nerves with lavish helpings of marmalade and sweetened tea. Otherwise food meant nothing to him. When the soldiers groused about a reduction in their meat ration, Hitler's reaction was to remind them that during the siege of Paris in 1870 the French ate rats.

He maintained his status as an artist with sporadic drawings and water colors of shell-damaged buildings and picturesque farmhouses. His work showed what one critic has called "a Philistine precision and neatness and an undeniable eye for structure," but otherwise it had no more character than any well-executed picture postcard. For the Regimental Adjutant, First Lieutenant Fritz Wiedemann, he once painted a dining room, evidently contributing artistic touches of his own to the décor. When, years afterward, Wiedemann reminded the then Chancellor of this incident, Hitler commented: "If Germany had not lost the war, I would not have become a politician, but a great architect like Michelangelo." This was an enduring delusion of the greatest destroyer of his age: that he was at heart a master builder.

But long before he or anyone else knew how the war was going to end, Pfc. Hitler's comrades at the front were well aware that his real passion was not art, but politics. It sometimes literally required an enemy barrage to stop one of his harangues, the shells coming as relief from his insistent oratory. "It was like in the Reichstag" when Hitler took the floor, one of the soldiers remembered, and Hitler took the floor often. The orderly room became his forum, as the beer table had previously been. The setting changed, but his themes remained the same, and they would not alter in any basic way as long as he lived.

In sudden seizures of agitation he would break into a group and smother the casual conversation with a political tirade. White-faced and intense, he spouted warnings of the manifold dangers that threatened the homeland from the sinister conspiracy of the Free Masons, from the menace of Marxism, and the machinations of the Catholic Church. But mainly, and incessantly, he harped on the dreadful threat of Jewry to Germany and all Aryan civilization. He used phrases that he would keep repeating in a thousand variations thereafter—"Jewish parasites," "racial despoilers," "international Jewish finance," and the like. On one occasion, Mend has recorded, he shouted, "If I had the power, I'd force all the Jews to go to Palestine!" He delivered this with such vehemence that his listeners laughed at him, but it was in embryo the attitude that led ultimately to the extermination camps.

Hitler was serving side by side with a Jewish soldier and under Jewish officers. By a little-known irony, the very officer who recommended him for his Iron Cross I was a Captain Hugo Gutmann, a Jew. There were no less than 100,000 Jews in German uniform on all the fronts, and they suffered about the same proportion of casualties as did the population as a whole. Of their number, official German war records would show, 35,000 were decorated for bravery, 23,000 were promoted, and 2,000 commissioned—remarkable figures, since the Prussian army had barred Jewish officers before the war. None of this made any impression on Adolf Hitler, whose prejudices were never affected by fact and reality, and who lived obsessively within the walls of fantasy he had erected around himself.

His ideas were often disregarded as *Quatsch,* nonsense, by the soldiers, and some thought him unbalanced, crazy. The List Regiment was composed largely of students and men of education to whom Hitler's more primitive outpourings may have seemed repellent. The unit also included a number of Social Democrats who sometimes countered his attacks on Marxism, which they equated with trade-unionism and social legislation. The fact that Hitler was an outsider, an Austrian among Bavarians, and a peculiar character in general, inclined still others to dismiss him as a crackpot. But not all.

The regiment was a microcosm, a sampling, of what he would encounter in Germany on a much vaster scale later. If, as afterward, there were those who laughed at him, and some who regarded him as not worth listening to, there were others whose attention he caught and held, who did listen and were persuaded. In retrospect, Hans Mend professed to see the origins of the Nazi Party in Hitler's impromptu orations to the men of the 16th Bavarian Infantry Regiment during its days at the front. "I may say," he wrote, "that Adolf Hitler won his first National Socialist followers in the billet we called 'Black Marie's' at Fournes in 1915 and 1916."

The regimental sergeant-major, Max Amann, was one such convert. He was a tough, burly Bavarian of the brawling sort that later became the core of Hitler's retinue in Munich. Uncouth but able, Amann was to do much toward organizing and managing the Nazi Party's business affairs. He was not the only List veteran to figure in the Nazi hierarchy. Lieutenant Wiedemann, the Regimental Adjutant for whom Pfc. Hitler did the interior decorating, became Chancellor Hitler's own adjutant and later his Consul-General in San Francisco. Another lieutenant in the regiment, Rudolf Hess, became a pillar of the Party and its deputy leader, though he and Hitler never met at the front.

The Army not only gave Hitler his first followers; his wartime experience first gave him the idea of becoming a speaker and entering politics. He had been at the front for two years without interruption, and even his enthusiasm for war lost its glow. "Horror had taken the place of the glamour of battle," he wrote of this period. "Ardor gradually cooled, and joyous exuberance was choked off by deathly fear." Casualties in the regiment, unusually severe from the start, mounted steadily. There had been occasions when it was pulled out of the line because its losses could no longer be sustained. In one such engagement, a sergeant was forced to take charge of a battalion and the medical officer assumed command of the regiment. Mend witnessed a mass burial in which corpses sprinkled with lime were being put into the earth in layers of thirty, with straw between, until one grave alone held more than 100 bodies. He could not understand how Hitler continued to escape death and injury, and once said to him: *"Mensch, für Dich gibt es keine Kugel!"*—"Man, they don't have a bullet with your name on it!"

So it seemed, though some of his calls were very close.

At the battle of Wytschaete, early in the war, he was in an attack with eight comrades when three of them were killed and another grievously wounded. Adolf Hitler was untouched. As a result of the action, the four men still able-bodied were summoned to the staff tent where a conference on possible decorations was being held. The tent became crowded and the enlisted men, including Private Hitler, were asked to step outside. They had left the tent less than five minutes when a shell hit it, killing almost everyone inside and crippling the rest. Adolf Hitler was untouched.

Anyone inclined to ponder the unfathomable ways of Providence might contemplate the fact that in a "generation predestined for death," as Ernst Jünger called it, when the Great War was destroying German manhood at the rate of one out of every thirty-two of the population; when 1,773,700 German battle deaths were being recorded; when nearly 9,000,000 were dying on both sides in the bloodiest and most indiscriminate slaughter ever known; when the finest and noblest of the world's youth— poets, artists, musicians, potential geniuses—were being mowed down in windrows, Adolf Hitler, who spent four years where the bullets flew thickest, was spared.

He was deeply impressed by this himself. It solidified his long-held conviction that destiny had marked him for her own, and that fate had reserved an unspecified but certain greatness for him. He was sure that he was being spared for a reason. The mysteriously powerful belief in himself with which he was born, and which had survived twenty-five years of failure and futility, was reinforced and enlarged by his war experience. He was not yet ready to say openly, as he would in a speech in 1938, "I regard myself as the instrument of Providence," but already as a mere private he was sufficiently certain of himself and his future to tell his fellow soldiers, including those who laughed at him, that one day they would assuredly hear more of Adolf Hitler.

He did not, however, escape entirely unscathed.

Toward the end of September 1916, he took part in the Battle of the Somme, which had been raging for months and which, he said, was "more hell than war." In this massive and prolonged British-French offensive, the Germans suffered 400,-000 casualties, and Hitler was among the wounded. On October fifth he was hit in the upper thigh of his left leg by a shell fragment.

For the first time in two years he left his regiment and the front. His wound was not serious, but he was brought to a military hospital in the town of Beelitz, near Berlin. "What a change!" he wrote. "From the mud of the Somme battle to the white beds of this wonderful place! One hardly dared to lie in them properly at first. One could only reaccustom oneself to this new world gradually." He did not, in fact, accustom himself to it at all. Its impact upon him was more violent and lasting than that of his wound.

He was familiar with the grousing and complaining of the men at the front, which seldom affected morale, and was largely routine. But in the hospital he first encountered serious symptoms of defeatism, all the more appalling to him because they were openly exhibited by other soldiers. There was, for example, the fellow patient who had contrived his way into one of the miraculous white beds by deliberately pulling his hand through a barbed-wire entanglement. He bragged about it, and he was not the only malingerer in the hospital. There was a cynical saying current about saving one's neck any way one could: "Better a coward for three minutes than dead the rest of your life." Defeatists in the wards were not being shouted down and repudiated, but were either listened to in silence or openly agreed with. "I was choked with disgust," said Adolf Hitler.

Outside the hospital the situation was worse. During his convalescence he visited Berlin for the first time. There he saw evidence of discontent, deterioration and actual hunger on every hand. The economic strain of the war, the catastrophic losses at the front and the British sea blockade were reducing the population to a sullen and sluggish human mass for whom the war was becoming an unbearable burden. Bread and potatoes were scarce, meat and fats almost unobtainable. Turnips, once used only for fodder, became the principal ingredient of almost every dish from sausages to marmalade. Millions of Germans would never afterward think of a turnip without retching. Children were so seldom properly fed that most had become pale and listless, and school sessions had to be curtailed. There were more and more beggars in the streets, and haggard faces everywhere.

War weariness was steadily spreading and deepening. In workingmen's cafés and restaurants soldiers were openly being urged not to return to the front. Many were overstaying their leaves. Agitation for peace was becoming increasingly insistent. Left-wing leaflets criticizing the Kaiser and denouncing the military leadership were being clandestinely printed and circulated in quantity. "Enough and more than enough of the slaughter!" one of them read. "Down with the war mongers on both sides of the border! Make an end to the mass murder!"

"That was 1917, when no one believed in anything any more," said George Grosz, who was also in Berlin then, and beginning to produce the merciless caricatures that made him perhaps the most trenchant of commentators on the Germany of his time. He, too, had volunteered and marched off to the Western Front in the mass delirium of the war's beginning. "The appeal of gun and helmet soon wore off," he wrote, "and war represented only the grim and the horrible. It came to mean filth, lice, idiocy, disease and deformity . . ."

Medically discharged from the Army, Grosz sat in his top-floor studio on the Stephen Strasse, and with stark and unerring pen strokes unmasked the essential beastliness of the times. From sketches dashed off while in the Army he made many of the finished drawings that now rank with Goya's *Disasters of War*—a medical orderly dumping fragments of a human body from a pail into a pit; a skeleton dressed as a recruit being examined for military duty; an insane soldier being forced into a straitjacket made from a horse blanket; crippled soldiers; soldiers without noses. He drew "lonely little men fleeing madly through empty streets," men raising clenched fists as they cursed at the moon, men drunk and men vomiting.

"What I saw filled me with disgust and aversion for mankind . . . ," said George Grosz. "My drawings expressed my despair, hate and disillusionment."

Despair, hate and disillusion were spreading epidemically through German society at all levels, and they were precisely the elements Adolf Hitler would need to assert himself when his time came. The war's social and psychic shocks were already opening the crevices in the structure of the German community through which he would eventually emerge from his obscurity.

His indignation at what he had seen in Berlin was increased when, after his discharge from the hospital, he was assigned to a replacement battalion in Munich. "I hardly thought I recognized the place," he said. "Anger, unrest and cursing wherever one went!"

The war was having a special impact on Bavaria, and the repercussions were most pronounced in the capital. Discontent took the form of castigating Berlin for the setbacks at the fronts and the hardships at home. The inbred antipathy of the south Germans for the north became increasingly virulent. Long-standing rivalries and jealousies between Bavaria and Prussia were being aggravated to a degree damaging to the whole war effort.

As a state with its own king, administration, foreign office and army, and with its own traditions and customs as well, Bavaria had always regarded itself as substantially independent within the framework of the German federation. Resistance to domination or interference by Prussia was strong, and particularism—the concept that Bavaria was entitled to special rights and privileges among the German states—was taken for granted. Even separatism, which called for breaking away from the Reich entirely and establishing a wholly independent nation, had its advocates.

In many Bavarians the blue and white of the state flag evoked a warmer and more primary allegiance than the black-white-red of the Reich itself. At one point a delegation of noblemen and prominent citizens called upon King Ludwig III in formal audience and urged him to wrest the leadership of the nation from Prussia and make Bavaria's the determining voice in the conduct of the war and the formulation of policy for the empire. In a paraphrase of the old saying that the world would find regeneration through the German nation, Germany itself was now to achieve salvation through Bavaria. It was an expression of the inveterate local chauvinism that, after the war, would manifest itself even more flagrantly and become a basic factor in the *Putsch* of Adolf Hitler.

In a similar anticipation of coming events, Munich became the assembly point of extremist opposition of every shade and gradation. Along with those who wished the war to end on almost any terms, there were organized and articulate factions that demanded it be extended and intensified. Pan-German agitation was particularly intense. It used speeches, leaflets, pamphlets and the press to demand a *"Totalisierung des Krieges,"* total war—a significant early use of the phrase. The Pan-Germans made no pretense of regarding the conflict as defensive, a war against enemy encirclement, which was the government line. For them it was frankly an opportunity for conquest and national aggrandizement.

Adolf Hitler, cured of his wound but not of his obsessions, saw nothing but the workings of the Jewish conspiracy in what he called "this accursed brawl among the German tribes." A Bavarian by choice, he was pro-Prussian and Pan-German by instinct. Since the antagonism of the two states was damaging to the German cause, he automatically assumed that it benefited the Jews and hence must have been inspired by them. As long ago as his days of reading the *Ostara* in Vienna cafés he had found the infallible formula that explained all the difficulties and complications of life and history, and he used it to explain the deplorable conditions he had found everywhere behind the lines: the Jew was responsible.

His stay in Munich was made even more disagreeable by his experience in the replacement battalion. Here he had a more plausible and human complaint. Like many another combat veteran, he was outraged to discover that his front-line status was not sufficiently appreciated by the training personnel of the rear. Aside from that, he found that in the battalion "the general mood was miserable; shirking was rated as almost a form of higher wisdom, while loyalty and steadfastness were regarded as signs of weakness and stupidity." As soon as he was able to arrange it, he was back with his regiment, where things were simple and the issues clear. The front was the one place he had yet found where he was more than a cipher. At home he was ignored. At the front he was decorated.

What he had seen at home and what he knew of the course of the war on the fronts caused him to ponder the reasons for Germany's precarious position after two and a half years of war. His conviction was unshakable that the German army was invincible, being composed entirely of dauntless heroes like himself who had won such spectacular early victories. There had to be some other explanation for the subsequent reversals and for the continued resistance of the enemy who, bafflingly, had not broken under the massive German blows. He concluded that the reason was not in the enemy's fortitude and fighting qualities but in the power and brilliance of its propaganda. It was propaganda, he decided that had bolstered the enemy after its initial defeats, and it was propaganda that was now undermining German morale at home and at the fronts. So effective were the enemy leaflets in playing on the yearning for peace, and seeking to separate the German people from their leadership, that Hitler feared the Army was learning "to think as the enemy wanted it to."

He was lastingly impressed by these feats of psychological warfare performed, he said, with "unheard of skill and truly inspired astuteness. I myself learned hugely from this enemy propaganda."

German propaganda, on the other hand, he regarded as wretchedly inept and ineffective—"a complete failure." It had neither destroyed the enemy's will to resist nor maintained the morale of the German people. Therein, he thought, lay a fundamental reason for Germany's failure to achieve the victory its soldiers so clearly deserved. "Day after day," he wrote, "I asked myself with mounting rage: Is there really no one at all who can put an end to this squandering of the army's heroism . . . this psychological mass murder?"

He believed he was the one who could do it if given the chance:

"More than once I was tormented by the thought that our battle with destiny would have turned out differently if Providence had put me in the place of these bunglers, these criminally incompetent scoundrels, of our propaganda service.

"For the first time, in these months, I felt the full treachery of fortune that had placed me at the front where any chance Negro could shoot me to pieces, while elsewhere I might have been able to perform quite different services for the Fatherland!

"For I was presumptuous enough even then to believe I could have succeeded in this.

"But I was only a nameless soldier among eight million!"

He was perhaps the one soldier among those eight million with sufficient self-confidence to imagine that he, singlehanded, could change the outcome of the war. What he did do to alter the course of history afterward, however, was hardly less astounding, and his discovery of the power of propaganda during the war helped him to do it.

He was wrong in believing that propaganda, whether good Allied or bad German, was the determining factor in the outcome of the war. But he was right in sensing that he had found a weapon that he was equipped to wield as few others have ever been.

His mind was coarse and he was in the deepest sense an ignorant man, and would remain so, but some subjects he was capable of grasping, analyzing and understanding with a mastery amounting to genius. Propaganda, its nature and uses, was one of them. He had first learned from the great demonstrations of the Social Democrats in Vienna, he said, that "the right use of propaganda is a true art." Only in the war, however, "did it become clear to what enormous results the correct application of propaganda could lead." He would learn how to apply propaganda correctly for his own ends. He would get enormous results.

Events that provided Hitler with one of his most effective propaganda themes began occurring soon after his return to the front. This theme was the postwar legend of the *Dolchstoss*—the "stab in the back"—which spread the belief that the German Army was never defeated in the field but was basely done to death by subversive elements behind the lines. Once this idea took hold, the blame for defeat could be shifted to civilian shoulders, absolving the military caste of responsibility for military disaster and leaving the cherished myth of Prussian invincibility unsmudged and intact for millions. By the *Dolchstoss* fabrication, a German historian has written, "All of Germany's postwar politics were poisoned at their roots and were therewith condemned to bankruptcy."

A cluster of developments early in 1917 contributed to the genesis of the legend. In March the outbreak of the Russian revolution and the abdication of the Czar had a stimulative effect on leftist labor circles in Germany, long restive at the course of the war and the postponement of promised social reforms at home. In April a meeting of dissident Social Democrats convened at Gotha and broke off from the main party, declaring themselves "in fundamental opposition to the current system of government and to the policies of the Reich." They also denounced the party leadership for its acquiescent attitude toward the government and the war. They called their new organization the Independent Social Democratic Party of Germany thus splitting the socialist camp in two. The parent body was thereafter known as the Majority Social Democrats.

Within the Independent group there was still another division. A small number of radical intellectuals designated themselves the Spartacus League and reserved freedom of future action for themselves, professing a more revolutionary Marxist philosophy than either of the other factions. From the Spartacists the German Communist Party would later evolve, adding further to the amoeba-like character of a workers' movement whose lack of unity was to prove fatal for democracy in postwar Germany. But at the time the emergence of the Independents and the Spartacists gave German labor a more militant and activist look.

This ferment of opposition to the regime coincided with a reduction in the bread ration. Inequalities in food distribution, and a progressive thinning out of supplies, had become a major cause of grumbling and resentment in industrial areas, and now a movement for an open protest was initiated. Leaders of the Independent Socialists, eager for the chance to prove their influence over the workers, sought to organize a kind of general strike. The Majority Socialists, unwilling to risk any further loss of leadership and face, supported the action.

Though the response was by no means general, the strike call was heeded by many munitions, metal and transport workers. In Berlin alone more than 200,000 men and women stayed away from their machines and benches. Parades and mass meetings developed into protests not only against the food shortages but also against the war and for immediate peace negotiations. What had long been seething beneath the surface broke momentarily into public view.

The strikes lasted only a few days. They were ended by a combination of military fiat and concessions from the authorities, including an agreement that a labor committee be consulted in the future on problems of food supply and distribution. The workers returned to the factories, and no essential damage had been done to the war effort. But these first major strikes were a forecast of larger and more significant ones to come. They generated lasting hatreds and divisions among the German people, accentuating and deepening the existing class antipathies. At the fronts thousands of soldiers asked themselves, as Adolf Hitler, did: "What was the army still fighting for if the homeland itself did not want victory? For whom were the enormous sacrifices and privations being made and endured? The soldier is supposed to fight for victory while the homeland strikes against it!" The troops were being stabbed in the back.

The raging resentment against Social Democrats and all Marxists that Hitler had conceived in Vienna was intensified during the war and brought to a pitch by the munitions strikes. He had not forgotten the workers who threatened to throw him from the scaffold for refusing to join their union. And for him "Marxism" had become synonymous with "Jewry." What was happening at home while he was at the front fed all his basic obsessions, and confirmed them.

There was, he thought, no party in all Germany equipped to take up the "ruthless struggle" that he considered necessary to destroy Social Democracy. He brooded about this at the front.

"I often spoke about it at length among my closer comrades," he said. "And in this connection the first thoughts came to me of engaging in political activity at a later date.

"It was just this that prompted me to assure the small circle of my friends that, in addition to my profession, I intended to become a speaker after the war. . . ."

But while the war continued he passionately wanted total victory for Germany. He did not then know that what he needed, first of all, for the unfolding of his own destiny was defeat.

And defeat was on the way.

It needed no stab in the back.

"Even before the first cavalry patrolmen swung foot into stirrup in August 1914, German diplomacy had lost the war," wrote a German historian who drew up a balance sheet of the statistics involved well after the event.

When all the participants had chosen sides and were counted up, twenty-nine nations comprising four-fifths of the earth's population were at war with Imperial Germany. Not all of them sent troops into the field, but, in one way or another, they all supported the major countries who did: France, Great Britain, Russia, Italy and, finally, the United States.

On the other side was Germany, which began with a single ally, Austro-Hungary, and later acquired two more: Turkey and Bulgaria. Thus 120 million Germans and Austrians were arrayed against an enemy 280 million strong, with 420 million more colonial peoples behind them.

The elements working toward defeat were hidden and slow to emerge, like the strangling effects of the British sea blockade, which was certain in the long run to do fatal damage to a country that normally imported one-fourth of its food and supplies. On the other hand, such feats as an unprecedented German advance of 250 miles in the West within two weeks, and the triumph at Tannenberg in the East, were immediate and spectacular. They proved that the traditional pride in Prussian power was not mistaken, and they seemed to be unmistakable preludes to inevitable victory. After a Tannenberg, who could doubt the invincibility of German arms?

Tannenberg was significant for another reason. From it emerged the two most famous German generals of the First World War, and one of them would later march at the side of Adolf Hitler in the *Putsch* that was an overture to the Second. His name was Erich Ludendorff.

When the summons to Tannenberg came, he was already a national figure, the first winner in the war of the *Pour le Mérite*. At a critical moment in the massive assault on Liège, he had performed a deed that stood out, vividly and romantically, even in the great surge of German victories.

The forts of the city had been thoroughly battered by heavy artillery, and most of the Belgian troops had withdrawn. Believing the main fort, the Citadel, to have fallen, Major General Ludendorff drove up to it in his staff car. But the Citadel had not fallen. He nevertheless pounded on the gates and, when they were opened, demanded that the fort surrender to him. It did, and Liège was in German hands.

Knocking on the gates of the Citadel at Liège opened the way for him to more than entry into a fort. It brought him onto the stage of German history where he was able to exert a baleful influence on the course of events long after the war was over. His singlehanded feat made him the hero of the western front, and when an acute crisis developed soon thereafter in the East, it was natural for the High Command to send him into the breach. He was forty-nine when his chance came.

While the Germans were exulting over their victories in Belgium and France, the Russians were breaking into East Prussia. Aside from his recent feat at Liège, Ludendorff was known as an exceptionally gifted strategist and organizer, having for years headed the war-plans division of the General Staff. He was thus judged to be eminently qualified "to keep the worst from happening" in the East and was named Chief of Staff of the Eighth Army there.

In the choice of a partner for Ludendorff a duet was created that dominated Germany for the rest of the war. The selection fell upon Lieutenant General Paul von Beneckendorff und von Hindenburg who, at sixty-seven, was on the retired list. He was chosen chiefly because of his imperturbable temperament. He could be relied upon to hold steady no matter what happened, and this was a rarer quality than might have been expected among the supposedly iron-willed warriors of the Prussian mode at the top of Germany's military establishment. The news from the East had been received in the High Command with something like panic. General Max von Prittwitz und Gaffron, the commander on the scene, was on the verge of hysteria when telephoning his intentions to retreat and his demands for reinforcements. And Erich Ludendorff, selected as the savior of the situation, was regarded by his superiors as "an extremely capricious person" whose nerves were not entirely reliable either, despite his bravura performance at Liège. Hindenburg was intended to be Ludendorff's sheet-anchor, holding him steady and on course during possible squalls.

Ludendorff contrasted with him in almost every way. He was of middle-class background, and it spoke for his ability that he had come so far in the Prussian army without any of the advantages that a *von* implied. Where Hindenburg was all imposing bulk and solidity, Ludendorff was driven by a compulsive energy that betrayed something unstable and erratic in his nature. His face was habitually set in a menacing glower designed to offset an inadequate chin. His manner was harsh and dictatorial. Men closely associated with him for years had never once seen him smile. But, of the two, Ludendorff had by far the quicker mind, the readier grasp of a situation and the more original way of responding to it. At Tannenberg the two developed a battle such as generals dream of, another Cannae. The Second Russian Army was wiped out. More than 90,000 prisoners and much booty were taken. Its commander became the first, and only, general of the war to commit suicide. Another Russian army was isolated and then routed in the Battle of the Masurian Lakes. East Prussia was cleared of the invader. There would be no march into Berlin from the East. Hindenburg and Ludendorff became the idols of the hour—"figures of superhuman grandeur" in the eyes of the German people. And with the war bogged down into the stalemated attrition of the trenches, Germany reverted to an ancient custom and established a military dictatorship so unlimited that its match had rarely been seen in a modern state. The two victors of Tannenberg were called upon to head it, Field Marshal Paul von Hindenburg as Chief of the Great General Staff, and Erich Ludendorff, now First Quartermaster General, as Chief of Staff to the Chief of Staff.

Constitutional procedures and civilian influence were shunted aside and virtually ignored. Kaiser Wilhelm, who had entered the war loudly proclaiming himself God's chosen instrument—"I am His sword, His Representative"—retained his byzantine title of All-Highest War Lord but lapsed into a barely tolerated figurehead. As the dominating and more dynamic partner in the new duumvirate, Erich Ludendorff, without a *von* to his name, became the real ruler of Imperial Germany, "the secret Kaiser."

Experts tend to agree that the First Quartermaster General was a peerless military technician. In the disposition and maneuvering of troops his mind worked with a mastery that approached genius. But it was a freakishly lopsided mind, and when not called upon to function militarily, it was shockingly limited. He had acquired control of what Lloyd George, the British Prime Minister, called "the most formidable military machine known in history," and within the combat zones he ran the machine perhaps as skillfully as any man could. But away from his war maps and logistics tables he was a blindly narrow Pan-German of the most primitive stripe. The same mind that could grasp and clarify the infinitely complex elements of a major offensive was also clouded by the phobias and cluttered with the absurdities of the *völkisch* beer halls. The famous First Quartermaster General, on whom the fate of four nations depended, shared the aberrations and outlook of the unknown Pfc. with whom he would one day make common cause.

In February of 1917, against the urgings of civilian advisers, Ludendorff and the High Command launched their campaign of unrestricted submarine warfare, a flagrant menace to the remaining neutral countries, including the United States. Two months later America was at war. If any single stab pierced the heart of Imperial Germany, it was this—and it was no stab in the back. Later in the year efforts by Pope Benedict XV to end by compromise the struggle that was making a human slaughterhouse out of Europe failed. Then, at Brest-Litovsk, the High Command revealed to the West, and to the German people, what kind of terms it intended to impose if Germany should be victorious. All remaining pretense that Germany was fighting a defensive war evaporated. All hopes of a compromise peace ended.

The preliminary to Brest-Litovsk was a paradoxical stroke by which Ludendorff, an archenemy of Marxism, contributed decisively to the establishment of the Bolshevik tyranny in Russia. The overthrow of Czar Nicholas II was accompanied by mutiny in the army, hunger riots in the cities and civil war. The German High Command naturally sought to exploit the turmoil and disintegration in an enemy country. A scheme was hit upon that turned out to be highly effective in its immediate results, but, like so many of Ludendorff's policies, disastrous in the long run.

The scheme was to transport the man who called himself Nicolai Lenin into Russia, where he could assume personal leadership of the extreme radical elements, intensify the turmoil, and take Russia out of the war. Lenin would be sent back to Russia for the same reason that shells and poison gas are dispatched into enemy trenches, as a High Command spokesman put it.

Lenin, still in exile, was then in Zurich, hopelessly separated from the revolution he had done so much to foment. With Ludendorff's approval, the German Government arranged to have him transported in a sealed railroad car from Switzerland across Germany and to Sweden. From Sweden he crossed by sleigh into Finland, and by train arrived at the Finland Station in Petrograd, where he was greeted by a Bolshevik delegation in a little waiting room that previously had been reserved for the Czar.

"Dear comrades, soldiers, sailors and workers," he said in

his first speech on Russian soil, "I am happy to greet you as the advance guard of the international proletarian army . . ." In private he said, "We will destroy everything, and on the ruins we will build our temple." He proceeded to do so. His *Iskra,* the spark he had sent flying from Munich and elsewhere during his exile, had helped start the blaze of revolution. Now, on the scene, he could fan it into conflagration. In less than a year, with another revolution of his own, he had overthrown the moderate Provisional Government, proclaimed the Union of Soviet Socialist Republics, established the dictatorship of the proletariat, and made the name "Communist" his own. And, as the High Command hoped, he removed Russia from the war against Germany.

At Brest-Litovsk, in March of 1918 the High Command forced Lenin to pay a staggering price for peace. More than 300,000 square miles of territory were ceded to Germany. This included 56,000,000 Russian subjects, or 32 percent of the entire population. Enormous amounts of natural and industrial resources were included, as well as an indemnity of six billion marks. It was, according to one sober historical appraisal, "a humiliation without precedent or equal in modern history."

Militarily, Brest-Litovsk was a success for the High Command, relieving the pressure on the German armed forces and releasing large troop contingents for action in the West. In every other way it was a catastrophe. It cemented, once and for all, the determination of the Allies to beat Germany to its knees rather than risk submission to another such German peace. Inside Germany, it caused a crisis in morale. Workers and Social Democratic leaders, sympathetic to the aspirations of their opposite numbers in Russia and yearning for signs of a reasonable settlement, were appalled at the ruthlessness of the conditions imposed by the High Command. A renewed wave of strikes swept the country, this time involving a million workers. In Berlin alone, more than 400,000 downed their tools. A state of siege was proclaimed, the military took over the factories, and strike leaders were arrested and sent to the front regardless of their physical condition or draft status. The main effect of this was to bring seasoned anti-war agitators into direct contact with the soldiers in the trenches, and spread disaffection.

In Munich the workers in the Krupp munitions plant also struck. The Schwabing Bohemian Kurt Eisner, of the Café Stefanie, had become the local leader of the Independent Socialist and was now an organizer of the strike movement. He, along with the whole strike committee, was arrested and thrown into jail. A young, dark-eyed poet named Ernst Toller, new to political agitation but eager to participate, distributed copies of his anti-war verses among the workers and their women. Toller had enlisted at the start of the war, requested action with the infantry, fought bloody battles as a machine gunner. Physically delicate and emotionally unstable, he had suffered a collapse and been given a medical discharge. His passion now was to bring an end to the horrors he had experienced at the front. Before he was arrested, jailed and put back into uniform, he addressed his first mass meeting and found that he had a ready tongue on the platform. The strike collapsed, but Ernst Toller, like Kurt Eisner, would be heard again.

In Munich, as elsewhere, only a fraction of the workers participated in the strike or sympathized with it. On January 9, 1918, during the labor unrest precipitated by the Brest-Litovsk negotiations, a toolmaker at the local railway yards wrote an article for the Munich-Augsburg *Abendzeitung* in which he sought to rally workingmen to support the war to the utmost, assuring them of ultimate and complete victory. Proletarian internationalism had failed, the article said; the idea of the universal brotherhood of workers was a myth. If the enemy were in as strong a position as Germany, he would never think of giving in. So the slogan of the German worker must be *"Durchhalten!"*—"Hold out!"—and all would eventually be well. The article was shallow and naïve, but it acquired a special significance. It was the first political utterance of Anton Drexler, founder of the minuscule party that became the instrument of Adolf Hitler's rise to power.

Drexler was one of those singular characters who, without any real weight or distinction of their own, achieve a kind of immortality by serving as the objects off which stronger characters ricochet into history.

No fiery agitator, heavy of mind and manner, Drexler was

ploddingly sincere in his conviction that a strong German peace would benefit the workingman. He saw his mission in spreading the Pan-German idea in labor circles. His trust was in the wisdom of established authority and the infallibility of the High Command, and he sought to wean his fellow workers away from their socialist tendencies and back to faith in the cause of the Fatherland. As in all Pan-German thinking, there was a pronounced streak of anti-Semitism in Drexler's outlook, but he was imbued with the German respect for order and opposed to political violence. Tall and bespectacled, without personal luster, he had a simple, direct way that attracted a small following among right-wing workers in the railroad machine shops.

On March seventh he was able to announce the formation of what he called the "Free Labor Committee for a Good Peace," by which he meant a peace the High Command would consider good. The group had about forty members and attracted no special notice, Munich being well supplied with parties and leagues of all political shades. The survival of this feeble newcomer seemed highly unlikely and, indeed, it accomplished nothing on its own. But in Anton Drexler's Free Labor Committee was the seed of Adolf Hitler's National Socialist Workers' Party.

Two weeks after this unnoticed event in Munich, the High Command committed itself to the greatest offensive ever mounted in a supreme effort to settle the war on its own terms. Ludendorff had long decided that Germany's sole chance of victory lay in "a gambler's throw" in the West, and this was his all-or-nothing roll of the dice. Inevitably, his last-ditch efforts failed and as the Allied pressure on all his fronts mounted, Ludendorff's nerves were visibly twitching. The imperious Prussian exterior began to crack, and now not even the wooden passivity of Hindenburg could steady him. On August eighth had occurred the "black day of the German Army," in Ludendorff's own phrase; the British had made a major advance with massed tanks—the tanks that the German Army had neglected to build for itself, though they had appeared on the battlefield long before. From the East came indications of the imminent collapse of Turkey, Bulgaria and Austria, Germany's only allies. The whole German position seemed on the brink of dissolution.

The First Quartermaster General, the "man of steel," was under the care of a psychiatrist. He was by turns morbidly irritable and sullenly apathetic, and, what was worst in a high commander, indecisive. His doctor ordered inhaling exercises and a daily period in his rose garden to induce relaxation and stave off hysteria. But more than deep breathing and the scent of flowers was needed to salvage the spirit of Erich Ludendorff. On September twenty-eighth his nerves gave way entirely. He threw in his hand.

Late in the afternoon Ludendorff entered the General Headquarters of the German Army in the Hotel Britannique at Spa, the Belgian watering resort. His face was ashen above the blue-and-white of the *Pour le Mérite* dangling from his throat. Escorted by aides, he made his way through the potted palms and up the stairs to the office of Field Marshal von Hindenburg, his nominal superior. There, his high voice quavering, he announced the reason for his mission. Germany's military situation was now so catastrophic, he said, that an immediate bid to the Allied Powers for an armistice was imperative. The basis for negotiations was to be the Fourteen Points proposed the previous January by President Woodrow Wilson. These demanded, among other fundamental conditions for a possible peace, evacuation of Alsace-Lorraine to France, an independent Poland, self-determination for the peoples of the Balkans, and disarmament—all of which the High Command had previously dismissed as unacceptable.

But now an appeal to Wilson for a cease-fire was so pressing, said Ludendorff, that it was imperative to dispatch it at once by wireless through Switzerland to Washington. Another forty-eight hours might be too late. By that time the German front might cave in, placing Germany in an impossible position in the coming peace negotiations. Hindenburg, though less panicky than his colleague, agreed with this estimate of the military situation. He also saw it as hopeless. He went unequivocally on record to that effect in a communication to Prince Max of Baden, the newest in the series of wartime German chancellors. Hindenburg wrote:

"The High Command abides by its request . . . that an immediate peace offer be made to the enemy. . . . In these circumstances it is desirable to break off the struggle in order to spare the German people and their allies useless sacrifices. Every day's delay will cost thousands of brave soldiers their lives." Signed: von Hindenburg.

In this key document, as in the utterances of Ludendorff at the time, there was no mention of a stab in the back, or of any failure of the home front, or betrayal by sinister elements in the rear. The only reasons given by Germany's two highest commanders for requesting an armistice were military: the German Army was beaten, and no alternative remained.

On October 3, 1918, the same day that von Hindenburg confirmed his request for an armistice, the Pan-German dream of a conqueror's peace was still being advanced at a meeting in Munich's Wagner Hall, where the toolmaker Anton Drexler was a principal speaker. This was the first sizable public function of his Free Labor Committee for a Good Peace, and it had been financed from private sources that still thought it worthwhile to rally workingmen behind the war effort. The theme of the speakers was expressed in Drexler's pet slogans: "Trust the regime! Hold out to the end!" The meeting won few, if any, converts, but it kept the Free Labor Committee alive, and fortified Anton Drexler in his belief that he was a man with a mission. He would be calling more meetings.

The man destined to benefit most from Drexler's political dabbling was still at the front, and needed no exhortations to hold out. Adolf Hitler and his regiment were keeping up the fight, though now they were back defending the same ground over which they had stormed in 1914. Still confident of victory, Hitler was nevertheless moved to melancholy brooding as he recalled how it was in those early days when, in one of his rare poetic phrases, "our young regiment went into battle as to a dance." Now he noted that, though the field of combat was the same, the men were different. Among the young recruits there was no longer the rousing patriotism of those early days. Now

there was what he called "politicking" in the ranks. He attributed it to "the poison of the homeland," which was penetrating
even the front lines.

These October weeks were the last of the war for him. During the night of October fourteenth he and some of his comrades
were caught in a British barrage and pinned to a hill south of a
place called Wervick. It turned out to be a gas attack.

Poison gas had been used first by the Germans in 1915 in
violation of International Law that prohibited the use of noxious
fumes as a weapon of war. It was then adopted by the Allies,
who thereby gained an advantage since the blockaded Germans
were unable to produce rubber masks. At Wervick the British sent
over yellow-cross, or mustard, gas, which was a strong vesicant,
having a blistering effect on the eyes and respiratory system. The
men of Hitler's regiment had never encountered it before.

"I was to become personally acquainted with it during this
night," he wrote afterward. "Already by midnight a number of
my comrades had dropped out of the fight, some of them forever. Toward morning I, too, was seized by a pain that grew
more intense every quarter hour, and at seven in the morning I
was stumbling and tottering back with burning eyes, carrying my
last dispatch of the war with me.

"A few hours later my eyes had become glowing coals, and
everything had grown dark around me."

He was temporarily blinded.

They took him to a military hospital. The fighting was over
for Adolf Hitler, but for him the First World War would never
really end.

About the time of the gas attack at Wervick, the military career of the First Quartermaster General was also drawing to a
close. In another emotional lurch he had decided that his hoisting of the white flag was premature, and that the war should
continue after all. Having made the irrecoverable blunder of dis-
closing the extent of Germany's military plight to Germany's enemies, he now made the quixotic attempt to resume his posture
as a man of steel. He protested that President Wilson's preliminary armistice conditions, which included immediate cessation

of submarine warfare, were unacceptable, and sent a ringing "Carry on!" message to the troops. This dizzying reversal put Chancellor Max von Baden completely off balance in the negotiations under way with Washington. It looked to the Chancellor like a crude maneuver to shift the blame for an inglorious end of the war from military shoulders, where it belonged, to those of the civilian officials who were frantically trying to pick up the pieces. Prince Max demanded that the emperor support him, and repudiate Ludendorff, on the issue of stopping submarine warfare. The Emperor agreed, and Ludendorff's position, already hopelessly compromised, became untenable. On October twenty-sixth he offered his resignation.

There was no shred left of the superhuman grandeur he had acquired at Liège and Tannenberg. He did not blow out his brains, but the wisps of glory that had gathered about his name were dissipated forever by the manner of his going. Turning his back on the chaos and collapse in his wake, he fled the country in a false beard and blue glasses. With a fake passport under the name of Lindström, he scurried into Sweden.

It would become symptomatic of the distortion of values in postwar Germany that Erich Ludendorff was able to return and be widely hailed as a national hero and potential savior. It would become part of the sinister farce of those times that thousands cheered him wildly on his way as he marched, openly and without disguise, to the *Feldherrnhalle* at the side of his former Pfc., offering himself again as a leader of the German nation. In a land where that could happen, anything could happen, including an Adolf Hitler.

He was lying in his hospital bed in the dark awaiting recovery, expecting the war to continue, still hoping for German victory. But even in the little Pomeranian town of Pasewalk, where the hospital was located, the warning tremors of coming events were being felt.

"For a long time," Hitler wrote of this period, "there was something vague but repulsive in the air. People were saying that in a couple of weeks things would 'break loose'—but I couldn't imagine what they meant by this. The first thing I thought of was a strike, like the one in the spring. Unfavorable rumors kept coming in about the Navy, which was supposed to be seething. But this also seemed to me to be the product of the imagination of a few rumor-mongers, rather than anything involving the broad masses. In the hospital everybody was talking hopefully about the approaching end of the war, but nobody thought it would happen immediately. I wasn't able to read the newspapers.

"In November the general tension mounted.

"And then one day, suddenly and without warning, the disaster struck. Truckloads of sailors appeared, shouting revolution. . . ."

5 "THE KAISER WENT. THE GENERALS STAYED."

"ICH ABER BESCHLOSS, POLITIKER ZU WERDEN." ("BUT I DECIDED TO BECOME A POLITICIAN.")

—ADOLF HITLER

BY THE TIME the German government opened serious negotiations with Washington for a cease-fire, peace sentiment had long been rampant in the fleet. Social Democratic literature and newspapers circulated through the squadrons, and organized cells with elected leaders were numerous, especially in the First Squadron, which had once been regarded as unconditionally loyal to the Kaiser. In some of the ships there had already been episodes of insubordination so flagrant that seventy-seven seamen were put under arrest, and two condemned to death.

Kiel, the country's major naval port, was populated by thousands of organized shipyard workers who were sympathetic to the rebellious sailors and militantly determined that the war should end. Mass demonstrations erupted. The revolution swept like a contagion from port to port and city to city—to Wilhelmshaven, the next greatest naval base, to Lübeck, Bremen and Hamburg, the second largest city in Germany. There 40,000 people demonstrated, and ten were killed in a clash at the Army barracks. But for a movement so tumultuous and involving so many thousands, there was little bloodshed. Soldiers in city after city disregarded their officers and joined in the demonstrations. Wherever the revolution flared up, it succeeded almost without opposition.

Adolf Hitler, following the progress of what he called "this

monstrous thing" from his hospital ward, clung to the hope that
it was only a localized affair, "a *Putsch* on the part of the Navy
that would be beaten down within a few days." He tried to
hearten his fellow inmates, especially the Bavarians, with this optimistic view. "I could not imagine," he said, "that the madness
would break out in Munich, too."

But it was Munich that now shook the nation. From the
edge of the water in the northwest, the revolution leaped south
to the foot of the Alps, where it set in motion a train of events
that hastened the end of the war and shaped the future of Germany.

Typically, the first street demonstrations in Munich were set
off by an increase in the price of beer. A simultaneous rise in the
cost of milk and butter was hardly noticed, but when six pfennig more were demanded for a liter of beer, citizens took to the
pavements in protest. There had long been grumbling about the
steadily deteriorating quality of the local brew, and the price rise
seemed a final outrage upon a population already heartily sick of
hardship and yearning for the comforts of peace.

Bavaria, being richly agricultural, had fared better during
the war years than most of Germany, but now there were long
queues before the food shops in Munich—"ragged figures," an
eye-witness reported, "with emaciated faces and eyes fierce with
hunger." Along the queues and around the city wild rumors were
circulated and believed, contributing to the air of desperation
and destroying the last remnants of morale. Stories were whispered of hidden hospitals full of victims of poison gas and horrible mutilations, and of entire units ravaged by venereal disease.
One rumor went that the Krupp steel interests were bribing the
generals of the High Command to keep the war going.

In Munich the list of the fallen had lengthened to 13,000,
and schools were being cleared of pupils to make room for more
wounded from the western front. Civilian hospitals were bursting
with victims of an influenza epidemic. A housing shortage made
living quarters scarce, crowded and costly. Italian planes had
flown over the city and dropped some scattered bombs, a new
and terrifying experience for a civilian population.

The people turned against King Ludwig, denouncing him as a weakling for his compliant attitude toward the north and sneering at him as the *"Milli-Bauer,"* or milk farmer, because cows from his estate supplied some of the local dairies. Once an empty milk can was tied to the royal carriage, and on another occasion Ludwig was hooted by soldiers from their barracks windows. He was seldom greeted any more on his walks through the city. A dead cat was hung on the palace with a rhymed note warning that the same thing would happen to the King if things didn't change.

When the explosion came, it assumed a characteristic Munich tint of the improbable and the theatrical. The nemesis of the House of Wittelsbach, kings in Bavaria for a thousand years, was the Schwabing journalist from the Café Stefanie, Kurt Eisner. The first German dynasty to topple, and the oldest one, was overthrown by a drama critic.

For the previous eight and a half months Eisner had been in jail on charges of treason because of his anti-war and strike activities. With discontent growing among the workers, the authorities judged that his release might have a soothing effect and placate the elements who were agitating for a liberalization of the government. He had been chosen as the candidate of the Independent Socialists in a by-election for a vacated seat in the Reichstag, and was released on October sixteenth to run for office.

Kurt Eisner emerged from prison as untidily bearded and generally disheveled as ever, peering nearsightedly from under his floppy black hat, a picture of the ink-stained wretch whose natural habitat is the café table and whose business is words, not action. To the solid burghers of the town, including those in the government, he seemed among the least of the dangers they were facing. But Kurt Eisner, every Philistine's idea of every Bohemian, proceeded to turn Munich upside down.

With his grating and monotonous voice—"his whole appearance," said a witness, "was that of a retired school-inspector or professor"—he began speaking in the beer halls and *Stuben* where so much of Munich's public opinion and political passion are generated, and he found listeners among workers, intellectuals, the wives of men at the front, and a scattering of soldiers from the local garrison. His first demonstration of strength came when he staged a rally on the outskirts of Munich, at the Stadelheim jail, where he had been imprisoned, demanding the release of fellow socialists. The prisoners were released.

Under the banner of "Truth, Freedom and Peace" Eisner spoke to large audiences in places like the Schwabinger Brauerei, which had been one of Hitler's prewar pubs. He demanded the abdication of the Kaiser and all the ruling princes of Germany, and called for a revolution, an immediate peace, and a republic with workers, peasants and soldiers at the helm. He ignored his own election campaign in favor of rally after rally for the revolution. In another beer hall, on November second, he predicted: "There will be no Reichstag elections as scheduled anyway. The revolution will come first." He was right, though when it came he was almost as surprised as everyone else.

As tension mounted in the town, attendance at Eisner's rallies increased, and sometimes a hall proved too small to hold everybody who sought admittance. Overflow meetings were held on the Theresa Meadow, a large grassy expanse not far from the center of the city and famous as the site of the annual October beer festival. A mass assembly was announced for the afternoon of November seventh on the Meadow under the joint sponsorship of the two Socialist parties.

The day was mild for late fall, the unions turned out their members, and by three o'clock something more than 100,000 people had gathered, spreading out from the enormous "Bavaria" statue that dominates the western edge of the area. The statue, a female figure cast in bronze and about ninety feet high, is a symbol of Bavarian patriotic pride with a sword in one hand, a wreath held over her own head with the other, and flanked by a lion. She made a hugely incongruous patroness for the gathering, whose temper was anything but conventionally patriotic. From a dozen speaker's platforms erected all around the Meadow, orators were urging the overthrow of the King and government, and an immediate end of the war. Workers from munitions factories were carrying signs demanding "Bread And Peace" and "Peace And The 8-Hour Day." Mingling in the crowds were sailors who had recently arrived from Kiel.

Erich Mühsam, the café anarchist and cabaret poet from Schwabing, was there, though he arrived late. He hadn't intended to come at all, and spent most of the afternoon as usual in the Café Stefanie playing chess with his friend Roda Roda, one of the star contributors to *Simplicissimus*. Mühsam had entertained no hopes of anything definite emerging from the meeting, regarding it as just another demonstration. But when reports reached the café that a huge throng had gathered on the Meadow and that something might be stirring after all, he decided to see for himself—not, however, until Roda Roda had checkmated him and ended the game. He arrived about five o'clock, when the gathering was breaking up.

The crowd divided into several separate columns for the march home, the Majority Socialists holding mostly together and parading off in good order. Other columns were less disciplined as they began streaming away from the Meadow and through streets posted with large yellow placards warning against any violence. Eisner led the largest column, escorted by the Kiel sailors, who had constituted themselves his Praetorian guard. And now, when the meeting was dispersing without apparently having achieved anything, the revolution began almost before anyone knew what was happening.

The Eisner column swelled and surged as it went along, acquiring momentum and an emotional charge that the meeting itself had not generated. Shouts arose for the revolution. A cry ran through the ranks to move on the Army barracks and call out the soldiers to join in. The pace and tempo of the column increased, sweeping Eisner along with it. "He was pale and gazed before him with passionate solemnity," one of the marchers reported afterward. "He did not speak a word. It almost seemed as though the suddenness of events had taken him unawares. Now and again he stared straight in front of him, half-anxious and half-bewildered. . . ." Red flags were being waved in the throng behind him.

Other columns, infected by the mounting excitement, split off in various directions, spreading uproar through the city. At the Army barracks in the Türken Strasse a fiery speech was being made to the soldiers from the back of a truck by a little man with a pointed reddish beard. It was Erich Mühsam, urging the soldiers to defy their officers, leave the barracks, and join the revolution. Mühsam, whom nobody took seriously but the police, was finally proving that the police were right. He was making revolution. The soldiers followed him, and together they went off to spread revolt among other soldiers in other barracks. Afterward Erich Mühsam claimed that it was he, fresh from his checkmate at the Café Stefanie, who really launched the Munich revolution, not Eisner.

Late that afternoon Ludwig III of the Royal House of Wittelsbach was taking his walk as usual, dressed like an ordinary citizen and looking, as usual, like somebody's benevolent little grandfather. He seemed unaware that anything unusual was afoot in his capital, but one of his subjects, a working man, was better informed. He approached the King during his stroll and said to him, "Your Majesty, you'd better get on home. Things look bad."

By the time Ludwig reached his palace a crowd was milling around the entrance, and he had to slip around the back way to enter. He had not been home long when the palace guards abandoned their posts and went over to the rebels. Even then the King seems not to have understood the gravity of the situation until two of his cabinet ministers called upon him with the news that not a single unit of loyal troops remained in the city. The ministers urged His Majesty to leave Munich as soon as possible. Wishing him well, they retired and left the royal family to shift for itself.

Queen Maria Theresia was seriously ill and all but helpless. The four princesses hurriedly threw together whatever was most urgently needed for the flight, one of them wrapping some of the family jewels in a handkerchief. The King himself tucked a box of cigars under his arm as he left the palace and led his family to the royal garage, where it was found that the royal chauffeur had also deserted, taking the gasoline supply with him. A private garage nearby had to furnish cars and drivers before the party, including one or two loyal aides, could set off to the south through streets noisy with the sounds of revolution. Beyond the city, in the countryside, the King's car lost the road in a fog, and drove onto a potato field, where it bogged down and had to be hauled back to the highway by farm horses. It was four in the morning when the exhausted King, aged seventy-three, finally reached his estate in the mountains at Wildenwarth. It was the first stop on a flight that eventually took him into exile in Hungary. He never returned to his capital alive.

Not a hand had been raised on behalf of King Ludwig III of Bavaria, not a shot had been fired in defense of a throne to which successive generations had pledged fealty and undying allegiance. A dynasty that had endured for a thousand years vanished into the fog of night—literally *"bei Nacht und Nebel,"* as the idiom has it—with an old man scurrying into the mountains, a box of cigars clutched under his arm. Ludwig produced no historic phrases to mark the passing of the House of Wittelsbach, but he made a prediction as he was fleeing, and in time it came true. "If it were someone else who was taking over, I wouldn't say anything," he remarked. "But as it is, nothing good can come of it. I am afraid there will be civil war."

In Munich Kurt Eisner was taking over.

Truckloads of soldiers waving red flags raced through the town, occupying the railway station and various ministries, and seizing newspaper plants. Machine guns were set up on street corners, but there was nothing to shoot at; no opposition to the revolt appeared from any quarter. The old regime had simply evaporated.

The new one was being formed in a beer hall called the Mathäser, one of Munich's largest and another favorite hangout of Adolf Hitler, who would later make beer-hall history of another kind. The Mathäser's casual guests on the evening of November seventh were surprised to find themselves part of a revolutionary assembly at which the future of Bavaria was being determined.

Kurt Eisner, now the central figure in a drama more bizarre than any he had ever reviewed for his newspaper, presided. The first order of business was the selection of a Workers' and Soldiers' Council, or soviet, a procedure that was becoming ritual all over Germany. Eisner himself was elected First Chairman of the Council.

A revolution can be made in a beer hall, but even proletarians crave the status of more appropriate surroundings in which to exercise authority. The Council accordingly rose and marched off in a body to the Bavarian Diet, acquiring a retinue from the streets as it went. At that hour the parliament building was locked, but after brief negotiations the doors were opened, and the workers and soldiers filed in and took possession of the assembly hall. It was after midnight when the first official session of the newborn government convened. The old regime was declared dissolved, the monarchy abolished. Bavaria was proclaimed a Free State. Kurt Eisner was named its Minister President.

Next morning the newspapers astonished the people of Munich by informing them that they were living in a republic. Most of the city, though conscious of yesterday's tumult in the streets, was unaware that a revolution had occurred during the night and was *fait accompli*. There had been no real "seizure" of power, since no one had offered to defend it. There was only a sudden proclamation by a dubious collection of restive workmen and deserting soldiers with a Schwabing Bohemian at their head. Afterward it was said that a single machine gun could have dispersed the Eisner revolution at any point. But nobody had mounted the gun and pulled the trigger, and now Kurt Eisner was master of Bavaria.

Nothing signaled the change so vividly, and to many so appallingly, as the red flags that flew on November eighth from the high twin domes of the Cathedral of Our Lady, the *Frauenkirche,* Munich's most famous landmark. There was, however, nothing excessively alarming about the program of the new government as announced in posters that appeared all over the city. They proclaimed that "fundamental social and political reforms"

124

would immediately be undertaken, but the predominating tone was conciliatory. Security of person and property was assured. Officers who did not "set themselves against the requirements of the new era" would not be disturbed in carrying out their duties. In a time of "wild, senseless murder" any further blood-letting would be abhorrent. "Every human life shall be holy." Everyone was invited to help make the forthcoming changes "quick, easy and peaceful." Citizens were admonished to "keep the peace and contribute to the rise of a new world." Long live the Bavarian Republic. Long live peace.

Kurt Eisner was obviously not asking, as Lenin was, "Do you really think we can emerge victoriously from the Revolution without the most rabid terror?" Eisner thought he could. He had come from his table at the Café Stefanie with no visions of violent class conflict and no lust for bloody purges. It was his lofty, and misty, intention to elevate the masses by spreading among them the idealism of Immanuel Kant, whom he admired more than Karl Marx. Peering over his wobbly pince-nez, a little bewildered but resolutely benevolent, he set about changing the world according to his lights.

What came of it turned out to be a classic instance of a man and a movement, with the best of good will, achieving the exact opposite of the goal intended. Eisner and his leftist uprising unwittingly steered Bavaria toward an eventual triumph of the Right. For later revolutionaries of a different breed, the spawn of other Munich beer halls, Kurt Eisner became "the grave-digger of Germany" and "the man who sealed Germany's fate," and thus a prime figure in the demonology that gave birth to National Socialism. The chain reaction set off in the Mathäser *Bierstube* has been summarized by students of the period in the facile, but not wholly invalid, formula of: "Without Eisner, no Hitler."

But the immediate effect of revolution in Munich was to accelerate upheaval in Berlin. Like Ludwig III, all twenty-two of Germany's lesser kings, princes, grand dukes and dukes had been deposed without opposition by the evening of November eighth, leaving only one throne occupied—the central one. Though secondary royalty had scurried for cover all across the land, Wilhelm II was still King of Prussia and Emperor of Germany. The Reich had crumbled inward from the edges, and only the core remained.

"The side possessing the better nerves will win," was another of the Kaiser's predictions, and now the hysteria that never seemed far from the surface of the German leadership was showing itself. Wilhelm himself had been teetering on the verge of breakdown ever since word came of red flags flying from troop trains and over the fleet. While orders were still going out to regiments in the line to fight to the last man, generals at Spa and ministers in Berlin appeared readier for the hospital or the asylum than for negotiations to end the war. Prince Max of Baden, who had become Chancellor when the situation was already beyond repair, sustained himself on sedatives and sleeping pills, being dangerously unsteady from strain and influenza. His predecessor, Count Georg von Hertling, had collapsed completely and requested the last rites. Of two ranking diplomatic officials it was said that "Wahnschaffe lost his head entirely, and Grünau had no head to lose in the first place." What the Germans call *Panikstimmung,* a mood of panic, prevailed in the Chancellery and at Army Headquarters. Even the seemingly unshakable Hindenburg broke down and cried.

A frantic attempt was made to conciliate the people and appease the Allies by liberalizing the government. Some voting reforms were hastily instituted, and Philipp Scheidemann, a newspaper writer and editor, became the first Social Democrat in history to be appointed to the Imperial Cabinet. Karl Liebknecht, the leader of the extreme left-wing Spartacus League, was released from jail, where he had been confined, like Eisner, for pacifist and strike activities. He was greeted by a crowd of 10,000 who escorted him triumphantly through the streets, and the unrest of the workers only increased.

After Munich it was inevitable that Berlin, too, would explode, and on November ninth it did. In the morning, leaflets were circulating on the streets and in factories and barracks, announcing that "The Hour of Decision Has Come" and calling workers and soldiers into the streets under the slogan of "Peace, Freedom and Bread." Soon the factories were empty and the barracks were restive. Huge lines of workers, some armed with automatic weapons and pistols, came streaming into the center of the city from the north and east, where the big Siemens, Borsig and other factories were located. Traffic stopped, the routine of the city was suspended, and Berlin became one enormous demonstration. The columns of workers flowed together into immense parades, at first grim and in military step, with the armed units in the vanguard. The city was studded with crack regiments picked for their reliability, and it was known that the High Command had long since perfected an elaborate plan for counteraction in case of just such an uprising as this. But, as in Munich, a kind of paralysis froze the authorities, and nothing happened.

Instead, troops that the Kaiser once expected to fire on their own parents at his command, troops of whom he had said, "Those are the gentlemen I can rely on"—units like the Fusilier Guards, and the Alexander Regiment, and the Naumburg *Jäger* —went over to the revolutionaries. There was some sporadic shooting, but no pitched battle anywhere, and few casualties. The disciplined parades dissolved into throngs of shouting and singing men and women flourishing red flags and wearing red arm bands. The demonstrations took on a riotous carnival air, and a reporter wrote: "The revolution in Berlin succeeded before it had really broken out." Social Democratic newspapers began printing extras announcing "the glorious victory of the Berlin proletariat."

It looked far from glorious to another eyewitness who was watching from a corner suite in the elegant Hotel Adlon, which afforded a view along Unter den Linden and across the Pariser Platz, both jammed with demonstrators. "It was all quite vulgar," was the verdict of Bernhard Prince von Bülow. He was watching the dissolution of the Imperial Germany he had served as Chancellor longer than anyone else except Bismarck, and his viewpoint was understandably jaundiced. It was he who had coined the celebrated phrase about Germany's deserving a "place in the sun," and it was he who had signed the treaty of Belgian neutrality, which, in another famous phrase, became a "scrap of paper" with the German invasion. Witty but superficial, cultivated but slippery—"*pomadig*," like hair oil, was a word often applied to him—he had done his share of history-making, and now he was a front-row spectator at an historic event being shaped by others. He was not impressed.

One or two storm battalions, he was sure, could have scattered the *canaille* (he used the word, borrowing from Napoleon at the Tuileries) and suppressed the revolution on the spot.

"*Ach*," he wrote in his memoirs, "the revolution brought forth no Gambetta to proclaim war to the knife and prolong resistance for another five months. Not even a Delescluze appeared to volunteer to die on the barricades."

This was a reactionary view and a muddled one as well, since the aim of the revolution was hardly to stir up fervor for prolonging the war. But the Prince was right in seeing that something fundamental was lacking in the German revolution. It had none of the *élan* that conviction and a sense of riding with destiny generate. Most of all it produced no personality of stature to hold the revolution together, define its goals, and inspire a following to carry it into the future. The vacuum of leadership that was to prove fatal to the German Republic occurred at its birth and continued until Adolf Hitler filled it.

The unopposed surge into the streets, the victory that came without fighting, the passing of power from the old regime to a new one by default, were making the revolution a hollow triumph from the start. The government that was falling was being toppled by the pressure of alien armies, not by German masses aflame with passion for a new social order.

There being no one to fight at the barricades, and indeed no barricades, the people in the streets adopted a symbolic gesture to express their feelings and give vent to the tension. Prince von Bülow observed it from his Adlon window, and it revolted him.

"I have never seen anything so disgusting and outrageous, and at the same time so cowardly, as the spectacle of half-grown oafs, sporting the red armband of the Social Democrats, as they crept up several at a time behind any officer wearing the Iron

Cross or the *Pour le Mérite,* pinned his elbows to his side to render him helpless, and then tore off his shoulder straps . . ."

It was happening all over Germany. Officers were stopped and seized, and the insignia of their rank ripped from their shoulders or slashed off with knives. The circular cockade with the imperial colors, worn on the military cap, was a special target of the street mobs, whether worn by officers or enlisted men. To tear it off and stamp it into the ground became a universal act of personal revolt against the war, the Army and the regime. The insignia and the cockade stood for the arbitrary authority of a bankrupt regime, for the brutal discipline of the parade ground and the inhuman hardships of the front, for all the years of killing and dying. Destroying the symbols brought a sense of liberation and relief.

Empty as the gesture was, it created a lasting bitterness, deep and widespread, that poisoned the atmosphere in Germany for years to come. Von Bülow's revulsion was shared throughout the officers corps and the ruling caste, which would always remember the revolution chiefly as a mass outrage in which the ultimate in indignity was inflicted on the nation's fighting men by craven civilians behind the lines.

"Young as I was," said one soldier afterward, "I determined I should never have anything to do with these people," and he spoke for thousands of his kind when he recalled what turned him against the revolution forever. "Beardless boys, dissolute deserters and whores tore off the shoulder bands of our front-line fighters, and spat upon their field-gray uniforms. At the same time they muttered something about liberty, equality and fraternity. Poor deluded people! Was this liberty and fraternity? People who never saw a battlefield, who had never heard the whine of a bullet, openly insulted men who through four and a half years had defied the world in arms, who had risked their lives in innumerable battles, with the sole desire to guard the country against this horror.

"For the first time I began to feel a burning hatred for this human scum that trod everything pure and clean underfoot . . ."

A future Storm Trooper, then only a boy, remembered all
his life an incident that occurred to him in Berlin on November
9, 1918. "I was wearing the cap of a choir student, adorned with
a black-white-red cockade," he recalled years later. "I had just
entered the Burg Strasse when two men approached me and,
though I was but a child, tore the cap from my head and boxed
my ears. The cockade was deemed sufficient provocation. . . .
The bitter resentment of that moment made a lasting impression
on me." Later in the day the boy was caught in a melee between
a gathering of revolutionists and some isolated loyalist soldiers.
A shot was fired, and he was trampled in the ensuing panic.
"The impression upon my youthful mind," he said, "was a
frightful one. I felt a profound hatred for these people. . . ." A
multitude of such impressions of the revolution seeped into the
consciousness of uncounted Germans and became rooted there.

At about noon on that same November day came the announcement that Wilhelm II, King of Prussia and Emperor of
Germany, had abdicated. The news was premature, but the Hohenzollern dynasty was just as thoroughly finished as if it had
been true. Prince Max of Baden turned over the office of Chancellor to the chairman of the Majority Socialist Party, and Germany's leader was now a commoner with protruding eyes and a
comfortable paunch who had begun his career as a saddle-maker
and spent most of his life in the trade-union movement. His
name was Fritz Ebert, and he was a decent, intelligent man, but
not one to say with Danton, *"De l'audace, encore l'audace, et
toujours de l'audace."* What Fritz Ebert said was: "I hate revolution like sin." He had lost two sons in the war, and he wanted it
to end, the Kaiser to go, and the government to change; but his
guiding principles were derived from the Prussian police manual
that demanded, first and foremost, *"Ruhe, Sicherheit und Ordnung"*—calm, security and order.

Fritz Ebert was sitting at lunch in the Reichstag building
with his deputy Philipp Scheidemann not long after the Chancellorship had been thrust upon him, when a tumultuous crowd
gathered outside. A delegation of workers came in with the news
that at the Imperial Palace, less than a mile away, Karl Lieb-

knecht was about to proclaim a German Soviet Republic to another crowd, mostly Spartacist extremists. If the Ebert-Scheidemann faction of moderate Socialists wanted to demonstrate their leadership of the workers and the revolution, something would have to be done at once. Philipp Scheidemann dropped his napkin, went out to the steps of the Reichstag building, and made a speech.

He said that the old regime was finished, that militarism was at last destroyed, and that Ebert was forming a new government. "The German people," he asserted, "have been victorious all down the line"—a sentence whose echo would plague him for years to come, but which was heartily cheered when he spoke it. Carried away by his own oratory and the enthusiasm of the throng, he then proclaimed the German Republic.

It was a spur-of-the moment announcement, and Scheidemann had no authority to make it, but once the word was spoken it could not be recalled. Ebert roundly scolded him for being so impetuous. "You ought not to have done that!" he is quoted as saying. "It is the business of the National Assembly to decide upon the form of the state." The German Republic, having come into being as an afterthought, began with a quibble.

Once there had been something known as *Kaiserwetter,* the sunny skies that so often smiled on Wilhelm II's gala days of reviewing troops and making speeches. But November ninth was bleak and cheerless at Spa, with wintry winds moaning around the turrets and gables of the Villa Fraineuse, the Kaiser's residence at High Command Headquarters. Not far from the villa was a simulated trench with barbed wire and sand bags where photographs were often taken of the Kaiser to make it appear that he was visiting the front. Most of his life had consisted of play-acting, but today the curtain was coming down. The generals were giving him his notice.

Wilhelm had become a burden and an embarrassment to everybody. While he was diminishing into a mere puppet of his generals, his stature as a symbol, paradoxically, loomed larger than ever. To the Allied nations, and much of the world besides, he was "the Beast of Berlin," the personification of the Hun, of blind autocracy and rampant militarism.

"A successor to Frederick the Great does not abdicate," said Wilhelm in one of the last outbursts of the stage rhetoric that he habitually mistook for historic pronouncements. But now he was informed that he no longer had a choice. His going was a pre-condition for any armistice the Allied Powers might grant, and for his generals the problem was no longer whether he should go, but how best to get rid of him. When he proposed staying in Spa until a cease-fire was agreed upon, and then leading the Army home himself, a spokesman for the High Command bluntly told him: "Sire, you no longer have an army."

Hindenburg wept openly as he confirmed what the spokesman was saying. As the Kaiser continued to vacillate, news arrived from Berlin that his abdication had already been announced, that the troops in the capital had deserted to the revolution, and that Ebert had taken over the government. Shortly afterward came the word that the German Republic had been proclaimed from the steps of the Reichstag. Wilhelm no longer had a throne to renounce. There was only a country to flee from.

The Kaiser fled into exile in the early hours of November tenth, boarding his cream-and-gold private train at the Spa railway station. Like Ludwig of Bavaria, he left *bei Nacht und Nebel,* a heavy fog adding to the furtiveness with which 507 years of rule by the House of Hohenzollern ended in its nineteenth generation. As Wilhelm crossed into Holland, there occurred a final touch of ignominy. Germany's All-Highest War Lord had to give up his sword to a customs official.

Another railroad car figured prominently in the last act of the Great War as the Kaiser was fleeing in his. This was the dining car of the Allied Command in the forest of Compiègne. The diner had been converted into a conference room for the reception of the German armistice delegation headed by Matthias Erzberger, a Catholic Centrist politician who was a member of the Reichstag and Secretary of State in the new government. Erzberger was a schoolteacher, a smallish, roundish man with some previous diplomatic experience as representative of the Imperial Government on missions in Italy, Rumania and elsewhere. But the principal feature of his present position was that he was a civilian.

At Compiègne there was no surrender of a German sword by a defeated general to a victorious Allied general. Instead there was a little politician with a pince-nez who would afterward be blamed—and not only blamed, but murdered—as the betrayer of the Fatherland behind the back of the Army. Ludendorff was in hiding in Sweden. The Kaiser was in flight to Holland. Hindenburg remained discreetly out of sight at Spa. No ranking officer of the High Command appeared at Compiègne to take public responsibility for Germany's defeat. The onus fell on a civilian.

With General Foch presiding, the Armistice terms were read out to the German delegation, and there was more weeping, this time by the young officer who acted as interpreter. The terms were harsh, designed to render further resistance impossible and make unmistakably clear that Germany had lost the war. They involved immediate evacuation of invaded territory in Belgium and France, and withdrawal from Alsace-Lorraine. The Rhineland would be occupied by Allied troops. The fleet would be surrendered and Germany's African colonies given up. The blockade would remain in effect.

Erzberger, appalled, wired to Spa for instructions. The reply from Hindenburg ordered him to dispute a number of the terms strenuously, but added that if protest was unavailing *"so wäre trotzdem abzuschliessen"*—sign anyway. The Field Marshal understood that Germany could no longer continue fighting no matter what terms the Allies imposed. But it was Erzberger whose name went on the surrender document.

The Armistice went into effect at 11 A.M. of November 11, 1918, and the Great War was over. Germany lay broken and exhausted, the mighty thrust toward glory and dominance ended in humiliation and despair. "The struggle was beyond our strength," as Hindenburg himself admitted.

Adolf Hitler learned of Germany's defeat in the hospital at Pasewalk, and the impact it made upon him became more crucial for the future of the world than any of the repercussions in the foreign offices of Paris, Rome, London and Washington, where statesmen imagined that the shape of history was being determined.

On the afternoon of November tenth, after weeks of wild rumors, came what Hitler described as "the most terrible certainty of my life." It was conveyed by the local minister, a dignified old gentleman who had been delegated to break the news to the wounded soldiers in the hospital hall. Hitler remembered that the minister was trembling as he began to tell of the fall of the Kaiser and the end of the monarchy, the proclamation of the Republic and the surrender of the German Army. Now a beaten and helpless Germany would have to rely on the magnanimity of its former enemies as it faced a dark and unpredictable future, the minister said. Soon he was weeping openly, and his audience with him.

"I could stand no more," says Hitler's account of the episode in his autobiography, Mein Kampf. "It was impossible for me to remain. As everything went black before my eyes again, I groped and tottered my way back to the ward and threw myself on the bed, burying my burning head in the pillow and blankets.

"I hadn't cried since I stood at the grave of my mother. . . . But now I could not help it.

"So it had all been in vain. All the sacrifices and privations. . . ."

There follows a long lament for all the squandered bravery, the useless agonies, the years of heroism, the two million fallen comrades. "Did all this happen only so that a swarm of miserable criminals could lay hands on the Fatherland?" he asked.

He had a vision of hundreds of thousands of graves opening and "sending back their heroes, silent and covered with mud and blood, as spirits of vengeance to the homeland that had so mockingly betrayed the highest sacrifice it is possible for a man on this earth to make for his people."

There is bathos in the passage, and many a rhetorical "Was it for this . . . ?" But the passion underlying-the stilted prose is unmistakable, and the impression made upon him by "this monstrous event," as he called it, was traumatic. "In these days and nights," he said, "hate grew within me, hate for those responsible for this deed." He saw it all not as military defeat but as betrayal by *Lumpen,* scoundrels, "in the pay of enemy propaganda who purloined the weapons from our hands, broke our moral backbone, and traded away the crippled Reich for thirty pieces of silver."

The Marxists and Jews were the criminals, and, he said, "There can be no dealing with Jews. There can only be the hard: 'either-or.' "

His career as an artist was forgotten; in view of what had happened to Germany, it seemed trivial, even laughable, to think of painting and drawing. In the "terrible days and worse nights" that followed, his own fate, he said, became known to him:

"Ich aber beschloss, Politker zu werden."

He decided to become a politician. Afterward, looking back at his own beginnings, he saw himself as "a man without a name," a half-blind cripple "taking the field against a world of enemies singlehanded." But in the world outside his hospital ward, events were multiplying that prepared his way for him.

In Berlin, and all over Germany, walls and kiosks were plastered with posters proclaiming that "The World Revolution Is on the March," and hailing the advent of a new order in which capitalism and imperialism were things of the past. Workers, peasants and soldiers were uged to form council-soviets, and to arm for battle against reaction. "Long Live the Republic!" said the posters. "Long Live the World Revolution!"

From his office in the Reichstag, Chancellor Fritz Ebert could hear the tumult of Spartacus throngs, which included armed. sailors and soldiers, and what they meant was a possibility he found intolerable: Bolshevism in Germany. He had no organized force at his command sufficient to assure his grip on the government and fend off the threat of civil war and anarchy.

On Fritz Ebert's desk was a telephone with a direct line to High Command Headquarters at Spa, and it rang when he wanted to hear it most. Over it came a call from General Wilhelm Gröner, a canny Swabian who was Ludendorff's successor as First Quartermaster General. With relief, Ebert learned that the High Command was still functioning, was still exercising authority, and was willing to bring the troops home in good order provided that the Government cooperated.

"What do you expect of us?" Ebert asked.

General Gröner wanted assurance that the regime would support the Officer Corps in maintaining discipline in the Army, would supply provisions and transport for the troops, and would oppose the spread of Bolshevism in Germany. The Officer Corps, on its part, would not take up arms against the regime or provoke civil war, and would make itself available in combating the Bolsheviks. The Field Marshal, Paul von Hindenburg himself, would remain at his post and do everything possible for the maintenance of order.

Ebert's answer was: "Convey to the Field Marshal the thanks of the Government."

So one of the first acts of Germany's new regime was to place its hope for survival in the armed strength of the old one. By his agreement with the High Command, Fritz Ebert weathered the initial crisis of his government, but he thereby canceled any hope of a fundamental reform of Germany's social structure. The prestige and authority of the Officer Corps had been acknowledged, and its continued existence assured. It would remain a bulwark against change and a rallying point for reaction. Designed to protect both parties from the radical Left, the pact yoked together two forces that would henceforth pull in opposite directions or clash against each other. A dichotomy and a contradiction had been created at the core of the Republic from which it never recovered. The red flag continued to fly from the Imperial Palace in Berlin, from the *Frauenkirche* in Munich, and across the land; the revolutionary posters with their prom-

ises of a new order remained up; but the Prussian sword was
never broken, and not even sheathed.

The Army came marching home from the front "like a
wounded lion," and all Germany was shaken by the spectacle. A
terrible power still resided in the disciplined columns of field-
gray, in the millions of haggard and embittered veterans who
were hailed as heroes as they goose-stepped through cities and
towns hung with banners that said "UNCONQUERED IN THE
FIELD" and "YOU WERE VICTORIOUS NEVERTHE-
LESS"—the same saying that would be echoed in the Odeon
Platz at Munich to salute the fallen men in the *Putsch* of Adolf
Hitler a few years later.

In the Moselle and the Rhineland, the best of the wine and
the last of the food were offered up by the local peasants as the
troops paraded by. When they marched as in triumph along Unter
den Linden in Berlin, the head of the Republic was standing at
the Brandenburg Gate to say to them: "I greet you as you return
unvanquished from the field of battle."

But shock and despair were dominant as rank upon rank
returned from the trenches, marching as in a trance, faces
wooden and eyes staring—"like ambassadors of death," said a
witness, "like envoys from a land of horror, and of the deadliest,
loneliest, iciest cold." The homeward march of the troops made
defeat concretely visible for the first time to the eyes of all Germany. "And," said another witness, "because the reality was past
bearing, because the defeat was not understood, the people took
refuge in a tragic intoxication. Never has Germany been more
German than she was during those days, living for yesterday and
the day after tomorrow, far from the reality of today."

The troops brought the front home with them. The battle
lines were now drawn inside Germany itself. At the end of the
march, the millions of soldiers dispersed into the population,
spreading their discontents, each continuing the war in his own
way. "The march home was the bitterest experience I have ever
had," said one soldier afterward. "Out of fear and courage, out
of storm, enthusiasm and defiance, out of blood and dirt, out of
hope and misery I returned, still with love in my heart. But when
we saw Germany, the ground sank under my feet. . . ."

They saw a Germany on the brink of chaos, its social institutions crumbling or paralyzed, hunger in the streets, and disorganization rampant where order and discipline had once been revered as the highest good. The Russia that had been defeated in battle seemed to be taking over Germany by infiltration and subversion in the wake of revolution. Soviets, or "Council Republics," were breaking out everywhere—"like ulcers," it seemed to these soldiers. Over and over again the question was being asked, as Hitler asked it: "Was it for this we fought?"

In Braunschweig a Soldiers and Workers Council turned out to greet the returning soldiers, and a squadron of Hussars rode them down with their horses. In Lennep, the Soldiers and Workers Council was dispersed by Sixth Army troops, the red flag was torn from the city hall, and the Prussian emblem hoisted again to the cheers of the people. There were clashes between returning troops and local leftists in Aachen, Cologne, Essen and elsewhere.

At the forest of Compiègne, the one concession Erzberger had been able to obtain from the Allied Command involved rifles and machine guns. When he heard how many were to be surrendered, he had blanched. "Why," he said, "then we are lost. How shall we defend ourselves against Bolshevism?" It was a point that registered with the conquerors. They allowed Germany to keep more weapons to preserve internal order, having no objection to Germans shooting each other. The elements of civil war were already rife beyond the Rhine: hatred and hostility to divide the people, and the weapons with which to fight among themselves. "It was," said George Grosz, "as if Germany had been split into two opposing factions—even as in the Siegfried saga."

A different metaphor was used by another observer to describe the aftermath of the war not only in Germany but in all of Europe. Ambassador Walter Hines Page, writing from London, turned to the Bible for images to suggest his dismay at what mankind had done to itself in the four and a half years just passed. In a letter to Woodrow Wilson, Ambassador Page wrote:

"You will recall more clearly than I certain horrible, cata-

138

strophic, universal-ruin passages in Revelation—monsters swallowing the universe, blood and fire and clouds and an eternal crash, rolling ruin, enveloping all things—well, that's all come. There are, perhaps, ten million men dead of this war, and perhaps one hundred million persons to whom death would be a blessing. The hills about Verdun are not blown to pieces worse than the whole social structure and intellectual and spiritual life of Europe. I wonder that anybody is sane."

A worse insanity was already on the way.

6 BLOOD ON THE STREETS

"IN A WAR OF IDEAS, IT IS PEOPLE WHO GET KILLED."
                              —STANISLAW LEC

ADOLF HITLER was released from the military hospital a few days after the war ended.

How seriously he was affected by the mustard gas may never be known. His medical report was missing from the Army archives when investigators subsequently sought to examine his case. Physically he seems to have suffered no permanent damage except for a recurring hoarseness. Though poison gas was perhaps the most dreaded of all the war's weapons, its terrors were much exaggerated and its effects were seldom lasting. The damage was often more psychological than organic. Doctors found that such consequences as protracted blindness or loss of speech were usually symptoms of a latent hysteria—"an unconsciously simulated disorder to escape the firing line." Hitler had been at the front almost steadily for more than four years, and the gas may have been a subconsciously welcome excuse to escape from the battlefield without running away from it. The "blindness" of which he made so much, and which was often played up in the mythology of the Nazi movement, was probably photophobia, a condition induced by mustard gas in which the victim recoils when bright light falls upon the eye.

The impact of poison gas was especially pronounced on hysterical personalities, and Hitler was in an abnormally agitated state when, at the hospital, he learned of Germany's defeat and the Armistice. Millions of others were shaken by the news, but Hitler received it with an intensity of shock peculiar to the violent emotionalism of his nature, and with a sense of personal outrage fed by the egomania that governed his reaction to everything. Germany's defeat became for him the most intolerable of all the rejections he had had to accept, the ultimate affront to his own person. In the war he had, for the first time, given of himself to the limit of what was in him, and it had come to as little as everything else he ever attempted. It counted for nothing.

The idea was insupportable.

November ninth remained for him the date of infamy forever after, the day of "the greatest villainy of the century." For the rest of his life he would pour a lexicon of vituperation onto this date: *Novemberschande,* the November shame; *November-verbrecher,* the November criminals; *November-Republik,* which became synonymous with *Juden-Republik,* the "Jew-Republic," and so on in a hundred hammering variations. The ninth of November became a shibboleth in the vocabulary of his emergence and rise, and he would seek to reverse the symbolism of it by choosing a November ninth for his *Putsch,* his own first thrust at power, when the time came.

He was twenty-nine years old when he left the hospital, his youth gone and his future without visible promise. His resolve to become a politician seemed hopelessly vague and insubstantial, on a par with his former dream of becoming a great painter or architect. That had disintegrated into peddling postcards on the street, and there was no reason to think that his newest aspiration was more firmly anchored in reality.

Nothing in his past indicated that he was anything more than another of those aimless outcasts who drift along the fringes of society without ever finding a place for themselves. Having never really begun a career, or formed any binding human associations, he had nothing to resume now that the war was over. He had no trade, job or profession to take up again. He had no home to go to. No wife or sweetheart, not a single relative or friend, awaited his return. He was, moreover, not only homeless but stateless, his service in the German Army having deprived him of his Austrian citizenship without gaining him German nationality. Adolf Hitler, when he left Pasewalk, was a man without roots, connections or prospects.

He stayed in the Army. Except for the fleeting warmth of the beer halls, it was the only haven he had found. Without a uniform he was in danger of sinking back into the unbearable anonymity of the slums and tenements, of being submerged again in the faceless welter of the masses he despised. The Army answered the needs of his tangled and clouded personality as nothing else had ever done. In the Army patterns of behavior were implacably set from above; everyone knew where he belonged and what he must do. The idea of hierarchy, of absolute authority and obedience, was central to his own view of how the world should be run. The haphazard procedures of civilian life, in which he was never able to feel at ease, were supplanted in the Army by an iron system of regulation. The Army was the embodiment of power, organized with a beautiful efficiency for the purpose of violence. Power and violence were the lodestones of his character. He would never completely break his tie to the Army.

From the hospital he was ordered back to the replacement battalion of his regiment, quartered in the Türken Strasse barracks in Munich. The barracks had been the first to participate in the Eisner revolution, and when Hitler arrived there toward the end of November he found it under the control of a Soldiers' Council. The place was crowded with undisciplined troops; many were staying in the Army merely for food and shelter, and because they had nothing else to do with themselves. Hitler found the situation repellent, and soon managed a transfer to a camp at Traunstein, about fifty kilometers outside the city.

Traunstein was a prisoner-of-war camp for Russians, and Hitler probably did guard duty there. He had chosen an isolated spot in a time of upheaval and change, uncertain of the future and of himself. "At this time," he wrote afterward, "plans chased themselves through my head, one after the other. For days I pondered what could be done, if anything at all. But at the end of every deliberation came the sobering thought that I, in my utter obscurity, had not even the slightest basis for any practical action." He was, so to speak, waiting in the wings, listening for a cue.

Munich at the time was the scene for a kind of political drama that Germany had never before experienced or imagined. For those not directly involved, it seemed a wholly implausible comedy, if not outright farce. The spectacle of an upstart *Schlawiner* from the Schwabing cafés functioning as the Minister President of Bavaria appeared preposterous even to many of Kurt Eisner's friends and associates. The news of his elevation was greeted with mingled incredulity and amusement at the Berlin *Vorwärts,* the country's leading Socialist newspaper on which he had once worked as political reporter and essayist.

"There wasn't a man among us who didn't love and cherish him from former times," *Vorwärts* wrote on December 2, 1918. "There wasn't one who wished him ill or despised him. Nevertheless: the news caused merriment among us, good-natured merriment, that spread from the editorial offices to the composing and press rooms. . . ." Eisner's judgment in the past, the article said, had been far from infallible on political matters, but nothing in his record matched the foolishness of having himself made a Minister President by his fellow dreamers from Munich's Bohemia. "You are living in a world of sweet delusion," *Vorwärts* informed him, "if you imagine you can put your confidence in the support of the Bavarian people—you, a literary immigrant from Berlin who never played a role in Bavaria's political life, a man virtually unknown to the public three weeks before taking office. . . . This minister-presidency of yours has nothing to do with the great gravity of our times. It stands in shattering contradiction to them. It is a Punch-and-Judy show in real life, freely adapted from Frank Wedekind by Kurt Eisner, with the author in the title role—homemade theater in the Munich-Schwabing style. In five minutes the curtain will come down, and it will all be over."

It seemed a sound enough estimate at the time. The editorial sages could not be expected to foresee that when the curtain was rung down it would be on a tragedy, not a farce. The Eisner era in Munich, begun with an aura of storybook unreality reminiscent of the regime of Lola Montez, was to be less a performance than a prologue, a blind preliminary to a larger drama.

After what Rainer Maria Rilke called the "confused monstrosity" of the war, peace in Germany had become a monstrous confusion. In Munich, for a time, it took on the aspects of a carnival, a *Gaudi* in the local idiom, with much demonstrating, hoisting of red flags, impassioned oratory, and a minimum of revolutionary violence. The brave new world of Kurt Eisner was being ushered in on sheer good will, lofty idealism, and something he designated as "communism of the spirit." His lifelong dream had been of a "Reich of light, beauty and reason," and now, by a turn of fortune that seldom falls to the lot of dreamers, he was in a position to shape a sorry world closer to the heart's desire.

As Minister President he preceded his major speeches with symphony concerts, and in executive sessions he philosophized at length on the inner nature of politics, which he held to be "exactly as much of an art as painting pictures or composing string quartets." His lieutenants and supporters in the new regime were men like the passionate young poet Ernst Toller, who was Vice Chairman of the Central Committee of the Workers-Soldiers-Peasants Council, and the café anarchist Erich Mühsam, whose major contribution to the new era was declaiming his own poetry from a roving truck to impromptu audiences on street corners where thousands of the idle lounged about as if, one witness noted, "a picnic and not a revolution were going on." Mühsam's specialty was an incendiary incantation called "The Sun of Liberty."

At the Hofbräuhaus, on the little square known as *am Platzl*, people were roaring with laughter at a song spoofing the revolution. It was sung by Weiss Ferdl, a moon-faced comic recently returned from the war and a local favorite. Weiss Ferdl's song, of his own composition, used the gross Bavarian dialect to make fun of the dawn of liberty's sun in Munich, and hooted at

such revolutionary manifestations as the widespread plundering
and the inglorious flight of the king. The gleeful refrain mocking
the new topsy-turvy state of affairs was soon on everybody's
lips—

> *Revoluzilazilizilazi hollaradium, alls drah ma um,*
> *Alls kehrn ma um, alls schmeiss ma um, bum bum!*

It was typical of the early stages of the Munich upheaval
that reds and reactionaries alike enjoyed Weiss Ferdl's jingle
("We're turning everything upside down, we're tearing it all to
pieces"), and that he was allowed to continue singing it without
censorship or even reproof. In the Eisner revolution there was no
censorship. The opposition newspapers, which predominated,
were scathing in their denunciations of the regime and its Minister President. Some of his more inflammable followers, led by
the unquenchable Mühsam, stormed into the offices of the Bavarian *Kurier* and the Munich *Tageblatt,* and occupied the
premises. They also forced their way into the home of Eisner's
principal political rival, the moderate Socialist Erhard Auer, and
forced him at gun point to resign his portfolio as a minister of
the government.

Eisner was appalled at this outburst of arbitrary action. He
hastened to countermand the confiscation of the newspapers, and
reinstated Auer. "I know you meant well," he admonished his
hotheads. "You acted out of love for me, but it was not a good
thing to do."

Power did not, despite the well-worn axiom, corrupt him,
but it did not leave him unaffected, either. A bureaucrat who addressed him as *"Excellenz"* noted maliciously that the leader of
the proletarian new order did not reject the honorific of the old,
and was visibly flattered on another occasion when shown his
picture on the cover of an illustrated weekly. The press was particularly caustic over Eisner's use of a private salon car on an official trip to Berlin, a luxury even Ludwig III had foregone. The
head of the workers' Republic found himself being referred to as
"Kurt I."

But it was his unshakable idealism, oddly mingled with a
grotesque misconception of his own importance on the interna-

tional scene, that proved his undoing. An impenetrable naïveté repeatedly betrayed him into actions that evoked either contemptuous laughter or furious hostility. Buoyed by his dreamer's faith in the invincibility of a high ideal, he saw himself as the instrument of reconciliation between Germany and the Allies, the potential architect of a better world. Acting on his belief that only through complete openness could international politics be purified, Eisner published secret papers from the diplomatic archives to show that Germany bore the sole responsibility for the war. His hope was that such an unprecedented *nostra culpa* would persuade the Allies at the peace table that a spiritual regeneration was taking place in Germany, with Bavaria as its source and Kurt Eisner as its messiah. In February of 1919 he repeated his proclamation of Germany's war guilt—"it can no longer be doubted"—at an international conference of Socialists in Berne. His speech also condoned the Allied policy of delaying the return of German war prisoners, and was generally a gratuitous display of sackcloth and ashes. His sweeping admissions were received with indignation by his countrymen, for whom they came like drips of acid in the open wounds of national humiliation.

With the purest of motives, Kurt Eisner was making himself the most hated man in Bavaria. Everything about him seemed calculated to outrage local pride and patriotism. Small and slovenly, with his shapeless slouch hat and Old Testament beard, his very appearance offended the Bavarian sense of fitness, always acute where the formalities were concerned. He neither looked nor behaved like a Minister President; he looked and behaved like a *Schlawiner,* and so did his closest associates. Worse, Eisner was both a Jew and an outsider, which made him doubly objectionable to the native chauvinists. It was frequently asserted that his real name was not Eisner but Kosmanowski, and that his family came from the East, from Galicia, a sufficient indictment in the eyes of most Bavarians. The fact that he had been born in Berlin and was a naturalized Bavarian did nothing to abate the antagonism against him as a foreigner. He was called "the Galician scribbler," and he seemed a sorry figure to take in exchange for a king.

The press became increasingly virulent in its attacks on the "dictatorship of the Schwabing Bohemians"; they were castigated as *Zugroaste*—strangers, carpetbaggers, Jews. "Bavaria for the Bavarians!" and "Bavarian men at the head of the Bavarian State!" became a battle cry of the opposition press. The *Fränkischer Kurier* dared to print arguments justifying tyrannicide.

Political murder was becoming more than an editorial threat. The multiple assassinations that would run like a red stain through the coming years began in Berlin in January of 1919, and it was a forecast of the brutalities in store for Germany that the pattern was set by a double murder that included the slaughter of a defenseless woman.

While Kurt Eisner in Munich was attempting, as one of his followers put it, "to change Germany by kindness", the real temper of the time was showing itself in Berlin, where half-hearted revolution had turned into sanguinary civil war. The government of Fritz Ebert was being hard pressed to maintain its authority and stave off the efforts of left-wing extremists to convert Germany into a sovietized state. Ebert's determination to establish an essentially bourgeois republic with a minimum of socialist trappings seemed like a gross betrayal to the Spartacists, who by now had founded the "Revolutionary Communist Workers' Party of Germany." A series of maneuvers and confusions had temporarily removed the extremists from the government, and the Workers and Soldiers Councils, which were to have been the key factors in the new proletarian order, had been shunted into a subsidiary role and virtual impotence. In protest, the extremists took to the streets in armed bands and converted the capital into a bloody chaos of pitched battles and guerrilla skirmishes. The revolutionaries, who had scarcely fired a shot in anger while overthrowing the regime of the Kaiser, fell to killing each other by the hundreds in a fratricidal conflict whose effect was suicidal for the entire German workers' movement. A revolution against the revolution was taking place, a struggle between two shades of radicalism, flaming red against faint pink.

Early in January insurrectionary mobs stormed the newspa-

148

per quarter and seized the editorial rooms and presses, including those of *Vorwärts,* the organ of the Majority Socialists. Heartened by this stroke, the extremists formed a Revolutionary Committee led by the most violent of the radicals. The Ebert regime was declared overthrown. A general strike was proclaimed. Masses of workers deserted the shops and factories and roamed the streets with weapons. Large sections of the city were wrested from the government and came under the domination of the Spartacists. Berlin verged on complete anarchy. The second revolution, the flaming red one, seemed about to succeed.

The leader of the Revolutionary Committee was Karl Liebknecht, son of one of the founders of Germany's Social Democratic Party, himself the founder of the Spartacist League, and the sole Social Democrat who had dared to vote against war credits in the Reichstag. He was co-author of the rousing Spartacus Manifesto that proclaimed to the workers: "Germany is pregnant with revolution. . . . The time for . . . high-sounding words has gone by! The hour of action has struck!"

But he himself was more a man of words than action. It was not physical courage he lacked; during the war he had stood in the Potsdamer Platz and shouted, "Down with the regime!" He was a vehement and effective speaker, with something of the ferocity typical of the intellectual extremist who, in his frenzy to right old wrongs, has no hesitation in committing new ones. But he had no gift for organizing, planning or decision. He was a wing-collar revolutionary.

His collaborator and co-leader of the Spartacus movement was the tiny but explosive Rosa Luxemburg, a revolutionary agitator from her youth and a veteran of Russian and German prison cells for her spirited defiance of authority. Barely five feet tall, full of fire and dauntless, she made herself a terror to the bourgeoisie with the power and brilliance of her pen and tongue. But she was woman enough to write poetry, carry a satin parasol, and send letters of almost girlish warmth to relatives and friends from her prison cells. Though schooled and skilled in Marxist theory, she was no fanatical follower of Soviet practice.

PRELUDE TO TERROR:
The Faces Behind the Putsch

Pomp and guns always surrounded Hitler. His Beer Hall *Putsch* of 1923 won support of a prestigious war hero, Field Marshal Erich Ludendorff (left). His storm troop army was run by men like Ernst Roehm, a homosexual (right), and other army veterans like Wilhelm Brueckner (rear).

A happy Hitler (in circle and inset) was in the crowd that cheered the outbreak of World War I in 1914 on Munich's *Odeonsplatz*. Nine years later, the same public square became the center of his abortive *Putsch*.

Public speakers were preaching hate and revolution throughout riot-torn Munich in 1923. Politics often erupted into open street-fighting.

Even in Bavarian costume (left) and during his stay in prison following his *Putsch* (top right), Hitler tried his best to look like a man touched by destiny. Since only a few fanatics then took Nazis seriously, followers like Herrmann Goering (in helmet) also wanted to appear forbidding.

As Hitler dreamed of power, a series of comic opera governments ruled the restless Bavarians. The pre-Nazi leaders included a left-wing poet, Ernst Toller (left) who became a general and ultimately committed suicide in New York; and Kurt Eisner (above), who became Prime Minister, opened political meetings with symphony music, and was assassinated. His previous experience had been as a drama critic.

The swastika was an ancient but still obscure emblem when these pioneer storm troopers first showed their colors on the outskirts of Munich in the days just before the *Putsch*. Hitler himself called his rise "a miracle."

A platoon of storm troopers named for *Fuehrer* Hitler sets out for action on the Munich streets. This was in the days before they wore brown shirts and these roughnecks were not as well organized and trained as they look.

Plenty of arms had found their way into the hands of the Nazis out of army supplies. Hitler ordered his *Putsch* marchers to unload their guns, but they did not all obey and nobody knows who fired the first shot.

As the *Putsch* began, Hitler's men started to arrest members of the Munich City Council. Although this time the established Government was able to restore order, it was a warning of the Nazi dictatorship to come.

Although Hitler's marchers were an oddly-assorted lot, some of them were smartly equipped and looked like regular army troops. Yet the confusion was such that not even the leaders knew their destination.

Heinrich Himmler (carrying flag) was 23 years old and had not yet joined the Nazi Party when he backed Hitler at the Munich barricades. Eventually the world knew him as chief of the Gestapo.

Proklamation

an das deutsche Volk!

Die Regierung der November-
verbrecher in Berlin ist heute
für abgesetzt erklärt worden.

Eine provisorische deutsche
National-Regierung
ist gebildet worden.

Diese besteht aus

General Ludendorff, Adolf Hitler

General von Lossow, Oberst von Seisser

Even as their *Putsch* fizzled, a Ludendorff-Hitler proclamation was issued declaring the overthrow of the "criminal" national Government in Berlin. It was wishful thinking, one decade premature.

"The atrocities of the Bolsheviki," she once said, "won't let me sleep nights."

They were an implausible pair, Rosa Luxemburg and Karl Liebknecht, to loom as the twin monsters threatening the foundations of German society, but they were so regarded by the embattled Right. Their mistake, it was said, was that they sought the salvation of mankind in the streets, where it was not to be found. But that is where their own fate was decided.

With control of the capital slipping away, and the authority of the government crumbling, Fritz Ebert turned again to the strong arm of the vanished Empire to bolster his faltering Republic. Invoking the telephone pact he had made with the Army, he summoned regular troops under their reactionary officers to suppress the unruly workers of Berlin. The Ebert socialists and the officers had in common only a common enemy, Bolshevism, the menace that was to shadow and distort the course of German politics far into the future. The threat of it would keep German democracy in bondage to the German Army, the natural foe of democracy, while the Army served as shield for a system it accepted only on sufferance, as a lesser evil. It was an unnatural and untenable alliance; the best the partners could say of each other was, "They are the enemies of our enemy." In the Berlin of January, 1919, the alliance broke the first uprising of the common enemy in what came to be called "the Battle of the Marne of the German revolution." As in the real Marne battle, the war went on for years, but the decision was not to be reversed.

The regular troops, led by the Potsdam Regiment, moved on the workers with tanks, trench mortars, flame-throwers and machine guns. The newspaper quarter was cleared, all public buildings were retaken, and the disciplined formations in their field-gray were cheered by a populace aching for the restoration of peace and some semblance of order. The Spartacists, poorly led and militarily outmatched, fought back for a time, and there was blood on the Berlin pavements, but on January thirteenth the Revolutionary Committee called on the insurgents to give up their resistance and go back to the shops and factories. The fighting subsided temporarily, and Fritz Ebert remained in power. Germany's revolutionary pregnancy became a stillbirth.

With the suppression of the uprising, the capital was combed for the ringleaders, several of whom had prudently fled Berlin to live and fight another day, if no more successfully. An armed patrol of citizens ferreted Rosa Luxemburg and Karl Liebknecht out of the private home in the Wilmersdorf section of the city where they were hiding. It was their misfortune that they were not delivered to the nearest police station, but were turned over to the military. German policemen might have observed the law even in a case involving the two foremost Spartacists; instead the prisoners were taken to the elegant Eden Hotel, the headquarters of the crack Guards Cavalry-Rifle Division, and fell into the hands of German officers.

The Eden Hotel in Berlin's west end was a hotbed of die-hard monarchists and reactionaries of all ranks and persuasions. Its halls resounded to the clatter of spurs and the stomp of jack boots. In its rooms men still fanatically loyal to a throne that no longer existed wove plots and formed cabals for the maintenance of their caste and privileges in a society that seemed in danger of slipping permanently from their control. The Cavalry Guards were the core of the regular troops who now dominated the city, and its officers saw themselves not only as saviors of Berlin but as the law in Germany.

They decided that Rosa Luxemburg and Karl Liebknecht should die, and that no court, judge, jury or legal verdict would be needed. The war was hardly more than two months past, and these were professional soldiers still saturated with the atmosphere of the battlefield, where one did not argue with the enemy. One killed him. They subscribed to an old German saying that went: *"Gegen Demokraten helfen nur Soldaten"*—"the only help against democrats is soldiers".

On the night of January fifteenth the prisoners were interrogated by the First Staff Officer of the Division, Captain Waldemar Pabst, an energetic and decisive soldier to whom legal refinements and humanitarian scruples would have seemed absurd in the circumstances. His only concern was to establish that he had

the right culprits. In Rosa Luxemburg's case this was not difficult. There was no mistaking that defiant and forward-thrusting
little figure. Liebknecht at first denied his identity, but admitted
it when a soldier pulled back his coat to reveal the monogram
"KL" on his shirt, an oddly elegant giveaway for a revolutionary.

Satisfied that he had the people he wanted, Captain Pabst
gave certain secret orders to his men, and then directed that the
prisoners be transported separately to the Moabit prison "for further investigation." Liebknecht was led away first.

On guard at the entrance of the hotel, where the doorman
stood in quieter times, was a hussar named Otto Runge, who had
not only been given special orders but also a sum of money for
what he was about to do. When Liebknecht was seated in the car
that was to take him away, Hussar Runge stepped forward from
his post and swung his rifle butt twice, smashing it against the
prisoner's skull. As the automobile drove away, Liebknecht was
semiconscious and bleeding profusely. In the Tiergarten Park,
one of the show places of Berlin, the car came to a halt at an
isolated and unlit spot. Liebknecht was dragged from the car,
hoisted to his feet and pushed along a wooded path in front of
his captors. As he tottered forward in the dark, bloodied and
unseeing, he was shot three times from behind, twice in the back
and once in the head.

The body was delivered to an emergency station at the
zoological gardens, where it was marked: "Unknown Spartacist."
Afterward the announcement was made that Liebknecht had
been "shot while attempting to escape," a phrase that became a
cynical stereotype to cover similar political murders well into the
Nazi era.

On the night of January fifteenth, however, the work of
Hussar Runge was not yet done. When Rosa Luxemburg was
brought out of the hotel, he was still at his post, and ready.
Again he swung his rifle, and Rosa Luxemburg was more dead
than alive when they dragged her to the car and heaved her into
the back like a sack of grain. This time there was not even the
pretense of an escape attempt. The officer in charge of the detail,
a Lieutenant Vogel, killed her as she lay unconscious on the seat

152

by putting a pistol bullet into her brain. Then, anticipating the techniques of the Chicago gangsters, they wrapped her body in wire, weighted it with stones, and threw it into the Landwehr Canal. It was not found for months, but that night Lieutenant Vogel's warriors returned to the Eden Hotel and passed around a tiny female shoe as a trophy in the crusade of the German Officer Corps to save the country from Bolshevism.

Numerically, two more deaths were as nothing compared to the millionfold massacre of the war and the continuing wave of killing and counter-killing that had come in the wake of the revolution. But the coldly savage slaughter of Karl Liebknecht and Rosa Luxemburg was a portent, a storm warning of the moral climate that would prevail in the political life of Germany through the coming years. Hitler, the obscure Private First Class, brooding and restive in his temporary retreat at Traunstein, could sniff the air from afar and sense that already the wind was beginning to blow in his direction.

"With this double murder in the year 1919," a leading German magazine wrote forty-three years later, "began that new historical period for Germany in which murder as a political means became an accepted fact and was legitimatized.

"It began with Liebknecht and Luxemburg and ended with millions of Jews, Poles, Russians. It became accepted as permissible and normal to slay anybody who stood in the way of one's own plans or policies. It began with the liquidation of two prisoners and ended with the liquidation of millions." *

---

* *Der Monat*, June 1962, in the lead article by Gerhard Zwerenz titled *"Vorschlag: Ein Orden fürs Morden"* ("Suggestion: A Medal for Murder"). The article was prompted by statements and interviews given the West German press, including the official information *Bulletin* of the Bonn government, by Major Waldemar Pabst (Ret.). Major Pabst, still energetic and decisive at the age of eighty-two, freely acknowledged his complicity in the Liebknecht-Luxemburg affair, though denying that he specifically gave the orders to Hussar Runge to assault the prisoners as they left the hotel. One of his officers, he said, bribed Runge "with a certain sum of money" to do so. Major Pabst did not, however, attempt to deny that his intention was to have the prisoners disposed of one way or another, and he had no more moral qualms about the matter in 1962 than in 1919. "The only point that matters," he said, "is this: was it necessary or was it not necessary?" (Interview in *Der Spiegel*, Nr. 16, 1962, pg 43) He still thought it was.

The shape of the German future was being determined even more decisively, if less apparently, in Munich than in Berlin. Events that seemed of only local significance were, in fact, beginning to trigger the chain reaction whose ultimate explosion would be felt throughout the world.

What Kurt Eisner called the "epidemic of mass madness" produced by civil war in the capital threatened to engulf the whole country, and in a public letter Eisner held the Ebert regime responsible. Everywhere in the south, he said, the indignation of the people was rising against Berlin. He added that at the same time "dark elements" were also at work in Bavaria. They were.

In several large rooms on an upper floor of the Munich hotel *Vier Jahreszeiten* ("The Four Seasons") a secret organization called the Thule Society had its headquarters. Ostensibly a literary and scholarly circle devoted to studying German history and customs, the society was actually the center of a counter-revolutionary conspiracy, a nest of reactionary elements constituting what a later generation would call a Fifth Column.

The name of the society derived from the mythological land believed to be the northernmost limit of the world, the ancient *ultima Thule,* the original homeland of the German race. The society itself was an offshoot of the *Germanenorden,* or Teutonic Order, whose base was Berlin and whose branches throughout Germany were patterned on the Masonic lodges. The Munich group had been founded during the war by an emissary from Berlin named Baron Rudolf von Sebottendorff, who was able to enlist 250 members locally and 1,500 in Bavaria, including a number of journalists, professors, aristocrats and army officers.

The objectives of the society were basically *völkisch,* embracing the usual twin concepts of racial superiority and anti-Semitism, as well as the related Pan-German dream of a coming Reich of unsurpassed power and grandeur that would bring all Europe under its sway. These notions, common to numerous other *völkisch* associations in Bavaria and throughout Germany, were tricked out with mystical connotations and bardic ritual in the Thule Society, many of whose tenets and trappings would be ready to Adolf Hitler's hand when he was ready to appropriate them. Though there was no organic connection between the two, the Thule Society in Munich and the cult of Lanz von Liebenfels, Hitler's mentor in Vienna, were of the same spiritual and intellectual spawn. Their symbols, slogans and aims were interchangeable; soon they would be indistinguishable from the ideological apparatus of National Socialism.

The symbol of the Thule Society was, again, the swastika. The society's letterheads and literature showed the emblem with the right-angles of its arms rounded off to give it the look of a circle or wheel. Superimposed on the swastika was a dagger, its naked blade pointed downward and intertwined with oak leaves. The slogans and sayings of the society anticipated the propaganda themes of National Socialism almost word for word, and its racial theories were another forecast of the Nuremberg Laws out of which the mass exterminations of Jews evolved. Only persons who were *rassenrein*—"racially pure"—through three generations could become members of the Thule Society, and the motto of the organization read: *"Gedenke, dass du ein Deutscher bist! Halte dein Blut rein!"*—"Remember that you are a German! Keep your blood pure!"

During the war the society concerned itself largely with combating "un-German tendencies" and promoting the extremist Pan-German line. But with the coming of the Revolution, a call for concretely subversive action was sounded by Sebottendorff. In a speech to the Thule membership, he characterized the Revolution as having been made by "racial inferiors for the purpose of destroying the *Germanen,* the Teutons." It was, he said, a triumph of "our deadly enemy: *Juda.* . . . From now on it must be an eye for an eye and a tooth for a tooth." The Thule offices became the headquarters of an extensive underground directed by an Action Committee; the upper floor of the Hotel Vier Jahreszeiten was the center of a kind of state within a state.

An elaborate spy system was organized, and Thule agents were filtered into the armed formations of the Eisner government and into its branches. Caches of arms were assembled and secret munition depots established. Identification papers, passes and documents of all kinds were forged, and official stamps and seals duplicated. With the hidden activities went a more or less open propaganda campaign that included the distribution of hundreds of thousands of anti-Semitic leaflets, often hurled broadcast into the streets by Thule members from speeding automobiles. A concerted effort was made to penetrate the mass of the population, especially the workers, who were thought, in the Thule view, to be "poisoned by Jewish internationalism" and needed to be recalled to the nationalist and racist camp. The war, and especially defeat and Revolution, had revealed a widening gap between the ruling and officer castes and the working man. It was an objective of the Thule Society to woo the workers across the spreading divide and bring them back to the side of the all-out nationalism of Germany's greatest days.

As a gesture in this direction, a Thule member named Karl Harrer formed a "Political Workers Circle." Neither Harrer, who was a journalist, nor anybody else on the predominantly bourgeois and aristocratic roster of the society, had any direct contact with the laboring class, and a Workers Circle did, after all, require some participation by workers. A proletarian go-between was needed to make the approaches of the Thule group palatable to the laboring class, someone who was at the same time a manual worker and an outright nationalist of the Pan-German stripe. Harrer found his man in Anton Drexler.

It was Harrer's newspaper that had first brought Drexler to public attention by publishing his article urging the workers to rally behind the High Command during the war. From this had grown Drexler's abortive Free Labor Committee for a Good Peace, the second stage of his unwitting progress toward a niche in history as a forerunner of Adolf Hitler. Like almost everyone else associated with the immediate origins of National Socialism, Anton Drexler was an instructive, and in many ways a dismaying, example of how shoddy the material can be of which history is made.

"From behind his spectacles," an associate noted, "his eyes

frequently looked out in honest despair," for he was haunted by a sense of secret and mysterious powers working for the destruction of Germany—powers whose sinister designs he had come to recognize and understand, but to which the workers remained stubbornly and stupidly blind. Sickly and unprepossessing, he had been pronounced unfit for combat and had, he said, chosen the home front as his battlefront.

In the Munich railroad yards, where he worked, Anton Drexler made it his mission to combat the inroads of socialism and expose the threat of the *"geheime Kräfte,"* as he called them —"the secret powers." These were international Jewry and Free Masonry, which, in league with each other and with international capitalism, were responsible for the plight of Germany and the distress of the German workman. He had suffered that distress himself in periods of unemployment when he was forced to play the zither in coffee houses to keep from starving, and this had first impelled him to ponder the flaws of the economic system and unriddle their true origins. He had also experienced the perfidy of the Jews at first hand. Once, during the war, in a conversation with a Jew from Antwerp, he defended Germany's position and aims. The Antwerp Jew had offered him strong wine, and Drexler claimed he lost consciousness and woke up in a hospital. The Jew had undoubtedly put something in the wine. The incident opened Anton Drexler's eyes to the menace of Jewry.

His Free Labor Committee for a Good Peace was his only organizational achievement and it had attracted no more than forty members. Germany's defeat made even this trifling showing obsolete. But destiny was on the side of Anton Drexler, and on the prompting of Karl Harrer he took the step that would embed him in the annals of National Socialism as "the original founder of the Party."

On January 5, 1919, the attention of all Germany, and of much of the western world, was focused on Berlin, where the Spartacists were threatening to depose the government and set the country on the road to communism. The really significant event for Germany's future, however, was occurring not in Berlin but in Munich, and it went unnoticed. That night, in a minor hotel called the Fürstenfelder Hof, the first meeting of something called the *Deutsche Arbeiterpartei,* the German Workers Party, was called to order by Anton Drexler. He read out a statement of principles that he and Harrer had jointly drawn up as guidelines of the new organization. These repudiated the idea of class war, but urged a struggle by the workers against the exploitations of stock-exchange capital and its alleged Jewish manipulators, and proposed that German labor make common cause with the farmer, the intellectual and the middle class against international Marxism and for a greater Germany. The slogan was, "Citizens and workers, unite!"

Only a handful of citizens and workers, less than Drexler's original forty, united themselves in the newborn party. Such fragmentary and splinter groups were being formed by the score in Munich at the time—they were "shooting out of the ground like mushrooms," in the German phrase—as the result of an unprecedented interest in political matters generated by defeat and revolution. Most of them soon withered away, and there was no reason to expect anything more of Anton Drexler's little association, whose leadership, program and membership were no more remarkable than any of the others. But Drexler had unknowingly created a nucleus. From his German Workers Party would grow the National Socialist German Workers Party—Adolf Hitler's Nazi movement.

In the streets of Munich the picnic aspects of the Revolution had disappeared. It had ceased to be a *Gaudi,* and there were scant signs of the new era of reason envisioned by Kurt Eisner. Symphony concerts and good will were proving insufficient to change a society obstinately unresponsive to the utopian ideals that had seemed so persuasive on the printed page, and so logical and inevitable in the all-night discussions of the social philosophers at the Café Stefanie. Eisner was discovering the truth in the words of Friedrich Engels: "People who imagined they had made a revolution always saw the next day that they did not know what they had been doing, and that the revolution they made was nothing like the one they had wanted to make."

Had Kurt Eisner been able to control and organize his revolution, and lead Bavaria along the humane and moderate way he dreamed of, the Private First Class waiting in the wings at Traunstein might never have stepped to the center of the stage. But Eisner had neither a program nor the firmness of character to carry one out. He had only a vague intent to turn away from the past and shape a future free of the cruelties and injustices that had always accompanied the exercise of authority. In shrinking from the arbitrary use of power he substituted only vacillation and uncertainty. While the economic and social situation deteriorated steadily, he never came to grips with the realities of governing.

In the 100 days of the Eisner regime practically no major legislation was put into effect, or even enacted. The revolution was mainly talk and appearance. Red flags flew from the public buildings. In the beer cellars, workingmen heard speakers herald the immediate abolition of capitalism and proclaim that now "everything belongs to everybody." The Worker-Soldier-Peasant Councils solemnly assembled and passed ringing resolutions. Even the high schools established Student Soviets, demanding the end of compulsory religious classes; and in one of the few concrete measures taken by the Eisner government the traditional supervision of the school system by the clergy was canceled. But nothing fundamental in the structure of society, or in the operation of the economic system, was changed. For a generation the radical element in the proletariat had hoped that revolution, once it came, would mean the redistribution of wealth through the breaking up of large estates and industrial monopolies, and the improvement of the workers' status with higher wages, more holidays, increased social benefits. Instead there was spreading unemployment, food and housing were scarcer than ever, and nobody seemed to be doing anything effective to improve matters.

The deepening disillusionment of the workers and intellectuals who had supported the revolution was reflected in a snatch of street dialogue recorded at the time by Oskar Maria Graf, a young Munich writer:

"Have you noticed any results of the revolution?"

"No, I haven't. But then it takes time."

"Nor have I. We're in the same muck as before . . ."

Factories were shut down for lack of coal and the general economic stagnation that followed defeat. Thousands of the jobless loitered aimlessly in the streets, restive and sullen. Kurt Eisner had been able to overthrow the monarchy, proclaim the Free State of Bavaria and make himself Minister President by leading mass demonstrations through the streets of Munich, and now the same streets became unruly with demonstrations that rocked the regime of Kurt Eisner. The champion of the workers' right to assemble and protest was forced to issue appeals to the workers to stop assembling and protesting, and he threatened reprisals if they did not. But the demonstrations continued.

Tensions were heightened by the agitation arising from the forthcoming elections to the Bavarian Diet. For the first time there was to be universal adult suffrage, including women. The town was plastered with posters, flooded with handbills, and, as modern innovations, airplanes dropped election leaflets from the sky while loud-speakers made party propaganda on the streets. A truckload of sailors coursed through the town beating drums and playing an amplified record that shouted, "Elect Eisner!" Three opposition parties issued a joint manifesto that said: "We stand on the brink of anarchy. . . . Does the regime lack the will to govern or does it lack the power?" It warned that Bavaria was in imminent danger of "sinking into the abyss of Bolshevism."

Aware of his precarious footing, Eisner had sought to postpone the elections as long as possible, and the results justified his worst misgivings. Election day, January twelfth, was a sunny Sunday. Citizens streamed to the polls by the hundreds of thousands and, in orderly fashion unmarred by violence, they annihilated Kurt Eisner politically. Despite war, defeat and revolution, Bavaria remained stubbornly conservative. The most seats in the Diet, sixty-six, were taken by the middle-class Bavarian People's Party, which reflected the traditional attitudes of the population with its predominantly Catholic and agricultural outlook. Eisner's own party trailed far behind the rest of the field with only 2.5 percent of the vote and a paltry three seats.

Eisner was isolated politically, left stranded by the ebbing of the tides that had swept him into power almost by accident. Again he was confronted by a reality he was unable to face or deal with. Though his refusal, or inability, to exercise power decisively was a major factor in his failure, he was now reluctant to let it go. He did not resign. He continued to drift and temporize, abandoned by the mass of the Left and unanimously hated by the Right. Reactionary officers and chauvinist students openly urged that he be dealt with as Berlin had dealt with Liebknecht and Luxemburg. The Thule Society secretly printed and circulated a handbill with a veiled but unmistakable threat against his life. It was couched in the language used in Schiller's *Wilhelm Tell* against the tyrant Gessler: *"Mach hurtig, Landvogt, deine Uhr ist abgelaufen"*—"Make haste, Governor, your time has run out."

Under the accumulating pressures, Eisner could not disregard the results of the election indefinitely, and at last agreed to convene the Diet on February twenty-first. The expectation was that he would resign and make way for a new government, but whether he intended to do so cannot be known for certain. He never reached the Diet.

On the morning of the twenty-first a young officer named Anton von Arco-Valley had himself wakened early by the chambermaid of his *pension*. He instructed her to lay out warm clothing while he bathed, because, he said, "it will probably be cold in the jail cell." She did not take the remark seriously. Anton Arco-Valley was a handsome young man and a Count; he frequently made scathing remarks about the unsatisfactory state of affairs in Munich and his intention to do something about it. Walburga Kästele, the maid, did not believe that so charming a youth as Count Anton, known as "Toni," actually intended to harm anyone. But he did.

He was twenty-two years old and had been a lieutenant in the 1st Bavarian Heavy Cavalry Regiment on the Russian front during the war, and was badly wounded and decorated. When the war ended, and while he was still weak from his wounds, he had been attacked on the street, and had his cockade ripped from his cap. To him the Revolution was visibly a *Dolchstoss*. Kurt Eisner became for him "the grave-digger of Germany" and, said Arco-Valley, "I despised and hated him from my heart."

His feelings were perhaps all the more intense because both King and Fatherland were adoptive, his birthplace having been Austria. He was, in addition, half Jewish on his mother's side, and had been rejected by the Thule Society as racially unfit. Not quite thoroughbred by the standards he most admired, not fully accepted where he most passionately wished to belong, Count Anton Arco-Valley resolved to prove himself the genuine article in the eyes of everyone, and his own.

Freshly bathed and warmly clothed, he telephoned the Diet and learned that Eisner was expected to arrive at about 10 A.M., when the session was scheduled to begin. At 9:45 Arco-Valley stationed himself in a doorway on the Promenade Platz where he knew the Minister President would pass on his way to the Diet. He took the safety catch off the revolver in his right-hand overcoat pocket, and waited.

Kurt Eisner had prepared a speech for the Diet in which he intended to give an account of his stewardship. One of its proudest sentences read: "Just as the revolution itself was achieved without bloodshed, so has Bavaria until now been preserved from serious and lasting internal convulsions." It was a comment that could not have been more ironic, in view of what was about to happen.

Toward 10 o'clock Eisner emerged from the Foreign Ministry on the Promenade Platz and began walking toward the Diet building in the nearby Pranner Strasse. His months in office had done nothing to improve his appearance. With his floppy black hat and flagrantly unkempt beard, he still looked like the eternal Bohemian heading for a favorite café, rather than a Minister President on his way to a crucial act of state. For escort, he was accompanied only by a sailor and by his secretary, the journalist Felix Fechenbach. About forty people were loitering around the area, some of them Spartacist followers of Eisner.

Spotting his quarry, Arco-Valley drew his revolver and darted from the doorway. He closed in swiftly from behind, and fired two shots. One bullet entered Eisner's brain, the other piercing his lungs through the back. He sank to the pavement and died on the spot in a pool of blood.

The sailor wheeled and began firing at Arco-Valley, hitting

him once where he stood and four more times as he lay on the sidewalk. Some of the bystanders who came swarming to the scene began kicking him in the face and body, and trampling him. They meant to kill him, and thought they had, but he survived.

Fechenbach collapsed sobbing over Eisner's body, which soldiers soon carried into the porter's lodge of the Foreign Ministry. The sailor, splattered with blood, rushed into the assembled Diet and shouted out the news of the murder. It had the impact of an exploding bomb. The meeting broke up in confusion. People poured into the Promenade Platz and milled about the spot where Eisner fell, some of the women crying hysterically and dipping handkerchiefs and scarves in the blood. The word ran through the crowd that Erhard Auer, the Minister of the Interior and Eisner's most influential opponent, had engineered the assassination. The rumor spread quickly and was widely believed.

Despite the turmoil, the Diet was reconvened at 11 o'clock. A dangerously overwrought audience packed the gallery, predominantly supporters of Eisner, many of them armed. The first speaker was Minister Auer, who delivered a eulogy of Eisner, praising him as "a man of the most unsullied idealism" and warning that unless the passions released by his murder were held in check, Bavaria faced the prospect of anarchy.

Auer had barely resumed his seat when the attention of the gathering was arrested by a man in a long gray overcoat who came stalking down the aisle to the front of the hall where the delegates sat. He was one of Kurt Eisner's most fervent followers, a saloon waiter and part-time butcher named Alois Lindner. He was carrying a Browning rifle.

Leveling the gun deliberately, he fired twice at point-blank range, and Auer toppled to the floor, severely wounded. Lindner then turned and walked toward an exit, firing two more shots at the delegate benches as he went. At the door a Major von Jahreiss attempted to block his way. Lindner shot him dead, and left the building unmolested. In the midst of the mounting panic inside the hall, a sudden hail of shots rattled down from the spectators' gallery. A delegate named Osel was killed as the others dove under desks, cowered behind benches, or jumped from the windows. Two cabinet ministers suffered nervous breakdowns. The Diet broke up in pandemonium. The government ceased to exist.

Kurt Eisner's assassination had exactly the opposite effect from what Arco-Valley's two pistol shots were intended to achieve. It caused a new and massive tilt to the Left. Coming just as Eisner's political importance was fading, the crime had combined brutality with pointlessness. Even such extremist groups as the Thule Society found it impossible to defend openly. It imposed a kind of paralysis on the Right, smothering the enemies of the Revolution in obloquy and rendering them temporarily ineffective. At the same time, the assassination set off an upsurge of radical sentiment such as Eisner was never able to generate when he was alive.

He was instantly elevated to the status of a proletarian saint. On orders of the Workers and Soldiers Council, the church bells of Catholic Munich were tolled for Kurt Eisner, the Jewish freethinker. An impromptu shrine was erected at the spot where he died. Soldiers made a pyramid of rifles and hung a wreath on it with Eisner's picture in the center. All passersby were compelled to take off their hats or salute. Streams of weeping women laid flowers on the sidewalk, where sawdust had been scattered over the blood stains. Official mourning was proclaimed throughout Bavaria. Tens of thousands who had turned from him when he lived rallied to him in death, and an immense procession followed him to his grave, led by black-clad miners and factory workers. He had become a martyr. Heinrich Mann delivered a memorial address hailing him as a historic figure and "the first truly spiritual man ever to head a German state."

As a renewed manifestation of the moral derangement that was gripping postwar Germany, the events in Bavaria produced a shock whose reverberations were felt throughout the nation. Following so closely on the Liebknecht-Luxemburg atrocities, the assassination of Kurt Eisner was interpreted as another warning flare revealing that reaction was ruthlessly at work to wipe out the Revolution and come back into power. The conviction was widespread that Arco-Valley had not acted on his own but was the agent of secret and sinister forces threatening to destroy the social order if they could not dominate it. The prevailing atmosphere of imminent chaos was intensified, and fear spread.

"The ground on which we stand is shaking," said Philipp Scheidemann, who spoke for the Reich Government. This was too restrained an estimate of Germany's situation for many. "We are not standing on ground at all," wrote the newspaper *Welt am Montag*. "We are hanging over an abyss."

In Munich the Worker-Soldier-Peasant Central Council assumed governmental power, and a state of siege was declared. Placards were posted warning citizens to stay indoors because of danger in the streets, and a 7 o'clock curfew was imposed. A general strike was called. The University, where students had hailed Arco-Valley as a hero, was shut down. Prominent citizens, aristocrats and officers were arrested and held as hostages. Newspaper plants were seized and a censorship imposed compared to which the wartime restrictions were mild. Public buildings, banks and even main hotels were occupied by Red troops and armed workers.

Feelings ran deeper and more dangerously than they ever had while the monarchy was being overthrown. An atmosphere of terror seized the city. Trucks with mounted machine guns roamed the streets, and speakers inflamed the corner crowds with the cry of *"Rache für Eisner!"*—"Vengeance for Eisner!"

The storm did not break at once. The passion behind the slogan *"Rache für Eisner!,"* however genuine, found no goal or target. No leader emerged capable of channeling it into action. Finding no immediate focus, it led to no immediate explosion. The hostages were not put against the wall and shot. Aside from some impromptu plundering, and a frenzied dance around a huge bonfire kindled from stacks of right-wing newspapers, no concerted outbreak of revolutionary violence occurred. But while the first surge of outrage that followed the assassination abated, it did not disappear. It continued to seethe and await an outlet.

For weeks Bavaria was without an effective government, and something close to the anarchy that Auer had foreseen set in. The Communist-Spartacist minority and its leaders became increasingly aggressive, but the Worker-Soldier-Peasant Councils that were nominally in control held their power only by default, and were able to do little to stem the general disorder. The state, shaky enough under Eisner, had been thrown out of kilter by his murder. The sequence of political lurches and lunges that now ensued ranged through unseemly farce to bloody violence, altering the emotional climate of Munich and Bavaria and making them susceptible to profounder upheavals still in store.

The sequence began with what seemed like a lurch back toward the center when the Diet reconvened on March seventeenth and elected Johannes Hoffmann as the new Minister President of Bavaria. He was a Majority Socialist, a former school-teacher, and an earnest man of good intent. He headed a coalition government with the Independent Socialists, and he hoped to restore order, preserve democracy, and keep the Spartacists in check. But the temper of the time was against him, and his policy was given no time to take hold.

Only four days after the start of the Hoffmann regime, the Munich revolutionaries were electrified by the news that Hungary had become a Soviet Republic. The dictatorship of the proletariat had been proclaimed, and the immediate nationalization of industry, banking and property was announced. The Hungarians had done what the Germans only talked about; they had gone all the way. In reality, the Hungarian Soviet under the fanatical Béla Kun was destined to be a gory fiasco. It would last for only 130 days of terror and economic collapse, bringing on a counter-terror from the Right that then dominated the country for a generation. But when the Hungarian Soviet Republic was proclaimed, it was joyously hailed by the Left extremists of Germany. In it they saw proof that a Soviet state was not necessarily a strictly Russian affair but was possible even beyond the borders of the Soviet Union. The Munich radicals promptly dispatched a telegram to their Hungarian comrades, congratulating them on their "mighty victory" and assuring them: *"Deutschland kommt bald nach!"*—"Germany will soon follow in your footsteps!"

The idea of establishing a Soviet Republic in Bavaria exerted a powerful appeal on the revolutionary dreamers of Munich. No popular basis for such a move existed; on the contrary, it ran violently counter to the character, traditions and bias of the overwhelming majority of the Bavarian people. But in the spring of 1919 it provided the readiest release for the emotional drives left over from the abortive Eisner revolution, and it offered an outlet for the social impulses reawakened and intensified by his murder. It took hold among unemployed workers and beer-table radicals, and talk of it grew into demonstrations and strikes.

The spreading ferment led to what was surely one of the most curious meetings in the history of revolutions. It took place on the night of April sixth in the bedroom of the former Queen of Bavaria in the Wittelsbach Palace, which had become the headquarters of the revolutionaries. The meeting included representatives of the two Socialist parties, union leaders, liberal democrats, anarchists, and assorted worker, soldier and peasant delegates. The Communists, though invited, were not represented as the meeting began. The chairman was Ernst Niekisch, another former schoolteacher, who headed the Workers' Central Council. In recalling the meeting afterward, the word he used most often to describe the proceedings was "grotesque."

Though the impulse had come from the ideological ferocity of Béla Kun's Hungary, the prevailing spirit in the queen's boudoir that night was still straight out of the Café Stefanie. Erich Mühsam was present and vocal. The young poet Ernst Toller was there, and the tone of the deliberations was set by a speaker whose character and outlook were, if anything, even more gentle and unworldly than Kurt Eisner's had been. This was Gustav Landauer who had also been a theater critic and was, besides, a Shakespearean scholar and a lecturer in literature and philosophy. Tall and richly bearded, with a deep and resonant voice, Landauer was cast in the mold of the Bohemian reformer whom Munich was producing at the time. He had a wide following among the workers who found something worthy of their respect in his forthright idealism and selflessness in their behalf. Landauer's social ideas were utopian and anarchistic, rejecting the concept of *Obrigkeit,* authority, in all its forms, and groping vaguely toward a society in which militarism and capitalism would be abolished and the common people at last come into their own and live happily ever after. Since the Soviet Union alone seemed determined to move in that direction, Gustav Landauer in his innocence believed that the cause of mankind could best be advanced by following the Russian example.

On Landauer's motion, the meeting voted to declare itself a constituent assembly authorized to revise Bavaria's form of government. It was conceded that there was no legal justification for this, but Landauer argued that revolution was always a "creative act" that must necessarily break abruptly with the past. It was decided to "conform to the will of the masses" and make Bavaria a Soviet Republic.

The cloudy idealism, the dreamy divorcement from reality that had marked the political activities of the Schwabing Bohemians from the start also characterized the birth of the new government. Its ministers were no longer to be called ministers but "People's Deputies," because this carried a more revolutionary ring. The meeting considered it an embarrassing joke when Erich Mühsam popped to his feet and unblushingly proposed himself for the post of People's Deputy for Foreign Affairs. Nobody could imagine this raffish little Don Quixote of the cafés in so responsible a role without either grinning or shuddering. Mühsam's self-nomination was declined with thanks, but the final choices turned out to be no less fantastic.

The portfolio of Foreign Affairs went to a Dr. Franz Lipp, largely because no other name was seriously offered. Few of those present had ever heard of him. He was supposed to have done diplomatic work of unspecified nature under the Kaiser, and was reputed to be a personal friend of the Pope. It was also held in his favor that he owned a gray frock coat and sported a well-tended beard of aristocratic cut. Later it developed that he was a mental case and had more than once been committed to asylums, but by that time he was already in office.

Economic and financial affairs were put into the hands of Sylvio Gsell, who believed in free money and free enterprise, and Dr. Otto Neurath, a doctrinaire Marxist. The two were somehow supposed to work together. The railroad and transportation portfolio was awarded to a Georg Paulukun, whose experience in the field consisted of occasional spells as a track maintenance worker. Military Affairs were entrusted to a former waiter. In the Bavarian Soviet Republic there were to be no distinctions between man and man, or job and job. Waiting on tables would be adequate training for running a ministry.

Misgivings arose, nevertheless, when Gustav Landauer was proposed as People's Deputy for Education and Instruction, a post for which his writings and scholarly background seemed to fit him. But this, after all, was still Bavaria, where the Catholic Church was a power whose special domain was education, and Landauer was not only not a Catholic but a Jew. He was, moreover, a non-Bavarian, another outsider. Some of the peasant delegates openly doubted whether he would be acceptable to either the Church or the people. Such objections gave the session pause, but were finally dismissed as reactionary and unworthy of consideration by a revolutionary council. Gustav Landauer was elected to the post.

Thus one step after another was taken to make the new government offensive to thousands of Bavarians. Having decisively rejected the Eisner regime as foreign and extreme, Bavaria was now to be confronted by a new one even more radical and just as dominated by outsiders and upstarts. And, before the night was over, it developed that the decisions of the council were unacceptable at the other end of the political spectrum as well.

Everyone present had felt uneasy about the absence of Communist delegates, since the founding of a Soviet Republic without them would indicate a glaring gap in its ideological basis. That such a gap existed became certain late in the evening with the appearance of Dr. Eugen Leviné, the dominant figure in the local Communist Party and editor of its newspaper, *The Red Banner*. Russian-born and a veteran agitator, Leviné had studied

at Heidelberg and become an agent of the German party apparatus whose Berlin headquarters had sent him to Munich. He
was gaunt and intense, an iron-hard advocate of the Leninist
way. For him the shapeless utopianism of the Eisners and the
Landauers was a childish evasion of the true revolution according to Marx that he and his comrades had pledged themselves to
bring about.

He told the meeting that the Communists of Munich had
no intention of supporting the so-called Soviet Republic about to
be proclaimed. Communists could not cooperate with Social
Democrats who, he said, had compromised themselves beyond
recovery by their backing of the war and would only damage the
Soviet idea by their participation in it. The Communists could
lend themselves only to undertakings in which they were the
leaders. Furthermore, said Leviné, a Soviet Republic could be
achieved only by class warfare, and not around a conference
table. He then departed.

His speech had a depressing effect on the meeting. There
was talk among the delegates of abandoning the whole idea of
proclaiming a Soviet Republic. The chairman himself, Ernst
Niekisch, urged this course. To him the proceedings had seemed
impossibly erratic. But none of the factions present wished to assume the onus of backing down, and as the meeting broke up in
the dawn of April seventh it was decided, on the suggestion of
Gustav Landauer, that all the church bells of Bavaria should be
rung that day to proclaim the birth of the *Räterepublik*—the
Bavarian Republic of Councils, or Soviets.

It was symptomatic of the ideological oddity of the new Soviet-style regime that church bells should announce its coming,
and it was indicative of the political fluidity in Bavaria that a
proclamation was sufficient to install a new government. "The
dictatorship of the proletariat has become a reality," the proclamation said. A Red Army would be organized. The press would
be socialized. A revolutionary court would deal ruthlessly with
all counterrevolutionary activity.

All this had a fiercely radical tone, and it was not immediately recognized that the flaming pronouncements, coming from

Toller and Landauer, were largely rhetorical. The effect was to alarm most of the population and cause the departure of the Hoffmann government from Munich. Hoffmann and his ministers fled northward to the city of Bamberg, where they, in turn, proclaimed themselves the only legitimate government.

The internal disarray of the Soviet-style regime was demonstrated at the outset when a new leader had to be found before the first day was out. Convinced that the enterprise was doomed, Ernst Niekisch resigned as Chairman of the Central Council. Ernst Toller was chosen as his successor, and nothing testified more vividly to the romantic and impractical nature of the new Bavarian Soviet Republic than that its highest post was awarded to a twenty-six-year-old poet.

For Ernst Toller, revolution was all emotion, fire and eloquence. Slim and graceful, with deep-glowing eyes and wavy dark hair above a high forehead, he had become a matinee idol of the proletariat. Along with his unfeigned passion for social justice went an actor's flair for dramatizing himself, a consciousness of the effect he was able to produce with his melodious voice and his writer's gift for the telling phrase. He could transfix an audience of workers with searing denunciations of injustice, or transport it with a poet's vision of the brotherhood and humanity that would one day set all things right. His youth and inexperience were redeemed from callowness by something somber and tragic in his looks—"the Jewish countenance on which the fate of that persecuted race is imprinted like the traces of a secret malady," as one observer said.

Like thousands of others of his time and place, Ernst Toller had become a rebel in the trenches. Shattered by what he had seen and endured there, he concluded that his world was "ripe for destruction." Salvation from the cruelties of the capitalist system lay in what he called "the saving power of socialism," for which he, like so many of his fellow rebels, had conceived a faith bordering on the mystical. But, like Eisner, and unlike the Russian revolutionaries, Toller was temperamentally incapable of a final commitment that would unhesitatingly hurt, kill and destroy for the good of the cause. "He was not the type," his friend

George Grosz wrote of him. "He confused his brilliant oratorical ability, which brought him a great deal of applause, with the true role of the leader. He was a fiery agitator. He must have visualized himself as another LaSalle and not one of those boring gray mass speakers who reported what was going on in the factories. He would stand beside a fluttering banner, his eyes fixed on the great, the beautiful and the ideal. He stood above the people and among them at the same time. He was of a romantic and sentimental nature. He lacked all the essentials of a genuine leader; he lacked firmness of will power and—innate to all real leaders—contempt for the masses. He viewed both swallows and people poetically, and confused poetry with politics."

There was more concern for poetry than for politics in the launching of the first Soviet Republic in Munich. Gustav Landauer gave the regime its characteristic thrust by taking charge of the University and announcing sweeping changes in its administration and policy. Henceforth examinations and degrees would be abolished. Any citizen would be admitted to the classrooms at the age of eighteen, regardless of previous schooling. The University would no longer be run by its governing senate, but by a Soviet of students. All faculties would be thoroughly revised along socialist lines to serve the requirements of the working class, and no longer those of the academic community. The traditional history courses were forbidden as being inimical to culture.

A passionate admirer and translator of Walt Whitman, Landauer proposed to make the American poet a major figure in the new culture that was to take root in the new society he and Toller and Mühsam were creating. "Every Bavarian child at the age of ten is going to know Walt Whitman by heart," Landauer told a foreign correspondent. "That is the cornerstone of my new educational program!" As Minister of Education and Instruction, he also ordered the newspapers to print German literary classics, such as the poetry of Hölderlin, on the front pages, side by side with revolutionary decrees and governmental proclamations. The theaters were thrown open free to the workers, and would hereafter be run for their benefit. "The world must become a meadow of flowers in which everyone can pick his share," was the motto of Gustav Landauer. It was as if Greenwich Village had moved into city hall en masse.

Dr. Lipp in his gray frock coat and elegant beard gave the administration an even more pronounced streak of the daft and quixotic. His principal activity as People's Deputy for Foreign Affairs was to issue a spray of dispatches that made Eisner's illusory statesmanship seem sound and hard-headed by comparison. In a cable to Moscow purporting to summarize the new political situation in Bavaria, Dr. Lipp took occasion to complain that his ministry's toilet key had been stolen by the Hoffmann regime in its flight to Bamberg. After accusing Prussia of bloody and repressive policies, Dr. Lipp's cable continued: "We want peace forever. Immanuel Kant, *On Eternal Peace,* 1795, Theses 2 to 5. Prussia wants to use the armistice to prepare a war of revenge. With fraternal greetings . . ."

Dr. Lipp also declared war on Württemberg and Switzerland "because these dogs refuse to lend me sixty locomotives. I am certain that we will be victorious. Besides, I will obtain the blessings of the Pope, with whom I am well acquainted . . ." When Toller, convinced that Dr. Lipp had become unhinged again, requested that the People's Deputy for Foreign Affairs resign, Dr. Lipp sighed, primped his beard, and did so with the remark: "What don't I do for the Revolution!"

The fraternal greetings sent by Munich to Moscow elicited a cable response from Nicolai Lenin himself. He must have recalled his own days in Munich when, as "Herr Meyer," he had launched the *Iskra* from the Schwabinger Café and his room on the Schleissheimer Strasse. Now that his spark had caught fire in Munich in a way he could hardly have foreseen, he wanted to ascertain how his revolution was progressing there. Ignoring the stolen toilet key and the theses of Immanuel Kant, Lenin's cable curtly demanded some hard facts. How did things stand with the agrarian program in the Bavarian Soviet Republic? he wanted to know. Did the "new order prevail fully and completely"?

There was no agrarian program, or any other in the Leninist sense, and the new order was far from prevailing. Most of the people, confused and disturbed by what was happening, were against it; the Majority Socialists, though part of the new government, were intriguing against it; and Lenin's own Communists on the scene were actively opposing it. Dr. Leviné's *Red Banner* branded the regime a "sham Soviet" that left the bourgeoisie firmly entrenched everywhere. While a blizzard of decrees and regulations, hurriedly copied from Russian and Hungarian models, issued from the Wittelsbach Palace, nothing was basically changed. The workers had not been armed. There was no dictatorship of the proletariat. There were only, the Communists charged, revolutionary phrases without revolutionary action.

Lacking support, cohesion and direction, the Toller-Landauer regime survived less than a week. Instead of contributing anything substantial to the brighter world of which it dreamed, the six days of its existence led in the end only to a deepening of the tensions and antagonisms that were steadily conditioning Bavaria for future violence and civil war.

The six days ended suddenly on Palm Sunday, April thirteenth, with a *Putsch,* an uprising of some troops of the Munich garrison who had remained partially loyal to the Bamberg government. The soldiers arrested a number of officials of the Soviet Republic, including Erich Mühsam, and held them prisoner at the main railroad station.

For a few hours the *Putschists* appeared to be in control and the Soviet Republic seemed ended, with the prospect of a return to moderation. But events turned the other way. The Spartacists, led by the hard-core Communists, reacted by marshaling their fighting elements on the Theresa Meadow—armed workers, revolutionary troops from the garrison, Red sailors. With rifles and machine guns, they marched into the city and fought the Hoffmann troops in the streets, battling from square to square and block by block. By evening the Hoffmann units had been pressed back into the railroad station, their last stronghold. There they were taken under heavy mortar fire by the Communists, which broke their resistance. That night they boarded a train and steamed off for Bamberg, taking their prisoners, including Erich Mühsam, with them.

The *Putsch* that was intended to drive the foreign radicals from power in Bavaria produced the opposite result in its aftermath. The Palm Sunday fighting swept the Toller-Landauer faction aside, but now the way was opened for the hard-core Communists to assert themselves. With Eugen Leviné at its head, an Action Committee dominated by Bolshevik extremists took control of the government. The second Bavarian Soviet Republic was proclaimed with a snarling declaration of war against the bourgeoisie—"the tigers and vampires of reaction"—who were now to be ruthlessly dealt with. A true dictatorship of the proletariat was to be established at last. The day of the Schwabing Bohemians was over; the hard-fisted Leninists had supplanted the poets and dreamers.

But there was something eccentric, a streak of the theatrical and immature, about the new set of revolutionaries also. Though Leviné himself had some intelligence and character, his closest lieutenants were, in their own way, almost as improbably cast for the roles assigned to them as their predecessors. The Bavarian propensity for breeding and attracting bizarre personalities was nearly as pronounced in the ruling clique of the second *Räterepublik* as in the first.

Max Levien, next in the new chain of command, was a swarthy, full-lipped Bolshevik with delusions of Napoleonic grandeur. He habitually strode about in high riding boots complete with spurs, and advertised his allegiance by affecting a red Russian tunic. His oratorical style was floridly belligerent, and even his ordinary conversation rang with the top-sergeant's tone of command. Moscow-born, like Leviné, he had fled Russia before the revolution to escape imprisonment, and was now a naturalized German. Obsessed and fanatical, he was fascinated by violence. He repeatedly called upon the proletariat to die for the cause and threatened all enemies of the working class with death. One of his projects was to organize an expedition to hunt down King Ludwig III in his mountain retreat and haul him back to Munich as a hostage. Nothing came of this.

The new Commandant of the City of Munich, and Commander in Chief of the regime's "Red Army," was a twenty-three-year-old sailor named Rudolf Egelhofer. His uniform for both positions was his sailor suit, a reminder to everyone that he had emerged as a revolutionary by participating in the mutinies in the fleet at Kiel. More recently he had distinguished himself by leading the assault on the railroad station that drove the Hoffmann troops from the city, and was thus the hero of the hour.

Egelhofer established himself in the War Ministry, surrounded himself with a numerous and swaggering bodyguard, and was soon notorious for his lordly style of living in public and private—"like an Asiatic prince," according to one description. He preferred champagne to the native brew, and his entourage of toothsome women disguised as secretaries and stenographers gave the War Ministry an incongruously convivial air. With unrestricted access to the city treasury, Egelhofer went far toward realizing the revolutionary ideal of "everything belongs to everybody" by distributing stacks of bank notes to his retinue, from adjutants to scrubwomen.

But Rudolf Egelhofer's personal *Gaudi* was only the lighter aspect of the second Soviet Republic on the Isar. Its more somber phase was personified by yet another Moscow-born revolutionist, the Commissar Tovia Axelrod. He had escaped from a Siberian prison camp under the Czar, returned to Russia to become a press and propaganda official under the Soviets, and then made his way to Munich where he attached himself in an unspecified capacity to the Eisner regime. His shadowy presence in the background of that experiment lent support to accusations from the Right that the Soviet Union had poured 164 million marks into Bavaria to turn it into a Bolshevik satellite. Tovia Axelrod was of the Leninist breed for whom destruction of the established order was a life's mission, and now the policy of Axelrod and his fellow commissars prevailed in Munich.

One of the first measures was to call a general strike, which had no apparent point except as a display of proletarian muscle, to show who was boss. Its chief effect was to cripple further the economy of a city already sinking into stagnation. Sweeping decrees for the confiscation of private and corporate bank accounts, business profits and food supplies were issued and put into effect. When raids on the banks of Munich and adjacent communities failed to replenish the depleted municipal coffers, the printing presses made up the difference by churning out paper money in the millions. Armed patrols fanned out through the city to search private homes for hoarded money and hidden guns. The patrols, many of them unauthorized, burst into houses at random and plundered at will, carting off whatever was handy and portable.

A pall pregnant with menace and uncertainty enveloped the city. During the day the nearly empty streets were dominated by grim workmen wearing red armbands and with rifles slung over their shoulders. Trucks full of soldiers of the new Red Army rumbled ominously to and fro on missions that could only be guessed at but that portended terror. After sundown a curfew was enforced with instant gunfire and, said one observer, "the dark city became hollow and silent," the people cowering in their homes behind barricaded doors. Something described by another resident as "a state of hysterical panic" gripped the middle and upper classes.

Egelhofer's Red Army, now master of Munich, consisted of some 20,000 men, workers from the Krupp and Maffei factories who had been liberally supplied with confiscated arms, and units of the garrison that had become little more than a uniformed mob as discipline disintegrated during the various revolutionary upheavals. In keeping with the new revolutionary era, the pay of the troops had been increased, and they were allowed to elect and depose their own officers, which only added to their unruliness. Hundreds of unemployed flocked into the ranks to enjoy the easy life of the barracks, where food and shelter were assured, and where the long duty-free hours were often enlivened by visits from women off the streets.

A few score Russian prisoners-of-war, released from the nearby camp at Pucheim, formed a special unit. This provided propaganda for both the Red regime and its opponents. The local Communists saw the Russian soldiers as symbols of the international scope of their revolution, but for most Bavarians, and most Germans as well, they were an appalling spectacle fraught with dreadful implications. What good was the glorious triumph at Tannenberg if armed Slavs were now marching on German soil? And if a Soviet regime could arm and maintain itself in Bavaria, how long would the rest of the nation be safe from the Red infection? Johannes Hoffmann, fuming with his fugitive government in Bamberg, was moved to act. He called the Bavarian people to arms and ordered his own soldiers to march on Munich. Civil war began.

In countering the military threat from the north, the leaders of the Soviet Republic, for all their stance of hard-headed realism, again betrayed the quixotic streak that so often characterized the Left in Bavaria. As field commander against the approaching Hoffmann troops, the choice fell on Ernst Toller, the poet.

During the turmoil of exchanging the first *Räterepublik* for the second, Toller had been put under arrest by the insurgent Communists, and there was even talk of having him shot. His popularity among the workers, however, preserved him as a possible asset to the new regime, and now his thirteen months in the ranks during the war were regarded as sufficient qualification for the role of commanding general of the Red Army. Borrowing a horse from a friendly cavalryman whom he had chanced to meet in a *Bierstube,* Ernst Toller trotted off to the front.

He went burdened with moral misgivings. "I hated force," he wrote afterward, "and I had sworn to submit to it rather than use it. Was I justified in breaking this vow, now that the Revolution was being attacked?" He decided that since the workers had put their confidence in him, and since he had accepted their confidence by assuming a position of leadership, he had no choice but to keep faith with them. "I should have considered the possibility of bloody consequences before taking office," he told himself, and rode on to the battle line. But he would not, and did not, waver from his conviction that "the revolution must be cleanly fought." Pure of heart, with the ghost of Sancho Panza at his side, Ernst Toller came to Dachau, which was being held by the Hoffmann troops.

A market town only fifteen kilometers from Munich, Dachau was fated to be lifted from the obscurity of centuries, and register itself in history, by two conflicting distinctions. It was about to become the scene of a victory for Bavaria's Red Army under Ernst Toller, and thus a significant early battleground in the clash of armed ideologies rending postwar Germany. But when the Tollers and all they stood for were ultimately crushed by forces even then gathering strength, Dachau would become permanently notorious for another reason. Under Adolf Hitler it became the site of the first concentration camp and set the pattern for all others. The defeat of the Tollers was a necessary precondition to the era of the concentration camps, and it was a cruelly ironic turn of history that the first of them, the one "with the curse of eternity on its creation," should have been established precisely where Ernst Toller won his greatest triumph.

Toller's victory at Dachau in the spring of 1919 was won despite scruples that would have seemed insanely softheaded to Private First Class Hitler, still marking time while the battle was being fought. Toller, wishing to avoid unnecessary destruction, ignored an order from Rudolf Egelhofer to bombard the town with artillery. He tore up another Egelhofer order directing that all captured "White" officers be shot, and he even sought to avoid battle altogether by first negotiating with the enemy. But when firing broke out anyway, Toller personally led his labor battalions in the attack on the town. Supported by other workers from a local munitions factory, the assault was successful and Dachau fell to the Red Army. The bloodletting was not extensive. The Hoffmann troops had little heart for the fray and surrendered readily or simply threw away their arms and went home, as they also did in another engagement at nearby Freising.

About a hundred prisoners and a few cannon were paraded through the streets of Munich to celebrate the exploit of the Red Army. Ernst Toller, the reluctant hero, found himself hailed as "the conqueror of Dachau," and was moved to issue a ringing communique proclaiming the triumph of the proletariat over what he called "the poisonous beast of reaction."

But the triumph was entirely Pyrrhic.

7 A BEGINNING

"I KNEW HOW TO SPEAK!"
—ADOLF HITLER

WHAT CAME to be known as *der Krieg nach dem Kriege,* the war after the war, was spreading all over Germany, and the poet Rilke expressed what thousands were feeling. "We've all been cheated of the deep breath of relief we were entitled to," he wrote to a friend. "The peace is falling out of everyone's hands and breaking into a thousand pieces."

Munich, he foresaw, would be "a harsh and turbulent place" from now on, and he noted the great vans rolling through the city as old residents packed up their goods, gave up their houses, and moved away.

Finding the situation "emotionally indescribable," he himself would soon be leaving Germany to become a permanent exile in Switzerland.

Pfc. Adolf Hitler was also finding conditions in Munich intolerable, but for his own reasons. The prison camp at Traunstein having been closed down, he returned to the barracks of the 2nd Bavarian Infantry Regiment in March of 1919. Everything he saw and experienced confirmed him in his hatred of the peace and the men who had made it. Something called "voluntary obedience" prevailed among the slipshod soldiers of his barracks, a travesty on the military traditions he adored. The Eisner regime and the Bavarian Soviet outraged his deepest convictions of what a German state should be. What he had learned to expect and fear from Lanz von Liebenfels and the *Ostara* in Vienna was occurring before his eyes: the Jewish world conspiracy, represented by the Eisners, Tollers and Levinés, was working its will in Germany. The *Tschandale* were taking over.

Everywhere he looked—even in the placards on the walls and kiosks—he saw symptoms of the spreading corruption brought by the revolution. In the avant-garde art and illustrations introduced into posters and newspapers by Gustav Landauer he detected what he called "the morbid excrescences of insane and degenerate men." For him, it all "bore the imprint not only of political but cultural decay." His resolve to become a politician and somehow shatter a system he loathed was hardened.

As in his prewar beer halls, and among his comrades at the front, his only emotional outlet was in explosive tirades delivered to anyone who would listen. One soldier remembered him afterward for his "inflated" way of talking, "like a man who has read a lot of books without digesting them." He was not taken seriously because word got around the barracks that he had come back from the front temporarily blind as a result of a nervous collapse. He was evidently regarded as still suffering from what, in World War I, was called shell shock.

But if, at this stage, Adolf Hitler's opposition to the new order in Germany was passive, others who felt as he did were acting with the ruthlessness that would set a pattern for Germany's future, and his own. In the opening days of this March of 1919, another Spartacus uprising was being shot to pieces by tanks, mortars and execution squads on the streets in Berlin. A government order was issued that any armed person caught resisting the new regime was to be shot immediately, and under the aegis of this open-season hunting license hundreds were put against the wall, singly, in pairs, and in groups. The Spartacists, for their part, were using gas shells and dumdum bullets. The bodies were "piled up like herring," said one contemporary account, and then carted off to corpse depots, where relatives came to sort out the remains of husbands, sons and brothers. Weirdly, incredibly, the bars, dance halls, and cabarets were open for business as usual, and placards all over the city announced a contest: *Wer hat die schönsten Beine von Berlin?*—"Who's got the prettiest legs in Berlin?"

In the state of Saxony radicals had seized power, defied the Berlin regime, and were terrorizing all opposition without being able to maintain order. In Dresden wounded veterans, infuriated by reports that their compensation was going to be reduced, hurled a Socialist minister into the Elbe River and shot him while he was struggling to save himself from drowning. In Stettin the police were overwhelmed and disarmed by radical mobs, and the jails were opened. A state of siege was proclaimed in the Ruhr.

After surveying the situation throughout the country, an American foreign correspondent summed it up in twelve words. Ben Hecht, representing the *Chicago Daily News* syndicate, cabled his managing editor:

"Germany is having a nervous breakdown. There is nothing sane to report."

Contemplating his countrymen in another turbulent time, Goethe was moved to exclaim: "May the good Lord help the Germans if ever a Napoleon appears among them!"

It was a profoundly prescient saying, but there was no sign of a Napoleonic figure as the leaders of the new Germany gathered in Goethe's town of Weimar to found the first German republic. They met in the neoclassical National Theater before whose entrance stood a joint statue of Goethe and Schiller. Weimar was a locale calculated to remind the world that there was, indeed, "another Germany," though the phrase itself had not yet been coined.

Johann Wolfgang von Goethe and Friedrich von Schiller, Johann Sebastian Bach and Franz Liszt, Lucas Cranach the Elder and Friedrich Nietzsche—much that was great and good in German literature, music, art, philosophy was associated with the lovely town on the River Ilm. From now on, Weimar and the quills of Goethe and Schiller were to displace Potsdam and the bayonets of Frederick the Great as symbols of the German spirit.

But Potsdam bayonets were, nevertheless, much in evidence as the delegates deliberated. The National Theater was surrounded by barbed wire and guarded by crack troops under General Ludwig Maercker, who wore the red stripe of the Imperial General Staff, a symbol nearer to the reality of the times than Goethe's quill. At Weimar, as everywhere else in Germany, the new Socialist state was depending for survival on the battalions of the old Empire.

Heinrich Hauser, one of General Maercker's riflemen, measured what he called "the masters of the new age" as they came and went. "Lots of belly and long beard," he noted. "Here were no saviors of Germany in her hour of need." Fritz Ebert, now confirmed as President of the Republic by popular vote, "held his slouch hat before his stomach with a dignity acquired at club functions."

The National Assembly stitched together a governing coalition dominated by the Majority Socialists and fashioned a constitution longer than the Constitution of the United States and embodying all the major features of the Bill of Rights and the Rights of Man.

But the most hotly debated issue involved Article 3, which provided for a new national flag. The Republic's colors were henceforth to be black-red-gold, recalling the liberal revolution of 1848 and signifying the dawning of a new era in German political life. Conservative and reactionary elements met the proposal with howls of protest. There was outrage at the abandonment of the imperial black-white-red under which the Reich had achieved unity and won the greatest military victories in German history. Discarding those colors seemed an unforgivable blasphemy. And it was not forgiven. For years to come the flag of the Republic would be despised by every *völkisch* patriot, and detested by all who gloried in what Adolf Hitler described as "German heroic grandeur." In the new Republican flag thousands promptly read their own symbolism: the black was for the future, the red was for the present—and the gold was for the past.

To many delegates, another saying of the Sage of Weimar

184

seemed particularly timely. It was from Goethe's *Belagerung von Mainz,* and it went: "It is better that injustices occur than that they should be removed in an unjust way. Therefore let everyone submit to the law." Far from submitting to the law, thousands of Germans were taking it into their own hands by rioting in the streets. The new Constitution and flag would be nothing but meaningless artifacts if the near-chaos in the country continued.

"Somebody has to be the bloodhound," said the new Minister of Defense, Gustav Noske, and he volunteered for the role. He was a broad, burly man, richly mustached, who sometimes affected a workingman's cap to advertise his proletarian background, which was authentic. The son of a basket-weaver, he had followed the butcher's trade, a calling whose implications his opponents made the most of in their attacks upon him. Equipped with peasant shrewdness and plenty of physical energy, he had made a name for himself in the trade-union movement and became the Socialist Party's expert on military matters. He had been sent to Kiel to restore order after the mutiny of the sailors, and he did so. It was he who set in motion the tanks and troops that subdued the Spartacists in Berlin and that were being deployed against insurgent Leftists everywhere else. No son of the working class, and certainly no Socialist, had ever wielded such military authority in Germany before. Gustav Noske was the nearest thing to a Strong Man that the German Revolution had produced.

Berlin in March had been bad, but the reports from Bavaria in April were worse. There an entire state seemed to be in convulsion, swept by turmoil that no longer was merely revolutionary but was carrying disorder to the point of madness: Eisner's assassination and its aftermath—Proclamation of a Soviet Republic—Russian-born Bolsheviks in the Wittelsbach palace—Red victory at Dachau.

From the exiled Hoffmann regime in Bamberg came anguished appeals for help, and they fell on receptive ears. "The Munich insane asylum must be put in order," said Gustav Noske, and he set about it.

The troops assembled at a former Army maneuver grounds, at Ohrdruf in Thuringia, and prepared to march on Munich. They were a special breed of soldier that was on the march all over Germany, mostly veterans for whom the war had never stopped. They were called the *Freikorps,* or Free Corps, and with the dissolution of the Imperial Army they were virtually the only combat-ready troops the government had. They had formed themselves into independent companies and battalions that were usually named for their commanders, or for the localities they represented—Freikorps Görlitz, Brigade Reinhard, Detachment Jena, Berlin Free Rifles. They thought of themselves as "cells of resistance against chaos," and to a man they endorsed the old saying about bullets being the only cure for democrats.

From Verdun to Tannenberg, many of them had fought the greatest battles the world had ever seen; none believed the German Army had been defeated in the field. As with Ernst Jünger, the war had entered into them like wine and they had never recovered from the intoxication. Some had gone directly from school to the front and knew no other way of life except the way of the trenches. For them the postwar world was an alien and unfamiliar place, barren of the virtues the army had taught them to value most—courage, comradeship and self-sacrifice. The Germany they had come back to was not the Germany they had marched away from, and what they now saw of civilian life made them despise it. The past was what mattered: one's own, which meant the ordeal of the trenches, and the nation's, which meant all its days of splendor. The Free Corps fought to arrest the future and recover the past.

At Ohrdruf so many dissident ex-officers volunteered that whole companies were formed of them. Established Free Corps units were augmented by loose-end students and demobilized noncoms who could find no other place for themselves in a disintegrating society. Freebooting drifters who would just as soon kill and plunder, having nothing better to do, joined the ranks, and toward the end of April 1919 a Noske army of some 20,-

000, under the command of a Prussian major general, began to move on Munich. By April twenty-ninth the city was surrounded.

Bavaria alone was subjected to every possible shock of the postwar German revolution, from the relatively innocent upheaval of Kurt Eisner's 100 days, through the hardening worker-soldier-peasant phase, and continuing with increasingly radical variations of the *Räte,* or Soviet, experiment and civil war. At no time did circumstances allow an orderly regime to coalesce and take root. Events were so colored and complicated by the native tendency to grotesquerie that even in a nation swept by turmoil, Munich seemed unreasonably volatile. And with the approach of the Noske troops, the situation in the Bavarian capital teetered on the edge of anarchy.

The only authority rested with the Red (Workers) Army, which was itself disorganized and disorderly. Its "General Staff" was issuing orders that reminded Ernst Toller of the dispatches of Dr. Lipp, and he resigned as field commander. Dachau fell, and panicky posters went up all over Munich: "The Prussian White Guard Is at the Gates! . . . Workers, Comrades! . . . The Enemy Is Merciless! . . . Prepare for a Battle to the Death!"

Rudolf Egelhofer, the young sailor who was now Commander in Chief and City Commandant, appealed to the regular troops of the Munich garrison to turn out and join the last-ditch defense of the capital. There was virtually no response from the undisciplined and largely reactionary units. At the barracks of the 2nd Infantry Regiment, as at some others, the soldiers were called together to vote on Egelhofer's appeal. There was a loud debate, which ended when Pfc. Hitler, wearing his Iron Cross First Class, mounted a chair and shouted: "Those who say we should remain neutral are right. After all, we're no pack of Revolutionary Guards for a lot of carpetbagging [*hergelaufene*] Jews." The soldiers were persuaded. The unit remained neutral.

Afterward Hitler told a story of how his behavior at this period came to the attention of the Red authorities, who sent three armed militiamen to arrest him. "But in the face of my leveled carbine," he said, "they couldn't summon the necessary courage, and all three of them went off the way they came."

It was a crucial incident, if it happened. All over the city Red Guards were rounding up agitators and conspirators, and there were many. Had Adolf Hitler actually been taken prisoner, he might well have been shot.

A raid by Red sailors on the headquarters of the Thule Society caught seven members and confiscated a mass of incriminating evidence: anti-Semitic leaflets, propaganda supporting the advancing White troops, forged seals and documents. The society had been recruiting for the Free Corps and producing false travel papers for volunteers. Among those arrested was the Countess Hella von Westarp, thirty-two years old, pretty, and the secretary of the society. She, with the others, was held as a hostage in the Luitpold High School, which the Red Army was using as both a barracks and jail.

Among the prisoners at Luitpold were two captured Hussars of the Guards Cavalry Rifle Division, the formation responsible for the murders of Karl Liebknecht and Rosa Luxemburg. Placards announced the approach of this unit as a warning to the population of terror to come if Munich should fall.

A White terror was, in fact, on the way. As the Free Corps marched on the city, fifty-two Russian prisoners of war at Pucheim, who had been freed by the Red regime, were rounded up and slaughtered in a stone quarry. A column of medics, overtaken as they prepared to succor Red Army wounded, was mowed down on the spot. At Perlach, near Munich, twelve noncombatant workers were shot in their tracks. Captured Red Army soldiers were executed out of hand. On the other side, the commander of a Red infantry regiment ordered that five hostages be executed for every one of its men killed in the fighting at Dachau.

On what turned out to be the last day of the Red regime in Bavaria, somebody ordered that the hostages in the Luitpold High School be shot. Nobody knows who issued the order, but it was obviously in reprisal for atrocities committed by the Noske troops. As such, and in every other way, it was utterly senseless, the product of panic and unreasoning rage. It could have no deterrent or punitive effect on the White army, which by now was victorious and beyond the reach of reprisals. No possible military, moral or propaganda benefit could result from carrying out the order, but it was carried out.

There was no consistency in the choice of the ten victims. Along with the two captured Hussars was an aging Jewish professor who had been caught tearing down a Red poster. He, of course, had no connection with the Thule Society, but was shot anyway. The seven Thule members included a prince, a sculptor, a painter, a baron, a railroad official, an industrial artist and the Countess Westarp—precisely the kind of people the average German was most inclined to respect and admire. They were put against a wall in the courtyard of the high school and executed by soldiers of a Red Army in the last stages of dissolution. At a window overlooking the scene, one report said, another soldier was playing the accordion. Staging the atrocity in a schoolyard added to the universal revulsion it evoked.*

It was useless to argue, then or later, that the shooting of the Luitpold hostages was no worse than innumerable similar acts by the Right, or that the murder of Rosa Luxemburg was every bit as atrocious as the killing of Hella von Westarp. Rosa Luxemburg was a dumpy, unattractive Polish Jewess, and a radical. The Countess Westarp was a gracious German lady and an aristocrat. The disposal of the one could be accepted by Germans with a shrug as an incident of the times. It might even be condoned. The murder of the other was an abomination and a horror. Everywhere *völkisch* patriots enshrined the Countess and her comrades as "the first blood witnesses of awakening Germany" to die under the symbol of Thule, the swastika.

There were multiple ironies as the White troops broke into the city from all sides on the day after the executions. The date was May 1, the traditional day of the worker. On the Red Square in Moscow, Nicolai Lenin was giving a speech, saying:

---

* Albert Einstein attended the Luitpold High School during his residence in Munich.

"The working class, which has liberated itself, now celebrates its day freely and openly not only in Soviet Russia but also in Soviet Bavaria . . ."

As the words were spoken, the Bavarian Soviet Republic was expiring and workers were dying in the streets under the guns of the White Army. In Schwabing, which once knew Nicolai Lenin as Herr Meyer, there was vicious fighting, for this was the breeding ground of the Bavarian revolt, the home of the detested *Schlawiner* whom the Free Corps types fell upon with particular fury. In the center of town, the Matthäser beer hall was in flames, under attack by mortars and hand grenades. The Matthäser, where Kurt Eisner had formed his first Workers and Peasants Council, became one of the last strongholds of Red Bavaria. In the smoke of its burning, the Free Corps and regular troops raged through the city.

Standrecht, martial law, drumhead executions, littered the streets with corpses. Spartacists, and suspected Spartacists, were hauled from their homes and hiding places and, as the phrase was, *"an die Wand gestellt,"* put against the wall. The soldiers, many in full field equipment, as in an enemy city, regarded the place as another Zabern on a titanic scale: mere civilians had dared to challenge authority, defy the uniform, and destroy what in Germany had always been sacrosanct and inviolable, *Ruhe und Ordnung,* civic peace and order. "Thirsting," as Nietzsche said, "for the pleasures of the knife" and inflamed by the Luitpold atrocity, they matched it and surpassed it with their own.

The members of a Catholic group called St. Joseph's Social Club were meeting in a hall to discuss putting on a play when normal activities could be resumed in Munich. The gathering was anonymously denounced to the military, who suspected that something subversive was afoot. Soldiers raided the hall, herded the club members into a cellar, and accused them of being Communist plotters. Twenty-one of the young Catholics were beaten to death with rifle butts, stabbed with bayonets and shot. The soldiers performed what court testimony later described as "a drunken Indian dance" on the bodies.

Gustav Landauer, gentlest of men who had once called

communism "the pestilence of our time," remonstrated with the Free Corps students who took him prisoner. He told them that he had always abhorred violence and militarism, whether from the Left or the Right, and he urged them to turn from violence themselves. An officer hit him in the face with the thick end of a riding whip, and the Free Corps boys beat him to the floor and shot him in the back. Seeing that he still twitched, they stomped him to death.

Rudolf Egelhofer was caught as he attempted to flee in an automobile. He was dragged from the car by a mob and beaten to death. Leviné was arrested later, put on trial, and executed. Axelrod and Levien managed to escape to Austria. A price of 10,000 marks was put on Ernst Toller's head. He was found, disguised with dyed hair and a false beard, in a Schwabing studio, where a woman betrayed him to the police under the guise of helping him escape. He was sentenced to five years' fortress arrest on charges of high treason. Not long after he began serving his sentence, he wrote to a friend:

"What will the coming years bring to Europe, to Germany? There are times when I want to scream and run away from the pictures of horror that haunt me like hallucinations." *

Few could read the signs so accurately then, but the signs were there. Handkerchiefs fluttered and there were cries of *"Hoch! Hoch!"* when the victorious government troops paraded along the broad Ludwig Strasse. One of the most impressive units was the Second Naval Brigade, trim, tough veterans of fighting in the Baltic and on the Polish border. Better known as the Ehrhardt Brigade, after its commander, it was a Free Corps unit with a reputation for absolute ruthlessness and efficiency, and it stirred in the spectators a surge of patriotic pride. Here again was *Zucht,* the old German manliness, the soldierly style and *élan* that contrasted so strikingly with the shuffling formations of the late Workers Army. *"Hoch!"*

---

* In jail Toller wrote several Expressionistic plays that were successfully produced in Berlin and elsewhere. They included *Maschinenstürmer* ("The Machine Wreckers") and *Die Wandlung* ("The Change"). Driven into exile when Hitler came to power, and despairing of the future, Toller committed suicide in a New York hotel room in 1939.

Along the route people noticed the curious emblem on the helmets of the Brigade, a symbol it had brought back from its battles in the Baltic. As they swung along, the Ehrhardt soldiers sang their marching song:

> *Hakenkreuz am Stahlhelm,*
> *Schwarz-weiss-rotes Band . . .*

"Swastika on helmet, Colors black-white-red . . ."

In the "liberation" of Munich, in May of 1919, the swastika won its first victory as a military emblem. Not very far in the future, on these same streets, other marching columns would adopt the song of the Ehrhardt Brigade and make it their own. They would call themselves Storm Troopers.

Pfc. Adolf Hitler might have been expected to seize his carbine and join the White troops in the battle for the city. He didn't. Years later Otto Strasser, who became one of his lieutenants and then broke with him, rebuked him publicly: "Where was Hitler that day? In what corner of Munich was the soldier hiding who should have been fighting in our ranks?"

He himself never disclosed what he was doing when the fate of Bavaria was being decided, and the Nazi Party literature glosses over the subject with evasions and fabrications. But the White victory provided a turning point in his career. His unwavering hostility to the Red regime had not gone unnoticed.

"A few days after the liberation of Munich," he wrote afterward, "I was ordered to report to the Commission of Inquiry on events in the 2nd Infantry Regiment during the revolution." His reports to the Commission on the behavior of his fellow soldiers were "mercilessly exact," an observer noted, and on the evidence supplied by Hitler many members of the regiment faced the firing squad. He was serving as an informer, but he saw his role in a different light.

"This," he would write in his autobiography, "was my first more or less purely political activity."

He had made a transition.

Though he continued to wear the uniform, his days as a

soldier were over. By singling him out for this special assignment, paltry as it was, the Army had lifted him out of the ruck
of military anonymity and moved him into a new arena of action. In his own eyes he was now beginning to redeem the pledge
he had made to himself in the hospital at Pasewalk: "I, however,
decided to become a politician."

Nothing at the National Assembly in Weimar, or in the Hall
of Mirrors at Versailles, where the Peace Treaty was being
signed, compared in importance for the future of Germany with
the change in status of the obscure Private First Class in the infantry barracks in Munich.

He had just turned thirty.

Munich, too, moved into a new phase when the Red flag
was hauled down from atop the Wittelsbach palace, the *Residenz,*
and the white-blue banner of Bavaria was hoisted again. It was
an event the steward of the palace had long been praying for,
but his joy was somewhat dampened when he saw that the victorious White troops, now occupying the *Residenz,* behaved no better than the Reds. "What we were able to protect from the Reds,"
the steward, a Herr Wimmer, observed, "was not especially respected by the Whites. They stole everything they came across,
and we could do nothing about it . . ."

Captain Manfred von Killinger commanded a company of
the Ehrhardt Brigade quartered in the palace. His men slept on
the floor in the throne room, which had to be illuminated with
candles, the electricity having failed. The first night Captain von
Killinger dimly made out an object on the seat of the throne,
something nestled between two damask cushions. A closer look
told him what it was. It was the company mascot, a dog named
Putsch.

Captain von Killinger found it both amusing and symbolic
that a Free Corps dog should occupy the throne of the Bavarian
kings. He thought it served the citizens of Munich right. For
years they had flabbily tolerated what he called "the international riffraff" of the Schwabing cafés, who openly spat upon
throne and flag until freebooting soldiers like himself were forced

to come and put things right again with fire and sword. But he had the grace to recall a line from a German poet of the wars against Napoleon: *"Gott schütze die Lande vor Zeiten, in denen wir nötig sind!"*—"God preserve any country from times in which the likes of us are necessary!" *

Not only the Wittelsbach palace but all Munich was now in charge of soldiers. The *Reichswehr,* the provisional Army allowed by the Versailles Treaty, was the sole authority; the legitimate Hoffmann regime still sat uncertainly in Bamberg. Though the business and industrial life of Munich was near paralysis (even the breweries were threatened with closing for lack of coal), the *Reichswehr's* priorities called for immediate action in another direction.

A bureau designated as *Abteilung I b/P* was organized and put in charge of an energetic General Staff officer named Karl Mayr. His assignment was to investigate and report on troop morale and political attitudes in the ranks. Many soldiers had succumbed to democratic or outright revolutionary ideas, making them unsuitable material for the army the General Staff envisioned for the future. They were also a source of possible infection for their fellows. Captain Mayr and his *Abteilung* were to detect and weed out the tainted elements and, by instruction and propaganda, keep the others firm in their allegiance to the standards of the old Imperial Army. For this, officers and men would be needed who were not only politically reliable but also capable of imparting their convictions to others.

The first extensive listing of candidates compiled by Captain Mayr included the name: Hittler, Adolf. The name was misspelled, but it definitely belonged on such a list, as events shortly proved. Adolf Hitler had advanced another step along his way.

He later described himself as an "Education Officer" in Captain Mayr's unit, but was actually listed as a *V-Mann.* This was short for *Vertrauens-Mann,* a designation for a minor un-

---

* Manfred von Killinger would afterward become a commander of Storm Troops for Adolf Hitler and Nazi *Gauleiter* of the State of Saxony. He also served as German Consul-General in San Francisco and then as Ambassador to Rumania. He committed suicide at the approach of the Russian army.

194

dercover agent or trusted intermediary. As such, he was sent to a series of indoctrination courses conducted by the Army at the University of Munich. There he made a discovery that laid the basis for his career from then on.

"One day," as he told it, "I asked for a chance to speak. Somebody had been holding the floor with a lengthy discourse in defense of the Jews. This stirred me to make a rebuttal. The overwhelming majority of those present at the course expressed themselves as agreeing with my standpoint . . ."

He never forgot the incident, and he interpreted its significance correctly in his autobiography. "All at once I was being offered an opportunity of speaking before larger groups of listeners, and what I had always sensed before, but had only assumed out of pure feeling, was now substantiated: I knew how to 'speak!' "

"Ich konnte 'reden!' "

It was a crucial discovery, and he was not the only one to make it. One of his instructors then was Professor Karl Alexander von Müller, a Munich historian, and he, too, was impressed by *V-Mann* Hitler's ability to compel others to listen when he spoke.

"After one of my lectures and the lively discussion that followed it, my attention was arrested by a little group in the empty hall," the professor wrote. "The men seemed spellbound by one of their number who was haranguing them with mounting passion in a strangely gutteral voice. I had the peculiar feeling that their excitement derived from him and that at the same time they, in turn, were inspiring him."

The man stayed in the professor's mind. He remembered "the pale, gaunt face under a disheveled and unsoldierly forelock, the close-cropped mustache, and the striking clear-blue eyes with a glow of cold fanaticism in them." At a subsequent lecture he asked Captain Mayr if he was aware that among the trainees there was "a natural-born orator."

"Where is he?" Captain Mayr wanted to know.

The professor indicated the seat.

"That's Hitler from the List Regiment," Captain Mayr said, and called out: "You, Hitler, come up here."

The professor remembered, too, how Hitler approached the podium: "awkwardly, with a kind of defiant embarrassment," still ill at ease with superiors. Nothing immediate came of the interview, but when Captain Mayr was choosing an "Instruction Commando" for a special mission outside of Munich, he included *V-Mann* Hitler.

Word had come in that at Camp Lechfeld, a compound for returning prisoners of war, the men were being infected with Spartacist ideas and a revolutionary mood was developing. The Instruction Commando was sent to arrest this trend and teach the men "to feel and think in a nationalist and patriotic way," as Hitler himself phrased it. He spent only five days at Lechfeld, but again his flair for political rhetoric asserted itself. He spoke to the men on "Who Is to Blame for the World War?" and "Political Slogans, Social and Political," and he led discussion groups on a variety of current issues. Reports sent back from the camp repeatedly stressed the success of *V-Mann* Hitler's performance. His talks were described as *temperamentvoll*, fiery, and as "sweeping the audiences along with him." He was called *"ein geborener Volksredner,"* a born people's orator, who "compels the attention of his listeners and makes them think his way." At Camp Lechfeld, in August of 1919, Adolf Hitler displayed to bedraggled groups of returning prisoners the beginnings of that mesmeric power that, later on, would enthrall millions and change the face of Germany.

It was at this time, too, that he composed his first political document. Captain Mayr had received a letter from one of his former agents, a man named Adolf Gemlich, who was concerned about one of the disputed issues of the day. What was he to think about the Jewish situation? Under the new government, Jews were given equal rights with all other citizens, and there were many Jews in the ruling Social Democratic party. How was this possible if, as was so often said, the Jews were a national danger?

More and more people were asking similar questions. Anti-Semitism in the south of Germany had always been less pronounced than in the north, but Bavaria's experience of the *Räte* period had intensified it and it was beginning to take on ugly proportions. Adolf Gemlich was not alone in wondering whether there might not be something to the talk about Jews being responsible for the lost war and the misery that had come in its train. The revolution had left Bavaria emotionally and economically exhausted. The Red Republic had infected the middle class with a paranoiac fear of Bolshevism, which to most meant any change, or threat of change, in the traditional social structure; and the advocates of social change, as the Bavarians saw it, always seemed to be Jews. Look at Eisner. Look at Axelrod. Who murdered all those splendid people in the Luitpold High School?

Captain Mayr thought the Gemlich letter deserved a full answer. He turned it over to *V-Mann* Hitler, who had demonstrated in his Lechfeld speeches that he was something of an authority on the subject. In the reply Hitler composed, dated 16 September 1919, he sounded all the notes that he would strike to the end. His letter to Gemlich contains phrases that he repeated, almost word for word, in the last will and testament he wrote in his Berlin bunker in April of 1945, just before committing suicide.

He began by warning against the superficial idea that anti-Semitism was based merely on a widespread dislike for the Jew as an individual. The causes ran deeper. Jewry, he said, was not a religious community but a *racial* one. As a race, the Jews were conspiring to accumulate all the earthly goods of the world, and thereby rule the world. Reacting against them emotionally could no doubt lead to pogroms (a word he misspelled). But that was no solution. True anti-Semitism should consist of a deliberate, planned campaign to deprive the Jews of the rights that they, unlike other foreigners, were enjoying in Germany. But that was not sufficient, either. For the anti-Semitism of the future, he said, "The final goal"—which later, in his days of power, became "the final solution"—must "unshakably" be the removal (*"Entfernung"*) of all Jews.

He concluded by saying that majority rule, such as existed currently in Germany, could not accomplish this desirable end. What was needed, he said, was strong and ruthless leadership to wage a fight on behalf of the betrayed and deluded German people.

The letter was badly written—the style would become notorious with the publication of *Mein Kampf*—but otherwise there was no reason for him to modify its text or tenor afterward. His first political document presaged his last.

Bureau I b/P was also charged with covertly observing, and reporting on, political activities in Munich with its more than fifty parties, associations and factions. They ranged from the Block of Revolutionary Students to the New Fatherland group, and from the Society of Communistic Socialists to the *Ostara Bund*. The Army was interested in what all of them were saying and doing, or intended to do.

"This was a time," as Hitler noted, "when everyone felt compelled to start a party if he was dissatisfied with the way things were going and had no faith in the already existing parties. These little groups sprouted like weeds and then, after a time, disappeared without a trace. Most of their founders had no idea at all what it means to make a party out of a group, let alone to make a movement. So these organizations were almost always strangled by their own ridiculous middle-class limitations."

But one of the weedlike parties, one of the least likely of them all, was fated to survive and grow beyond its most delirious dreams because Adolf Hitler, in his capacity as undercover army agent, chanced to attend a meeting on the evening of September 12, 1919.

It was the party founded ineffectually during the war and still led by the plodding railroad mechanic, Anton Drexler. Now he was calling it the German Workers Party—*Deutsche Arbeiter-*

198

partei, or **DAP**. The meeting was held in a back room of a beer cellar, the Sterneckerbräu. Forty-six people were present as Adolf Hitler, wearing civilian clothes and his newly cropped mustache, took his seat.

The speaker was a Munich engineer and writer named Gottfried Feder, a member of the Thule Society. He was a man of some education and background, and something of a dandy. Hitler was familiar with him, having heard him lecture in the training courses at the University. Swarthy and intense, Feder was obsessed with the idea that "breaking the slavery of interest," and the elimination of international loan capital, would solve all the economic difficulties of the world. Hitler admired what he called the "ruthless brutality" of Feder's arguments, and he approved of breaking "interest slavery" as a weapon against international finance, which meant Jewry.

On this occasion, however, Hitler was bored by the talk, having heard it all before, and intended to leave as soon as possible. But a Professor Baumann requested the floor and began a speech advocating the separation of Bavaria from Prussia. Bavaria would then affiliate with Austria to their mutual benefit, and a better and more peaceful world would result.

Hitler could not allow anything so politically heretical to pass unchallenged. He took the floor himself. In fifteen minutes he disposed of the professor's arguments so effectively that Anton Drexler whispered to the member sitting next to him: *"Mensch,* he's got the gift! That one could be useful." As Hitler was about to leave, Drexler hurried after him, introduced himself, and pressed a brochure in his hand. It was Drexler's account of his career as founder and leader of his party. He called it *My Political Awakening.*

Hitler hadn't caught Drexler's name, but he was glad to have the pamphlet, because it would spare him another meeting of what he called "this dreary society." The pamphlet would tell him all he needed to know about it. Few pieces of reading matter have ever had more enormous consequences.

At that time Hitler was living in a room of his own at the 2nd Infantry barracks. Then, as for the rest of his life, he had trouble sleeping. "Since I was used to waking up mornings before five o'clock," he tells us, "I amused myself by scattering a few crumbs or leftover crusts on the floor for the mice that played about the little room. Then I would watch as the comical little beasts scampered after these choice morsels. I myself had experienced so much want in my life that I could understand the hunger, and therefore also the pleasure, of the little creatures only too well." The man who was to be responsible for the death of thirty million human beings had a fellow-feeling for mice.

On the night after the DAP meeting, unable to sleep, he thought of the pamphlet and began reading it. "Once I began, I read the little brochure through with interest, for it mirrored an experience similar to what I myself had passed through twelve years earlier. Involuntarily I saw my own development brought to life before my eyes."

Drexler's forty-page pamphlet with its pale pink cover was, in fact, a feeble forerunner of Hitler's *Mein Kampf*. In the *Political Awakening* of the Munich railroad mechanic the future *Führer* of Germany saw many of his fundamental ideas expressed in language he would adopt as his own, though he would use that language with a power and impact far beyond the capabilities of an Anton Drexler. The words *"National-Sozialismus,"* National Socialism, were used in the pamphlet, as were most of the political stereotypes attributing defeat in the war and Germany's postwar plight to the machinations of Jews and Free Masons. Drexler, further, urged a "new world order," as Hitler himself also would do, and predicted the rise of a new political party that would embrace the embittered and disillusioned in the lower middle class, in the civil service, and among the workers —the elements to which Hitler's National Socialist Party would one day most strongly appeal.

Most of all, Drexler's particular bid to the workers, his idea of winning them away from the left and enlisting them in the ranks of the nationalists, coincided with Hitler's own conception of what a new party must do. Such a party, he thought, must first of all "offer the possibility of access to the broad masses, for without this element the whole effort would be pointless and superfluous."

The pamphlet did not prompt him to take any specific action, and he was surprised when, a week later, he received a postcard informing him that he had been accepted as a member of the German Workers Party and inviting him to attend a committee meeting the following week. He thought it a curious way of enrolling members, and didn't know whether to be irritated or to laugh. "I had no intention of joining an existing party, but wanted to found one of my own." Nevertheless, moved by curiosity and an impulse to tell the committee what he thought of its methods, he attended the meeting. It confirmed his worst misgivings.

The meeting place this time was the back room of a shabby restaurant called "Altes Rosenbad." Hitler described his reception: "In the murky light of a broken gas lamp four young people were sitting around a table. One of them was the author of the little pamphlet. He immediately greeted me most joyfully, and welcomed me as a new member of the German Workers Party. I must say, I was somewhat taken aback . . ."

He was introduced to Karl Harrer, the journalist from the Thule Society, who was "chairman of the national organization." And this time he learned Anton Drexler's name. He then sat back and observed the proceedings. The minutes of the last meeting were read and a vote of confidence for the secretary was recorded. The treasurer's report disclosed that the Party had seven marks, fifty pfennig, on hand. This was entered in the minutes, with a vote of confidence for the treasurer. The chairman read out answers to letters, one each from Kiel, Düsseldorf and Berlin. This flow of correspondence was regarded with satisfaction as a sign of the Party's increasing importance, and considerable time was spent discussing how the new letters should be answered.

"Dreadful, dreadful!" was how the potential new member regarded the session. "This was political club life on the lowest possible level. And this was the group I was supposed to join?"

He asked some questions, and found that "aside from a few broad paragraphs, the party had no program, no leaflet, no printed matter of any kind, no regular membership cards, not even a miserable rubber stamp . . ." Hopeless.

Two days later he nevertheless made what he called "the most crucial decision of my life." He registered as a member of the German Workers Party, and received a certificate of membership.

His motive for joining was probably more instinctive than reasoned, but he cited plausible arguments for it afterward. "This absurd little group with its handful of members," he wrote, "seemed to me to have the advantage that it was not petrified into an 'organization,' but offered the individual an opportunity of truly personal activity. . . . The conviction had grown in me that it was just through such a little movement that the renewal of the nation could be achieved. . . ." What was needed, he thought, was not merely new election slogans but an all-new philosophy that the established parties would not tolerate, being hopelessly frozen into their own outmoded concepts.

What he saw in the German Workers Party was an instrument, a tool. It advocated ideas he agreed with, and it offered him, for the first time in his life, an opportunity for leadership. He knew that, once he joined the party, he would soon control it. His nearly unerring aptitude for sensing the defects and weaknesses of others told him immediately that Anton Drexler and Karl Harrer would be no match for him in a confrontation. On the other hand, his status in any solidly organized and functioning party would be low. His lack of education and social background, of which he was acutely conscious, would automatically relegate him to a subsidiary role. Among the Drexlers and Harrers he was at no such disadvantage and, from what he had already observed of them, he was far from being under any intellectual handicap, either. Why undertake the laborious, and almost certainly frustrating, task of organizing a new party when the DAP was already there, ready to be dominated and manipulated as he saw fit?

"What preliminary qualifications did I bring to this challenge?" he asked himself. He ticked off his drawbacks. Being poor and without resources seemed to him to be the least of his disadvantages. It was harder, he thought, that he was "counted among the nameless," one of the millions whom "chance allows to live or shunts out of existence without causing even those at one's elbow to take any notice."

This was part of his later pose as an isolated crusader who "stood utterly alone" ("*ganz mutterseelenallein*") as he started on an "inconceivably difficult way" and "took the field against a world of enemies singlehanded." But he was not, in fact, alone. He was part of the Army, the most powerful political force in the Germany of the time, and he could rely on its backing for his political activities into the indefinite future. He was about to become the public advocate of an outlook and a set of beliefs that, as he knew, were shared by many Germans, and he had recently been given cause to believe that he had a special talent for expounding those beliefs in a way that would draw response. The social disintegration in the wake of the war was, he sensed, the right ambience for the flowering of what would accurately be called his "hideous genius." And he was further supported by his own inexplicable conviction that he had the seeds of greatness in him, that fate intended him for leadership. Nothing in his career up to now had given him any cause to believe it, but he never doubted it.

Ever afterward he cultivated a *mystique* about the beginnings of his movement, and this included a myth about his membership card. The Party literature, and later the world press, had it that his membership number was seven. Seven is a mystical number; through the ages it has had an aura of magic about it. The fact is that Adolf Hitler became the seventh member of a key Party committee, but his membership card bore the number 555, a figure without distinction. Even that was a fraud. The membership listing of the DAP began with No. 501, a contrivance to make the Party roll look longer than it actually was. The substitution of No. 7 for No. 555 was among the first of the deliberate distortions that contributed to the building of a Hitler legend.

But what he went on to accomplish after joining that "absurd little group," the German Workers Party, was sufficiently astounding without any mythological embellishments.

8 BIRTH OF A WOLF

"INTO THE DECAYING AND COWARDLY BOURGEOIS WORLD . . . A NEW POWER PHENOMENON WAS ENTERING . . ."

—ADOLF HITLER

THE VERSAILLES PEACE TREATY went into effect at 4:15 P.M. on January 10, 1920, officially ending the conflict in which 2,300,000 Germans had perished. That evening a German nobleman, who was also a radical democrat and an acute observer of his times, made an entry in his diary.

"Today the peace was ratified in Paris . . . ," Count Harry Kessler wrote. "A terrible time is beginning for Europe, a sultry, pre-storm period that will end in an explosion that will probably be even more frightful than the World War."

Writing in Berlin, Count Harry Kessler, a publisher of books and a patron of art, had never heard of the Munich nonentity Adolf Hitler, who would do more than anyone else to make the Count's prediction come true. And Adolf Hitler, too, was looking into the future. Though the two men, the cultivated Count and the Munich nonentity, forecast what was coming from widely separated angles of vision, they were, in fact, foreseeing eye to eye. Time would prove them both right.

In his new capacity as member of the German Workers Party, Adolf Hitler was also using the metaphor of a storm to come, but he did not speak of it in warning. He welcomed it. "We are approaching grave times," he said in an early speech to a Munich beer-hall audience. "The day is coming when this will be true: 'The *Volk,* the people, will rise up and the storm will break!' "

Hitler's enrollment in the DAP had given him a focus and a cause. A formidable energy, long suppressed and unused, was released and channeled, and the moribund little party began to feel the first faint twitches of resuscitation. From the start his aim was grandiose: "To build a movement that would one day succeed in re-creating a German Reich of greater might and glory, where the bigger and more powerful mass parties have hitherto failed."

The first task, as he saw it, was to make the Party known "at all costs." What he had seen in Vienna of the possibilities of marshaling the workers into disciplined ranks, and his brooding in the trenches on the impact of enemy propaganda, had convinced him that the masses could be manipulated at will if only they could be reached.

Using the company typewriter in his barracks, he began by tapping out announcements of forthcoming DAP meetings— little slips of paper inviting the recipients to come and listen to the next scheduled speaker. Some he wrote by hand and dropped before dawn into the mail boxes of people thought to be likely prospects for meetings or for membership.

Once a week he met with the so-called Work Committee, which consisted of the only six men who were at all active in the Party. Hitler was the seventh. The meetings were held in the Café Gasteig, a Vienna-style coffee house where the same corner table was reserved every Wednesday evening. The corner and the table would afterward be pictured as a National Socialist shrine —"Here sat the first seven of the Movement."

A Czech historian once observed that if the ceiling of a restaurant in which a certain group of men were dining one night had fallen on them, there would have been no Czech nationalist movement. Had the roof collapsed on the seven men at the corner table in the Café Gasteig, the difference to the history of the entire world would have been incalculable. But the roof did not fall.

Hitler found the meetings depressing. He saw the same six

uninspiring faces every week—"all nameless poor devils," known to nobody in Munich except a few friends and a handful of supporters. "We would have been happy then," he wrote afterward, "if only we had been attacked, or even laughed at. But what was most oppressive was the utter lack of attention paid us. It was that which caused us the most despair." And he added: "I suffered most of all."

He acquired the party title of *Werbeobmann*, or propagandist and publicity man, and began to carry out its functions "ruthlessly," a favorite word of his, then and later. The results of the typed and handwritten announcements had been, as he put it, "miserable." Almost nobody responded. He stepped up the style and number of announcements by having them mimeographed in a Munich stationery store and scattering them broadside. A few more people began to turn up. New faces were painstakingly counted: eleven at one meeting, thirteen more at the next. With another batch of mimeographed announcements, newcomers mounted from twenty-three to thirty-four.

A collection among the "poor devils" who were the core of the party produced enough money for a major advance in Hitler's campaign to attract public attention. A small advertisement was inserted in the *Völkischer Beobachter*, a rabidly nationalist sheet representing the views of the Thule Society. The result was not only gratifying but amazing. The meeting advertised was to be held in a cellar room of the Hofbräuhaus, the largest beer hall in the world. The room could accommodate about 130 people, which seemed enormous to Hitler and his colleagues. His, and the party's, constant anxiety at the time was: "Will they come?" But he himself had what he called the "unshakable conviction" that if only people could be induced to come and listen, they would surely be won over to the cause. In response to the first advertisement 111 people appeared, the largest audience the DAP had yet achieved.

Hitler saw to it that at every meeting there were now tables covered with pamphlets, leaflets and party literature that could be taken home and studied, as he himself had done with Drexler's *Political Awakening*. One of his sayings, which guided him

to the end, was: "Propaganda, propaganda! Everything depends
on propaganda."

His debut as a major speaker for the party came on November 13, 1919, at a beer cellar called the Eberlbräu. Some 300
people were in the hall. All had paid a fifty-pfennig admission
charge, an innovation in Munich politics. There were few workers, but many students, shopkeepers and army officers.

His subject was the Treaty of Versailles as contrasted with
the Treaty of Brest-Litovsk, a theme he was to pursue with ham-
mer-blow insistence in many meetings to come. The police report on his Eberlbräu performance described it as "masterful."
He pictured Versailles as a monstrous oppression on the German
people with its unconscionable burden of reparations and its humiliating provisions depriving Germany of her colonies and reducing her armed forces—the glory of the Reich—to a pitiful
100,000 men. The Treaty of Brest-Litovsk was in every way reasonable and humane, but the economic sanctions imposed at
Versailles were, in contrast, grinding Germany down into want,
misery and despair. He denounced the "hunger blockade" imposed during the war by the British Navy, and referred to the alleged remark of French Premier Clemenceau that there were
twenty million too many Germans in the world, a saying that
was causing indignation and outrage throughout Germany.

He closed with the type of threat and forecast that would
never be absent from his speeches: "We must stand up and fight
for the idea that things cannot go on this way. German misery
must be broken by German iron. This day must come."

The speech, said the police report, was received with "tumultuous applause."

It was followed by comment from the chairman, Karl Harrer, who explained that Germany's plight was caused not by war
and defeat but by "the Jews, the Free Masons, and the Social
Democrats." He urged everyone to come to the next meeting,
and bring at least three others along.

Meetings were now held every fourteen days, but attendance was often disappointing. Hitler nevertheless urged using a
larger hall, the *Deutsches Reich* on the Dachau Strasse. When

the place was not filled, other committee members became alarmed and began to oppose his ideas as rash, if not calamitous. But the *Deutsches Reich* was near an Army barracks, and the meetings there began to attract soldiers, who were welcome additions to the Party's following. Hitler's impatience with what he called the "eternal doubters" on the committee mounted. He increasingly took the management of the Party's affairs into his own hands.

He scouted the Munich restaurants and taverns for a headquarters for the Party, whose total equipment consisted of a cigar box to keep its funds in, and a few stamps and envelopes for such correspondence as there was. He found a dismal, vaulted room available in the Sterneckerbräu, the same tavern where he had attended his first DAP meeting. The rent was fifty marks a month. This was regarded as an exorbitant sum by the committee, even though the mark, which had been sinking steadily since the end of the war, was valued at 56.62 to the dollar. He was one of the signers of the lease, giving his occupation as *Maler,* or painter. He was still clinging, however emptily, to the idea that he was an artist.

There was only one window in the new headquarters, and it faced an alley so narrow that practically no sunlight penetrated, giving the place, as he said, "more the look of a funeral vault than an office." A table and a few borrowed chairs were installed, then a telephone, and a safe in which the Party's card index and membership records were kept. The cigar box could now be discarded, though there was as yet little money to put in the safe beyond the scattered contributions that were beginning to trickle in. From time to time Hitler made donations to the Party treasury out of small savings from his army pay. At Hitler's urging the Party also acquired a piece of equipment without which no self-respecting German organization could hope to function, a rubber stamp. Another major acquisition at this time was a small Adler typewriter, the party's first.

The Adler was contributed by Rudolph Schüssler, who became business manager of the party and its first paid employee. He was a comrade of Hitler from the barracks of the Infantry

Regiment. Schüssler, a sergeant, was one of several ex-soldiers whom Hitler was infiltrating into the party to build his own clique as a counterweight to the stodgier and more conservative elements, represented by Drexler and Harrer. Hitler saw what lay ahead of him not as political activity in the traditional sense but as combat, and this period of party growth would one day be officially known as the *Kampfzeit,* the time of battle. What he wanted around him, whenever possible, were men who had served at the front and were, as he put it, "swift as greyhounds, tough as leather, and hard as Krupp steel."

The description hardly applied to Karl Harrer, the "First Chairman" of the party and head of its national organization (which was virtually nonexistent.) He was an unimposing figure, with nothing at all of the greyhound in him. Clubfooted and shabbily dressed, he had become dominant in the little group by virtue of being a founder and through his connection with the older and more firmly rooted Thule Society. He was inclined to caution and deliberation, comfortable in discussion groups in dimly-lit back rooms but uneasy in the tumult of a mass meeting.

Hitler's impetuosity and extremism disturbed him. Though a convinced anti-Semite and an outright nationalist, Harrer was more for talking things over and examining them theoretically than for taking specific action. He was afraid that Hitler's head-long drive for mass attention would bring the party into disrepute and probably ruin it. A hesitant and uninspiring speaker himself, he was also repelled by Hitler's unbridled oratorical style.

Hitler, for his part, regarded Harrer with contempt as a "little journalist" who lacked every essential for the leadership of a party, let alone a movement. With the support of the new and radical members he had recruited into his own faction, Hitler was able to make Harrer's position of caution and restraint untenable. Toward the end of 1919, the First Chairman and national head of the German Workers Party resigned.

In less than four months since joining the DAP Hitler had made himself its dominant personality, begun to inch the Party out of its total obscurity and toward the limelight. And now he had deposed its ranking official. The qualities that he found lacking in Harrer and Anton Drexler, the founders, he himself was demonstrating at every opportunity—what he called "the invincible will and energy, and if necessary the brutal ruthlessness, to sweep aside any opposition . . ." With his disposal of Harrer, he had made a stride toward taking over the Party and making himself a factor in Bavarian politics.

By January of 1920 the German Workers Party of Munich had achieved a membership of 190. Most of them were mechanics and locksmiths, the fruits of Anton Drexler's proselytizing among his fellow workers in the railroad shops. There was also a scattering of minor civil servants, students and grade-school teachers. Seven of the members were associated with journalism and publishing, six were engineers, three were doctors and four were Army officers. Though the military element in the Party, officers and men, represented only 13 percent of the membership, it was the most significant for the future. The Army's interest in the DAP had by no means ended with sending *V-Mann* Hitler to spy on it. Meanwhile, the name of member No. 555 was down on the first Party roll as Hittler, misspelled again.

No. 555 was aware that a group of less than 200 did not seem imposing, or even promising, in a city, to say nothing of a nation. But from meeting to meeting he made a point of boasting that the Party was growing, and it was, if only fitfully. Money was as acute a problem as membership, and Hitler made regular appeals to his listeners for donations that would be gratefully accepted as the audience filed out. Occasionally there were windfalls, such as the contribution of 300 marks by a Fräulein Dornberg, who may have been the first of the many women to succumb to Hitler's oratory and open their purses to his cause. Her donation made possible a spurt in the Party's propaganda campaign.

Munich began to be sporadically aware of a new kind of leaflet circulating in the town, and of posters on walls and kiosks that the eye could hardly avoid. The color was predominantly red, "screaming" red (*knallrot*). The hue was the choice of the propaganda chief of the DAP, who had his reasons. "We used red on principle," he explained. "It is the most exciting and provocative color. We knew it would irritate and enrage our opponents, and thereby bring us to their attention, willy-nilly, and make us stick in their minds." Red, of course, was the special color of the Left, and if the leaflets and posters provoked Communists to come to the DAP meetings and cause an uproar, that was counted as a plus. It attracted attention. It caused talk. It spread the name of the Party.

Munich was beginning to witness the onset of a political agitation that Germany had never seen before. The world's greatest demagogue was performing preliminary finger exercises in what would become a fully orchestrated assault on the German mind. The *Werbeobmann* of the German Workers Party was in the process of evolving, and putting into practice, the theories of propaganda and mass appeal that would prompt the liberal-left journal *Weltbühne* to say of him: "God knows who his spiritual forefather may have been, but his teacher in propaganda was Barnum." Afterward others would note that he was the first European politician to see the applicability of American advertising techniques to politics. In his own discussions of his propaganda procedures the word *Reklame,* commercial advertising, would frequently occur. Already his avowed purpose was "the tearing down of a world and the building a new one in its place," but he never hesitated to descend to the methods of the promoter and pitchman to achieve his goal. Like no other German politician, he was aware of what he called "the most powerful factor of our time, public opinion," and like no other anywhere, he developed techniques for manipulating it.

The first mass impact of the Party on the Munich public came in February of 1920, and was proclaimed by a red poster that did not carry Hitler's name. He was not yet considered enough of a draw for the contemplated meeting, the biggest venture to date of the DAP. It was to be held in the banquet hall of the huge Hofbräuhaus. Hitler was again assailed by his then usual doubts as to whether anyone would turn out. An empty hall would be a catastrophe, because the meeting was to be the occasion for the first reading of the Party's official program, Twenty-Five Theses elaborated chiefly by Hitler and Anton Drexler.

But Hitler had done his advance publicity and promotion work well, and when the meeting began at 7:30 P.M. on the evening of February twenty-fourth, more than 2,000 people were assembled in the Hofbräuhaus banquet hall, by far the largest gathering the DAP had ever attracted. As it soon turned out, however, the hall was by no means filled entirely by well-wishers.

The speaker of the evening was a Dr. Johannes Dingfelder, a *völkisch* orator of some reknown in the Munich area. His topic was "What Is Urgently Needed," a speech he had delivered many times before. It was heavy with the usual *völkisch* clichés and patriotic pieties. He attacked the Jews, but decorously avoided mentioning them by name, though voices in the audience let him know that his drift was being caught. (There were calls of "Out with the Jews!") He quoted Shakespeare and Schiller, and referred to the shooting of the Luitpold hostages as a symptom of the disorder and degeneration of the times. With the ringing prediction that Germany would one day awake and the world find regeneration through the German nation, Dr. Dingfelder retired.

He was followed by "a thin man with a mustache," Adolf Hitler, and the tone of the meeting ceased to be decorous. The new speaker, who was also chairman of the meeting, had no delicacy about denouncing the Jews by name. *Ostjuden,* Jews from the East, the kind who had first repelled him in Vienna, were his special targets. His excoriation of them won "lively applause," according to the police report of the meeting. (Now *his* meetings were being spied on.) The speaker also abused the government for its indifference in the face of spreading want and misery, and for its acquiescence in the outrages inflicted on the German nation by the Versailles Treaty.

But the uproar began when he proceeded to the reading of the Party program. A sizable section of the audience consisted of Communists and Independent Socialists who had come to disrupt the first major meeting of the rabidly nationalist DAP. The political atmosphere in Munich was explosive. Only three days before, the Left had staged mass meetings to commemorate the murder of Kurt Eisner, and the opposing factions, Left and Right, had been clashing in the beer halls and abusing each other in the press.

Hitler afterward, in *Mein Kampf*, pictured his presentation of the new Party platform as a personal triumph in which he won over a hostile audience and imbued it with "a new conviction, a new belief, a new will." Actually, his program was met with organized howls of protest and catcalls. The reporter of the Police Department feared that physical violence would break out momentarily. Before the meeting was over, men were leaping on tables and chairs and there was, the reporter noted, *"ungeheurer Tumult"*—a monstrous uproar. But Hitler had liberally laced the audience with his own adherents, "faithful war comrades and other supporters," who overmatched the opposition in shouts and threats, and succeeded in restoring enough order for the meeting to proceed. It was a foretaste of what was to come at many a subsequent meeting, where brute force would be as much a part of the agenda as speeches and resolutions.

The twenty-five points of the Party program were predictably in line with the thinking of the *völkisch,* rightist, nationalist tendencies in the Germany of the time. The language smacked more of the plodding Drexler than of the tempestuous Hitler. There was little evidence of the extreme political philosophy he was already privately envisioning and would, before very long, describe as "a declaration of war against the established order."

Instead, the twenty-five points were calculated to appeal to a wide spectrum of the embittered and discontented, to disgruntled war veterans, to Pan-German fanatics, to the economically endangered, and to the growing anti-Semitic elements diffused through the middle and lower classes—in short, the components of the German population to which Hitler would appeal, and on whose emotions he would play, from then on. The first two points demanded the "right of self-determination" for Germany (a sardonic borrowing from Woodrow Wilson's Fourteen Points) and called for the abolition of the Versailles Treaty. Point Three demanded the return of German colonies, and Point Four proclaimed: "None but those of German blood, whatever their creed, may be members of the nation. No Jew, therefore, may be a member of the nation." There were demands for land reform and the nationalization of trusts and large enterprises. This was to benefit "small traders" and "small purveyors," with the aim of "creating and maintaining a healthy middle class." A strong central government was called for, and controls on the press. Profiteers and usurers, "criminals against the nation," were to be punished by death.

The program was not destined to play any substantial role in the future of the Party, its more radical provisions, such as land reform and nationalization of trusts, remaining dead letters to the end. It did little to win new members, since nothing in the twenty-five points was sufficiently new or different from what other nationalist parties were also offering. The future and growth of the DAP, as events would increasingly show, depended on one man, and the rank and file would, with time, reduce the matter to the saying: "Our program, in two words, is: Adolf Hitler."

Though the Hofbräuhaus meeting was not the unalloyed triumph Hitler afterward described, a significant milestone for the Party had been passed. The first mass meeting had been staged; a program had been drawn up and promulgated; an impact had been made on the public. None of this could have been imagined before Hitler's entrance into the Party only a few months before. As he watched the great hall empty that night he sensed, correctly, that new possibilities were opening for him, and afterward he twice attempted to put down in words the significance of the event as he saw it. In one version he pictured the meeting as the kindling of a fire in which a new sword of Siegfried would be forged for the liberation of Germany and vengeance on her betrayers. In a more vivid and less mythological metaphor, he wrote:

"When I finally closed the meeting, I was not alone in thinking that a wolf had been born that was destined to break into the herd of deceivers and misleaders of the people."

The imagery of the wolf, the beast of prey, suited his temperament. His name itself, Adolf, was the Teutonic equivalent of "noble wolf," and it seemed appropriate for a man who saw the world as a jungle where the law of fang and claw prevailed. From time to time he would assume the pseudonym *Herr Wolf,* and at the height of his power as warlord of Europe his secret military headquarters in East Prussia was called the *Wolfschanze,* or wolf's lair. His followers took up the imagery. Years later his Propaganda Minister would openly warn the democratic world that the Party intended to destroy: "We come as enemies! We come like the wolf breaking into the fold. . . ."

The wolf's birth was scantily noticed at the time. There were brief reports of the Hofbräuhaus meeting in some of the papers, with Hitler's name mentioned only fleetingly. *Der Kampf,* the organ of the Independent Socialists of Munich, characterized the twenty-five points as "A Stolen Program," and in a subsequent article dismissed the DAP as "handymen for the Prussian Junkers and militarists." It was not the Party program but the personality of Adolf Hitler that began attracting supporters capable of giving the movement further impetus.

Two, especially, joined him early and contributed psychological and political support without which he and the DAP might not have developed as it did, or survived at all. One was an Army officer, a latent homosexual whose energy and soldierly drive propelled Hitler and the Party into feats of organization without which the group might have disintegrated. His name was Ernst Roehm. The other was what the Germans call a *Dichter,* a poet, a bard, a man of letters, and he came to be recognized as "the spiritual father" of the Hitler movement. He was also tutor, coach and companion to Hitler himself. His name was Dietrich Eckart.

Eckart was twenty-one years older than Hitler, and different from him in almost every way. He was big, burly and gregarious, with a boisterous humor and an insatiable relish for the cafés and *Bierstuben,* where he spent most of his time. His blue eyes peered sharply out of a totally bald head, and his language was often blunt and coarse in the native Bavarian manner.

218

Bluntness and coarseness also characterized the paper he edited and published. It was called *Auf gut Deutsch* ("In Plain German"), had a circulation of about 30,000 and took the usual nationalist, Pan-German and anti-Semitic line.

But he had also made something of a name for himself as a writer and poet. His translation of "Peer Gynt" was brilliant and became the standard version, bringing him a steady income in royalties. He had written plays of his own and, like the Marquis de Sade, staged some of them in an insane asylum, using the inmates as actors. His poetry tended toward the nordic and mystical, with variations on the Nibelungen theme. In 1919 before he (or anybody) had heard of Hitler, he composed a bardic verse in archaic German in which the coming of a national redeemer was predicted—a hero "familiar and foreign at the same time, a nameless one." This was later, in the mythology of the Party, made to apply to Hitler, especially since Eckart also forecast "the hour of vengeance," which was Hitler language before Hitler. On another occasion Eckart gave a much earthier sketch of the man he thought was needed to save Germany: somebody who could "stand the sound of a machine gun," but not an officer, because Eckart felt that they no longer had the respect of the people. "A worker who knew how to talk" would be best. He would have to be able to "put fear into the pants of the rabble." He wouldn't have to know much, politics being a stupid business at best. But he must be someone who could "give the Reds a juicy answer, and won't run when people start swinging table legs." The final requirement was: "He's got to be a bachelor. Then we'll get the women!"

Adolf Hitler met Eckart's specifications with uncanny precision, and they soon became an oddly matched twosome on the Munich scene. Eckart took Hitler about with him and showed him something of the ways of the world, how people dressed and behaved outside an army barracks or beer hall. Hitler, born in a backwater, reared in a provincial town, a common soldier most of his adult life, was devoid of social style or breeding. He had never been in a drawing room or dined in a first-class restaurant. The marks of the *Schlawiner* were still pronounced in his dress, looks and manners. Eckart began to introduce him to the better bars and cafés of Munich, to polish up his language, and improve his appearance. He gave Hitler his first trench coat, which became his trademark. Eckart was the first educated person, the first man of the world, to concern himself with Hitler as an individual, and the incipient *Führer* responded with a gratitude he displayed toward no one else throughout his life.

Hitler's usual attitude toward the well-bred, the educated, the intellectual, was one of instinctive hostility expressed in snarling contempt. But in Eckart he found a kindred spirit with whom he could feel at ease, despite the difference in education and background. To offset the superiority conferred by college degree, poems and books, Eckart was, like Hitler, essentially a Bohemian, rootless and antisocial. He was drunk a good deal of the time, and a morphine addict. His ideas and outlook were congenial to Hitler's own. Eckart, too, was a reader of *Ostara*, subscribed to its ideas, and was even accused by Lanz von Liebenfels of plagiarism.

Eckart did more than socialize with Hitler and pick up his tabs at the Munich pubs. He contributed generously to the Party treasury, and his flair for strong, colorful language was of inestimable propaganda value to the Party in its early days. He wrote a battle song for the movement—*"Sturm! Sturm! Sturm!"* ("Storm! Storm! Storm!")—full of feverish references to burning and killing and redeeming vengeance. Every verse ended with a two-word refrain that became the slogan of the Nazi Party and appeared on its standards and banners all through the ensuing years: *"Deutschland erwache!"*—"Germany, awake!"

It was not strange that when Hitler came to write *Mein Kampf*, in which he "set down for all time" his philosophy, testament and blueprint for power, he dedicated it to Dietrich Eckart.

There is no mention at all of Ernst Roehm in *Mein Kampf*, though no objective account of Hitler's rise could be complete without him. If Eckart was the "spiritual father" of the movement, then Roehm was the organizing genius of the Party (always allowing for the fact that without Hitler himself there would have been no movement to be father of, or Party to organize.)

Roehm succeeded Captain Mayr, who had unwittingly launched Hitler into politics, as press and propaganda officer for the Bavarian *Reichswehr* (*Abteilung Ib/P*). It is a definitive comment on the course of Adolf Hitler's career that both of these men, without whom his rise would have been impossible, were destined to end as victims of the system they helped create. Mayr, who later turned Left and opposed Hitler, would perish in the concentration camp at Buchenwald. Roehm would die in the "night of the long knives," the Hitler purge of 1934.

Ernst Roehm had served at the front as a Company Commander in the 10th Bavarian Infantry, was wounded three times, and was sorry when the war was over. He had never wanted to be anything but a soldier, and never intended to stop being one. "Since I am a wicked and immature man," he once said, "war and unrest, like it or not, appeal to me more than the orderly life of your respectable burgher." He regarded the peace of 1918 as an obligation to continue the war by other means.

Despite his bluff Bavarian manner and earthy style, he was a gifted intriguer and political manipulator, and his influence was much wider than his rank of captain indicated. He was active, openly and behind the scenes, in political and military matters, inseparable in the Bavaria of the time. He organized para-military units as local defense forces that could be quickly rallied in case of further Spartacist threats to the Hoffmann government, which by now had ventured to return to Munich from its exile in Bamberg, but was still dependent on the Army to keep order in Bavaria. Roehm also directed the clandestine movement of surplus World War armaments away from the Allied Control Commission to secret hiding places to await the ultimate confrontation with Weimar that the Army was, sooner or later, anticipating. Thousands of rifles, machine guns, grenades and mortars—and even trucks and armored cars—were stockpiled under Roehm's supervision in remote forests, pits and parks. The same thing was happening in other parts of Germany to circumvent the disarmament provisions of the Versailles Treaty and build a "black" *Reichswehr* that would be a standing, if surreptitious, reinforcement to the reduced legitimate Army. The stockpiling was often done with the tacit consent of the Allies, and of the Bavarian government, both frightened by the threat of renewed Red revolution.

It was inevitable that Roehm, aware of all the agitation in Munich, should come into contact with the DAP and Adolf Hitler. They first met at sessions of a secret society called "The Iron Fist," and Roehm sensed almost at once that in Hitler he had found a personality worth cultivating and supporting. He joined the DAP (membership No. 623), and began attending meetings regularly. He discreetly siphoned certain Army funds into the Party treasury. And he greatly strengthened the Party by recruiting new members from his own political and military cadres—Free Corps characters spoiling for action and violence; ex-officers steeled in the trenches and seething with resentments against the Republic; veterans embittered by unemployment and soured by defeat; serving soldiers dreaming of future victories in an Army restored to glory. The infusion of the Roehm recruits into the DAP gave it muscle, fortifying it with the brawn needed for many a beer-hall brawl and gutter melee. The Drexler-Harrer style of playing at politics in back rooms with turgid resolutions and pedantic discussion became obsolete with the sheer physical vitality imparted by Roehm and the propaganda momentum supplied by Hitler. Between them they were forging a movement that was about to burst into the streets and make Munich aware that a political phenomenon was taking form.

While Eckart was making Hitler more acceptable socially, Roehm was introducing the unknown agitator into military and political circles. Roehm offered Hitler the intimacy of the *Du,* the familiar form of address, which in turn gave Hitler some status with Roehm's fellow officers. Roehm set little store by social distinctions. It was enough for him if a man had served at the front and was opposed to the Republic. He himself was hardly a model of military elegance and style. He was under medium height and far from svelte, and his face, unhandsome to begin with, was mutilated by his wounds. The upper part of his nose had been shot away, and a deep bullet scar marred one cheek. He had a blunt, agressive manner that bordered on the rowdy, and few at this time suspected that he harbored homosexual tendencies. These emerged later and caused a scandal, but did nothing to diminish the soldierly toughness of his bearing or his qualities as a leader. He had been shaken to his depths (*"aufs tiefste erschüttert"*) by the abdication of the Kaiser. On his return to Munich from the front, a sergeant wearing the red armband of the Revolution had accosted him with the demand that he remove the imperial cockade from his cap. He refused, and swore to himself that he would never remove it as long as he was in the Army, and he never did.

Whatever else might be said of him, he could not be accused of hypocrisy and self-delusion. He made little effort to conceal his objectives, and he had a clear conception of his own personality. He spoke for thousands of like-minded German officers when he said: "I am a soldier. I consider the world from my soldier's viewpoint. Consciously one-sided." And: "Europe—the whole world—can go up in flames. What is that to us? Germany must live and be free."

In the analysis of Konrad Heiden, the sharpest eyewitness of Hitler's rise, the German Workers Party was becoming the "gun-carriage for moving the cannon of Munich's anti-Weimar officers into the civilian sphere." But barely three weeks after Hitler's announcement of his Party's program in the Hofbräuhaus, German officers in Berlin unlimbered their cannon literally in the first overt attempt, the first *Putsch,* to overthrow the Weimar Republic.

On March 13, 1920, a proclamation was issued from the Wilhelm Strasse:

BE IT KNOWN!

The Reich government hitherto in office has ceased to exist. The full state power has devolved on Commissioner Dr. Kapp of Königsberg as Reich Chancellor and Minister President of Prussia . . . A new regime of order, freedom and action is being organized.

The proclamation was signed by Baron von Lüttwitz, General of Infantry, and Commissioner Kapp.

It was appropriate that the general's name came first. The event became known as the *Kapp Putsch*, after its most prominent civilian figure, but its inspiration and execution were military. The Berlin officers, always restive as servants of the Republic, had been goaded into action when the Allied Control Commission began putting into effect some of the more pride-wounding provisions of the Versailles Treaty.

Already sullen at the change in the national colors, the abolition of orders and decorations, and the reduction of the Army, the officer corps was outraged when, in February, an Allied note demanded the delivery of almost 900 German leaders for trial as war criminals. Almost every name, military and civilian, revered by the German nation was on the list—names like von Hindenburg, Ludendorff, von Mackensen, von Tirpitz, von Falkenhayn and the Hohenzollern Crown Prince himself, not to mention Rupprecht, Crown Prince of Bavaria. Never before had a War Guilt clause been part of a peace treaty, nor had defeated officers and statesmen been summoned to the victor's judgment seat as war criminals. The so-called "shame paragraphs" of Article 231 aroused indignation amounting to frenzy not only among the officers and troops but also throughout the civilian population. Some officers advocated resistance to the point of war, if necessary. And in Munich Adolf Hitler saw in the alleged injustices of Versailles, and in the War Guilt question, "a precondition for the success of our movement in the future."

The Berlin officers were further incensed with the Allied demand for immediate demobilizaton of 60,000 members of the armed forces, including 20,000 officers. At the same time, the German Government moved to dissolve the Free Corps as a drain on the treasury and a menace to the stability of the State. One Free Corps unit, the best, strongest and most disciplined of them all, decided to resist dissolution, no matter what the consequence.

224

This was the 2nd Marine Brigade, under the redoubtable Commander Ehrhardt. After its participation in the "liberation" of Munich, the Brigade was now stationed at Döberitz, some twenty-five kilometers outside Berlin. The attitude in the Brigade was so menacing that once when Reichstag delegates demanded it be disarmed, a government spokesman replied: "May I invite the gentlemen to try it themselves?"

For Ehrhardt and his men the idea of dissolving the unit was intolerable. Hadn't they fought against the Poles and Bolsheviks, holding back the Red flood not only from Germany but from western Europe? Hadn't they, and their comrades-in-arms, suppressed the Red uprisings inside the Reich itself, assuring the very survival of the Republic? And were they now to be dismissed out of hand, officers and men, like so many discharged clerks from a department store? It was another *Dolchstoss,* another stab in the back, like the one that lost the war for Germany in the first place.

Through General von Lüttwitz, who commanded the Berlin military district, an ultimatum was delivered to the government: further disbanding of troops must be suspended; new elections must be held; suppression of strikes; censorship of the press; restoration of the old Imperial colors. In short, a turning back of the clock. The ultimatum was rejected, and the 2nd Marine Brigade marched on Berlin, augmented as it went by other Free Corps elements in the area.

It marched in column of route, under full pack, preceded by its assault company and a field artillery battery. They went singing the song of the Ehrhardt Brigade, to an English music-hall tune, "Good-bye, My Bluebell," the same tune to which American troops had marched into Cuba in 1898. But here the words were distinctively German, and more ominous:

> *Swastika on our helmets*
> *Black-white-red our band*
> *The Brigade of Ehrhardt*
> *Is known throughout the land. . . .*

And then the threat:

Worker, worker, what's to become of you
When the Brigade is ready to fight?
The Ehrhardt Brigade smashes everything to bits,
So woe, woe, woe to you, you worker son-of-a-bitch!

The Brigade marched by night, and dawn was breaking when the column entered the capital. There was no resistance. Colonel-General Hans von Seeckt, the Chief of the General Staff known as "the Sphinx with a monocle," did not approve of the *Putsch,* but took no action against it. "Our troops do not fire on our troops," he said, and let the march go on. The Ebert government, including its strong man, Noske, had fled the city at 5 o'clock that morning for Dresden and later for Stuttgart, which became the temporary capital of the Reich.

As the Brigade goose-stepped through the Brandenburg Gate, it was greeted by a figure every officer and soldier recognized at once: Erich Ludendorff, who, as he explained afterward, "quite by chance" happened to be taking a stroll there that morning. On hand also was Dr. Wolfgang Kapp, resplendent in top hat, morning coat, striped trousers and spats, as befitted a man about to be proclaimed chief of a reborn Germany. The old Imperial colors were unfurled, the band struck up *Deutschland, Deutschland über alles,* and Dr. Kapp led the way along Unter den Linden to the government offices, accompanied by Erich Ludendorff and General von Lüttwitz. Backed by the singing soldiers with the swastikas on their helmets, the new regime took over.

It was a fiasco from the start.

When it came to making a revolution, the hardheaded Prussian officials and the disciplined *Reichswehr* generals proved a match for the dreamy Bohemians of Schwabing in disorganization and ineptitude. Unfortunately for Germany, and the world, the only postwar government capable of acting with effect once it got into office would, when the time came, turn out to be that of Adolf Hitler.

The Kapp people couldn't find a typist, to begin with. It was a Saturday, and nobody had come to work at the Chancellery. Fräulein Kapp, the new Chancellor's daughter, was called upon to type out the manifesto of the new regime, but by the time that essential chore was done, the deadline for the Sunday papers had passed, and Berlin went through the week-end without official notice as to what had happened or what the intentions of the new government might be. Confusion and uncertainty set in at once, and were never dissipated.

Kapp himself was almost a caricature of the Prussian bureaucrat. With his pince-nez perched on a beefily undistinguished face and the creases at the back of his head nakedly exposed by the barber's clippers, he might have stepped out of a cartoon in *Simplicissimus*. He had, curiously, been born in New York, the grandson of immigrant parents who were liberals. Emigrating back to Germany, Kapp became a district commissioner in the East Prussian agricultural administration, a not very exalted post. But during the war he was a flaming jingo, supporting the most extreme of the Pan-German war aims and helping to found the Fatherland Front that gave support in the Reichstag to the expansionist objectives of the High Command. This made him a likely possibility for the military to turn to when a civilian figurehead for the *Putsch* was required. But for all his fire-eating, Dr. Kapp presented a wavering front when his *Putsch* came under pressure, which it did immediately.

Though widely approved by the military, the seizure of the government did not have the highest Army sanction as long as Hans von Seeckt stood aside, observing the proceedings icily through his monocle but taking no part. The civil service, the rigidly traditional *Beamten,* took no part either, ignoring Kapp's appointments and directives and paralyzing the bureaucracy. (One Privy Councillor hid the official rubber stamps required on all documents, a crippling blow!) Kapp issued orders, canceled them, and then repeated the process. When the soldiers supporting him demanded pay, Kapp was shaken to discover that he had no money at his disposal. He suggested to Ehrhardt that it be taken by force from the State Bank. "Certainly not!" said Ehrhardt. "I'm an officer, not a bank robber." In the "new regime of order, freedom and action," nothing worked.

Others were acting more decisively. From Stuttgart, the seat of the legitimate government, a general strike was proclaimed against "the bloody freebooter elements" who had taken over Berlin. Some twelve million union workers, employees and civil servants were summoned to preserve the Republic by stopping work. The response was overwhelming, and the greatest general strike in German history resulted. Trains and streetcars stopped. Factories shut down. Offices and stores closed. Civil servants left their bureaus. In Berlin the electric power stations ceased functioning and the lights went out. Subways stopped. The water supply dried up. Waiters walked away from their tables. Garbage collections were halted. Traffic was paralyzed. The metropolis ceased to function.

Commander Ehrhardt was for arresting the strike leaders and shooting them, along with as many workers as necessary. Orders to that effect were issued by Dr. Kapp and his Cabinet, but their nerves failed them, and the orders were rescinded. On top of the strike came a mutiny of troops and security police, who announced their allegiance to the Ebert government. The *Putsch* collapsed. It had lasted four and a half days.

On the afternoon of March seventeenth, Dr. Kapp issued a hollow farewell manifesto, scurried into a waiting taxicab, and was driven to Tempelhof airport. He fled to Sweden, as Erich Ludendorff had done before in another moment of collapse and defeat.

All Berlin knew the *Putsch* was over when the 2nd Marine Brigade formed up for its march back to camp at Döberitz. The band was silent now and there was no singing, as a largely hostile crowd watched it go. The troopers were sullen and seething at their defeat. When a boy in the crowd ventured to hoot, two of the soldiers broke ranks and clubbed him down with their rifle butts and then kicked him to death with their hobnailed boots. The crowd protested. An officer snarled an order, and the column opened fire with rifles and machine guns. When the column re-formed, dead and dying littered Unter den Linden. The groans and screams of the wounded were drowned out as the troopers struck up their song again—

228

> *Swastika on our helmets*
> *Black-white-red our band . . .*

The dead on the Berlin streets were symptomatic of what was happening all over Germany as aftermath of the Kapp *Putsch*. In the Ruhr the general strike developed into an uprising in which a Red Army of 60,000 workers fought pitched battles against *Reichswehr* units, with casualties in the hundreds. A Soviet Republic was proclaimed in the industrial region of Saxony; it terrorized the population by threatening to burn down whole cities and "slaughter the bourgeoisie regardless of sex or age" if government troops dared interfere. Middle Germany verged on anarchy, and atrocities of the bloodiest and most savage kind were committed by troops on both sides, Red and government.

In a nation desperately in need of reconciliation and recovery, the Kapp *Putsch* increased tensions, deepened hatreds and multiplied the symptoms of sickness and suspicion between German and German. It intensified the murderous antagonisms between Right and Left, and it coarsened the sensibilities of a public growing accustomed to violence and brutality in civil life.

Back in their camp at Döberitz, the men of Ehrhardt's Brigade rapidly recovered their spirits. *"Putsch ist futsch . . . ,"* one of their jingles now went: "The *Putsch* is a flop." But the verse continued jauntily:

> *But don't you worry and don't you cry*
> *There'll be another one by and by.*

And Kurt Tucholsky, perhaps the most brilliant journalist of his time in Germany, agreed. He put it another way in one of his articles in the *Weltbühne:*

"The Kapp *Putsch* was an unsuccessful dress rehearsal. Opening night has been postponed."

9 FEVER CHART

"... THOSE WERE FANTASTIC TIMES."
—GEORGE GROSZ

WHILE THE KAPP *Putsch* was collapsing, a small bi-plane labored through heavy weather toward Berlin, and one of the passengers was getting sick. It was Adolf Hitler, on his first flight.* He was also on his first political mission outside Bavaria. He and Dietrich Eckart had been commissioned by *Abteilung Ib/P* to sound out the situation in Berlin and bring back a report on how the counterrevolution was progressing there.

By the time the plane landed, the *Putsch* was over and Kapp had fled, leaving the two contact men from Munich with no mission. They were privately advised by Kapp's press secretary, a certain Trebitsch-Lincoln, to make themselves inconspicuous if they didn't want to be arrested. The visitors were appalled to discover that Trebitsch-Lincoln, who was on the way to becoming notorious in his own right as an international impostor and swindler, was a Hungarian Jew, a black mark against the Kapp enterprise in the eyes of the two Bavarian anti-Semites.

But if the *Putsch* mission proved futile, the flight to Berlin turned out to be highly advantageous to Adolf Hitler in other ways. He made contact with north German rightist groups like

---

* The pilot was Lieutenant Ritter von Greim, a *Pour-le-Mérite* World War I ace who would become the last Commander in Chief of Hitler's Air Force in World War II.

the *Stahlhelm,* a reactionary veterans' association that was growing into political power. He met radical Free Corps activists like Lieutenant Leo Schlageter who, within two years, would organize the first Berlin branch of Hitler's party. He was introduced to *völkisch* circles that had access to financial support from major industrialists like the locomotive magnate von Borsig; in time he would be able to tap such resources himself.

Dietrich Eckart provided the entrée into levels of Berlin society where Hitler could not, as yet, hope to be received on his own. Eckart presented him to the salon of Frau Helene Bechstein as "Germany's young Messiah," and she received him as such. The wife of a wealthy piano manufacturer, she had strong *völkisch* tendencies and high social standing. Helene Bechstein was the first of the grand ladies of German society to make Adolf Hitler *salonfähig,* acceptable in the salon. Despite his lack of polish in such routine amenities as hand-kissing, Helene Bechstein, like others of her kind after her, found something irresistible in his very crudity. About him, one German writer has said, these women detected "the smell of a barbaric wildness" that stirred them as their own groomed and tailored men did not. Frau Bechstein had a pet name for him. She called him *Wölfchen,* little wolf.

What must have been the most memorable moment of his visit, however, was his introduction to Erich Ludendorff. The revered First Quartermaster General, "the tower that defied the world," had come back from Sweden calling himself "Karl Neumann," and his suite at the Hotel Adlon had a private exit to spare him the distress of encountering Allied officers in the lobby. The broken man of Spa in 1918, who had fled the country in dark glasses and false whiskers, was now the hero of the nationalist Right. The same officers who had noted the details of his breakdown in their diaries while it was occurring were now flatly denying that it ever happened.

It must have inspired something like awe in the Pfc. from Munich (who was still in the Army though not in uniform) to shake the hand of the hero of Liège and Tannenberg. It would have seemed wildly unlikely to either of them that, before very long, they would be marching side by side in another *Putsch* of far greater consequence for history than the sorry Kapp affair.

Profitable as the Berlin visit was for his present and future career, Adolf Hitler did not warm to the city, and never would. Again, as on his first visit during the war, he was "choked with disgust," if for other reasons. What he had seen of life in the capital only confirmed him in the hatred that he had been voicing in his Munich speeches. Not only was it the seat of the government he wished to destroy; he saw it also as the center of a spreading corruption eating away the fiber of the Reich.

In his Hofbräuhaus speech he had denounced moral laxity and made it a part of his indictment against the Weimar Republic. His meetings rang with attacks on the *"Vergnügungswut,"* the universal madness for pleasure, which he castigated as a plot to undermine the nation. "We dance and pursue pleasure to forget our misery," he said. "It is no accident that more and more kinds of diversion are constantly being invented." The nerves of the people were being deliberately lacerated, the moral decay was being engineered by the enemies of hereditary values and traditional concepts. Life in Germany, he charged, was becoming a "hothouse of sexual imagery and stimulation" threatening to engulf the whole culture in "the suffocating perfume of modern eroticism."

When Hitler called Berlin "the great Babylonian whore," he was using the nation's *Vergnügungswut* as grist for his political mill, but he was not alone in his estimate of the place. Another visitor from Munich, younger and more sensitive, also recorded his impressions of postwar Berlin in the early 1920's, and it all but took his breath away. To Klaus Mann, the son of Thomas and a fledgling author himself, the city was an enormous sexual circus:

" 'Look at me!' the German capital trumpets, boastful even in its desperation. 'I am Babylon, the monster among cities. Sodom and Gomorrah together were not half so degenerate, not half so horrible as I am! Step right up, ladies and gentlemen, with me anything goes and no holds barred! The night life of

Berlin—man alive, the world has never seen anything like it! Vices you never even heard of! Once we had an unsurpassed army; now we have unsurpassed perversities! A tremendous selection! There's something doing here, believe me! Don't miss it!' " What Georges Clemenceau predicted for the French came true for Germany: "You will live the gamy peace of decadence . . . It will be filthy and delicious . . . as when the ancients opened their veins in a bath of milk."

To George Grosz, Berlin looked like "a stone-gray corpse," and there were some who called it the ugliest city in the world. It had never been to Germany what Paris was to France and London to England, being a late-comer as a capital, with something raw and unfinished about it. Only the war had given it a recognizable stature as a world metropolis, and now the aftermath of collapse and defeat had infected it with a communal hysteria, or what the Germans themselves called a "delirium of desperation."

Berlin had never danced so much. Jazz and ragtime, brought in by black musicians from America, created a craze whose only previous parallel was the St. Vitus mania of the Middle Ages. Dancing had been forbidden during the war, and in a panic of relief that the war was over, a wave of physical agitation swept over Berlin and much of the rest of Germany. Two-step, fox-trot, tango and shimmy replaced the waltz and gavotte; banjo and saxophone obliterated the violin. A favorite number was "Everybody Shimmies Now," and everybody did. The shimmy, also imported from America, was a shaking of the body from shoulders to knees, suggesting a prolonged shudder. It was almost as if the nation were shuddering to music over the slaughter it had passed through and at horrors to come.

The feverish beat of the dance halls and cabarets pervaded the streets as well. What would later be called "permissiveness" burst out on a scale Germany had never known before, as if some secret, but universally recognized, signal had been given that all restrictions and repressions of the past were canceled and everything was now allowed. Along Berlin's Broadway, the Kurfürstendamm, pimps and prostitutes paraded by day and night, proclaiming the eruption of the underworld to the surface of

German life. In the Markgraf and Puttkamer streets, painted girls lounged in open windows and called to passing men. (On the Reeperbahn in Hamburg, whores leaned out of the windows with their naked breasts painted with eyes, noses and mouths, so that each girl offered three faces to the passerby.) In the Nollendorf Platz there were houses of accommodation for both men and women. The women could choose male or female partners, according to preference. Middle-aged women made themselves available, housewives of fifty and over whose lives had been ruined by the war and who found their customers among youngsters seeking a mother-type, or aging men who felt inadequate with girls.

The Friedrich Strasse was like a pulsing artery running string-straight and narrow through the heart of Berlin. It had been built by Frederick II as a march route for the Berlin garrison to the parade ground at Tempelhof. Now, at night, it presented a spectacle that tourists from many countries came to gape at. In the eerie half-glow of the gas lights, wounded veterans sat on the sidewalks, showing their stumps and mutilations and begging. The silk stockings of the whores brushed against the beggars' caps extended for alms. There was a constant to-and-fro surging and jostling, in the shadowy gulch between the buildings. Hawkers elbowed each other offering dope, pornography, women. *"Kokain gefällig?"*—"Care for some cocaine?" It was also called *Koks* and *Schnee,* snow. Peddlers flashed packets of obscene photographs, while others tempted passersby with: "Want to see naked dancers? Guaranteed stark-naked ladies. Guaranteed!"

Little girls of ten and eleven, rouged and wearing short baby dresses, promenaded the gully from midnight to dawn in competition with lush blondes swathed in furs. Amazon types in high lacquered boots of green and red stroked the cheeks of passing males with riding crops, and whispered: "Would you like to be my slave?" Even during the uprisings and street battles, when mortar fire thundered and blood ran in the gutters of Berlin, the parade of the prostitutes never stopped.

In the Mikado Café, in the Puttkamer Strasse, male prosti-

tutes gathered with transvestites and homosexuals of every shade
and variety. The Mikado was only one of the many homosexual
bars of Berlin, an added attraction for foreign tourists. The
spread, and open display, of homosexuality seemed to many another alarming symptom of the degeneracy of the times that
cried for correction. Here, again, the war had created a social
problem, but now the Republic was blamed for it. Revolutionary
sailors had established a homosexual enclave in Berlin, and the
postwar slackening of inhibitions had brought the aberration
into the open, where it came as a shock to the general public.
(The aberration itself, of course, was nothing new in Germany.
There had been a homosexual camarilla around the Kaiser, and
a major court scandal as a result.) The police allowed transves-
tite clubs to operate without interference. Ben Hecht remembered a group of homosexual aviators, who were not unique in
the Berlin of the time—"elegant fellows, perfumed and monocled and usually full of heroin or cocaine. They made love to
one another, openly kissing in the café booths. . . ." Transves-
tite dances with the men dressed as women and the women as
men became orgies for the participants and spectacles for onlookers who sought them out as one of the major attractions of
the town. Special resorts catered to perversions of every kind: a
club for sadists, one for exhibitionists, another for masochists.
Painted boys with plucked eyebrows solicited on the side streets,
competing with the whores for customers. Officials high in government and industry came regularly to certain bars to pick up
drunken sailors.

In the cabaret called *Schall und Rauch* (Noise and Smoke)
a popular chanteuse named Trude Hesterberg sang a song that
went:

> *Take off your clothes, Petronella, take 'em off!*
> *It's the only way to be famous . . .*

Nude dancing and nude revues became a vogue. The Apollo
Theater featured seventeen young women strewn about the stage,
naked above the hips and only wispily covered around them. A
girl from Frankfort named Henny Hiebel, who was billed as La

Jana, became the sensation of Berlin when she was carried through the audience nude on a huge silver platter borne by twelve men in armor.

There was often something deliberately morbid, a straining for shock that went deeper than mere nudity. In a cabaret called the White Mouse, on the Friedrich Strasse, a dancer named Anita Berber came to symbolize in her own lithe and undulating person all the pleasure-lust and sexual obsession of the period. A face dead white and frozen under flaming red hair made her seem bereft of all human emotion as she writhed, naked, in the spotlight. With her partner, Sebastian Droste, she performed "dance legends"—"The Hanged Man and the Vicious Woman," "The Corpse on the Dissecting Table," "Coitus." Night after night she packed the White Mouse with jaded Berliners, thrill-hunters from the provinces and gasping tourists—"Philistines gone wild," as a chronicler of the times called them. She destroyed herself with cognac and cocaine, and was dead before she was thirty.

Throughout Germany nudism became a form of protest, a defiance of convention and a refuge from the drabness and distress of postwar life. "Back to nature" (*"Zurück zur Natur"*) became a slogan that justified the flight into nakedness, an attitude reflected in Hans Fallada's celebrated novel of Germany in 1920's, *Little Man, What Now?* A character named Heilbutt tries to recruit the young Pinneberg, the "little man" of the title, into a nudist club. "Do you think I could stand it all," says Heilbutt, "—this miserable job . . . the whole filthy mess Germany is in, if I didn't have this [nudism]? A man could despair, but I know that some day things will be different. And this helps, Pinneberg, this helps. . . ."

Whatever promised to help was indulged in without restraint. "A universal insecurity and confusion has seized the people," a tract on postwar morality lamented. "Everything that only a short time ago was regarded as sacred heritage has suddenly become invalid." Virginity had lost its value and became a joke; a *virgo intacta* at sixteen was an object of ridicule. Promiscuity was the style, and nightclub singers like Ilse Bois warbled their approval of it—

> *I don't sleep with only one.*
> *I sleep with a whole damn crew—*
> *'Cause that's the modern thing to do!*

Wife-swapping (*"Austausch der Ehegatten"*) was rumored to be prevalent in high society, and the spread of lesbianism was acknowledged as a contributing cause of the skyrocketing divorce statistics. Contraceptives were openly available everywhere, including grocery stores, where they were sold along with jam and shoe polish. A favorite brand featured the trademark of a stork with its beak tied closed by a ribbon and a bow. Women, for the first time, were demanding the "right to one's own body," and the number of abortions soared beyond anything known before. In the cabarets, leering little songs were sung about that, too. The cynical cabaret songs were an accurate reflection of the atmosphere of dissolution, social and economic, that characterized postwar German society. In the night spots along the Kurfürstendamm and on the Friedrich Strasse, even the ominous plummeting of the mark was the occasion for another frivolous couplet: *Dear corpse, dance around your coffin and holler/ Your three hundred seventy marks are worth a dollar . . .*

"All the old, great bourgeois virtues and forces had broken down," George Grosz noted, "even as had the middle class itself."

Nothing portrayed the breakdown more vividly than the drawings of George Grosz. His gallery of German life in the 1920's remains to this day a classic commentary on a society in disintegration, a chamber of social horrors rendered in caricature and cartoon. The "disgust and aversion for mankind," which had inspired his war drawings were, if anything, intensified by what he saw and experienced in civilian life. His portrayals of the types that dominated German society—the monocled Prussian officer unchanged by war and defeat; the bloated industrialist with his fat cigar; the bureaucrat squinting contemptuously through his eyeglasses; the thick-necked profiteer with his shaved skull surmounted by a tiny tuft of meticulously parted hair— were so savagely accurate that people recognized them in the flesh on the streets and in restaurants: "Look! There's a George Grosz!"

The alienation of intellectuals like Grosz was finding its wildest expression in the Dada movement, which was started by a group of poets, painters and musicians in the Café Voltaire in Zurich during the war. *Dada,* the word, was chanced upon in a French dictionary. It meant hobby-horse, and the nursery-non-sensical sound of it was exactly in keeping with the spirit of the movement. The idea was to mock, deride and spit at all the beliefs and standards of a system that had brought mankind to the bloody catastrophe of a world war.

Dada staged art exhibitions that would have been acceptable to an Andy Warhol a generation later: old rags, rusty nails and cigar butts were pasted on canvas and offered as *Merzbilder* ("garbage pictures"). They were seriously reviewed by critics and sold to collectors. A huge collection of assorted newspaper clippings and photo-montages was assembled, pasted in a scrapbook, and called the *Dadacon.* It was proclaimed to be greater than the Bible, and offered for sale for $35,000. Words would be clipped from books and newspapers, tossed into a hat, and then drawn out at random. The result was offered as a new kind of poetry. But when poetry readings were held, discordant music came crashing from the wings so that not a line could be understood or even heard.

But the Dadaist sensed that something was terribly wrong and that something even more terrible was brewing. Some of them spoke more prophetically than they could have known at the time. Walter Mehring, who went on to become one of modern Germany's most brilliant satirical poets, composed an early Dada rhyme in racy, big-city slang, and called it *berlin simultan.* The tone reflects the jaunty cynicism of the Kurfürstendamm and the Alexander Platz, and the slang makes it largely untranslatable, but the burden of the verse is: *"C'mon, boys, let's all go . . . Off to the pogrom with a ho-ho-ho . . . Pull in your bellies*

and throw out the Jews . . . With swastika and poison gas . . .
*Let's have a go at murder in the mass . . ." **

The moral and artistic excesses of the time evoked dismay, approval or indifference in varying degrees among the public, but Adolf Hitler spoke for a broad area of German opinion when he expressed his revulsion. "Sixty years ago," he wrote, "an exhibition of so-called Dadaistic 'experiences' would have seemed simply impossible and the organizers would have been put away in the madhouse . . ." He was not alone in detecting a strain of madness in what was being offered the public under the guise of art and free expression. Leo Lania, a journalist and writer at the opposite political pole from Adolf Hitler, wrote: "Amid the roaring cannons the poets had lost the power of speech. They could only stammer, pant and scream." The drama of Expressionism struck out wildly at German mores and traditions, exposing deep antagonisms between class and class and generation and generation. In a play called *Vatermord* ("Patricide") by Arnolt Bronnen the widening gap separating German fathers and sons was dramatized, and ugly emotional undercurrents in family life were probed and exposed. *Vatermord* began with a scene reeking of sexual perversion between two young men, continued with a murderous confrontation between father and son, and went on to sensationally frank sexual scenes between son and mother.

On other stages the flaming proletarian dramas of Ernst Toller, still in his Bavarian jail, were being shown, and in Munich a young playwright named Bertolt Brecht wrote a play called *Drums in the Night,* his first to be produced. It dealt with a returning soldier who finds his girl pregnant and the world he

---

* The verse was first published in 1919 in *Der blutige Ernst,* edited by George Grosz and Carl Einstein. It seems an astounding prophecy at that early date, with its mention of swastika, gas and mass murder (*"Massenmord"*) so accurately forecasting the concentration camps of the Nazis and Hitler's "final solution" of the Jewish problem. Queried about how it was possible to foresee such things so clearly and so early, Walter Mehring wrote the author: "At those times, and under the circumstances I wrote, I could not help being aware of coming turmoil and terrors." It is not a very satisfactory explanation. A better one, perhaps, is that poets are often prophets without knowing how they do it.—R.H.

knew collapsing to the accompaniment of gunfire mowing down the Spartacists. "Brecht," said a Berlin critic, "is impregnated with the horror of this age in his nerves, in his blood. . . . Brecht physically feels the chaos and putrid decay of the times."

But millions of Germans who did not write plays, or even go to the theater, could remember when things were disciplined and orderly, not chaotic, and when the national mood was one of self-confidence and advancement, not decay, and when the times were not called putrid but *herrlich,* glorious. That was before the war. For increasing numbers it was being phrased differently: "That was before the Republic . . ." The yearning to turn the clock back deepened.

The symptoms were becoming more and more visible on the streets. Groups were marching. *"Juda verrecke!"*—"Jewry perish!"—was being shouted by one band of marchers, while another raised its fists and chanted, *"Heil Moskau!"* There were few enough who marched and shouted and sang in support of Weimar.

"Since it was founded," Adolf Hitler was saying contemptuously, "no one has defended this Republic."

In Munich his campaign to destroy it was gaining momentum.

10 MAGIC OF THE SPOKEN WORD

"HARKEN TO THE VOICE OF THE PROPHET THAT HAS BEEN
SENT TO YOU! AND THEN, GERMAN PEOPLE, THEN RISE UP!"
— ADOLF-VIKTOR VON KOERBER (1923)

MUNICH'S easygoing style through the years had prompted the joke that even the end of the world would occur there a week later than anywhere else. So it became a paradox and a puzzle that Munich, of all places, should be the first to feel, and respond to, the impact of so apocalyptic a movement. But events had vitiated the easygoing atmosphere of the city on the Isar. Red revolution and White terror had left it tense and apprehensive, dangerously fertile for renewed outbursts of the emotional violence that was never very far below its surface. It was an atmosphere in which an Adolf Hitler could function with maximum effect.

On his return from Berlin, on March 31, 1920, he took another decisive step. After almost six years as a soldier, he left the Army, pocketing the fifty-mark demobilization pay and signing out from his barracks for the last time. He did not, however, make any real break with the *Reichswehr*. It had launched him, it would continue to support him, and he would be in its debt the rest of his life. He never, in fact, became a civilian in any acceptable sense of the word. He was perpetually waging his own private war with society, guerrilla or open, in uniform and out. He was as much at war when he left the barracks a civilian as he would be when, not many years later, he became Commander in Chief of the same army that never ranked him higher than Private First Class.

He rented a dingy furnished room on the Thiersch Strasse, No. 41, where he lived "like a down-at-heels clerk," as one of his visitors remarked. He made no effort to find a job, having already assumed in his own eyes his predestined role as *Politiker*. He spent most of his time at the headquarters of the DAP at the Sterneckerbräu and took his meals there, dining frugally on its meager menu. He was not a paid employee of the Party, and how he supported himself caused speculation that later swelled into controversy. His landlady found him a brooding, uncommunicative type with erratic habits, "a regular Bohemian."

His change in status from soldier to civilian coincided roughly with a change in the name of the Party. The German Workers Party (DAP) became the National Socialist German Workers Party—*Nationalsozialistische Deutsche Arbeiterpartei (NSDAP)*. One reason for the change was to make certain that no suggestion of Marxism would attach to this particular "workers" party. The designation "National Socialist," actually a contradiction in terms, was not original, having been used by right-wing groups in the Sudetenland as early as 1896, and the combination was not new even then.* *National,* with its connotation of Pan-German attitudes, was almost obligatory, but *sozialistisch* had its special reasons. The war had left a widespread revulsion against capitalism, especially among workers, so that "socialist" had acquired a definite appeal among people the Party hoped to win over. The fraternity of battle tended to break down traditional barriers between class and class. Something called "socialism of the trenches" had been experienced, and even career officers like Roehm acknowledged it and welcomed it. Roehm privately laughed at the obsessive anti-Semitism of the movement and tolerated it merely as a propaganda device, but he took the "socialism" in the Party's new title seriously, and so did many others. Hitler, on the other hand, objected to the "socialist" part of the DAP's new name, and agreed to it only, again, for propaganda purposes. What the words "National So-

* It would perhaps have given Hitler and his fellow Party members pause to know that *"national-sozial"* was used by Moses Hess, the founder of socialistic Zionism, circa 1860.

cialist German Workers Party" meant precisely was never fully clarified, then or later. The key words in the new name were foggy or patently inaccurate. *Socialist* was regarded as a theft and a fraud by real socialists. *German* was hyperbole, since the party was not yet even Bavarian in scope, and was known to few even in Munich. *Workers* was equally dubious, since its membership proved more middle class than proletarian. Even *Party* was disputed, since Hitler himself insisted it was not a political party in the traditional sense, but a movement. *National* in the current German meaning of nationalistic, super-patriotic, was the only word in the label that could be called honest.

Now the Party was holding meetings regularly every eight days. With each meeting a scattering of new members were added to the rolls, and the socialist press began to cock an indignant ear at what was going on at the NSDAP rallies. Deploring the flagrant anti-Semitic tone of the speeches, the Munich *Post* singled out one speaker for special comment: "Adolf Hitler behaved like a comedian, and his speech was like a vaudeville turn, with the same refrain coming every three sentences: Hebrews are to blame for everything." Not long afterward the same paper said: "One thing Hitler has going for him, and it has to be admitted—he's the most artful and cunning of all the rabble-rousers now spreading their poisons around Munich."

The sneer that he was merely a *Komiker,* a comedian, was one that he would hear often during his career until, at the end, it would be said, "The story of Hitler's rise is the story of how he was underestimated." There *was* something ridiculous about him. His toothbrush mustache became a world joke, reminding millions of Charlie Chaplin. It was barely as wide as the nose, and he may have adopted it to conceal his unpleasantly large nostrils. There was the *Stirnlocke,* the forelock, which kept falling down in moments of agitation, and when he spoke he was always agitated. He was, as more than one observer saw him, "all corners and angles," and he had a receding forehead, which bothered even enthusiasts eager to subscribe to his theories of racial superiority. Receding foreheads and ridiculous mustaches are not ordinarily associated with superior racial types. At first sight, some who became his devoted followers were put off by what one of them called his "utterly mediocre" appearance. It was only afterward that more erudite observers recalled some appropriate words from Aristophanes' *The Knights* and applied them to the Adolf Hitler of the early 1920's: *"Now mean and unregarded; but tomorrow / The mightiest of the mighty . . . The sovereign and ruler of them all / Of assemblies and tribunals, fleets and armies . . ."*

As unlikely as that seemed at the time, there were signs that the principal orator of the National Socialist German Workers Party possessed some quality that, though impossible to define, set him apart from his competitors. More and more frequently on the streets of Munich, in the cafés and restaurants, one man asked another: "Have you heard this fellow Hitler? I tell you, he's got something."

What he had was oratorical power, an inborn gift of personal projection. First the Munich beer halls, and then all Germany, became aware of what his boyhood friend Gustl Kubizek had noted in that room they shared in the Stumper Alley in Vienna: Adolf Hitler had an "overwhelming gift of persuasion." Where it came from, exactly what it consisted of, how he was able to generate and exert it, remains one of the mysteries of the human personality that no amount of psychiatric speculation has, until now, been able to unravel. It resided in his voice, presence and passion when he spoke. It showed itself in what the novelist John O'Hara, writing of the same quality in certain stage personalities, called "that terrible power of complete command over an audience."

A meeting would be announced on shrieking red placards and by leaflets distributed on the streets or hurled broadside from trucks by shouting young Party members and, later, by Storm Troopers. At meeting time, the Kindl-Keller with its large L-shaped hall, say, or the capacious banquet room of the Bürgerbräu, would look more like the scene of a social gathering than a political rally. The audience would be seated at well-scrubbed wooden tables, drinking beer out of heavy steins or mugs, the room filling with smoke and the din of male conversation. The beer halls were all connected with the local breweries, and the beer could be relied upon to be up to Munich standards, which were high. It was served in generous portions, sometimes by waitresses carrying ten mugs at a time without a tray. Congenial as the atmosphere was, everybody present recognized that the meeting was a serious affair; there was no incongruity between savory, relaxing beer and important politics. *Biertischpolitik,* beer-table politics, was a powerful factor in the public life of Bavaria, and when Hitler made the beer halls and cellars his gateways to public attention and, ultimately, power, he was choosing his route with a knowing eye.

He was never in the hall at the time announced for the meeting. He made a point of appearing late and, if possible, unexpectedly from a side entrance, so that the audience seldom quite knew how and when he arrived. Suddenly he was there.

He never mingled with the crowd, either before or after his speeches. At this stage he sometimes took a mug of beer, but when he drank, it was to ease his throat, which often became dry, perhaps as a result of his wartime gassing. The man who became the idol of the beer halls, and used them as corridors to eminence, had no passion for the brew on which his movement was floated.

He usually spoke from a platform at the end of the room, or at one side, where a band might otherwise be playing, or sometimes from atop a table. It is not easy to quiet a room full of men who are drinking, talking, and making a clatter with beer mugs on wooden tables, but Hitler from the first was able to impose his personality on his listeners and establish an immediate rapport with them. This mysterious rapport, which often built into a frenzy that speaker and audience shared, was the core of his success as orator and agitator.

He would seem to sniff the air, sensing and absorbing the atmosphere of the particular hall and audience. The speech would begin hesitantly, as if he were still feeling his way, groping for the right tone, the right note. Before long a sentence that began quietly, and on a low key, would acquire power as it continued, and end with emphasis. His eyes took on a glow, his breath came faster. He had got the feel. He had made contact and closed the circuit between himself and the audience. The speech gathered pace, assurance, momentum, until it came pounding from the platform in verbal avalanche, battering the audience, subduing it, overwhelming it. "In this unlikely looking creature," said Konrad Heiden, who heard him many times, "there dwelt a miracle: his voice." Heiden called it "a gutteral thunder."

"His words go like an arrow to their target," said Otto Strasser, once his follower and later his enemy. "He touches each private wound in the raw, liberating the mass unconscious, expressing its innermost aspirations, telling it what it most wants to hear."

Hitler's impact on an audience has also been described by unsympathetic eyewitnesses such as Hubertus zu Löwenstein who was born a Bavarian prince but became a crusading democrat. At a typical meeting in the Bürgerbräu, the scene of Hitler's coming *Putsch,* the Prince studied an audience that seemed, he said, "intoxicated" by the oratory: ". . . men staring at the speaker with wide-open, distorted mouths—murderers, I thought; and others, pale, desperate, hollow-eyed, in ragged uniforms. From them nothing new would come; they would follow anyone who made them promises.

"And others again—their weighty forms filled up whole rows, their heavy hands clasped around their beer mugs as though they were sacred relics. Their pendant mustaches, dripping with the froth of beer, quivered with emotion . . ."

The Prince himself was impressed by the speech against his will "if only on account of the elemental passion with which it was delivered." Fuming and flailing, clutching his heart, thrusting his hand into the air with widespread fingers, the speaker made the Prince see the pictures he wanted the whole audience to see: "Germany trodden in the mire, its weak government, the country surrounded by foes bristling with weapons and ready to hurl themselves on us afresh, the people led astray by maundering about peace and the criminal policy of 'fulfillment' [of Allied reparations demands]."

248

If the liberal, democratic Prince had to check himself so as not to succumb to the speaker's spell, those who heard the echo of their own discontents and terrors in the speaker's words succumbed without reservation.

Sometimes a speech would end on a note of sheer hysteria, with Hitler staring trancelike at his audience and shouting, *"Deutschland! Deutschland! Deutschland!"* in a hoarse chant. There would be a moment of silence, the audience sitting transfixed. The clatter of beer mugs had long since ceased under the spell of the oratory. Men sat motionless, staring at the speaker as if hypnotized. Women went slack at the mouth, and breathed heavily, as if in the grip of sexual excitement. The speaker stood sweating, in his shabby blue suit and his high, tight collar, panting as if he had just run a hard race.

Then the applause would sweep over him—an "outburst of frenzied cheering, hand-clapping, and a cannonade of table-pounding. It sounded like the demoniacal rattle of thousands of hailstones on the surface of a gigantic drum," as another observer, overwhelmed himself, described it. The observer was Ernst Hanfstaengl, scion of a wealthy family of Munich art dealers and educated at Harvard. Aristocratic, a snob, Hanfstaengl had come to observe Hitler in action as a curiosity of Munich's political underworld. He came away "impressed beyond measure" by Hitler, and a convert to his cause.*

There were more and more converts as the size and frequency of the meetings increased and Hitler's mastery of the techniques of mass persuasion grew. His oratorical gift would have been remarkable anywhere, but it was especially effective in postwar Bavaria. He had, in the first place, no serious competition. The speakers for the rival parties were in the traditional German mode, which meant that they were dull. People left their meetings disappointed and empty, and began casting about for a message to which they could respond. Hitler was making his ap-

---

* Hanfstaengl subsequently joined the Party and, when Hitler came to power, was made Foreign Press Chief of the NSDAP. He antagonized Hitler through some critical remarks, and in 1937 had to flee for his life to Switzerland and exile. He was known as "Putzi."

peal precisely to people who felt themselves ignored or slighted by the established parties—"to those," he said, "who are suffering and tormented, those without peace, the unhappy and discontented"—and he was doing it with a demagogic flair such as Germany had not experienced since the Drummer of Niklashausen 400 years before. Political parties customarily used pamphlets, newspapers and books to make their views known and attract supporters. Speeches were habitually read from manuscripts, usually in a steady drone and with soporific effect. The manuscript, not the speech, was considered the important factor. In Germany there was a universal reverence for print, and orating to mass audiences was considered *infra dig,* a rather demeaning business for a leader. But Hitler ignored all that, and was deliberately building his following on what he called "the magical power of the spoken word."

He argued that every major movement in history, whether religious or political, owed its growth and spread to great speakers, and never to writers. What he called the "volcanic eruptions of human passions" had been brought about through the ages either by widespread misery or, in his belief, "by the firebrand of the word hurled among the masses." Not even communism, he held, owed its spread to Marxist texts and pamphlets, or to the printed manifestoes of its founders and disciples. What won communism its huge following among the workers, he argued, was the hundreds of *speakers* in its behalf, from its major apostles to the anonymous agitators in factories, shops, discussion groups and meetings. "The newspaper flood, and all the books turned out year after year by the intelligentsia," said Hitler, "roll off the lower-class millions like water from oiled leather." Only spoken words can "open the gates to the hearts of a people—words like hammer blows."

This was largely rationalization, since his ability as a writer was minimal, while his gift as a speaker was unmatched for his time and place. His words did fall like hammer blows on his audiences and affected listeners in a way that a later generation of Germans, looking back from a changed historical perspective, could scarcely comprehend. Even his diction and accent were exactly right for his purpose. Though born an Austrian, there was something unmistakably Bavarian in the quality and rhythm of his speech. He was at home in the earthy Bavarian dialect, having absorbed it as a boy in Passau, in Lower Bavaria, where his father was stationed for three years. Service in a Bavarian regiment further bolstered his claim to being a true *Bajuvar,* an authentic product of the native soil. He never overcame a vulgar flattening of the "t" sound into a "d." Educated listeners, especially north Germans, winced at the coarseness of his diction and the crudity of his accent, but his Bavarian listeners were struck familiarly, and therefore agreeably. Polished diction and an educated accent would have been fatal for his purposes.

What his purpose was he announced plainly, over and over, in his earliest speeches. All the tendencies, goals and ideological impulses that led to mass murder and world war when he came to power were implicit in what he was saying in the beer halls before anybody outside Bavaria knew he existed. Nothing that Adolf Hitler said or did after he became Chancellor of Germany, and master of Europe, could have come as a shock to anyone who paid attention to his speeches in his Munich days. But nobody outside Bavaria was paying attention.

As early as April of 1920, in a Hofbräuhaus meeting, he was threatening a *Putsch* against the government, a full-scale revolution, if necessary, to achieve his goals. The Weimar Republic was not much more than a year old when he was publicly calling for a dictator in Germany and foreseeing the day when his Party would come to power and trample over the opposition "like a herd of buffaloes." One of his axioms was: "The cruder and more brutal your language, the larger the crowd who will be ready to listen to you."

He made a study of the accoustics of all the principal halls of Munich. He found that more voice was required in the Hackerbräu and the Kindl-Keller than in the Hofbräuhaus, and adjusted his vocal projection accordingly. He went to the "Platzl," the domain of the popular Munich comedian Weiss Ferdl, and studied Ferdl's tricks for holding the attention of a crowd despite the racket and bustle of a room full of uninhibited drinkers. Hitler also took lessons in delivery and gesture from a prominent local actor named Basil, and he practiced his gestures for hours before a full-length mirror. He was aware of how much of the theatrical, of the rehearsed and contrived, would enter into his political performances.

He tested halls and *Bierstuben* for their quality of warmth, and found that some resisted the creation of mood, for reasons that could not be fathomed, while others seemed to have an inherent glow favorable to a speaker. He spoke at all hours and ascertained that the time of day had a definite effect on the receptivity of an audience. But, he said, the most brilliant propaganda will fail unless one basic and unalterable rule is followed: "It must confine itself to a few points only, and repeat those points endlessly." This "thousandfold repetition of a few simple ideas" is necessary because propaganda is not made for the intelligent and educated but for the masses, and the masses are stupid and forgetful.

Once a speaker has mastered the psychological principles of mass persuasion, he can convince the masses of anything he likes. "Nothing is so absurd that it will not be believed if it is presented with enough conviction," he would write, unconsciously echoing a saying of Marcus Tullius Cicero's centuries before: "Nothing is so difficult to believe that oratory cannot make it acceptable . . ." Hitler followed what he called "the very sound principle" that a big lie is always more credible than a little one. In "the primitive simplicity of their souls," he said, people are more easily victimized by the big lie "since they themselves sometimes lie in small matters, but would be ashamed to lie on too large a scale." They cannot conceive that anyone would venture a truly monstrous falsehood, and will therefore be inclined to believe that there must be some truth in such a statement. "Thus," said Hitler, "something of even the most shameless prevarication will find lodging, and stick . . ."

After emphasizing and deploring Germany's manifold miseries, with the audience seething and shouting its indignation, Hitler would promise a day of reckoning, a time of revenge: ". . . clench your fists! Bite your teeth together! Hope, pray, work that the day will soon come when the people, the *Volk*, rises up against the despoilers of Germany within and without. . . . Then victory will not fail us!" Where would a beaten and disarmed nation find the means to rise up and strike? Never mind. What counted was spiritual rearmament. The rest would follow. "When sixty million people have the one single will to act together in a fanatically nationalist way—then the weapons will well up out of their fists by themselves . . . !"

The more violent the speech, the more inflammatory the language, the greater was the response, which, in turn, prompted even more excessive language at the next meeting. The printed texts of the speeches were pocked with notations like [tremendous storm of applause] and [jubilant ovation] and [raging approval from audience]. It was a wonder of the human personality that Adolf Hitler, who as an individual made no contact with anyone, who remained wrapped untouchably inside the barriers he had built around himself, could establish a miraculous affinity with a crowd. The relationship that was impossible for him as a man vis-à-vis another man became surpassingly intimate and intense between him and an audience. In his own person, he had only rebuff and withdrawal for those around him, but as a speaker before a mass of listeners he radiated warmth, intimacy and passion. "What he says and the way he says it," a contemporary report tells us, "sings to the heart and echoes there. What lies buried deepest in one's innermost being he brings to the surface. He welds together the most diverse elements of his audience with the hammer blows of his ideas and the fire of his personal intensity. Soon everyone present feels himself a member of one community."

Sometimes his perorations had the effect of trumpet blasts and marching orders. The audience would come to its feet in unison, and stream out of the hall shoulder to shoulder, carrying the meeting into the streets, singing patriotic songs or the *Sturm* verses of Dietrich Eckart. Columns would form and march through downtown Munich, bellowing *Pogromlieder,* pogrom songs, as they went.

One of the most popular had the refrain: *"We don't want any Jew republic."*

Events were steadily conspiring to add impact to the tirades of Adolf Hitler in the beer halls. Though a fiasco in Berlin, the Kapp *Putsch* had scored an unforeseen success in Bavaria. The march of the Ehrhardt Brigade, and the flight of the Reich government, had reverberated through the country with an intensity that reached crisis proportions in Munich. During the few days that Kapp was in office, and the Republic seemed doomed, a fateful change had occurred in Bavaria. The local military, prompted by events in Berlin, acted on its own. The socialist regime of Johannes Hoffmann was confronted with what amounted to an ultimatum: in view of the crucial situation in the Reich capital, and to prevent local uprisings of either Right or Left, Hoffmann and his cabinet were invited to resign. In the interests of *Ruhe und Ordnung,* peace and order, the military would temporarily take over. Outside the building where this proposal was made, armed troops were pointedly marching up and down. The Hoffmann government, never certain of itself and now faced with what looked like a military coup, hesitated only briefly before bowing out. At one stroke the government of Bavaria was purged of socialists and supporters of the Republic, leaving the way free and clear for an upsurge of rightist and reactionary agitation such as was possible nowhere else in the Reich.

Wolfgang Kapp, nursing his wounds in Sweden, could congratulate himself on one victory, at least, and one that would have consequences far beyond what he could have foreseen that morning when Hermann Ehrhardt's troops escorted him in his cutaway and spats to the government offices in the Wilhelm Strasse. Munich became mecca and magnet for freebooting anti-Weimar elements from all over the country. Whoever felt in danger of arrest or restraint for subversive activity against the Republic headed for Bavaria, certain of welcome and accommodation. Free Corps activists, their units now dissolved, were provided with jobs as agricultural workers and supervisors on the great estates of the countryside, or given cover employment in the city, and supplied with forged papers and passports when necessary. Ehrhardt and his Brigade were invited to establish themselves in Munich by no less a personage than Ernst Poehner, the Police President, and did so.

The very pillar of German nationalism himself, Erich Ludendorff, moved to Munich after the Kapp *Putsch*. An admirer presented him with a villa in the suburb of Ludwigshöhe, and troopers of the Ehrhardt Brigade established a day-and-night guard around it. The villa became a shrine of the counterrevolution, and nationalist conspirators from all over Germany, but especially from Munich, made regular pilgrimages there to consult with the gray eminence of the *völkisch* movement. In between he carried on his obsessive investigations into the world machinations of Jewry, the Catholic Church, and Free Masonry —what he called the "supra-state powers"—and bided his time.

Adolf Hitler visited the villa at Ludwigshöhe, and the oftener he came the more he impressed the former Quartermaster General. The Kapp failure had disillusioned Ludendorff on the possibilities of salvation for the nation through the officers corps. Nothing, he concluded, could be expected of the "upper 10,-000." There must, he now felt, be a mass basis for any future action, and this Hitler, by all reports, had the stuff of a real *Volksredner,* an orator of the people. "What a combination!" a fellow conspirator named Kurt Ludecke exclaimed. "Ludendorff, the General, with all that name implied of caste and authority, and Hitler, the dynamic corporal coming from the people!" It seemed an ideal combination for a *Putsch,* when the time should come. And should it succeed, Ludendorff had no qualms about how to proceed. "The greatest blunder of the revolutionaries," he said more than once, "was to leave us alive. If once I get back to power, there will be no pardon. I will hang Ebert, Scheidemann and the whole pack with a perfectly clear conscience, and watch them dangle."

In Bavaria he would have had plenty of company to help produce such a spectacle. The place had become a breeding ground for secret organizations and paramilitary units whose attitudes ranged from honestly conservative to rabidly rightist. Their members supplied numerous recruits, speakers and supporters for Adolf Hitler's expanding National Socialist Party, and the meetings of the NSDAP took on increasingly aggressive tones. The anti-Semitism of the speeches brought from the audiences shouts of *"Totschlagen!"* and *"Aufhängen!"*—"Kill them!" and "String them up!" When an observer from the police department expressed fears that the National Socialists were stirring up the people dangerously in such difficult times, Hitler's public reply was: "Yes! We want to stir up the people, and keep on inciting them, for we're hoping for the day when this race of foreign parasites must leave the country forever. Not until then will law and order return, and the man from the police department can sleep peacefully in his office!" [Stormy Applause].

There was the whiff of coming gas ovens and genocide in such speeches, and he made them day after day. He sometimes spoke for two and a half hours on end ("and," said one listener, "we could have listened to him much longer"). Sometimes he reached such a pitch of fury that his voice became a scream that the rear rows could not understand. When the discussion period was reached at the end of an evening, he was sometimes so hoarse that he could not participate. Often the halls had to be closed by the police long before the meeting started because of overcrowding, and when he spoke against the Jews, time and again the auditorium would be full to bursting—*"zum brechen voll,"* as the police reports had it.

He was not alone in his attacks on the Jews, not in Bavaria, where the Thule Society had long flourished and where the local tendency toward anti-Semitism had been intensified by the Jewish element in the Eisner upheaval and the *Räte* period. Few organs of opinion, even so, were as openly rabid as a little twice-weekly sheet that called itself the *Völkischer Beobachter*.* It had once, under another title, been a trade journal for butchers, a gruesomely appropriate phase of its existence, in view of what

---

* Here, again, the impossibility of translating *völkisch* accurately makes it difficult to render the title of the paper in English. It is usually given as *Racial Observer*, which, again, is inadequate, but suggestive.

was to come. It was later owned by Rudolf von Sebottendorf, the leader of the Thule Society, under whom it became a general organ of the *völkisch* movement and openly advocated measures that were, in retrospect, unmistakable stages along the road to Auschwitz, Buchenwald, Dachau and the murder of 6,000,000. In a front-page story on March 10, 1920, the *Völkischer Beobachter* was already urging a "final solution" (called *Endziel,* final goal) for the elimination of Jews from Germany. The headline on the story read CLEAN OUT THE JEWS ONCE AND FOR ALL! (*"Macht ganze Arbeit mit den Juden!"*) and the text proposed using the "most ruthless measures," including concentration camps (*"Sammellager"*) and "sweeping out the Jewish vermin with an iron broom."

Before the year 1920 was out, Hitler's National Socialists had, by means not entirely clear, acquired this paper as the official organ of the Party. A major factor in the transaction was an initial payment of 60,000 marks made to the owners by Dietrich Eckart. The money, it seems certain, came originally from the treasury of the *Reichswehr* and was supplemented by contributions from others.

The paper appeared in an unattractive three-column format, had a circulation of about 7,000, and practically no advertising; but it represented an enormous gain for the young Party, and contributed appreciably to its growth. It was not, and never became, a newspaper in the accepted sense. The *Völkischer Beobachter* was, and remained, purely a propaganda vehicle. It did not even call itself a newspaper, but a *Kampfblatt,* a battle paper. Hitler used it to implement in print his principle that the masses could never be won over by "a feeble insistence on so-called objectivity but only through a ruthless and fanatically one-sided orientation toward the goal to be reached." * The *Beobachter* was an extension of the Party leaflet and placard, and its style was poundingly polemical, like Hitler's speeches. What it had to say, observers noted, was "more spoken than writ-

---

* Hitler called this "the very first fundamental of all propaganda activity." What would one say, he asked, "about an advertising poster that was supposed to praise a new soap but also described other soaps as 'good'?"

ten." Even in print, Adolf Hitler managed to maintain the tone of the spoken word.

With the spread of political extremism in Bavaria, and with the increasing hostility toward Berlin, something approaching a civil war atmosphere began to prevail. A Berlin newspaper printed news from the south of Germany under the headline: ATROCITY STORIES FROM A SAVAGE LAND. And the *Weltbühne* published the warning: "Travelers, Avoid Bavaria!" In many a speech, at every opportunity, Adolf Hitler exacerbated the bitterness between Bavaria and Berlin, outdoing himself in vituperation against the "November Republic," the "November criminals," the "Berlin ghetto" and the "Berlin Asiatics." Among the *völkisch,* according to the code of the nationalists, loyalty to the elected, legal government was equal to treason to the "real" Germany, the Germany of the past.

Down at the "Platzl," in midtown Munich, Weiss Ferdl was singing a satirical song about Bavaria as the *Ordnungszelle,* the cell of order, in the Reich. The burghers of the town, and the peasants in from the countryside, clattered their beer mugs and laughed approvingly. But now Munich was being called by another name as well—*Mörderzentrale,* murderers' center. The men whose *Putsch* had failed in Berlin found the atmosphere in Munich, where a Hitler could flourish, congenial for their purposes. They were men who had less faith in the power of the word than in the efficacy of action. And they knew only one kind of action: violent.

A young correspondent from America who signed himself Ernest M. (for Miller) Hemingway was in Germany in the early 1920's, and witnessed the violence as it erupted. He wrote about it afterward: ". . . those who had never accepted a military defeat hated those who had, and started to do away with the ablest of them by the vilest program of assassination the world has ever known. They started immediately after the war, by killing Karl Liebknecht and Rosa Luxemburg, and they killed on, steadily eliminating revolutionary and liberal alike . . ."

The story was told with relish, by Ernst Roehm among others, that a worried citizen came to the Munich Police President,

258

Ernst Poehner, and whispered: *"Herr Polizeipräsident,* are you aware that there are political murder gangs operating in Bavaria?"

The Police President, a towering figure, looked down coolly through his pince-nez for a moment before replying: "Yes. But not enough of them."

11 THE FEME

ON OCTOBER 6, 1920, the body of a woman was found under a tree in Forstenrieder Park, outside Munich. She had been strangled. A note was fastened to the tree above the body. "You lousy bitch," it said, "you have betrayed your Fatherland. The Black Hand has judged you."

Police established that the dead woman was Marie Sandmeier, a servant girl, who had recently come to Munich looking for work, having been dismissed from her job at a manor in Upper Bavaria. Wandering around the city, she had noticed placards of the Allied Disarmament Commission ordering all stores of arms and ammunition to be turned in forthwith. Marie Sandmeier remembered seeing arms cached in the manor where she'd worked. Having no love for her former employer, she decided to report what she knew, but by mistake told her story at the shop where the posters were printed instead of at the Disarmament Commission. Her story was relayed to a member of the rightist Citizens Defense Corps, who traced her to her new address in Munich. On October fifth, a man who said he was from the Disarmament Commission called on her and requested her to come with him and give her report. She went readily. The next morning her body was found in the park.

Not long afterward, a waiter named Hartung came to Munich from Halle, where he had been used by the Citizens Defense

Corps as a stool pigeon among the Communists. Hartung made a connection with the Munich Citizens Corps, but was dismissed when he began demanding more money than he was thought to be worth. "You'd better be careful, I know plenty," Hartung said as he left. The next day he was heard boasting that he meant to get a truck and clean out an arms cache he knew about. The following day his body was found in a river with eleven pistol bullets in it and weighted with paving stones.

The paving stones were found to have come from an army parade ground, and a Defense Corps truck with two officers had been seen near the river the night before the body was found. The two officers, both lieutenants, were identified by name, and it was established that they had also been involved in the disappearance of Marie Sandmeier. Just as they were about to be arrested, Police President Poehner intervened, and shifted the case to another department, thereby delaying matters long enough for the suspects to flee. In neither the Sandmeier nor the Hartung case was anybody convicted and punished, though evidence pointing to the Citizens Defense Corps and army officers associated with it was plentiful.

The murders did not stop at servant girls and waiters. On the night of June 9, 1921, Karl Gareis, the leader of the Independent Socialists in Bavaria, was returning to his home in Schwabing from a meeting at which he had been the principal speaker. As he said good-night to a friend at his front gate, four shots were fired out of the dark, and Gareis fell to the ground with a bullet behind his ear. Three-quarters of an hour later he was dead. His killer was never caught. Afterward nationalist youth had another song to sing:

> *O hero brave whose shot made Gareis fall*
> *And brought deliverance again to all*
> *From the Socialist swine . . .*

Before the war, political murder was virtually unknown in Germany, and organized assassination unheard of. All through the long and turbulent rule of Kaiser Wilhelm II, no attempt was ever made on his life nor on that of any other German leader.

But in the first four years of the Weimar Republic, from 1919 to 1922, there were nearly 400 political murders, many of them unsolved and almost all unpunished. It became "open season," as one journalist put it, on officials and supporters of the Republic. As with the Mafia in America at a later time, there was at first a tendency to doubt whether a specific organization was behind the multiple murderings, choosing the victims and directing the execution of the death sentences. But such an organization existed. It was whispered about, when mentioned at all, by its initials only: *"O.C."*

Organization Consul was founded in Munich by Commander Ehrhardt with some of the ranking officers of his Brigade. He had fled to Hungary after the collapse of the Berlin *Putsch,* but made his way back to Germany with forged papers provided for him by Police President Poehner. The papers identified him as "Consul H. von Eschwege," and from the false title he took the name of his organization. Its purpose was to continue in secret what the Brigade had been doing in the open until the Kapp debacle: undermine the Republic and further the nationalist cause by any means. In a document describing Organization Consul's laws and regulations, one statute read:

"Verräter verfallen der Feme"—"Traitors will fall afoul of the *Feme."*

The *Feme* was an irregular tribunal that originated in medieval Germany at a time when the government was too weak to maintain order and administer justice. Such courts met in secret and exercised great power, often imposing death sentences that minions of the court then carried out. There was no appeal or recourse from the verdict of the *Feme,* and its own members were under threat of death should any detail of its functions or membership be revealed. Ehrhardt's "O.C.," and the *Feme* over which he presided, acquired a legendary reputation as the unseen force behind many of the murders and much of the subversion that afflicted the Republic in its early years, and there was enough hard evidence to give substance to the legends.

The first of the *Feme* assaults on prominent personalities of the Weimar Republic occurred in the Black Forest on August 26,

1921, when Matthias Erzberger was shot by two of Ehrhardt's gunmen. The bullets that cut him down were the climax of a long campaign of vilification to which Hitler and his National Socialists had contributed heavily. In speech after speech in the Munich beer halls Erzberger had been denounced as a criminal and a traitor, and consigned to the gallows. In the Black Forest rhetoric was translated into action.

What was principally held against Matthias Erzberger by nationalists of all shadings was that he was the man who signed the Armistice in the railway car in Compiègne. It counted for nothing that Erzberger had gone there on the plea of Field Marshal von Hindenburg at a time when the German armies had collapsed, when the First Quartermaster General was hiding in Sweden, and when the Kaiser was in flight to Holland. What was remembered, and never forgiven, was that he was the civilian who put his signature to the document that acknowledged Germany's defeat.

There were other charges in the indictment against Erzberger. He had, in 1917, introduced a peace resolution into the Reichstag. He advocated compliance with the Versailles Peace Treaty. And he dared to blame the fanatics of Pan-Germanism, and not the Republic, for Germany's plight. The scroll was charged full with the crimes of Matthias Erzberger, former schoolteacher, former Finance Minister of the Republic, and now, as he took his morning stroll in the woods with a friend, private citizen.

On their way back, they were accosted by two young men who at first seemed to be casual strollers also. But one of them suddenly pulled a pistol from his pocket and shot Matthias Erzberger in the stomach. Erzberger's friend made a defensive gesture with his umbrella, and was shot point-blank and badly wounded. Erzberger attempted to flee into the woods, but the second assassin gunned him down, and then bent over him and put two bullets in his head.

Police investigation quickly established the identities of the two killers, who had been observed in the vicinity of Erzberger's hotel for several days. Their baggage was found to contain hand

264

grenades and pistol ammunition. Their names were ascertained: Heinrich Tillessen and Heinrich Schulz. It was found that they had both been officers in the Ehrhardt Brigade, and that they returned to Munich after the assassination. Nevertheless, they were able to elude arrest and, with forged papers provided by the "O.C.," escape to Hungary, where authorities refused to extradite them.*

Now the nationalist students in their drinking clubs had a new song to sing, a sacrilegious adaptation of the old Protestant hymn of thanksgiving: *Nun danket alle Gott/für diesen braven Mord*—"Now thank we all our God/For this most splendid murder." And the Nuremberg-Munich *Volksstimme* ("People's Voice") commented editorially: ". . . the only wonder is that it took so long for a bullet to find its way into his body."

There were widespread demonstrations of shock and indignation. Berlin reacted by declaring a state of emergency in the country and invoking Article 48 of the Constitution to prohibit incitations to violence in the press and attacks on leaders of the Republic. But nothing like the strong-arm measures that had been taken against uprisings from the Left were put into effect. Gustav Noske, the Defense Minister, had lost his post as a result of the Kapp *Putsch,* and no new "bloodhound" emerged, then or later, to enforce the will of the government. Demands that Bavaria clean house and purge itself of extremist elements were defied by the current Minister President, Gustav Kahr, a reactionary monarchist and a champion of the Citizens Defense. The uproar over the Erzberger assassination brought about his resignation, and he was replaced by the more moderate Count Hugo Lerchenfeld, but the situation remained fundamentally unchanged. The operations of the *Feme* continued as before.

On June 4, 1922, a Sunday, Philipp Scheidemann went for a walk with his daughter and granddaughter through a wooded area near the city of Kassel, where he was Lord Mayor. With his

* After World War II, more than twenty-five years after the assassination, Tillessen and Schulz were brought to trial in a German court and sentenced to fifteen and twelve years imprisonment, respectively. They were pardoned in 1952.

white hair, neat goatee, and cutaway coat, he seemed the ideal German paterfamilias, courtly and distinguished. But under his cutaway coat Philipp Scheidemann was carrying a revolver.

He always did. As the man who said, "Better an end with terror than terror without end" to stop the fighting, as the man who proclaimed the Republic from the steps of the Reichstag, as the Republic's first Chancellor, he was a particular target for the hatred of the Right. His sins were not canceled by virtue of also having said, "May the hand wither that signs this paper," meaning the Versailles Treaty, and resigning from the government in protest. The nationalist press kept up a drumfire of personal abuse against him, denouncing him as a grafter who enriched himself in office and lived like a lord, though in fact his circumstances were modest and his means limited. His house was smeared with filth, and vicious slanders were scrawled on it. His life was repeatedly threatened. Philipp Scheidemann had reason to carry a gun, even on a Sunday stroll in the summertime.

His daughter and granddaughter left him briefly to pick some flowers. At that moment a young man wearing wrap-around leggings jumped out from behind a hedge and attacked him with perhaps the most curious weapon ever used in an assassination attempt. It was a syringe activated by a red rubber bulb. With it the attacker squirted prussic acid into Philipp Scheidemann's face. Terrified, and temporarily blinded, Scheidemann managed to pull his revolver before losing consciousness, and fired two shots. Neither hit, but they caused his assailant to run away, together with a comrade who had been lurking nearby.

Scheidemann was not seriously hurt, a strong wind having dissipated the impact of the acid and his mustache preventing it from reaching the mucous membranes of his nose. Again the assailants proved to be members of the O.C. This time, however, the usual pattern was broken, and they were quickly caught and tried. They were given sentences of six and eight years, but were amnestied before their terms were up, and went on to assume high government posts when Adolf Hitler came to power ten years later.

Despite the failure of the Scheidemann assassination and a

swelling chorus of indignation in the legitimate press, Ehrhardt's *Feme* proceeded with its program undeterred. Less than three weeks after the attempt on Scheidemann, the young assassins of Organization Consul struck again, and this time on the highest level they had so far dared to assault.

Walther Rathenau was the most brilliant mind, the strongest character, the most cultivated personality, in the leadership of the Weimar Republic. This was sufficient cause to mark him for assassination, but there was another. He was a Jew.

He came from a wealthy and distinguished Berlin family. His father, Emil, had early grasped the enormous possibilities of the incandescent light, and founded the German Edison Company, which grew into a great electrical complex known internationally as the AEG. Walther studied physics and chemistry, but also literature and philosophy. He took his doctorate with a dissertation on "The Light Absorption of Metals" and, after studying banking as well, he became a member of the board of AEG and then its president.

He was one of many Jews on the higher levels of German life who considered themselves more German than Jew, and he took the aristocratic Junker as his ideal. This tendency showed itself in a stiffly erect bearing and a Prussian rigidity of manner. He was tall, handsome and vain, and his outlook was more autocratic than democratic, but his loyalty to the Republic was not in doubt.

During the war he organized and headed the government's War Materials Division and performed prodigies of improvisation and resourcefulness, such as adopting a method of making nitrogen from the air that saved the German armies from running out of explosives during the crucial battles of the war. As the war progressed, his bureau came to control the economic life of Germany, and Rathenau emerged as one of the most powerful men in the country. When collapse was imminent, he advocated a *levée en masse,* an armed uprising of the people against the Allied armies as a means of carrying on the war, but Ludendorff, by then in a state of collapse himself, had no heart for the plan. No taint of stab-in-the-back could reasonably attach to Walther Rathenau.

He was the Foreign Minister of the Republic when he went to Genoa in April of 1922 to attend an economic conference arranged by the British. On the sixteenth he and the Russian Commissar of Foreign Affairs, Georgi Chicherin, quietly left the conference, drove to the Riviera town of Rapallo, and signed a treaty re-establishing diplomatic relations between their two countries. The treaty also provided for closer economic relations between Germany and Soviet Russia, and mutually renounced reparations. The Rapallo Treaty came as a severe jolt to the Allied powers. It unexpectedly brought together the two defeated pariah nations of Europe, and it signaled the end of Germany's postwar isolation and the start of an independent foreign policy. It was widely hailed in Germany as a great coup, but reactionary elements condemned it as unwarranted *rapprochement* with the hated Bolsheviks.

Actually, the treaty was a boon to the German Army and warmly welcomed by General Hans von Seeckt, since it prepared the way for secret cooperation between the High Command and the Communists for years to come—the Germans providing money and specialists for the Red Army, while Russia built the tanks and guns for Germany that the Versailles Treaty prohibited. But none of this was credited to the account of Walther Rathenau, who survived his Rapallo Treaty by hardly more than two months.

What was chiefly held against him, aside from being a Jew, was his support of the policy of "fulfillment," or compliance with the Allied reparation demands. These amounted to 132 billion gold marks, or about thirty-five billion dollars, and to most Germans this seemed a cruelly exorbitant burden. Rathenau's idea was to undertake "fulfillment" with the objective of showing that the terms were impossible and would have to be modified. This did not diminish the campaign of vilification against him, either. He was savagely denounced in the Reichstag for ruining the economy and "pulverizing our middle class." In Munich Adolf Hitler was attacking him for reducing Germany to the status of "a colony of foreign powers." The nationalist press seethed with the same incitements that preceded the deaths of Gareis and Erzberger. The National Socialists publicly jeered at him as "the un-crowned king of the Jews," and another murderous jingle appeared in print repeatedly:

> *Knallt ab den Walther Rathenau,*
> *die gottverfluchte Judensau.*

[Shoot down Walther Rathenau
That God-damned Jewish sow.]

He, also, never left his house without a pistol, but they gave him no chance to use it. On the morning of June twenty-fourth, Rathenau left his villa in a residential suburb of Berlin for the Foreign Office. He was riding alone in the back seat of an open car driven by a chauffeur. Some construction workers along the road noticed the car and its occupant as they passed. The workmen also observed, and with special interest, a powerful six-seater touring car, dark gray and open, that followed. What caught their attention was the splendid new leather coats worn by the two men in the back seat of the touring car. One of the men, the workers noted, had an open, clean-cut look—"what we call an 'officer's face.' " He was indeed an officer, formerly in the Navy and more recently in the Ehrhardt Brigade. His name was Erwin Kern, he was twenty-four years old, and he was about to murder Walther Rathenau.

When the Foreign Minister's driver slowed down for an S-curve in the road, the long touring car accelerated, overtook the machine ahead, forced it to the side of the road, and cut it off. As Rathenau leaned out to see what was happening, Erwin Kern stood up in his handsome leather coat, put a Lewis submachine gun to his shoulder and squeezed off a nine-bullet burst point-blank. Walther Rathenau crumpled together and fell over unconscious. The other young man in a leather coat then took an egg grenade from his pocket, and pulled the pin. He was Hermann Fischer, another ex-officer and a member of the Berlin arm of the O.C. He lobbed the grenade with professional competence, and the workmen, frozen where they stood since the first shot, watched it go off. They saw how the explosion lifted "the gentleman in the tonneau" momentarily into the air and seemed to make the whole car jump. Then the gray touring car, driven by a young student named Ernst Werner Techow, roared away.

Rathenau's chauffeur, miraculously unhurt by either bullet or grenade, sped his bleeding passenger home, where a doctor pronounced him dead.

Walther Rathenau had been Foreign Minister only five months, and was the first high official of the Weimar Republic to be killed in office.

"When political murders occur *en masse*," Dr. Fredric Wertham writes in his study of the subject, "they are a sure indication of long-range political trends." In postwar Germany the indication and the trend set in simultaneously, and the assassination of Walther Rathenau was not merely a symptom but the disease itself. "A world begins to stink," was Kurt Tucholsky's comment on the continuing terror from the Right, and in another of his prophetic dissections of his own society he wrote: "The foundations are shaking . . . I sense it numbly: something is creeping up that threatens to destroy us. . . . Listen: You will hear the pulse-beat of a new time." There was a sense of horror at the Rathenau death that went beyond what even a political murder would normally cause. "Your accursed deed," said a Berlin newspaper, addressing the killers, "has not only struck the man Rathenau; it has struck Germany in her entirety. . . . You have slain one man but wounded sixty million." There were mass demonstrations such as Germany had never seen before, 700,000 assembling in grief and protest in Berlin alone. In the Reichstag Dr. Joseph Wirth, the current Chancellor, delivered an impassioned speech in which he lamented that political life in Germany had degenerated to the animal level. He turned dramatically to the right side of the house and said: "There stands the enemy that is dripping his poisons into the wounds of our people. The enemy stands on the Right!" There were shouts of "Out with the murderers! Out with the murderers!" until the delegates of the German National Party had to withdraw from the hall.

The retreat was temporary, and applause was not entirely unanimous when Rathenau's killers were run to earth. Trapped in the tower of an isolated castle, where they were hiding, Kern was shot by police, and Fischer killed himself after shouting a last *"Hoch!"* out the window for his leader, Ehrhardt. In nationalist circles the two assassins were hailed as martyrs who had died gallantly in a great cause, and the surviving accomplices were described at their trial as idealists who acted out of motives "both noble and patriotic." In Bavaria, Gustav Kahr took the widely accepted position that "if there were no radical anti-national leftists there would obviously be no need for radical right-wing nationalists." And Erich Ludendorff argued that the assassinations of Erzberger and "the Jew Rathenau" were the inevitable result of the misery into which the country had been plunged and were simply expressions of the nation's "will to defend itself." Young Techow, the driver of the murder car, was sentenced to fifteen years, the severest penalty imposed in any of the right-extremist murders. He charged at his trial that Rathenau was one of the 300 "Elders of Zion" whose secret "protocols" proved the existence of a Jewish conspiracy to dominate the world. The protocols, a notorious forgery stemming from czarist Russia, were then circulating by the hundreds of thousands in Germany, and Techow's accusation was taken seriously. Rathenau's murder coincided with the summer solstice, and it became known that young German sun-worshipers had "gathered on hilltops to celebrate simultaneously the turning of the year and the destruction of one who symbolized the power of darkness."

It was only nine days after the death of Rathenau that the O.C., as if to show that it was uncowed by demonstrations and protests, struck in the same Berlin suburb where Rathenau had been killed. The publicist Maximilian Harden, who had been urging acceptance of the Versailles Treaty and friendship with Russia, was returning to his home in Grunewald after mailing a letter to an American friend. In it he had expressed fears that his life was in danger. Not far from his home he was set upon from the rear by two men who assaulted him with an iron bar, striking him on the head no less than eight times. His cries brought a neighbor to the scene, and Harden's life was saved as his attackers fled. They were caught and brought to trial, where it turned out that the iron bar had been wielded by an agent of the O.C., who was, again, an ex-Army officer. He and his accomplice in the murder attempt were sentenced to a year apiece. "The meaning of the sentences is clear," wrote Kurt Tucholsky, who covered the trial. "The meaning is: *Weitermachen!*"—Continue as before. Assaults on the officials and defenders of the Republic had become so routine, and the pattern so well set, that Tucholsky suggested a handy little brochure might be published for the guidance of future assassins: "How To Be an Expert Nationalist Murderer in Eight Easy Lessons."

Maximilian Harden was sixty-one at the time of the attack, from which he never fully recovered, and one of his statements in court was a despairing commentary on how the Germany he knew had changed. "I fought against the Kaiser from the first," Harden said, "but under his regime they didn't kill you for it."

The revelation at the trial that arrangements for the attack on him had been made in Munich surprised no one.

On the day Walther Rathenau was murdered, Adolf Hitler was sitting in a jail cell at Stadelheim, where he spent four weeks for breaching the peace. He and several of his National Socialists had broken up the meeting of a rival party, his first use of terror tactics against a political rival. His confinement was somewhat eased by the special consideration accorded him by the prison guards, a cell with a private toilet, and the knowledge that the incident had won him a burst of the publicity he regarded as essential to his Party's growth. On the other hand, the sentence muzzled him, and kept him out of the public eye, at a time of great political turmoil of the kind he would have liked to exploit and manipulate.

Neither he nor his Party had overtly participated in the *Feme* activities of the O.C., though a number of National Socialists were involved on their own. Hitler was opposed to individual acts of retaliation and revenge, not on ethical or humanitarian grounds, but because they seemed too petty to meet the situation as he saw it. "It is laughably illogical to kill some fellow who has betrayed a cannon," he said, "while nearby sit dogs in high office who have sold out an entire nation, who have two millions uselessly dead on their conscience, who are responsible for millions of cripples, but who meanwhile go serenely about their republican business." He looked forward to the day when a German nationalist court would execute not one or two dozen traitors but "10,000 of the criminals responsible for the November treason." Nothing lasting, he said, could be accomplished by a handful of conspirators using "dagger and poison and pistol." What was needed was "a hundred thousand, and again a hundred thousand, fanatical fighters for our view of life. The work must be done not in secret conventicles, but in overwhelming mass demonstrations . . . in the conquest of the streets." He was out of prison in time to play a leading role in one of the greatest mass demonstrations Munich had ever seen.

As a result of the Rathenau assassination, Berlin had passed a "Law for the Protection of the Republic," a statute intended to give the government new powers to halt the terror from the Right. It provided measures to control the extremist agitation of nationalist groups and their press, prohibit subversive meetings, and punish desecrations of the flag. Some organizations were ordered to disband, and a number of viciously anti-republican newspapers were shut down. But, as with the measures taken after the Erzberger murder, nothing fundamental changed. The prevailing passions were by now too deep-seated and long-established to yield to legislation. The principal result of the new law was to widen the gap between Bavaria and Berlin. Bavaria opposed the measure as an unwarranted infringement on its sovereignty as a Free State, and Hitler's National Socialists promptly labeled the Rathenau statute a "Law for the Protection of Jewry." While workers in Berlin carried a gallows through the streets with an effigy of Ludendorff dangling from it, posters went up and handbills were distributed in Munich calling for a quite different protest meeting in one of the city's principal squares, the Königsplatz, under the auspices of the United Fatherland Leagues, the successors to the Defense Corps.

An outpouring of more than 50,000 filled the square to hear the Law for the Protection of the Republic denounced, and Munich saw for the first time a spectacle with ominous implications for its future: 600 marching men in matching caps and jackets representing the National Socialist Party of Adolf Hitler. On their left arms they wore red bands with white circles inside which were black swastikas. They carried flags of the same design. The date was August 16, 1922, and the marching men—six columns of 100 each, with fifteen flags and two military bands—formed the first public parade of Adolf Hitler's Storm Troops. The National Socialists were the only group to appear at the rally to the sound of drums and trumpets, and with banners flying. They were greeted with enormous enthusiasm.

Hitler had never addressed so huge a gathering, and he made the most of it in a virtuoso performance that marked a high point of his oratory to date. His theme was "Free State or Slavery?" but, as he often did, he used the immediate occasion to launch into a sweeping indictment of the whole social structure, picturing the world as locked in a pitiless struggle between national aims and ideals and the predatory designs of an "intangible, international supra-state" organized and dominated by Jews. He ranged through centuries of history, quoting Voltaire, Rousseau and Fichte. He referred to the disappearance of previous civilizations—"vanished without a trace"—and warned that confused and misguided Germans were helping to bring a similar fate upon their own country by not resisting the trend of events. He reminded his audience of Bismarck's saying that the fate of peoples is never determined by the resolutions of the majority, but by "blood and iron" only. "What Germany needs, and deeply yearns for today," he said, "is a symbol of power and strength."

To many, he himself was becoming such a symbol.

An indication of the impact of the Königsplatz speech comes from one of the 50,000 listeners who left a record of his impressions and reactions that day. He was Kurt Ludecke, who

274

had seen a good deal of the world and, in various business and personal adventures that took him to England, France and the Balkans, had acquired a sheen of cynicism and sophistication. He was nationalist in outlook, having sampled the racist writings of Gobineau, Lagarde and Houston Stewart Chamberlain. He was thirty-two, restless and at loose ends when he drifted to Munich. Lured by one of the screaming red posters of the National Socialists, he attended the Königsplatz rally and had his first view of Hitler.

"Critically I studied this slight, pale man, his brown hair parted on one side and falling again and again over his sweating brow. Threatening and beseeching, with small pleading hands and flaming, steel-blue eyes, he had the look of a fanatic." Far from being repelled by Hitler's fanaticism, Ludecke was enthralled: "His words were like a scourge. When he spoke of the disgrace of Germany, I felt ready to spring on any enemy. His appeal to German manhood was like a call to arms, the gospel he preached a sacred truth. He seemed another Luther. I forgot everything but the man. Then, glancing around, I saw that his magnetism was holding these thousands as one."

Kurt Ludecke, cosmopolitan and sophisticated, experienced what he called "an exaltation that could be likened only to religious conversion." Upon meeting Hitler and joining the Party, he made a solemn commitment: "I had given him my soul." *

Additional rallies at which Hitler also spoke kept the public in a state of ferment, and resulted in a pronounced increase in the membership of the National Socialist Party. An official from Württemberg reported back to his government that "the leader [*Führer*] Hitler must be a fascinating personality" and that, with the continuing growth of the National Socialists, "it is by no means impossible that they will attempt a *Putsch* in the near future. . . ." Should such a *Putsch* occur, the report continued, it

* Ludecke rose high in the ranks of the Party, and became "foreign-affairs adviser" to Hitler. But when Hitler came to power in 1933, he had Ludecke arrested and thrown into a concentration camp. With the help of Roehm, Ludecke escaped and fled to America. As he got off the boat, Ludecke learned that Roehm himself had been murdered in the 1934 Hitler purge.

was highly unlikely that the *Reichswehr* and the police would do anything to prevent it, but would in all probability join it.

So, in the end, the operations of the O.C., and the terror of the *Feme,* instead of producing a ground swell of positive counter-action, brought about an increase in rightist sentiment and activity. The murder of Rathenau, aside from the immediate demonstrations and outcries in the left-liberal press, did nothing lasting to strengthen the hand of the Republic against its internal enemies. The first great upsurge of indignation might have been expected to produce a leader from among the Social Democrats and trade unions to rally public opinion and solidify it into an invincible popular front against the Right. But the leadership vacuum, fatal to the Republic from the first, would continue to the end.

The only personality of real consequence for the future whose emergence was furthered by the assassination of Walther Rathenau was Adolf Hitler. The authorities evaluating the post-Rathenau situation agreed that Adolf Hitler had now become a *"Machtfaktor,"* a power factor, to reckon with "such as had not appeared on the scene in a long time." And at the year's end the Directory of the Munich Police Department compiled a report that concluded:

"There can be no doubt that the National Socialist idea—perhaps especially because its propaganda activity emphasizes the nationalist idea so strongly—has today, already, taken root, in all circles and levels of the population, and the Party must be regarded as a powerful element in our political life."

12 "THE KING OF MUNICH"

"HOW STRANGE AND INHUMANELY ABNORMAL THINGS STAND WITH US TODAY IN THIS LAND OF OURS!"

—THOMAS MANN (1922)

A YOUNG Foreign Service Officer named Robert Daniel Murphy was put in charge of the American Consulate in Munich when it reopened after the war in November of 1921. He was rather junior, at twenty-seven, to be the ranking United States diplomat in Bavaria, but, as he observed afterward, "the evidence suggests that our Government did not think it mattered much who represented it in Munich." Like almost all other observers then on the scene, he found it impossible to believe that "the demagogue Hitler, so unconvincing to me, would ever amount to much."

This was not the obtuseness of an outsider unequipped to judge an unfamiliar political situation. Robert Murphy's assistant was a German named Paul Drey, who had a comprehensive knowledge of local politics and personalities. They attended a number of the early Hitlerite rallies together, and after one of them Murphy, the foreigner, asked Paul Drey, the knowledgeable native: "Do you think these agitators will ever get anywhere?"

"Of course not!" Drey answered. "The German people are too intelligent to be taken in by such scamps!"

Robert Murphy's superiors in Washington were not impressed by the Munich agitators, either. His reports became increasingly urgent, but they were ignored. "During my Munich years," Murphy has written, "I saw nothing to indicate that the American government or people were even mildly interested

278

in the political developments which seemed so ominous and significant to us on the spot." Not even Hitler's *Putsch,* when it came, stirred any interest in the State Department, elicited any queries, evoked any response. "Yet," says Robert Murphy, "we were dealing with the origins of World War II." *

The movement's warlike trappings began with the design of the banner that was to become the symbol of conquest and terror for tens of millions. Afterward it came to be called "probably the most brutal and powerful design ever invented for a flag," and its potential for violence and bloodshed was recognized from the first in the place of its birth. "The swastika," said the Munich *Post* in June of 1920, "is an incitation to race murder." But for Hitler the flag he designed was "young and new, like the movement itself . . . it had the effect of a flaming torch." In its eye-arresting vividness and simplicity of impact, the swastika flag was one of his most effective creations. In his view, the trappings of the Party—flags, insignia, armbands, standards, symbols, uniforms, ceremonies—were of the utmost importance from the outset. "An effective insignia," he said, "can give the first stimulus toward interest in a movement for hundreds of thousands."

He pondered the colors of his flag, and their arrangement, with the greatest care. He wished to retain the old black-white-red of the Imperial emblem—"the most glorious war flag of all times"—but not in the old combination, which, however grand, represented the past. After considering and discarding dozens of ideas submitted by Party members, he finally singled out a design from a man named Friedrich Krohn, a dentist, and modified it into the pattern that became the Party standard. The red of the field predominated, the same flaming red he had stolen from the Communists for his posters as "the most exciting and provocative" color. Into the red he set a white disk, and in the center of the disk a black swastika.

* When World War II duly came, Robert Murphy served as personal emissary for President Franklin D. Roosevelt on several crucial military missions, and was elevated to the rank of Ambassador. Paul Drey died in the Dachau concentration camp.

280

The dentist Krohn, too, had centered his design around the swastika, having been a member of the Thule Society and written a monograph on the symbol. But Hitler made the sign larger, stronger and coarser, and decreed that its top arm would be pointed to the right instead of to the left as Krohn had it. Hitler emphasized the swastika, and made it the particular symbol of his movement, in the belief that it was a peculiarly "Aryan" rune, the sign of the pure-blooded Nordic races in contrast to the Semitic. But not only had the swastika been the property of many races and colors for thousands of years around the globe, it was also a Jewish symbol, having appeared on ancient Palestine pottery and even on synagogues excavated in the Holy Land. From the time the swastika was first flown on the red-white-black banners of Adolf Hitler, the mystic and immemorial symbol became tainted and would forever afterward be associated with millions dead by deliberate extermination. From symbolizing the wheel of the sun and the cycle of life, it would henceforth signify only darkness and death.*

At the same time, Hitler designed the Party brassards and lapel insignia, and issued orders that all members wear their Party pins constantly and that the swastika armbands be displayed on the left sleeve at all meetings by sergeants-at-arms and others delegated to keep order, not only as identification but "to strengthen the feeling of solidarity." What he wanted to create among his followers, and especially among his meeting guards, was the kind of esprit that prevails in combat units at the front. "From its first day," he said, "the young movement took the position that its idea was to be promulgated spiritually and intellectually, but when necessary, it was to be defended by muscle and fist." In the political warfare he was waging, Hitler meant to have the heaviest battalions on his side, and the result was the formation of his Storm Troops.

Like almost everything else in the Hitler upheaval that rocked the world, the Storm Troops originated in the Munich beer halls. They were an outgrowth of the first handful of National Socialist brawlers appointed to keep order at Party meet-

* The word 'swastika' comes from the Sanskrit and means "all is well". . . !

ings and prevent them from being disrupted by Communist and Social Democrat intruders. A kind of guerrilla warfare developed among the rival political factions, the one determined to keep the other from putting its views unmolested before the public. At first the National Socialist rallies relied largely on the support of *Reichswehr* personnel like the 19th Bavarian Mortar Company, almost all of whom were members of the Party in addition to being members of the German Army. They turned out for the Hitlerite meetings and stood ready to break up any opposition. The Army also supplied manpower and weapons for NS raids on Social Democrat and Communist assemblies. Gradually the Party, under Hitler's guidance, organized its own strong-arm units, which, at first, were disguised as sport and gymnastic clubs. At the start, Ernst Roehm was active in the formation of the National Socialist muscle squads, and their ranks were largely filled by former members of the Ehrhardt Brigade, ex-Free Corps men, and brawny recruits from the Citizens Defense and the Fatherland Leagues.

The first Party units were formed before Hitler gave them the name by which they would go down in history. Their commander was a naval lieutenant named Johann Ulrich Klintzsch, who qualified for his post by being a fugitive Kapp *putschist,* a former Ehrhardt officer, and a conspirator in the Erzberger assassination. Field exercises being forbidden by the Versailles Treaty, the units drilled on country roads and out-of-the-way vacant lots, sometimes with canes or sticks in lieu of rifles. But often they were given access to Army facilities, parade grounds, weapons and rifle ranges. Before they were organized into regulation regiments and battalions, they were divided into so-called *Hundertschaften,* or one-hundred units, even when they could not muster sufficient numbers to live up to the title.

Their first uniform was the swastika armband and any available scrap of leftover Army outfit, or nothing else at all. The early units were so tatterdemalion that the Munich *Post* hooted at them as "Hitler's Foreign Legion," and afterward Hitler himself, looking back, said that anyone seeing a squad of his in those days would ask: "What workhouse have they escaped from?" But he was insistent on the value of a uniform for achieving the sense of solidarity he was seeking, and gradually a rough similarity of dress evolved. Ski caps, because they were cheap, and gray wind jackets, were adopted, with only the Party cockade and brassard to announce the affiliation of the wearer. The brown shirt and uniform that the world came to know, massed in serried ranks of tens of thousands at Party demonstrations, were still in the future.

In his *Hundertschaften* Hitler began to accumulate followers who came nearer to living up to his ideal of what they should be: "swift as greyhounds, tough as leather, hard as Krupp steel." For new recruits he set the same age limit as the old Army's, between seventeen and twenty-three. He deliberately made joining seem a dangerous commitment—*"auf Biegen und Brechen,"* risk your neck, come what may. In a fight, he said, nobody would leave the hall "unless carried out dead." Anyone who showed cowardice, he promised, would have armband and insignia torn off by Hitler himself. What he demanded was the same *Kadavergehorsam,* the blind obedience, that was the ideal of the Frederick William who had first made Prussia a military power. What Hitler wanted to wield through his private army was, he said, "the weapon of brutal force, applied persistently and ruthlessly" as the only certain means of making his political philosophy prevail. The marching songs of the National Socialists expressed the bloodlust of the movement with astonishing frankness. After first adopting the song of the Ehrhardt Brigade (substituting Hitler's name for Ehrhardt's) the NS marching formation went on to songs with lines like *"Whet your knives on the curbstone / And cut the Jewish bodies to the bone!"* . . . *"When the hour of vengeances comes / We'll be ready for any mass murder"* . . . *"Everything will be so much better / When Jewish blood spurts from our knives . . . !"* It was one of the most glaring symptoms of weakness in the Weimar Republic that an avowed enemy of the state was permitted to organize and maintain, without serious interference from the authorities, an armed force whose open purpose was the overthrow of the government and the extermination of fellow citizens.

The Left organized strong-arm squads to counteract the terror from the Right. The Socialists called their defense unit the Erhard Auer Guards, after the party leader who almost lost his life during the shooting affray in the Bavarian Parliament at the time of the Eisner assassination. The Auer guards also wore uniforms and sometimes helmets, used military commands, and wore red armbands. So in Munich the elements for a miniature civil war confronted each other along ideological lines, a reflection and intensification of the divisions racking all Germany.

Organized assaults on rival political meetings became a fixed feature of the Munich scene and were given a standard name—*Saalschlachten,* hall battles. They were fought with beer mugs, chair legs, billy clubs and blackjacks. Many a hall was left looking like a battlefield, strewn with wreckage and smeared with the blood of the contestants. In one such encounter, on November 4, 1921, the *Hundertschaften* won the name by which they would afterward be known around the world.

On the day of the meeting the atmosphere was particularly tense, since an attempt had been made on the life of Erhard Auer by unknown assailants, and the Left was determined to avenge itself by breaking up the National Socialist gathering scheduled for the banquet hall of the Hofbräuhaus. Hitler had gotten word that his meeting would come under attack, and he prepared his forty-six-man guard for the worst, instructing them to move in at once at the slightest sign of disturbance and to fight to the death if necessary. The response from his guards was a threefold *"Heil!,"* a greeting and tribute the Party had recently taken over from the *völkisch* movement in Austria.

The hall was filled when Hitler began to speak, and he soon sensed what he called an atmosphere of "sullen hatred" and menace. In the audience, numbering about 800, his own people were far outnumbered by hostile workers from the Maffei factory, the Isaria Meters Works and other industrial sites. His platform was a beer table along one wall, and he was thus in the midst of the audience. He was able to speak for an hour and a half without a serious break, and he noticed that his opponents were using an old trick of beer-hall warriors: they kept ordering beer, but instead of returning the mugs they stored them under the table as an arsenal for the coming fight. It came when a leader of the opposition leaped upon his table and shouted the signal *"Freiheit!"*—"Freedom!," the greeting and slogan of the Social Democrats.

"In seconds," Hitler reported, "the whole hall was a mass of roaring, yelling men over which innumerable beer mugs were flying like howitzer shells, with the cracking of chair legs, the splintering of the mugs, and much howling and bawling and screaming." He kept standing on his table, watching the spectacle and, perhaps, seeing it as another confirmation of what he believed to be "a law of nature—that all living things mutually devour one another," and that "only force rules; force is the first law." He watched especially to see how his hall guards were performing. He had taught them to concentrate their attacks on limited objectives, and to attack from table to table instead of dissipating their energies by striking out at random. He was pleased to see that his boys were falling upon the enemy "like wolves" in packs of eight or ten, and were actually thrashing their opponents out of the hall—probably with the considerable help of volunteers from a *Reichswehr* mortar company, who are not mentioned in the Party version of the incident nor in Hitler's own account. At the entrance some shooting broke out, and several shots were directed toward the platform, with no effect except to make the speaker's heart "almost jump with joy at such a reminder of old war experiences." The police came, the meeting resumed, and Hitler finished his speech. The Hofbräuhaus *Saalschlacht* went down in Party history as a notable triumph for the movement, and thereafter its meetings were largely free from disruption by the Left. And from then on, as an honor won that night, the National Socialist marching and guard formations were, by Hitler's decree, to be called *Sturm Abteilungen,* or Assault Detachments. He took the name from the German Army's designation for shock troops, and it carried over into civilian life the brotherhood of violence born on the battlefields of the World War. In the Party, members of the *Sturm Abteilungen*

were called "S.A." men. The world would know them as Storm
Troopers.

The excesses of the National Socialists, in uniform and out,
which turned the streets of Munich into a battleground could
have been checked by application of the lawful restraints available to any civilized community. The restraints were not applied,
or only desultorily and sporadically, because the Bavarian authorities wished to see the young Party succeed. At the Munich
Police Directory sat a certain Dr. Wilhelm Frick who afterward
testified:

"We recognized that this movement, the National Socialist
Party, which then was still young—in 1919 and 1920 it would
have been an easy thing to suppress it—should not be suppressed. We did not do that, and we refrained deliberately, because we saw in the Party the seeds of Germany's renewal, because we were convinced from the start that this movement was
the one most likely to take root among workers infected with the
Marxist plague and win them back into the nationalist camp.
That is why we held our protecting hands over the National Socialist Party and Herr Hitler."

Once, in a rare moment of unqualified generosity, Hitler
acknowledged Frick's services to the Party and to himself. Without Frick, said Hitler in a private conversation at the height of
his power, the early activity of the Party would not have been
possible. And, he added, without Frick, he would never have
gotten out of jail (*"aus dem Kittchen"*—"out of the can").

As head of the Political Division of the Munich Police Pre-
sidium, Dr. Frick was well situated to extend helping and protective hands to the National Socialists. He was in charge of the
censorship of political placards, and almost anything Hitler
chose to put on his inflammatory red posters was permitted. In
concert with his superior, Ernst Poehner, Dr. Frick was able to
suppress complaints to the police against National Socialist
breaches of the peace and other acts of violence, and to see that
such police action as was begun against the Party and its mem-

286

bers came to nothing. Inside the Department there were Party members who regularly warned Hitler of pending police actions and other measures that might affect his activities. Hitler and his cohorts were never entirely immune from police interference, but for them the arm of the law was sufficiently crippled so that, by and large, they could proceed as they wished while their political opponents were obliged to keep strictly within the statutes. This was an enormous advantage bestowed largely by Dr. Wilhelm Frick, who, with his high stiff collar, close-cropped hair and severely puritanical manner, gave the impression of an unbending guardian of law and order.*

With a virtual green light from the authorities, Hitler proceeded with his program, which he summarized by saying: "We will incite the people, and not only incite: we will lash them to a frenzy." It became an axiom of National Socialist strategy that "whoever conquers the streets conquers the masses, and whoever conquers the masses conquers the state." Hitler's campaign to carry out this concept began early and was greatly furthered by his private army. He continually sent trucks plastered with his red posters and Party flags through the streets, and from them squads of S.A. men shouted Party slogans in unison and scattered leaflets as they went. Other S.A. men roamed the streets tearing down placards of rival political parties, beating up anyone who objected, painting swastikas on public buildings and private homes.

Packets of leaflets were fastened on the roofs of the city's white-blue streetcars in such a way that the wind scattered them along the route as the trolleys worked up speed. Leaflets came fluttering down from the twin spires of the cathedral, the *Frauenkirche,* and from the tower of City Hall in the Marien-

* As Chancellor of the Greater German Reich, Adolf Hitler never forgot his debt to the provincial official who made his beginning possible. Frick became Reich Minister of the Interior in the first Hitler Cabinet; Prussian Minister of the Interior; General Plenipotentiary for the Administration of the Reich; member of the Ministerial Council for the Defense of the Reich; and Reich Protector of the conquered provinces of Bohemia and Moravia. As a consequence of these honors and activities, Dr. Wilhelm Frick was sentenced to be hanged by the Allied War Crimes Tribunal at Nuremberg in October of 1946.

platz when the carved figures of its famous clock were activated on the hour. Natives and visitors to the annual October Beer Festival found themselves inundated with propaganda broadsides tossed from the cabins of the Ferris wheels and the cars of roller coasters. Small boys and girls, who had no idea of what they were doing, were paid by strangers to take bundles of leaflets and scatter them about. The leaflets were usually viciously anti-Semitic and full of threats against politicians and officials of the Left and Center. It was a *Gaudi* such as Munich's political life had never seen before, and it reached such proportions that, from time to time, the police were forced to intervene. Hitler himself was fleetingly arrested in connection with some of the more virulent anti-Semitic excesses in the leaflet campaign, but he was released "for lack of sufficient evidence."

Even reactionary newspapers were sometimes shocked by what the Bavarian *Kurier* called the "unbelievable roughness and brutality" of "half-grown National Socialists" who, the paper said, were damaging the repute of the entire *völkisch*-Fatherland movement.

Jewish religious services were broken up and synagogues desecrated. The windows of the Socialist *Post* itself were smashed. The flag of the Republic was burned in public places, such as the main railroad station. The National Socialist rowdies came to be known as *Hakenkreuzler,* from the German name for the swastika ("hooked cross"). Their disruptions of political assemblies became so commonplce that rival parties could scarcely schedule a meeting with any assurance that it would run its course without a *Saalschlacht.* Persons who looked Jewish were stopped on the street, abused, insulted and beaten up. An American visitor was seized and his trousers torn open to see whether he was circumcised. What was called the National Socialist *Sturmarmee,* or assault army, did not hesitate to breach police barriers and attack any rival group it chose. At an NS meeting in the Bürgerbräu a young *Hakenkreuzler* circulated through the audience carrying a cardboard box with the inscription: CONTRIBUTE FOR THE JEW MASSACRE. When a man protested, he was beaten to the floor with rubber truncheons.

In March of 1922 a serious movement was launched to stem National Socialist extremism. This did not originate with the Munich police, but in the Bavarian parliament, and took the form of attacking Hitler on the basis that he was not, after all, a German citizen. Having been convicted of a crime, and served time in jail, he was susceptible to deportation to his birthplace, Austria. This was the most serious threat he had been confronted with; he could readily have been banished to the relative obscurity of his native soil, where conditions were not merely less favorable for his advancement to power than in Germany but virtually impossible for his purposes. Banishment might well have meant the end of his career.

As an outsider, he had plenty of historical precedent. Alexander was not a Greek, but a Macedonian. Napoleon was not a Frenchman, but a Corsican. Stalin was not a Russian, but a Georgian. But Hitler passionately felt that he *was* a German, and pointed out that he was born only 250 meters from the Bavarian border in an area which, with the geographical fluctuations of history, could well be called as German as any place within the Reich, having, in fact, been part of Bavaria a few centuries before. When the matter of his banishment as an alien first came up, he wrote an impassioned letter to Count von Lerchenfeld, the Bavarian Minister President, pointing to his service in a Bavarian regiment where he had "staked his blood for his Germanism." Only the letter of "our present Jewish law," he said, could classify him as a foreigner.

What saved him in the end was the application of the liberal and democratic principles that he despised and would, as he repeatedly proclaimed, instantly abolish if he had the power. When the matter came to a final decision at a meeting of leaders of the principal Bavarian parties, they all agreed that public policy and civic order required that Adolf Hitler be deported—all except one. This was Erhard Auer, the Socialist leader. He argued that if the constitutional tenets of free speech and democratic freedom meant anything, they must apply to this case also. Arbitrary methods should not be applied because one did not agree with what Hitler was saying and doing. Besides, said Auer, this Hitler was *"nur eine komische Figur"*—only a comical figure.

Auer's argument carried the day, since none of the other party leaders wanted to assume responsibility for an action against Hitler that the Socialists themselves declined to take. "Thus," said Ernst Niekisch, himself a prominent Socialist who was present at the meeting, "it came about that the Social Democrats won the 'honor' of preserving Adolf Hitler for the German people." *

It was the second crisis he had survived within a year's time. The previous July he had spent six weeks in Berlin, conferring with nationalist groups of the north and addressing the prestigious National Club, where he favorably impressed an audience of upper-class and industrial types. But while he was away from Munich, a factional revolt erupted in the Party with him as its target. Some early members of the Working Committee, long resentful of being disregarded while Hitler ran the Party as he pleased, circulated an anonymous leaflet against him. It called him a demagogue with a "lust for power" who, "relying only on his gift as a speaker," intended to mislead the German people and wreck the Party in the process, thereby doing the work of the Jews and their supporters. Moreover, he was conducting his inner-Party intrigues in a manner *"echt jüdisch,"* or like a real Jew. This was language Hitler used about his opponents, but was unaccustomed to hearing about himself. The leaflet charged that there was something unsavory about how he supported himself, since questions on the subject got no answer, but only "threw him into fits of rage and excitement." He was accused of "excessive association with women"—where did he get the money for it?—to whom he often spoke of himself as the "King of Munich." The royal title he gave himself was also used as the heading of a placard that the anti-Hitler faction wished to post throughout the city. It was rejected by the police censors on the ground that it dealt with internal Party strife of no concern to the pub-

* Hitler did not become a German citizen until 1932, the year before he became Chancellor.

lic. But 3,000 of the leaflets were circulated, and it was printed in two Munich newspapers.

Hitler promptly sued the papers, and submitted his resignation to the Party, confident that it would be rejected. It was. No one denied that without him the Party would, in all probability, collapse or shrivel into the insignificance that was its lot before he brought it members, money and public attention. Aware that he now had the upper hand, Hitler revised the structure of the Party along the authoritarian lines he had envisioned from the start. He became the "First Chairman," or president; Anton Drexler, the founder, was put on the shelf as "Honorary Chairman." Hitler wiped from the books all provisions for majority rule and parliamentary process. From now on, his decision alone would prevail. It was his earliest application of the *Führerprinzip,* or "leader principle," by which all members of the organization deferred to the man at the top in blind obedience and carried out his will without question. The Party became a pyramidal arrangement designed to convey the decisions made at the apex down through the various levels of the structure to the broadest possible base with the least possible deviation en route. The leader principle, introduced into the National Socialist Party in Munich in 1921 as the consequence of a scurrilous leaflet, became the basis on which Hitler's European empire was governed at the peak of its power, and to its end.

Führer in the German dictionaries meant "leader, guide, conductor, manager, chief, driver, pilot (of an airplane) and, in music, fugue-theme." It took on a new, and eventually a worldwide, significance after it was applied to Adolf Hitler by one of his followers, Hermann Esser, a staunch supporter in the Party crisis of 1921. Esser was one of the drifting and unstable postwar characters who were beginning to coalesce around Hitler and his movement. The son of a railroad official, Esser started out as a left-wing radical who advocated hanging the bourgeoisie, and he worked on a Social Democrat newspaper at the outset of his career. The *Räte* period, however, repelled him and, like many another radical, he swung over to the opposite camp and became a ravening reactionary and anti-Semite. He met Hitler through Ernst Roehm, and soon displayed a yellow-journal flair for propaganda, written and spoken. He, too, subscribed to the "big lie" theory, and demonstrated in his own newspaper articles that if only the distortion was huge enough, some of it was certain to stick. He once threatened, in the *Völkischer Beobachter,* that if the government did not act as the National Socialists demanded, the Hitlerites would send portable gallows to work up and down the streets of Munich.

He was considered the best Party orator after Hitler himself. He sometimes "warmed up" audiences as a preliminary speaker to Hitler, and it was after a particularly successful session of mass hysteria that Esser bestowed the title of *Führer* on Hitler. He gave the epithet a certain personal warmth by making it initially *"unser Führer"*—"our Leader"—a valuable touch that endured. Hitler privately despised Esser, as he did most of his early associates, and said of him: "I know he's a scoundrel, but I must use him until I find somebody better."

It was also about this time that the word "Nazi" came into use. The word derives from the first two syllables of *National,* as pronounced in German, and thus served as a handy abbreviation for the Party's name, *Nationalsozialistische Deutsche Arbeiter Partei* (NSDAP.) By coincidence, the syllables had a familiar ring to Bavarians, since "Nazi" and "Nazl" were traditional diminutives for Ignatz, a given name common in those parts. Acquiring a nickname was a sign that the NSDAP had impressed itself on the man in the street as an element of everyday life in Munich. With Hitler's increasing aggressiveness as a mob orator, the impression could hardly be avoided. He had burst out of the beer halls, and was staging overflow meetings in the city's largest public arena, the Krone Circus, which could hold 8,000 people. Though the power he exerted was a function of personality, and could only be explained by the ill-defined and cloudy word *charisma*—a word coined at this time by the German sociologist Max Weber—Hitler himself was an extremely shrewd analyst of its effect. He understood the mass hysteria he was capable of creating, and its usefulness to him. "If I come to a mass audience with carefully weighed concepts, it won't understand me. But when I stir up corresponding emotions in the audience, then it follows the simple slogans that I gave it. In a mass assembly, thinking is eliminated." Thus he deliberately became one of the *terribles simplificateurs,* the "terrible simplifiers," of whom the historian Jakob Burckhardt had warned a half century before.

As a speaker, Hitler never tried to prove his assertions; he used statements as triggers for emotion. Changing the wrestling-match image, he thought of an audience as a woman who was to be first emotionally aroused and then seduced and made to yield. "The last eight to ten minutes of a speech," said Ernst Hanfstaengl, "resembled an orgasm of words." But if the means were emotional, the ends were always political. The mass meetings were designed to make the individual "from his little workshop or big factory where he feels very small" (as Hitler put it) believe that he amounted to something, after all, that he had a spiritual home. "By the magic influence of what we call 'mass suggestion,'" Hitler said, the little man absorbed strength and confidence from the thousands with whom he shared his experience. "The National Socialist movement must never forget this," he said, and it never did.

The epithets "King of Munich" and "His Majesty Adolf I" were inspired not only by Hitler's increasing prominence as a public figure but also by his acquisition of an inner circle of henchmen, over which he presided with sovereign authority. The court assembled nightly in the cafés, restaurants and beer parlors of Munich. The Bratwurstglöckl, behind the Church of Our Lady in the center of town, was a favorite spot, and there the host was an S.A. man. Another regular gathering place was the Café Osteria Bavaria, near the *Beobachter* office and not far from that of *Simplicissimus,* which was beginning to print satirical sketches of Hitler, another sign of his breakthrough into public attention. A particular favorite was the Café Heck in the Galerie Strasse. Here Hitler had a reserved table, a *Stammtisch,* in a dimly lit corner of the long, narrow room where he could sit with no one behind him and see everyone who entered and all that was going on. He could not bear solitude, and his court served him as audience, sounding board and distraction until he was forced to retire alone to his dreary room in the Thiersch Strasse. Amid the famous *Gemütlichkeit* of the Munich cafés and restaurants, in this atmosphere of ease and congeniality, Adolf Hitler was able to mature the plans by which he meant to foment a revolution.

His court consisted of seething antisocial characters like himself—"a collection of little Hitlers," in the sardonic phrase of one who knew the circle well. They were Bohemians of the Right, failed citizens and, often, frustrated intellectuals who mistook a private sense of grievance and a smoldering resentment against society for revolutionary passion. They were Hitler's "true believers," the born followers who, in Eric Hoffer's analysis, transmute their self-contempt into flaming hatred of others. They were Nietzsche's *Zu-kurz-Gekommene,* the ones short-changed from birth, who take it out on the world in anti-Semitic fulminations and tantrums of destruction. But they saw themselves differently. In the words of one of them, they were "a tiny group of determined men against a world full of stupidity and evil." Or, again, they were "men who, in a dark time, shake the world with their fanaticism." They found their place in the Hitler movement, and Hitler's political genius would one day elevate them into a modern phenomenon: the punk as history-maker, the thug as politician.

There was Alfred Rosenberg, who, like Hitler himself, was an outsider, a non-native of dubious background. Like Hitler, he did not like to have his ancestry discussed. He was a German Balt, born in Estonia, who drifted into Munich after the World War. He was a student of architecture, which made something of a bond between him and Hitler when they were introduced by Dietrich Eckart. Rosenberg brought the "Protocols of the Elders of Zion" with him from anti-Semitic circles in the Baltic, and these, too, impressed Adolf Hitler, who subsequently mentioned them with approval in *Mein Kampf.* Another frustrated artist, Rosenberg had experienced the bitterness of having his paintings rejected and the humiliation of standing in line for a handout of cabbage soup at a Munich charity kitchen. Sallow, slovenly and

294

"cold as the tip of a dog's nose," he was unanimously unloved, if not despised, by the more robust Party specimens, some of whom suspected him of Jewish blood (a favorite intramural sneer among members of the inner circle). Rosenberg had read the classics, like Goethe and Tolstoi, and wrote in a turgid style that impressed Hitler as scholarly. He made Rosenberg editor of the *Völkischer Beobachter* and later elevated him to the post of chief philosopher and theoretician of the Nazi Party. For his part, Rosenberg at first found something "volcanic, explosive, unbalanced" in Hitler, and had misgivings about his receding forehead. But in the end he became a faithful henchman of his *Führer* without whom he might never have risen above the anonymity of the soup kitchen.*

Rudolf Hess needed no handouts, being the son of a prosperous exporter whose base was Alexandria, Egypt, where Rudolf was born. He had served as an officer in the same regiment where Hitler was a dispatch runner, but they never met in the field. In civilian life the relationship of officer to private was reversed; Hess became the underling and took orders. He had gone through the usual stages of indoctrination for a right-radical activist, having worked in the underground for the Thule Society and fought as a Free Corps volunteer in the White assault on Munich. He was a formidable street fighter, in spite of a ponderous and pedantic manner and in spite of his intra-Party nickname of *Fräulein* Hess, which he earned through his doglike and undisguised devotion to Hitler.

Among those of the inner circle, Hess had the most solid and respectable background. He had attended good schools. He studied at the University of Munich, specializing in geopolitics under the famous Professor Karl Haushofer. He wrote poetry. He composed an essay, which won a prize, on "What Must the Man Be Like Who Will Lead Germany Back to the Heights?" (It was, of course, a word portrait of Adolf Hitler.) There was

* When he came to power, Hitler appointed Rosenberg his Minister for the Occupied Eastern Territories, where his policies of slave labor and mass exterminations resulted in Rosenberg's death by hanging at the Allied War Crimes Tribunal in Nuremberg.

something introverted and morose in his appearance, in the darkly beetling brows, the deep-set eyes, and the massive jaws. But what some called his reserve and introversion others called heaviness and stupidity. His brutality and bovine fanaticism appealed to Hitler, who, in time, made him Deputy *Führer* and thus one of the most important men in the Third Reich. Ultimately his eminence in the Party led to a life sentence in the Spandau Military Prison in Berlin. He was an ardent believer in astrology, but his horoscope failed to show what was in store for him when he first took his place as the most devoted and unwavering member of the King of Munich's court in 1920.

Hitler himself took to carrying a heavy dog whip as a scepter, a symbol of authority. It dangled from a loop around his wrist, and was made of hippopotamus hide, or, some said, rhinocerous. The whip betrayed an impulse in him that was always close to the surface—the impulse to lash out, to exert power, to demonstrate what he meant by his favorite words, "ruthless" and "brutal." He was usually dressed in the trench coat Dietrich Eckart had bought for him, and topped it with a slouch hat. The ensemble—the trench coat, the hat, the whip—should have given a swaggering, dashing impression, as it was no doubt intended to do. But the effect did not come off. There was always a certain awkwardness about him, as if he hadn't been put together right, and an air of what in his native land was called *Schlamperei*, an Austrian sloppiness. His figure was bad. The torso was too long and the legs too short. He had no grace of movement and no physical style. As long as he was able, he avoided having his picture taken for the press. There was always an S.A. man ready to smash a camera, if necessary.

Dog whip or no, Hitler walked the streets of Munich with a certain wariness, half convinced that an assassin was ready to spring at him from every doorway. Everywhere he went he was accompanied by his bodyguard, a young butcher named Ulrich Graf, who seldom left his side in public. Graf was a redoubtable beer-hall brawler, and organized the first squad of three or four men selected to protect Hitler during his speeches. Ulrich Graf was sometimes called "the first S.A. man," a distinction also bestowed on another member of the court, Emil Maurice. Maurice was dark and of French descent and was suspected, in the usual inner circle back-biting, of having Jewish blood. He was an ex-convict, and his taste for savagery in a *Saalschlacht* endeared him to Hitler, who made him his personal chauffeur.

Of a similar stripe was Christian Weber, a part-time horse dealer and nighttime bouncer in some of the more questionable dives of Munich, where he was suspected of pimping on the side. He was a bulky, brawny creature—"apelike," in one description —who joined the Party early and became another favorite of Hitler's. Physical violence was always an attraction for the *Führer,* and he was ready with admiration for anyone who could inflict it and endure it. The more men of the Graf-Maurice-Weber type he could gather around him, the surer he felt of himself and of the survival of his Party. And he was attracting more of them all the time, enough to risk a Storm Troop foray outside Munich.

For a *völkisch* "German Day" observance in the town of Coburg, he hired a special train and led 800 of his S.A. men through the streets in defiance of an order by the local authorities that such a display of uniformed men was not to be permitted. The S.A. men marched anyway, with swastikas flying and a forty-two-piece band playing. Coburg was a stronghold of independent Socialists and Communists, and the Storm Troop parade was an outright provocation to the populace. It was, in fact, a calculated gesture on Hitler's part to show that he could now march anywhere in Bavaria he chose to. His column was attacked with hurled bricks and cobblestones, and the S.A. fought back with knives, rubber truncheons, and alpenstocks wielded by Nazi roughnecks in leather shorts and knee stockings. The Storm Troopers prevailed, the town and its officials were cowed.

Almost the whole of Hitler's court was on the scene and shared in the triumph—Ludecke, Eckart, Rosenberg, Graf, Weber, Esser. The Coburg affair was like a frontier raid, like something out of Karl May with Hitler in the role of Old Shatterhand, but it came to be called "one of the most important milestones in Nazi history." Kurt Ludecke wrote of it: "For the first time, the authorities were openly defied; and for the first time outside Munich the Nazis carried their fight into the streets."

The morale of the S.A. was further stimulated at this time by the acquisition of a new member whose presence exhilarated everyone from Hitler down to the newest recruit. His name was Hermann Goering.

Goering had been the last commander of the Richthofen Squadron, the "Flying Circus", famous on both sides of the lines for its skill and elan. As a successor to Manfred von Richthofen, the fabled "Red Baron," young Capt. Goering became a national celebrity over night. He had already earned the title of hero by winning the highest of all German decorations, the *Pour le Mérite*. He was several times an ace with twenty-two kills to his credit.

Despising the Republic and contemptuous of civilian life, he became a barnstorming stunt pilot in Scandinavia after the Armistice. One of Sweden's early airlines hired him as a pilot, and there he met and fell in love with the Baroness Karin von Kantzow. She was tall, willowy, and five years older than he.

The Baroness responded to his courting. Flyers were glamorous, and Capt. Goering was not only a pilot but a war hero. There was a difficulty, however—she was married. He felt he should be able to offer her something more substantial than a stunt flyer's life before asking her to leave her husband to come away to Germany with him. He gave up flying and enrolled at the University of Munich to study political science and history. But he was temperamentally unsuited to the classroom, and the current political tumult in Munich attracted him far more than any lecture.

It was not, he said afterwards, the oratory of Adolf Hitler that won him over to National Socialism. It was the dynamism he sensed in the Party's program. "I knew the overthrow of the Republic would be done by dissatisfied men, veterans, who didn't like a peace where there were no jobs, no food, no shoes. So I looked over the parties to see which one showed promise. I decided to join the National Socialist Party. It was small—that

meant I could soon be a big man in it. It appealed to the unhappy veterans—that meant it would have the manpower for a
Putsch . . ." He saw in the Party's attacks on Versailles and in
its anti-Semitism a powerful emotional element that would win
followers of all political persuasions. After hearing Hitler speak
once or twice, Goering went to Party headquarters for an interview. He was received by the *Führer* with open arms. ("A war
ace with the *Pour le Mérite!*" Hitler afterwards rejoiced to Ludecke. "Imagine it! Excellent propaganda!")

Goering was not mistaken in thinking that he would soon
be a big man in the Party. Within a few months he was put in
command of the Storm Troops. Though a native Bavarian,
Goering had been hardened as a cadet by the harshest Prussian
infantry training, and he began to put the Storm Troops through
the same kind of merciless parade-ground discipline. He raised
the S.A. to a new level of efficiency and gave it more military
gloss than it had known before.

One of Goering's innovations was to organize an elite corps
called the *Stabswache,* the Staff Watch. The men were distinguished from the ordinary Storm Troopers by black ski caps
with a death's head insignia. The swastika on the brassards they
wore were also rimmed in black. The *Stabswache* then developed into the *Stosstrupp Hitler,* the Hitler Shock Troop, a combination of commando unit and palace guard. From these formations the most dreaded elements in the Nazi terror apparatus
evolved: the S.S., the Elite Guard uniformed in black, and its
combat arm, the *Waffen-SS.*

Hermann Goering's energy and exuberance introduced a
new note into the Hitler court. He added a cosmopolitan touch
to the entourage that Putzi Hanfstaengl, for one, welcomed.
Goering shared Hanfstaengl's barely disguised contempt for the
provincial clods who made up most of Hitler's retinue. Goering
had something of the world beyond Bavaria about him, a style
acquired in casinos where pilots drank more vintage wine than
beer, and in foreign capitals like Stockholm and Copenhagen
where he had been feted and admired. "An attractive, rollicking
fellow," Putzi called him. But others had another description for

him. They called him "a brutal egoist who didn't give a damn about Germany, as long as he could amount to something." The world came to know how much of the brute there was in rollicking Hermann Goering.*

In November of 1922, not long after the Coburg episode, the American Embassy in Berlin sent an observer to Munich "to assess the developing strength of the National Socialist movement." Foreign diplomats saw no special significance in what was going on in Bavaria, and Hitler himself was, in the words of one of them, regarded as "an uneducated madman." But United States Ambassador Alanson B. Houghton was curious. He wanted to know more, and dispatched his Assistant Military Attaché, Captain Truman Smith, to Munich. Young Captain Smith was impressed.

At first he thought Hitler "a pure and simple adventurer," but before he was through he was calling him "a marvelous demagogue." Captain Smith interviewed him at length, noting that the eyes, "gleaming with fanaticism, intense and unceasing," were all that saved the Leader from looking commonplace. Several sources assured Captain Smith that Hitler was not really as radical as his speeches made him out to be (an error of judgment that would be repeated many times during Hitler's career), and Captain Smith did not think Hitler was big enough to take the lead in a German national movement. But he saw, and sensed, enough to give him pause.

A march-past of Storm Troops was staged for him, and he was bowled over. The S.A. lined up in Cornelius Strasse, in a poor section of town where the new, and larger, headquarters of the Party was located. The American officer watched them pass in review before Hitler, and noted that they were armed with pis-

---

* Goering became the No. 2 man in the Third Reich. He organized the secret police system, established the first concentration camps, and as economic dictator launched the slave labor program. His Air Force, the *Luftwaffe*, introduced the indiscriminate bombing of cities—Warsaw, Rotterdam, London, Coventry—as a routine practice of war. "He was the leading war aggressor," said the verdict pronounced on him by the Nuremberg Tribunal. He committed suicide by taking poison before he could be hanged.

tols and clubs. "Twelve hundred of the toughest roughnecks I have ever seen in my life," Captain Smith reported. "A remarkable sight indeed." He noted that the Party was buying trucks to transport the Troopers from city to city, and "such purchases cannot be carried out today without considerable capital." He heard that the money was coming from certain unnamed industrialists.

"Critics and scoffers," he noted, were dismissing Hitler's doctrine as "bunkum," which the German people would certainly reject once the economy was stabilized. Captain Smith thought the scoffers were being too optimistic, and, in an acutely perceptive summary of the German situation at the end of 1922, he wrote:

"The material and moral chaos has been too great in Germany since the war for sober thought to be sure of victory, and we must not underestimate how deeply the racialist program and the Hitler imagery have bitten into the consciousness of the shopkeeper and mechanic. . . .

"In the past three years in particular, reason and reality have faded further and further. New and fantastic dreams have arisen, in which constantly figure Barbarossa and his two-edged sword awakening from his rock-bound sleep to put to flight the enemies of Germany. . . ."

It was sagacious to detect this strain of Teutonic mysticism in the passions of the extreme Right, and to stress that, even at that early date, the aim of the Hitler movement was "control of the Reich, not just Bavaria." The report to the Berlin Embassy was forwarded to Washington, where, like the earlier warnings of Robert Murphy, it was filed and forgotten. The next time Captain Truman Smith, U.S.A., saw Adolf Hitler was in 1935, when some of the "fantastic dreams," and many of his predictions, had come true. Hitler, as Chancellor of the Third Reich, was addressing an audience of 70,000 at a Nuremberg "Party Day" rally . . .

The report of 1922, for all its accurate, long-range analysis, had not failed to note a more immediate issue that was working for Hitler and his movement. It was a development that was shaking the Republic like no other since the end of the war. The catastrophic decline of the mark was turning Germany into an economic madhouse and reducing the morale of the people to depths of despair unplumbed even in the worst days of the war. Wars, after all, were in the nature of things, and to be expected. What was happening now was both unnatural and unprecedented. The correspondent Ernest M. Hemingway, in one of his dispatches, noted the "dogged sullenness" and "hysterical desperation" of the Germans as they watched "the plunge to worthlessness of their currency."

But for Adolf Hitler the debacle of the mark was not a disaster. It was an opportunity.

13 ONE EGG:
80 BILLION MARKS

". . . SOMETHING STUPENDOUS TOOK PLACE. THE INDESTRUCTI-
BLE FAITH IN MONEY WAS SHAKEN AND DESTROYED."

—GEORGE GROSZ

On the day the Armistice was signed in the forest of Com-
piègne, November 11, 1918, the German mark stood at 7.45 to
the dollar.

Five years later, in November of 1923, the German mark
stood at 4,210,500,000,000 to the dollar—four trillion, two
hundred and ten billion, five hundred million.

Long before it was over it ceased to be economics and
passed into the realm of phantasmagoria. The explanations for
what was happening never caught up with what actually did happen, and a nightmarish unreality pervaded the most taken-for-
granted transactions of everyday living. No currency in history
had ever depreciated like the German mark, and the toboggan
slide of its descent was a disaster that turned into the wildest ab-
surdity without becoming any less disastrous. Strings of ciphers
that had hitherto applied only to astronomical distances now applied to pocket money; the number of marks needed to buy a newspaper reached figures that only the mind of a trained mathematic-
ian could hope to comprehend. The government, through its National Bank, kept 300 paper mills and 2,000 printing presses
working day and night turning out paper money that, when it
reached the consumer, was literally worth less than the paper it
was printed on. An egg that cost twenty-five pfennigs in 1918

came to 80,000,000,000 (billion) marks in 1923, and what was once a seventeen-pfennig glass of beer was priced at 150 billion marks. Based on the value of the prewar mark, a 1923 postage stamp would have cost $11,900,000,000 in American money.

The German inflation was an economic convulsion that unhinged itself from economics and drifted into sheer delirium, taking the German people with it.

It began during the war. In England the war effort was financed largely by increased taxation, but in Germany no comparable measures were taken to limit individual incomes and reduce the flow of currency. Mounting expenditures were met by printing and circulating more and more bank notes. The process accelerated after the war. By the summer of 1919 the mark stood at 15.51 to the dollar; by the fall it was 24.74; by the end of the year 35.45. Two years after the Armistice it was 87.75.

The disruptions of revolution and civil disorder, added to the enormous burden of reparations, gave the economy no chance to recover from the shocks of war. The depletion of gold reserves, the flight of private capital abroad to avoid attachment as reparations, the widening gap between revenue and expenditures, all contributed to the malfunctioning of the economy and fed the financial chaos. Then the assassination of Walther Rathenau undermined whatever confidence there was abroad in Germany's prospects for a viable future. At the time of Rathenau's death, in June of 1922, the mark stood at 272 to the dollar. A week later it was 401. In ten more days it was 527. At the end of the year it was 6,750.

For many Germans the surest sign that a cataclysm was upon them, and not merely an economic disturbance, came with the deterioration of the thousand-mark note. This bill, brown and elegantly etched, was the largest in circulation, and therefore looked upon with a respect verging on reverence. It seemed nothing short of sacrilegious when this magnificent piece of currency declined to the point where it barely sufficed for tram fare.

"With the belief in this venerated symbol of wealth and security," said Fritz Schoenberner, the editor of *Simplicissimus* who saw it happen, "the whole moral world order of the little bour-

geois had broken down." More was crumbling in Germany than
the value of the mark.

On January 11, 1923, the German economy was again severely shaken when French and Belgian troops occupied the
Ruhr, creating not only an industrial crisis but emotional and
political turmoil as well. The occupation was set off by the failure of Germany to deliver 135,000 telegraph poles and a quantity of coal to France on the date required in the reparations
agreement. *Le Boche payera*—the Boche must pay—was the attitude of the French, who tolerated no recalcitrance from the
Germans. They were glad of an excuse to move in and take over
an area that had produced so many of the guns and shells that
almost brought France to her knees. The occupiers were met by
crowds singing the *Wacht am Rhein*, by acts of resistance, and by
expressions of hatred that were like a renewed declaration of
war. The French turned their machine guns on crowds of demonstrating workmen. In Essen, at the Krupp factory, thirteen
were killed and thirty wounded. Five hundred thousand Germans turned out for the funerals, and the whole nation was in
mourning.

Encouraged by the Berlin government, the workers of the
Ruhr organized a "passive resistance." No German moved a
hand to turn a factory wheel, lift a shovel in the coal mines, or
pull the throttle of a locomotive. The most productive and effi-
cient industrial complex in Europe was paralyzed.

In the end, passive resistance caused the French more difficulties than the occupation was worth, but it also seriously damaged the already wavering German Republic. The government
was forced to pour financial support into the Ruhr for the
hundreds of thousands whom resistance had put out of work,
and the only way to meet this enormous new obligation was to
print more money.

At the bar of the swank Hotel Adlon in Berlin a patron,
who had been abroad for some time, ordered a glass of beer and
asked how much it cost these days.

"Three-fifty," said the waiter.

The patron got some idea of the progress of the inflation since he was last in Germany when he learned that "three-fifty" meant not three marks, fifty pfennig but 3,500,000 marks.

In the Adlon dining room, the menus had to be drastically altered with every meal—not the dishes, but the prices. The cost of a full dinner one evening would barely pay for a cup of coffee at breakfast.

Nothing seemed able to stop the avalanche. Not even a strike by the men who printed the money held it up for long. They resumed feeding the paper into the presses, paper that was hardly more negotiable when it came out as money than when it went in blank.

The number of marks required to buy anything became so enormous that people carried their money in knapsacks when they went shopping, and then in wheelbarrows. An industrial worker had to haul six weeks' pay to the store to buy a pair of shoes, and twenty weeks' pay for a suit of clothes. A woman who took a basketful of marks to the butcher shop turned her back on it as she stood in the queue, and when she looked around again the marks had been dumped on the pavement but the basket had been stolen.

Every passing minute meant an increase in price. The cost of a chicken, or a rabbit, or a chop, would mount by several million marks in the time it took to walk from home to the store. Shoppers needed bigger bags to take their money to the store than to carry their purchases away from it. A student might set out for his university with a check to cover his board and tuition for the coming semester. When he arrived, the check wouldn't buy a book. In some banks the money was not counted out; it was weighed on a scale, and handed over with a rubber band around it, like a packet of handbills.

The factories began paying three times a week, because the value of the wage diminished so drastically from Monday to Saturday. On paydays, the wives, mothers and sweethearts of the workers waited outside the factory gates. As soon as the men were paid, they rushed out and gave the money to their women-folk, who hurried off to the nearest store to buy something, anything, before the money's value went down further. The store-keeper then continued the panic by trying to pass along *his* money for something concrete before it evaporated in his cash box. It reached the point where teachers, who were usually paid monthly, received their salaries weekly, then daily, and finally twice daily. Everybody was desperate to get rid of today's money —"as if it were poisonous or on fire"—before tomorrow at one o'clock, when the new figures on the relative standing of the dollar came in from the New York Stock Exchange. But no device or stratagem could keep up with the decline of the mark.

Factories, firms and assorted enterprises began printing their own *Notgeld,* emergency money backed by whatever they were producing—shoes, sugar, coal, potatoes. Almost every part of the country had its own currency, and at one time there was an estimated 172 kinds of money circulating, including railroad marks and vegetable marks. In some sections the monetary system broke down so completely that people reverted to barter, as their ancestors had done before any organized society was established. Professional people, finding it impossible to support themselves with incomes eroded by the inflation, took menial jobs wherever they could find them. Lawyers became messenger boys. Professors drove cabs. Teachers waited on tables. Something called the "academic proletariat" sprang up.

The price of vice mounted with the price of everything else. On the Kurfürstendamm the whores were asking six billion marks and a cigarette for the mistress-slave perversion ("Come along, dearie. A bargain!"). The song that swept the country was a piece of musical idiocy imported, like jazz and the shimmy, from America—*"Yes! We Have No Bananas"* or, in German, *"Ausgerechnet Bananen."*

Foreigners, or those who had access to foreign exchange, could accumulate staggering sums of German money for very little of their own and consequently live like royalty on comparatively meager resources. Common soldiers could hire housemaids. "This miracle of exchange makes a swinish spectacle," Ernest Hemingway wrote, describing how the French youth of Strasbourg crossed a bridge and "ate themselves sick" in the

German pastry shops for trifling sums of francs. In another dispatch Hemingway reported spending four days at a resort hotel in a party of four. The bill, including tips, came to twenty cents a day apiece.

A whole caste of "inflation profiteers" sprang up. People driven to the wall by the economic collapse put up their property for a stated price at a time when the mark still had some value. By the time legal formalities were completed and the sale consummated, the worth of the mark had deteriorated to the point where the purchaser acquired, say, a $50,000 apartment house for the equivalent of $20. Men with larger resources and unlimited credit took advantage of these conditions to accumulate huge holdings at virtually no cost to themselves. A financier or industrialist would arrange to buy a factory for ten million marks on a six-month basis. When the six months elapsed, and it was time to pay, ten million marks bought no more than a bus ride; a factory changed hands for the price of a bus ticket. Mortgages could be paid off, bonds retired in worthless money, large debts wiped from the books with the transfer of astronomical sums representing a pittance in real worth. By unlimited and unscrupulous variations of these procedures, a financier named Hugo Stinnes became one of the richest men on earth, acquiring coal mines, steel mills, real estate, newspapers and factories until he controlled nearly a sixth of all German industry.

Swarms of lesser manipulators flourished, and the theaters and nightclubs were filled with newly-rich who were given a generic name: *Raffkes*. A Raffke was anyone who overnight had "money like hay" or of whom it was said "he stinks of money." Mocking jokes by the dozens circulated about them—

Frau Raffke: "Our house is full of Titians."

Herr Neureich (Mr. Newrich): "Why don't you call an exterminator?"

—but there was bitterness and hatred when the thousands ruined by inflation saw the manipulators, the *Schieber,* parading in finery and crowding the restaurants.

Hardest hit were the provident, the ones who had lived according to the rules. Those who had prudently put away something for the future found that all their years of thrift had been futile. The savings of the middle class were wiped out, erased like chalk marks from a blackboard. Pensions, the support of retirement and age, melted away to nothing. War bonds, patriotically purchased and stored away for the future, turned out to be worthless, and the shock of the government's betrayal of trust was for some as painful as the monetary loss.

A typical breakfast consisted of turnip coffee, mildewed bread and synthetic honey, and some had less. "We were always hungry," George Grosz remembered, and he was not as badly off as many others. Crowds went through the streets with signs demanding "Bread for the Proletariat!" and "Open the Coal Bins! We Are Freezing!" Trains and trucks carrying food to the famished cities were stopped and pillaged. Frequently farmers refused to sell their food at all, spurning the worthless paper that was supposed to pass for money. In Hanover the novelist Vicki Baum saw mobs storm the grocery stores and butcher shops, while her own larder consisted of one last crust of bread that she divided between her two small children.

As hunger and poverty made deeper and deeper inroads into the ranks of the middle class, the old dread of sinking into the proletariat intensified. The possible loss of status was an appalling thing in a caste-ridden society, and hostility grew against the social system that had brought such a thing about. Few stopped to sort out the causes of the inflation and trace its roots to the war that imperial Germany had entered into. What was obvious to millions was that under the Kaiser the nation had been prosperous, confident and respected; now, under the Republic, everything that had once been stable was falling apart. Whatever faith there was in democracy, moderation and the liberal promise of Weimar was severly damaged, and millions became more receptive to extremist propaganda than ever before. The Communists made gains among the workers, but the far Left continued to be largely repellent to the Middle, whose sense of status survived even the degradations inflicted upon it by the inflation. The extreme Right benefited the most. What agitators like Adolf

Hitler had been saying all along seemed to be clearly substantiated by events.

Robert Murphy would write: "Inflation, in my opinion, did more than any other factor to make Hitlerism possible."

As the value of the mark went down, the membership of the National Socialist Party went up. Munich was especially hard hit because of its large population of white-collar workers, retired persons living on pensions, storekeepers and caterers to the tourist trade. A mood of desperation pervaded the city. There were hundreds of suicides. Even the children of Thomas Mann, who was well established as one of Germany's foremost authors, often were hungry, and went barefoot because no shoes were available. Monika Mann has recorded how she and her brothers and sister "quarreled like sea gulls" over an extra piece of bread, and only escaped outright malnutrition through the resourceful foraging of their mother, who was not above dealing in the black market to feed her children. Others were driven to crime and despair. At the Platzl the comedian Weiss Ferdl was singing a new song in Bavarian dialect, voicing the lament of the market women about skyrocketing prices and featuring the refrain:

> *A so kann's nimma weita gehn* . . .
> "It can't go on like this."

This was also the theme of Adolf Hitler's propaganda. He pictured the country as "on the brink of a hellish abyss" and called for a dictatorship as the only way to stave off national collapse. He alternately wept with the people in their misery and chided them for accepting it so passively. "The people are a lot of children. You can only press million-mark notes into the hands of a childish public!" But the note he struck most often was one of apocalypse, of imminent and utter disaster: "A great desolation and bitterness has seized our whole German people. One sees no light anywhere. The end appears to have come . . ." Now, he said, the great polarity had taken place, the ultimate either-or: Swastika or Star of David. Another enemy was symbolized by another star, the Red Star of Marxism, but that also was Jewish. He left no doubt about who the enemy was.

Where, and to whom, could Germany look for salvation in the hour of utmost need? "Already, millions feel that redemption is to be found in our movement. That has already become almost a new religious belief!"

Christian, nationalist Bavaria would fulfill its predestined mission of redeeming Jewish, Marxist Berlin. The saying of a Munich official went from mouth to mouth: "The behind of a Frenchman is preferable to the face of a Prussian." When Friedrich Ebert, the President of the Republic, came to Munich on an official visit, he had to be isolated from the public as much as possible to spare him the insults of hooting mobs and possible harm. Chancellor Joseph Wirth was warned by his advisers not to stop off at Munich when passing through on the train. It became almost suicidal for an official from Berlin to appear in Munich, but when Field Marshal von Hindenburg visited the Bavarian capital, he was greeted with cheers and ovations by great crowds. And when the body of Ludwig III, the last Wittelsbach monarch, was brought back from Hungarian exile for burial, the whole city turned out to mourn. Nobody had offered to defend him when Revolution came, but now there was a serious movement to restore the monarchy by putting his son, the Crown Prince Rupprecht, on the throne.

As the Republic reeled under the successive blows of the inflation, the Ruhr occupation and the growing division between Berlin and Bavaria, Adolf Hitler began to sniff the air and hold up a moistened finger in the wind. He was beginning to weigh possibilities, and wonder whether the time was ripening sooner than he had expected. As early as April of 1920, in a speech in the Hofbräuhaus, he had vaguely threatened a *Putsch* if conditions in Germany did not change—"and even another revolution if necessary." Then it was part of the inflammatory talk he used to charge up his listeners and make them forget for the moment that they were only an insignificant group. Now that the Party had grown spectacularly, in membership, backing and

confidence, and the strength of the government seemed less and
less formidable, Hitler again threatened imminent revolution, and
the words took on an ominous ring of probability that they did
not have before.

"*Jawohl!*" he was saying. "The November Republic is in
danger!" He could hear the sound of creaking, as in the beams
of a building about to collapse. "Today this never very proud
structure is beginning to totter," he announced. The very name
of the Republic, he said, was becoming a hated thing, and a
cause for shame, among wider and wider sections of the public.
As the inflation continued to rage unabated, he suggested that
people save their final fistful of plummeting marks to buy rope to
hang 10,000 of the men who had betrayed them.

In August of 1922 Hitler gave his support to preparations
for a *Putsch* organized by a Dr. Otto Pittinger, a public health
official who headed one of the anti-Weimar "Fatherland
Leagues." Pittinger's idea was to seize the government and
bring Gustav von Kahr back into power as dictator of Bavaria.
Through blundering organization and internal disunity, the attempt came to nothing. Its failure created a lasting contempt in
Hitler for the leadership of the Bavarian rightists. "No more Pit-
tingers, no more Fatherland societies," he said to Ludecke.
"From now on I go my way alone." The conviction was growing
in him that he was far better qualified to lead a revolt than any
of his rivals. "If nobody else dares to bring it off, I'll do it myself," he told Ludecke.

But at the end of 1922 his Party, in spite of its phenomenal
rise, was little known outside of Bavaria. Its estimated membership in Munich was, according to police reports, 10,000. There
was a scattering of branches, and small clusters of followers,
here and there in the Reich, but National Socialism was still far
from being a national movement. Crisis or no, how could Hitler
and his Party hope to make a significant impact on the nation,
let alone dream of taking over the government?

"We don't believe in majorities," Hitler was telling his followers at this time. "We believe in the energy of the minority." He
reminded them that the "Jewish revolution" of 1918 had been

made by a handful of agitators, and advocated what he called the *Stosstrupp,* or shock troop, method of jolting the broad majority out of its lethargy. In many variations he repeated something he had said at Coburg: "For as long as the world has stood, history has been made by minorities."

He was not, yet, ready to put his *Stosstrupp* theory to the test, but events outside Germany confirmed him in his conviction that it was possible for a minority to deal fatal blows to an established system. On October twenty-eighth Benito Mussolini staged his march on Rome, and began the Fascist era in Italy. In November Mustafa Kemal overthrew the Sultan of Turkey and drove him into exile.

The triumph of the *Fascisti* in Italy was immensely encouraging to the Nazis. The Fascists also had a charismatic leader, an ex-corporal with a gift for oratory and propaganda. Mussolini's country, too, found itself in economic distress, and his appeal was to the masses, to those oppressed by inadequate wages and intolerable living conditions. To them Mussolini had become *Il Duce,* which was Italian for *Führer.*

He also used incendiary oratory, propaganda, parades and violence in assaulting the established order, and his aim was a monolithic state with an absolute dictator, himself, at its head. He, too, had Storm Troopers—squads of young men in black shirts, many of them veterans, who rampaged through the industrial cities of Italy, beating down all opposition and conducting guerrilla warfare against Communists and Socialists with fists, clubs and bombs. As the disorder grew and the Fascist movement spread, it was backed by the Army and by industrialists eager to support a Strong Man who promised to suppress radicals and restore order and stability.

The parallels were many, and the Nazis savored them all. A few days after Mussolini's "March on Rome," Hermann Esser, the man who had bestowed the title of *Führer* on Hitler, said in a speech: "What a band of courageous men was able to do in Italy, that we can do in Bavaria also. We, too, have Italy's Mussolini. His name is Adolf Hitler."

What happened in Turkey was a further encouragement.

Mustafa Kemal Pasha (like Hitler, the son of a customs' officer) proclaimed the abolition of the sultanate and made himself the most powerful man in Turkey from his base in Ankara, where he had set up a rival government to the one in the capital, Constantinople. To the National Socialists of Bavaria, this was an event charged with significance. For them it meant that a corrupt and entrenched system could be toppled from outside its capital. "Constantinople" they read as "Berlin." For "Ankara" they read "Munich."

In the mood of the times in Germany, inflation raged in more than the currency. There was an explosive inflation of rancor and resentment. For Adolf Hitler and his followers, in 1923, there was a mounting wildness in the dream of power.

14 AT THE SHRINE

"... WE ARE ON THE VERGE OF ANOTHER REVOLUTION."
—ADOLF HITLER

ERICH LUDENDORFF, brooding darkly in his walled villa at Ludwigshöhe, greeted the new year with foreboding. Nineteen hundred and twenty-three, he knew, would not turn out well. It would be what he called a *Jahwehjahr,* a Year of Yahweh. His studies in the occult told him that Jewish cabalists had long been looking forward to this particular year as favorable to their malign purposes. It was easy for someone like himself, with a knowledge of such matters, to see why.

He noted that the numerals 1 9 2 3, like those of the fateful year 1 9 1 4, added up to 15, which included within itself 10 and 5. And according to the mystical Jewish system of numerology known as *gematria,* these figures were the equivalents of the first two consonants in the name of Yahweh, the Lord God Jehovah of the Jews.

Clearly, the omens were ominous.

Newly-born *Time* magazine, surveying the German scene from 3,000 miles away, agreed. In one of its earliest issues it called Germany a country "gone sick with misery" and the most likely leader of a potential revolt was Erich Ludendorff—"a solitary phantom striding the earth with noiseless, slippery, dreadful steps." But the dreadful steps were then being taken, and far from noiselessly, by Adolf Hitler whom *Time,* and most of the rest of the world, regarded as merely the leader of the "Bavarian Fascisti", a local agitator subordinate to Erich Ludendorff.

Hitler began the year in a way calculated to let everyone know that he did not feel himself subordinate to anybody. He proclaimed the first "Reich Party Day" of the NSDAP, and set the date for January 27–29. Delegates and guests were invited to Munich from all over Germany, and an elaborate program of assemblies and observances was announced, including twelve mass meetings and a march and ceremony of Storm Troops in the open. In view of the tenseness of the political situation in Munich, the authorities declared a State of Emergency, forbade the Storm Troop demonstration, and restricted other phases of the Nazi observance which, it was feared, might lead to disturbances and disorder.

It would have been a serious, if not crippling, blow for Hitler to cancel or curtail his first "Party Day" program after announcing it with fanfares to the faithful. Instead, he responded with a warning to the authorities that he intended to hold his Storm Troop ceremony regardless of any prohibition. If the police were ordered to shoot to stop it, he, himself, would take the first bullet. For the blood bath that would certainly follow, the authorities would be held responsible.

"Two hours after the first shot," he warned, "the regime would be finished."

It was a measure of Hitler's influence in Munich that the highest officials of the Bavarian State backed down and let his Party Day observance proceed rather than risk a confrontation with him. On his word of honor that he did not intend to *putsch,* to take overt action against the state, the Party Day program was allowed to proceed on the basis that the twelve mass meetings be cut to six, and that the S.A. ceremony take place inside, in the Krone Circus. But Hitler staged his twelve meetings anyway, racing from one to the other by car and speaking at each. One observer, a non-Party member, was stunned by the menacing atmosphere of the assemblies with their inflammatory speeches and the continuous blare of martial music—"a strange mixture of the military and the revolutionary." The witness noted that most of the audience was comprised not of workers, as the Party name might lead one to expect, but of members of "the deteriorating middle class."

On January 28, the Storm Troop ceremony was held in the open, too, as Hitler wished it from the first. In the clear, cold winter air, some 6,000 S.A. men stood in rigid formation, a first forecast of the tens of thousands that would amaze the world in the enormous Party Day rallies at Nuremberg when the Party came to power.

His sway as "King of Munich" was not undisputed, however. When he attempted an armed foray against a May Day demonstration of leftists, he ran headlong into *Reichswehr* opposition, and was decisively blocked. The Army commander for Bavaria, General Otto Hermann von Lossow, left Hitler "almost foaming at the mouth" by ordering him to disarm his assembled troops and send them home.

The setback, though humiliating, turned out to be only temporary. With an unpredictability that his inner circle would come to recognize as a fundamental trait, he disappeared from Munich's political turmoil for several months. He went off to Berchtesgaden, to the Obersalzberg, a thousand meters high in the Bavarian Alps not far to the southeast of the city. It would be his favorite retreat when he came to power, his "Eagle's Nest," but now he lived in the same modest boarding house as Dietrich Eckart who had introduced him to the place. He assumed the name of "Herr Wolf" and, as he afterwards recounted, enjoyed listening to what people were saying around the dinner table about "that crazy monster Adolf Hitler," whom none recognized as being present.

Down below, events were steadily shaping themselves in his favor—events that he neither instigated, guided or controlled, but that were nevertheless working for him. On the evening of May Day, despite his surrender to von Lossow, he had addressed a mass meeting at the Krone Circus and spoken with his usual power. He predicted that Germany's hour of decision was coming, and coming soon. "Everything is falling away," he said, "everything is becoming decayed and rotten . . ."

It was an unconscious prose paraphrase of the poem written not very long before (in 1920) by William Butler Yeats in other circumstances—

> *Things fall apart; the centre cannot hold;*
> *Mere anarchy is loosed upon the world. . . .*

And two later lines in the same poem applied with startling aptness to the situation that was rapidly heading toward crisis in Germany—

> *The best lack all conviction, while the worst*
> *Are full of passionate intensity.*

"In this summer of 1923," says Carl Landauer, a journalist and historian who was there, "Bavaria was a witches' cauldron of conspiracy, terror and treason." On May 9th the Munich Residenz Theater presented the first performance of Bertolt Brecht's *Im Dickicht der Städte*—"In the Jungle of Cities"— which he set in Chicago. Its theme of men attacking each other with "the irrational, impersonal anger of beasts" could more appropriately have had Brecht's own city of Munich as its background. Critics would afterward recognize in the play "not really Chicago, but the abyss before Hitler."

In a series of observances called "German Days", the primitive patriotism of *Deutschland über alles* was systematically churned up in what amounted to a coordinated propaganda campaign against the Republic. More than 100,000 people poured into Nuremberg on Sept. 1st and 2nd for the largest and most emotional German Day, highlighted by a march of uniformed veterans and ex-officers, by "Fatherland" groups and assorted militants. They paraded for two hours through streets thickly bedecked with the flags of Imperial Germany and the banners of "the old army". Nothing like it, said the official police report, had been seen since the year 1914, nor like the masses of hysterically cheering spectators. Nuremberg generated the feeling among thousands that a momentum had been started, that something portentous was in the offing. "In a few weeks,"

said Adolf Hitler in his speech at Nuremberg, "the dice will roll
. . . What is in the making today will be greater than the World
War. It will be fought out on German soil for the whole
world."

The Nuremberg German Day powerfully enhanced Hitler's
stature with all elements of the dissident Right. He had been on
public display side by side with Erich Ludendorff, the center-
piece of the celebration, and the Quartermaster General took the
occasion to announce his formal support of Hitler's movement,
an invaluable endorsement. At Nuremberg, too, something
called the German Fighting Union ("*Kampfbund*") was formed,
an alliance of the National Socialists with two other para-military organizations, the Reich Flag and the Oberland League.
Hitler was chosen political leader of the new organization, which
put new resources of manpower and prestige at his disposal.
"After Nuremberg," said Gen. von Lossow later, "Hitler regarded himself as the German Mussolini, the German Gambetta.
His following dubbed him the German Messiah. For them he
was *der Berufene,* the chosen one . . ."

The National Socialists were not alone in looking for a Messiah, for some sort of Chosen One, to deliver the nation from its
multiplying ills in the Fall of 1923. All the established methods
of governing a state and maintaining its health and dignity appeared to have broken down as the country lurched from one catastrophe to the next. Now the wildest plunges of the mark were
occurring and its relation to the dollar was beginning to be reckoned in the trillions.

The feeling that the center was not holding, that things
were falling apart, was deepened when Berlin announced that
the passive resistance to the French in the Ruhr was a failure
and would end officially on Sept. 26th. Resistance, it was explained, had become unbearably costly and was not accomplishing its purpose. The men were ordered back into the mills and
mines to work under French supervision. Payment of reparations
to France and Belgium was resumed. For Germany it was yet
another humiliation, another defeat, "the second capitulation
since 1918."

The public reaction was explosive. The government was bombarded with new salvos of abuse from both Left and Right while finding few defenders and no effective ones. Crises were now occurring with such frequency that crisis seemed a permanent condition. In Bavaria an official State of Emergency was proclaimed. The administration of Minister President Eugen von Knilling, foreseeing political turbulence with which it could not cope, turned its powers over to a "State Commissioner General" with dictatorial powers. The man chosen for one-man rule in Bavaria was Gustav von Kahr who had already served as premier and resigned in the aftermath of the Erzberger assassination. A career politician, von Kahr was an unwavering monarchist, a pillar of the Bavarian Right and a champion of the Fatherland Leagues.

Squat, swarthy and with a massive head set between hunched shoulders, Dr. Gustav Ritter von Kahr gave off no sparks. But his appointment as dictator of Bavaria was a warning flare that relations with Berlin would deteriorate and that subversion of the Republic from the south would intensify. In response, Berlin proclaimed a State of Emergency throughout the country and prepared for the worst. "The position as between Bavaria and the Reich now comes to a head," the newest German Chancellor, the seventh in five years, wrote in his diary. He was Gustav Stresemann, the head of the centrist People's Party, who had taken office in an atmosphere of impending insurrection from both Right and Left. He was a man of courage and character, but he was not many weeks in office before he confided to a party caucus: "I am sick of this dog's life, with treason on every side. If the nationalists come marching into Berlin I am not going to run off to Stuttgart (as was done during the Kapp *Putsch*.) If they come, they can shoot me down right here, in the place where I have every right to sit."

What the Communists designated as "ARS"—an acute revolutionary situation—prevailed in the industrial areas of Saxony and Thuringia. In Hamburg a Red uprising was ruthlessly put down in two days of bloody street fighting. There was fighting, too, in the Rhineland where Separatists proclaimed a "Rhenish

324

Republic" independent from the rest of the Reich. The green-white-red flags of separatism flew briefly from municipal buildings in Aachen. "Rhenish troops" occupied the Town Hall of Wiesbaden and there was separatist rioting in the streets of Krefeld, Rheydt, Mühlheim and Coblenz.

The Republic did, indeed, seem to be creaking and groaning in its beams and joints, as in a building teetering on collapse. "The nation was poised for drastic change," as Kurt Ludecke saw it. "Whoever pulled the first prop from under Berlin might very well succeed, because all Germany would spring up to topple the government . . ."

Adolf Hitler appeared at a "German Day" rally in the Bavarian town of Bayreuth on September thirtieth. He gave the usual speech, followed by the customary march-past of Storm Troopers, but the journey to Bayreuth was, for him, a pilgrimage.

Ever since his *Rienzi* night in Linz ("In that hour it began") Richard Wagner had been a dominant influence in his life, and would continue to be until the end. Adolf Hitler did not eat meat, or touch hard liquor, or indulge in the "dirty habit" of smoking, because Richard Wagner's example had guided him in that direction. "With almost hysterical excitement," he had discovered not only that Wagner's music affected him profoundly but that Wagner's ideas in writing also corresponded exactly with his, Adolf Hitler's, inmost beliefs.

Now, in the fall of 1923, he sensed the imminence of Wagnerian events in which he, like another Siegfried, would play a leading role, and he turned instinctively to the shrine of the Master as if in preparation. More, he was received into the very home of the Master, entering through the high, grilled gate into the Villa Wahnfried, where he was presented to the Mistress of Bayreuth herself, to Cosima, aged eighty-six, widow of Richard.

And he met the Master's son-in-law, one of the most curious characters in the intellectual life of his time. Houston Stewart Chamberlain, born in England and schooled in France, was one of the most passionate prophets of Germany's mission to dominate the world by virtue of her god-given superiority to all the other races of the earth. He was old and paralyzed now, confined to a wheel chair and scarcely able to utter an intelligible sentence, but his influence had been great and would survive him. His chief work, a book called *Foundations of the Nineteenth Century,* set forth his theories of race and history with a turgid plausibility that had caught and convinced readers over two generations. He used the trappings of scholarship, and the ingenuity of a sometimes brilliant if always erratic mind, to argue his thesis that the Teutons are the "bearers of light" for all mankind and that "the higher development of humanity is bound up with . . . a mighty Germany spreading her sacred heritage across the earth. . . ." The corollary that other races and nations were necessarily inferior to the "Aryan" was repeatedly stated and always implied. In short, the same racist fantasies that Lanz von Liebensfeld and his kind spread through the low cafés and beer parlors were touched up and tricked out with historical references and learned footnotes by Houston Stewart Chamberlain, and achieved circulation and acceptance in exalted circles. The Kaiser himself admired Chamberlain's work, had invited him to court, and made him a correspondent and friend.

It was particularly gratifying to Germans that their nation's greatness and natural right to dominate were substantiated by an Englishman, and not just any Englishman either. Houston Stewart Chamberlain was the son of an admiral of the Royal Navy and the nephew of two generals and a field marshal of the British Army. The nervous affliction from which he suffered for years, and his repeated breakdowns, were less frequently mentioned.

Chamberlain was a model of the intellectual whom Adolf Hitler ordinarily despised—a sheltered, bookish theoretician with no experience of the world's realities, and a pitifully inadequate physical specimen to boot. But as documentarian of the Master's own racial theories he merited the greatest respect. Accordingly Hitler put himself out to impress the palsied invalid and the circle at the Villa Wahnfried, which included Wagner's son Siegfried and his wife Winifred, who was also English. Hitler was, in his own view, on holy ground. Remote from the turmoil of the Munich streets and beer halls, he was in a realm permeated by the "great, dark chords of Wagnerian ecstasy." He was seeking assurance that he was engaged in something more significant than the crudities of Bavarian politics. His curious conviction that he was somehow destined for greatness, deep-rooted as it was, needed periodic confirmation, and at the Bayreuth shrine he hoped to find it.

The reassurance was forthcoming in full measure when, on his return to Munich, he received a letter from Chamberlain. "You have mighty things to do," it said. "That Germany in the hour of her greatest need can produce a Hitler testifies to her vitality. . . . The sublime Ludendorff openly joins you and adheres to the movement: what glorious confirmation! . . . May God protect you!" And more in the same fervent vein of verbal anointment.

For Hitler, still torn by doubts as to whether he was the German Messiah or only, as he once said, *"eine kleine Johannisnatur"*—"a little John-the-Baptist type"—this was glorious confirmation. At one remove, so to speak, it was accolade and approval from the Master Wagner himself, and it bolstered his conviction that destiny had indeed chosen him for mighty deeds. Before long he would be speaking and writing not merely of Ruhr and Rhine, and Munich and Berlin, but of a "new Germanic march" to the East "along the road of the Teutonic knights of old." Even gaudier dreams would take shape as his vision of the future, and his role in it, became more and more grandiose, more and more Wagnerian. Beyond Germany, beyond Europe, he would see as his mission "the vast process of re-ordering the world" in accordance with the heroic conceptions of the Master of Bayreuth, and on the racial foundations of Houston Stewart Chamberlain. After Bayreuth, there were few moments when he did not hear the great, dark chords of destiny reverberating in the background.

But in the fall of 1923 events were forcing him toward what he afterward called "the most desperately daring decision of my life . . . in the eyes of many an almost insane decision."

There was a general air of irrationality about affairs in Bavaria at the time. Gustav von Kahr, for all his reputed conservatism and stolidity, was defying Berlin with abandon. A decisive, and perhaps irrevocable, break seemed imminent, and the saying in the streets was: *"Wann geht's los?"*—"When's it going to start?"

Von Kahr's rule as Commissioner General of the State, meanwhile, rested largely on the support of the local armed forces. His regime became virtually a triumvirate in which he was flanked on one side by General von Lossow and the 7th (Bavarian) *Reichswehr* Division, and on the other by Colonel Hans Ritter von Seisser, the commander of the Bavarian State Police. Except for one disturbing element, the triumvirate would have been in confident control of the situation in Bavaria.

The disturbing element was Adolf Hitler and his Nazis. Though they all agreed in general outlook and had the destruction of the Republic as their common goal, a rivalry that amounted to open hostility existed between the two camps. For Gustav von Kahr, as for most of the Bavarian ruling class, Hitler was an acceptable drum-beater and rabble-rouser, but hardly of the stature to play a leading role in the government of Bavaria, much less of the Reich.

Hitler, strengthened at Nuremberg and inspired by Bayreuth, had no intention of being held in check by what he called a "high-collar politician." The violence of his agitation increased, and his *Völkischer Beobachter* surpassed itself in vituperation. The *VB* was now a daily paper appearing in a new and larger "American" format, thanks to the financial assistance of Putzi Hanfstaengl, who got the money from his family's Fifth Avenue art store. Late in September the paper attacked Colonel-General Hans von Seeckt, the Chief of Staff of the German Armed Forces, as an enemy of the *völkisch* movement, a lackey of the Weimar Republic and a pawn of sinister Jewish-Masonic elements. Worse, he was charged with being under the political influence of his own wife, a Jewess (*"nee* Jacobsohn," as the paper noted.) The Chancellor, Stresemann, was similarly reviled. In Berlin the article was considered extreme even for the unbridled journalism of Bavaria. The whole country having been proclaimed to be in a State of Emergency, the ordinary guarantees of press freedom could be suspended at will by the government. Accordingly, the Defense Ministry ordered General von Lossow, as its ranking officer in Munich, to forbid publication of the *Völkischer Beobachter* indefinitely—by force, if necessary.

After consulting with Kahr, the General notified Berlin that he was refusing to carry out the order. To do so, he said, would endanger public security. He did not wish to commit any act that would bring the *Reichswehr* into conflict with local authorities —*i.e.,* Kahr, who regarded the order as another intrusion of the federal government into Bavarian affairs. Von Lossow's act was open insubordination. The Defense Minister promptly asked him to resign. He refused to do that also. Kahr announced that, regardless of Berlin, General von Lossow would remain in command of the local *Reichswehr*. Kahr went further: He insisted that the Bavarian regiments of the federal army take an oath of allegiance to the State Government, and they did so. It was an action unprecedented in the history of the German Army. What was at stake, Kahr and his faction believed, was Germany's future. It would be determined by the outcome of the struggle between the "nationalist-German" (his) concept and the "internationalist Marxist-Jewish" (Berlin's). Ideologically and emotionally, there was little to choose between Kahr's motivations and Hitler's.

But neither intended to allow the other precedence in delivering the decisive blow against the Republic and reaping the glory of it. That a blow would be struck no one doubted. The air was thick with *Putsch*-rumors, and the slogan *"Los von Berlin!"* —"Break away from Berlin!"—was discarded as too mild. It was replaced by *"Auf nach Berlin!"*—"On to Berlin!"—an unmistakable call to aggression. The communications passing back and forth between Munich and Berlin now reminded Erich Ludendorff of the notes exchanged between two hostile nations on the brink of war. "I knew that the hour of Germany's destiny was approaching," Adolf Hitler wrote of this period afterward. "I formed the resolution to strike."

Destiny was all very well to parade as a motive in retrospect, but at the time Hitler was prompted more by an elementary instinct for political self-preservation. He had repeatedly called for a dictatorship—a "brutal" one. But now that a political explosion seemed certain, he was in danger of being blown away in it unless he could set if off himself and take charge of the wreckage. He could not delay much longer. Too many others were extending lighted matches toward the fuse. Even the philosopher Oswald Spengler was involved in the intrigue and subversion preliminary to a *Putsch*. Like Hitler at the hospital in Pasewalk, Spengler had also wept when he learned of Germany's capitulation in 1918. Like Hitler, he, too, had then resolved to enter politics to do what he could to stay the decline of the West. But he was supporting the colorless Gustav von Kahr. So deeply was Spengler involved in the plotting to overthrow the Republic that he attended secret meetings, wrote coded letters to fellow conspirators and saw himself as Minister of Culture or Press Chief in the dictatorship-to-be.* "It is time," he wrote on October 30, 1923, "that the Right Wing pulled itself together and took action."

Hitler thought so, too, but could not make up his mind what action to take. As long ago as the previous August the *Völkischer Beobachter* had run a front-page headline that asked: WHAT WILL HITLER DO? The question, said the paper, was being heard everywhere, not only in Munich and Bavaria but in Saxony, in the Ruhr and Rhineland, and even in Prussia. It was also being asked of Hitler by his own lieutenants, one of whom warned him bluntly that if something didn't happen soon the Storm Troops would drift away and follow the first leader who struck a blow. There had been much talk of "Bavarian fists setting things right in Berlin," and Hitler had made the forecast that in the coming battle "heads will roll, either ours or theirs," but no heads were rolling.

When a plan was finally hit upon, it came not from Hitler, or

---

* When Hitler came to power and began to substantiate Spengler's predictions of Caesarism in the modern state, the philosopher briefly supported the *Führer*. He soon became disillusioned, however, and wrote and spoke scathingly of Hitler and National Socialism. He died in despair in 1936, condemned to silence by the Nazis for whom his philosophy had helped prepare the way.

from one of the Party firebrands like Roehm and Goering. It came from the pale and pompous intellectual, Alfred Rosenberg. He suggested that November fourth, the German Memorial Day, would provide the opportunity for a coup. The leading dignitaries of the State—Kahr, Lossow, Seisser and Prince Rupprecht as well—would be present at the ceremonies and would review a military march-past, including a contingent of Storm Troops. The reviewing stand would be in front of the *Residenz* Church on the Marstall Strasse, a short connective street that could readily be blocked at both ends. Rosenberg's idea was to have a strong formation of Storm Troopers arrive early, before the other parading units, seal off the street and make Kahr, Rupprecht and the others prisoners. Then the *Führer* would respectfully approach the Prince, apologize for disrupting the ceremonies, and explain the situation. He would inform Rupprecht and the others that he was taking over the government, acting in the best interests of Germany to prevent Bolshevik chaos and forestall the separation of Bavaria from the Reich. Thus, with a *Putsch* "both short and painless," as Rosenberg put it, the Hitler revolution would at last be launched, presumably with the support of the dignitaries trapped in the side street.

This implausible scheme was adopted, but when *der Tag* came for the National Socialist revolution the would-be *Putschists* were dismayed to find that the ceremonies were protected by an unusually large turnout of armed police. The Marstall Strasse, and the adjacent Court Garden, were swarming with troops and security guards, making the Rosenberg plan of a quick and bloodless sealing-off of the street impossible, and frustrating the whole plan. But only four days later Hitler made the lunge for power that marked a milestone in history. In the backward perspective of time, his *Putsch* would be likened to the raising of a curtain on a new epoch. It would be called the prologue to the Second World War. None, or few, saw it in any such terms at the time. It was, instead, a "Munich political carnival," a *"Ganovenstück"*—a gangster melodrama.

A fiasco when it happened, it turned out to be the foundation of his eventual rise to power.

15 THE PUTSCH

"IT IS A NECESSITY FOR GERMANS TO ABUSE THE GOVERNMENT OVER THEIR BEER."

—BISMARCK

THE PREFERRED TIME for staging a coup is the weekend, when the apparatus of government slows down to a standstill. Offices and bureaus are deserted. Officials whose hands usually grip the levers of power are away. The police and military establishments go slack. One's own people, on the other hand, are unfettered by shop and factory and can more readily assemble to devote themselves to the business at hand, such as marching, shooting and occupying buildings. The streets, furthermore, are not congested with working-day traffic, so one's own transport can move freely while marching columns maneuver unimpeded. Saturday is the day to start your *Putsch,* Sunday the day to solidify it. By Monday you are entrenched in the seat of government.

This was roughly the strategy Adolf Hitler decided on. He picked the weekend of November 10–11 and issued secret orders accordingly. The directive for Sunday morning included the phrase *"Einrücken mit Musik":* March in with music. There would be good reason for bands to be playing. Sunday would be the eleventh of November, the fifth anniversary of the unforgotten and unforgiven surrender of 1918. How glorious it would be to tear down the flag of the republic on that very day, and run up, once and for all, the old Imperial black-white-red! The "scene of disgrace" in the forest of Compiègne would be obliterated by the *Putsch* of Adolf Hitler in Munich . . .

But at almost the last minute he was forced to choose another time. This erratic choosing and canceling of dates, of making and revising plans, of issuing and rescinding orders, was an outgrowth of the fluidity of the political situation, and of Hitler's inveterate tendency to react impulsively and emotionally at critical moments. Abruptly, he chose the evening of November eighth as his hour to strike.

What changed his mind was an invitation to attend a meeting where the Commissioner General von Kahr was to outline his economic and governmental plans for the future. Everyone who amounted to anything in the upper echelons of Bavarian life would be there. In itself such a speech, even before such an audience, was not a matter of much concern to Hitler and his captains, but in the context of Munich politics the meeting was freighted with implications of intrigue and double cross. Kahr had been increasingly cool to Hitler, and suspicion was growing into certainty that he was maneuvering toward his own coup, from which the National Socialists would be excluded. The meeting and speech, whatever their announced purpose, might well be the occasion for proclaiming Bavaria's final break with Berlin, the restoration of the Wittelsbach monarchy, and Kahr's public anointment as the true Messiah of the nationalist cause.

Hitler did not intend to be caught sitting mutely on the sidelines while history passed him by. A council of war was accordingly held on the seventh with all the ranking Nazis, including Goering and Roehm, assembled in secret session. They met at the home of Dr. Max Erwin von Scheubner-Richter, who functioned as a political chief of staff to the *Führer*.

He was, like Rosenberg, a refugee from the Baltic, and his background was such that one newspaper demanded he be thrown out of Bavaria. His name, his "von," and his doctor title were all dubious. During the war he had been a German agent in Turkey, and he was now, among other things, the Party's liaison with Munich's colony of White Russians, whom he sought to integrate into the Nazi movement. A notable intriguer, he had participated in the Kapp *Putsch* and was highly regarded by Hitler for his political shrewdness and his contacts with industry and the Church. He strongly supported Hitler's plan for using the Kahr meeting as the occasion for the long-awaited *Putsch*. Many factors combined to favor the idea.

It was certain, for one thing, that the ruling triumvirate—Kahr, Lossow, Seisser—would be together on the rostrum, so that all three could be promptly rounded up and presented with a *fait accompli*. The elite of the entire community would be gathered in one room, where they could either become participants and supporters of the coup or be dealt with summarily if they acted otherwise. When the council broke up at 3 A.M. on November eighth, the decision to act was unanimous. All previous orders would be canceled. A new alert would be sent out to the Storm Troops and to the *Kampfbund,* the Fighting Union. Tonight, at the appointed hour, the future of Germany would be decided.

And, since this was the City of Munich in the State of Bavaria, the future of Germany would be decided in a beer hall.

The Bürgerbräu was situated on the south bank of the Isar River, on the outskirts of Munich, about a half mile from the center of town. By convention, like most beer halls, it was called a *Keller* (cellar), but it was in fact a commodious structure with gardens around it and a variety of dining rooms and bars inside. It favored the hearty, heavy dishes of the area—*Ochsenfleisch mit Weinkraut und Salzkartoffel, Sauerbraten mit Kloss,* and the like—but it was also capable of serving more discriminating tastes, and was therefore much frequented by the *bon ton* of the town. Its essential feature was its main hall, the largest in Munich outside the Krone Circus. It could accommodate 3,000 beer drinkers at its roughhewed wooden tables, and was frequently used for civic and political gatherings.

The Nazis knew it well. Hitler had held many a stormy meeting there, and the Party used it for social and fraternal evenings. The Bürgerbräukeller, a Nazi stamping ground, was about to become a Nazi landmark and, ultimately, a Nazi shrine.

That something significant was afoot on the eighth, a Thursday, was sensed by many as the day progressed, but only a few of those involved were informed of what was about to happen. Alfred Rosenberg was one of the few. At 11:30 in the morning he received a surprise visit from Adolf Hitler. "Rosenberg," said the *Führer*, "tonight is the night. Kahr is giving an official speech in the Bürgerbräu, and we'll catch them all together. Do you want to come along?" Rosenberg's answer was "Of course!" Immediately he set about preparing a proclamation to the public for the next day's issue of the *Völkischer Beobachter*, of which he was now editor. Hermann Esser, sick abed with yellow jaundice, was similarly told by the *Führer* personally that the blow would be struck that night. Sick or not, Esser promised to be there.

All through the day, by letter, phone and word of mouth, S.A. men were alerted for the evening's action without being given any details of what the action would entail. Some thought they were being summoned to one of the maneuvers that were constantly being held, but many guessed that this occasion was special. Afterward, looking back, they would repeat the same phrase: *"Es lag in der Luft"* —"There was something in the air."

Cycling home from work, a former soldier and current Storm Trooper named Karl Kessler stopped off briefly at S.A. headquarters in the Schelling Strasse. A certain amount of activity was noticeable there, but nothing unusual enough to cause comment. Nobody said anything to Kessler about an impending *Putsch*. But when he got home he found a typed slip of paper in an envelope on the table:

"2nd Company assembles tonight, 8 P.M., at the Arzberger Keller. Uniform!"

All over the city hundreds of other S.A. men were taking off their work clothes and putting on uniforms in response to similar summonses, and then hastening to designated assembly points. "Uniform" meant field-gray windbreaker with swastika brassard, field-gray ski cap, and revolver belt. For some the word came over the telephone with a curt *"Auf Gehts!"* —"This is it!"—which was enough. A shoemaker named Josef Richter was having supper when a comrade came to the door and shouted: *"Alarm!"* Richter got up from the table and hurried to his assembly point, the Hofbräuhaus Keller, where a rifle and ammunition was issued to him. Hours later, after much pointless milling about, his company was marched off in the direction of the Bürgerbräu, still in the dark as to what was going on.

For Karl Heinlein, Sr., a combat veteran of the Western Front, the *Putsch* became a family affair. He was ordered to report to the same assembly station as Richter with "steel helmet and other necessary accouterments," and did so promptly. But even before he left home, his two sons, Jakob and Karl, Jr., were already off to join their own paramilitary formation, the *Bund Oberland*. This was an outgrowth of the Thule Society, a "Fatherland" organization which once was a Free Corps, but now called itself a *Bund,* or league. The insignia of the Oberlanders was a spray of edelweiss on the cap, instead of the swastika. They were inclined to be rustic types in Bavarian mountain hats and high woolen stockings, though there were more smartly turned-out Oberlanders as well.

All such formations were part of the Fighting Union formed at the Nuremberg German Day under the military command of Lieutenant Colonel Hermann Kriebel, who was now directing the mobilization of the *Putsch*. Like General Ludendorff, on whose staff he had served, Kriebel had a receding chin, which did not add to his impressiveness as a military figure. But he was an enemy of the Republic to be reckoned with, a formidable proponent of the stab-in-the-back legend. When Germany surrendered in 1918, he had shaken his fist at a Belgian mob and shouted from the train that was taking him back to Germany: "*Auf Wiedersehen* in a few years!" Now, as his Fatherland units from all over Munich and the surrounding towns moved into position, Lieutenant Colonel Hermann Kriebel was confident that his promised *Wiedersehen* with the Belgians was only a matter of time.

The mobilization did not function flawlessly. The S.A. man Georg Zacherl had put in a hard day at the machine shop, and went to bed early. No summons or alert had reached him, and he was soon asleep. It chanced that he lived across the street

from the Bürgerbräu, and the first he knew of anything unusual
going on there was when the sound of shouted commands woke
him up. Looking out of the window, he could see men swarming
around the entrance of the beer hall, a coming and going of uniformed men and police, cars driving up and important person-
ages getting out. An S.A. comrade shouted up at him from the
street: *"Putsch!"*

Georg Zacherl's parents were surprised, moments later,
when he rushed headlong from the house. In uniform.

The hall was packed and Commissioner von Kahr had been
speaking for about twenty minutes when Adolf Hitler arrived at
the Bürgerbräu on the night of November 8, 1923. He drove up
in a red Benz touring car the Party had recently acquired, and
he was accompanied by his bodyguard, Ulrich Graf, by Alfred
Rosenberg with a pistol in his pocket, and by Anton Drexler, the
founder of the NSDAP and now its honorary chairman. Drexler
thought they were all on their way to attend a meeting in the
suburbs, and was not told the true situation until Hitler abruptly
informed him as they neared the beer hall. Perhaps Drexler had
never realized how inconsequential he had become in his own
Party until that moment. "I wish you luck," he said tonelessly,
and figured no further in the events that he had originally set in
motion.

Hitler, in his usual trench coat, was recognized by the
guards at the door and was promptly admitted with his group,
even though admittance had been cut off because of overcrowding in the hall. Inside, the numerous top hats, elegant overcoats,
officers' caps and swords in the cloak room testified to the quality of the audience. The aristocracy of the Isar was there, as anticipated.

Awaiting Hitler's arrival in the lobby were Scheubner-
Richter, Lieutenant Colonel Kriebel and several other instigators
and managers of the *Putsch*. They now stood about tensely, listening to the voice of the speaker, which reached them through
the doors to the auditorium. "Does anybody know what he's

talking about?" Hitler asked the group sarcastically. Nobody did. They looked repeatedly at their watches, more and more often as 8:30 approached.

Inside, Gustav von Kahr was reading his remarks in a dry monotone. It was not Kahr's oratorical style or his speech, with its curious title, *Vom Volk zur Nation*—"From the People to the Nation"—that had filled every chair and table in the pillared hall, now redolent of beer fumes and hazy with smoke drifts. Speculation, rife for days, had infused a basically tiresome occasion with the electric possibility of something unexpected. Even Kahr, stolid as he usually was, had sensed something overactive about the town that night and wondered why so many people, most of them young, were milling about the hall as he drove up. A reporter, made suspicious by the number of armed and uniformed men in the streets, had come near to stopping Kahr's automobile and warning him to turn back. But the Commissioner had arrived at eight o'clock, mounted the podium, and promptly begun his droning speech, which had now reached the sentence—

"Not even a man equipped with the greatest executive powers can rescue the *Volk,* the people, without the nationalist spirit and energetic help of the people themselves . . ."

It was shortly after 8:30, and he got no further.

At 8:30 the group waiting in the lobby heard the rumble of a heavy truck approaching the building, and they knew what it meant. The first contingent of the *Stosstrupp Hitler,* the Shock Troop of the S.A., was arriving on schedule. Other trucks followed instantly and were parked crosswise in the middle of the street to block off further traffic. Out of the trucks leaped armed men in combat dress and steel helmets. They swarmed around the entrance of the building, threatening the police guards with their rifles and shouldering them aside. Others surrounded the building, blocked its approaches, and occupied the adjacent gardens and the kitchens.

Simultaneously a squad of about fifteen, armed with machine pistols and led by Captain Hermann Goering, stormed through the lobby and burst open the folding doors to the hall. With them they carried a heavy machine gun, which they set up in the doorway, pointed at the audience.

At first Kahr thought his meeting was being disrupted by the Communists, whom he had been denouncing in his speech. He stepped away from the lectern and stood quietly next to General von Lossow and Colonel von Seisser as uproar erupted in the hall. Men leaped onto their chairs and jumped on tables to see what was happening. Women screamed and fainted at the sight of the steel helmets and the machine gun. The aisles were blocked, and there was an eddy of shoving as somebody tried to force his way from the rear of the hall to the speaker's platform.

It was Adolf Hitler.

He had a pistol in his hand. Even with the help of Graf and Goering, he was having difficulty forcing his way forward. When his progress continued to be blocked, he climbed on a chair and shouted into the hubbub: *"Ruhe! Ruhe!"* Then, when quiet did not ensue, he pointed his pistol to the ceiling and fired.

The hall froze into silence.

"The national revolution has broken out!" Hitler shouted. "This hall is occupied by six hundred heavily armed men, and no one may leave it.

"The Bavarian government and the Reich government are deposed. The barracks of the *Reichswehr* and the State Police have been occupied. *Reichswehr* and State Police are advancing under the banners of the swastika."

Almost none of this was true, and Hitler did not make a very imposing figure as he stood on the chair shouting it. His looks and behavior showed nothing of that "ice-cold self-possession" that he himself considered the sign of the true hero. He was pale and sweating and his hair was falling over his forehead. Some thought he had the look of a madman, and something erratic in his manner made others guess he was drunk.

To at least one observer he simply looked foolish. He had taken off his trench coat and, apparently in deference to the high significance of the occasion, was wearing a cutaway. Of all possible garments, this suited his ungainly figure least. Paul von

Hintze, admiral and diplomat, was sitting nearby and afterward related: "When I saw him jump on the chair in that ridiculous costume, I thought, *'armes Kellnerlein!'* "—poor little waiter . . .

But steel helmets had taken up positions along the walls of the hall and in the gallery around it, and they were crouching behind the machine gun in the doorway. No one was disposed to confront Adolf Hitler in his cutaway. The police stationed in the hall stood motionless. They were not only outnumbered and outarmed, but several police officials in mufti were seen to pull on swastika brassards, letting the men know where their sympathies lay. One of them had even helped put the machine gun in place. Police reinforcements, stationed in the area on riot alert, were not dispatched to the Bürgerbräu. At police headquarters Wilhelm Frick was in control, which meant that everything possible would be done, and was done, to forestall serious interference with Adolf Hitler's *Putsch.*

Climbing over a table, Adolf Hitler reached the speaker's platform where the triumvirate—Kahr, Lossow, Seisser—were standing, rigid and expressionless. Hitler, still flourishing his pistol, asked the three to accompany him into an adjacent room. As they went off, General von Lossow—according to his story later—muttered to his colleagues: "Put on an act!" *"Komödie spielen!"*

Once in the room, Hitler appeared even more agitated than before. He barked an order for a stein of beer and took several gulps, unusual for him. The dryness of throat caused by his wartime gassing was evidently intensified by the tension of the moment. When Colonel von Seisser accused him of breaking his pledged word that he would not make a *Putsch,* he apologized: "I did it for the good of Germany. Forgive me." Otherwise he was not notably polite. He forbade his captives to speak to each other on pain of being shot. He explained that he was building a new regime in Bavaria to be a springboard for a new regime for the Reich. Everyone would, on pain of death, have to accept the post assigned him. "I have four bullets in my pistol," he said. "Three for you, my colleagues, if you fail me. The last one for myself." According to Kahr, several armed Storm Troopers were hovering in the background, and Hitler was continually flourishing his pistol, so the threat did not seem to be an empty one.

Out in the hall, no one had been permitted to leave, and the 3,000 people began to feel trapped. Murmurs of protest swelled into mutinous rumble. It took another shot into the ceiling, this time from Captain Goering's pistol, to bring a measure of quiet. He then mounted the podium and, with what one witness called "a certain brutal energy," bellowed a short speech explaining that Kahr and his colleagues were in no danger, that matters would shortly be clarified, and that it was all being done for a greater Germany. "And anyway," he concluded, "you've got your beer. What are you worrying about?"

But beer in itself was not necessarily enough, even for a Munich audience. Disorder was threatening again when Hitler appeared from the side room and went to the podium. He still seemed awkward and uneasy—"like a provincial bridegroom," as Putzi Hanfstaengl saw him. Then he began to speak, and his magic with an audience began to work again. "It was," said Hanfstaengl, who was there, "like the difference between a Stradivarius lying in its case, just a few bits of wood and lengths of catgut, and the same violin being played by a master." The audience, like so many other audiences before it, and after, was electrified.

He again proclaimed a new provisional government for Bavaria and declared the "November criminals" in Berlin finished and ousted. Ludendorff would head a new National Army and he, Hitler, would take over the political leadership of the new national government. In the new administration there would be high office for Kahr, Lossow, Seisser and other Bavarian stalwarts of the Right. "The mission of the provisional regime," he said, "is to begin the march against Berlin, that sink of iniquity, with all the might of this State and the accumulated power of every province in Germany."

Not self-aggrandizement and personal ambition was motivating him and his comrades. No, at the eleventh hour they were taking up the struggle for a renewal of the German Fatherland in which Bavaria would have the place that was due it. "Tomorrow," he concluded, "will find either a nationalist regime in Germany, or us dead."

When he went back into the side room, he had the entire assemblage behind him. As one of his entranced listeners described it, he had turned the mood of the audience "inside out, like a glove."

The effect of the speech was to give the gathering, for the first time, the sense of being present at a momentous occasion instead of being enmeshed in an unseemly political tumult involving characters one would rather not associate with. At first there had been contemptuous hoots of "Side show!" and *"Mexiko!"*, as if a banana-republic travesty were being staged. Now the hall rang with calls of *"Achtung!"* and shouts of *"Heil!"* and the men in steel helmets cracked their heels together as they presented arms. Ringed by a reverent escort of S.A. men, the Quartermaster General was entering the Bürgerbräu.

Erich Ludendorff's formidable scowl was, if anything, more thunderous than usual. Having been rushed to the hall through the foggy night at eighty kilometers an hour in Scheubner-Richter's car, the General was not in the best of moods. He was not arrayed in the full uniform and spiked helmet he usually affected on ceremonial occasions; he was dressed in the old tweed hunting jacket he had been wearing when hauled away suddenly from his suburban villa. Hitler received him, as always, with the enlisted man's wary respect for a general officer, and addressed him as *Excellenz*. He led the General into the room where the triumvirate was still confined.

The audience saw none of them for more than an hour, but the situation in the hall did not remain static. The "blue" police assigned to keep order at the meeting had long since been intimidated by the armed Hitlerites. Now the police were summarily ordered out with the command: *"Blaue Polizei heraus!"* They went. Then, under the direction of Scheubner-Richter, the highest-ranking officials of the Bavarian government were singled out in the audience, taken into custody by Storm Troopers, and led from the hall as prisoners. They included the Minister President of Bavaria, von Knilling, the current Police President of Munich, Karl Mantel, and a Count von Soden, chief adviser to Crown Prince Rupprecht. Even before they completed their seizure of the state, the Nazis were turning Bavaria into a police state.

Outside the hall a terror was being launched against officials, Communists, Social Democrats and Jews. Several S.A. men led by Rudolf Hess kidnapped two ministers of the government, drove them out of town and into the mountains, and tortured them all night long with the expectation of death by dragging them from tree to tree as if they were about to be hanged. Storm Troopers broke into the home of Erhard Auer, the Socialist who had been shot almost fatally at the time of Eisner's death and often threatened with assassination since. Now he was threatened again and physically abused while his gray-haired wife was brutally mishandled by the S.A. men. His son-in-law was seized and held prisoner, along with those abducted from Bürgerbräu. All night long Jews were rounded up by S.A. and Oberland raiding partners, and held hostage. Many of the victims were chosen from the phone book for no other reason but that their names looked Jewish.

The Shock Troop descended on the Socialist Munich *Post,* used their rifle butts to smash windows and beat down anyone they encountered. Editorial offices and press room were indiscriminately and thoroughly vandalized. "A Marxist poison kitchen," the Nazis called the place, and the vandals in uniform raged through it, breaking furniture, throwing typewriters from the windows and—in anticipation of the book-burnings that later appalled the world—making a street bonfire of newspapers, files and Socialist brochures. The devastation stopped only when a police official arrived and suggested that the newspaper plant would be useful to the Nationalist cause when the new regime took power. The Shock Troopers hadn't thought of that. They spared what was left of the *Post,* and set off to harass and arrest Jews.

The shock waves that went out from the Bürgerbräu were an accurate foreshadowing of what the Third Reich of Adolf Hitler would be like, but that night Adolf Hitler's *Putsch* was in danger of expiring in the beer hall where it was born. Able to sway the thousands in the main hall, Hitler was getting nowhere with the three men in the side room. Kahr was sullen and silent, nursing injured feelings over the interruption of his speech and the public disgrace of being herded off the platform at pistol point. The two military men were cool and curt. If a National Socialist bandwagon had indeed been set rolling by the events in the adjacent banquet hall, the triumvirate showed no signs of leaping aboard it. And without their cooperation Hitler's hope of succeeding with his revolt were of the dimmest.

The 50,000 members of his Party, however fanatical, were not a strong enough base from which to launch a national movement. His S.A., capable enough for occupying beer halls and intimidating civilians, would be no match in a serious collision with *Reichswehr* and police. What Hitler needed desperately was the support of just those components of the state that the triumvirate represented: the civil service, army and police. He had been frustrated on May first because they opposed his march against the Reds of Munich. How could he hope to march on Berlin without their support?

Ludendorff's arrival was an enormous relief. However coolly, or even defiantly, the triumvirate might choose to treat a Hitler, dealing with a Ludendorff was another matter. The Quartermaster General was thoroughly irked that Hitler had so completely taken charge of affairs and apprised him of the *Putsch* only after it was under way. He was further irritated to learn that Adolf Hitler was to be the dictator of Germany, not Erich Ludendorff. Being made commander of a new National Army, the role assigned to him, seemed hardly exalted enough, and he showed how he felt by cutting Hitler dead as he entered the room. He addressed himself to the triumvirate, saying in effect that he was as surprised as they were by the *Putsch,* but since it had started, the only thing to do was go along with it for the sake of the Fatherland and the good of the *völkisch* cause. He may have thought that the upstart Pfc. could be disposed of later.

Hitler's argument, too, was that matters had progressed so

far that the only possible way to go was forward. "This has already become a world-historic event," he said. "There is no turning back." Ludendorff's approach was gruffer. Soldier to soldier, he turned to Lossow, the general, and Seisser, the colonel: "All right, gentlemen, come along with us, and give me your hand on it." At no time during the discussion, before Ludendorff's arrival or afterward, was there any mention of the fact that everybody involved in the *Putsch* was committing high treason. The tacit assumption by all concerned was that any attempt to overthrow the Republic must be a meritorious undertaking. The only questions on which right-thinking men could differ involved how, when and by whom.

In response to the appeal of the Quartermaster General, Lossow now thrust out his hand, and, according to his own version, signified his agreement with one syllable: "Good." Afterward, it was said and printed that, with his eyes moist and his voice quivering, he said: *"Excellenz,* your wish is my command." But to the last, Lossow claimed he was playing a part and never for a moment considered supporting the *Putsch.* When he was offered the post of Minister of Defense in the new regime, he did not, he claimed, take it seriously. "I thought they were like children playing at 'You be the Emperor and I'll be the Pope.'" Seisser, in turn, was offered the nonexistent office of Reich Minister of Police, and he also gave Ludendorff his hand without qualification.

It took a little longer to get Gustav von Kahr to pledge himself to the *Putsch.* Having contemplated one of his own, he was not keen about being relegated to a minor role in somebody else's.

When finally, after much persuasion, he gave in, he made one proviso touching the topic he felt most deeply about. He would consent to take the post of chief administrator of the new government, he said, if it were understood that he would act at all times as representative of His Majesty the King, by which he meant Rupprecht. As far as he was concerned, the revolt was to be merely a preliminary to the restoration of the monarchy. Hitler hastened to assure him that he, too, was passionately con-

346

cerned with righting the wrong that "a mob of common criminals" had done to the Wittelsbach dynasty five years before. Kahr gave Hitler his hand.

Exactly what was in the mind of Gustav Ritter von Kahr when he did this, and what motivated him through the mental and moral convolutions of that strange evening, may never be clarified. For the moment it sufficed Hitler that all three of the triumvirate had expressed their willingness to march with him against the Republic. When he led Ludendorff, Kahr, Lossow and Seisser out of the side room and back onto the stage before the packed hall, he was "beaming with joy," as one witness described it, and aglow "with a kind of childish happiness." His *Putsch* was succeeding, his hour was striking.

Kahr's heavy face, it was noted by many, was like a mask; but some said they detected in Lossow's expression a hint of detachment and indifference, a kind of facial shrug. Seisser was pale and appeared not fully in control of himself. Ludendorff, deadly earnest, launched into a speech in which he described the events of the night as "a turning point in our German history and in world history." He said he was putting himself at the disposal of the new nationalist regime in the hope that honor would again be restored "to the old black-white-red cockade" that the revolution of 1918 had disgraced. But it was Hitler, again, who stirred the audience to emotional response. He described the pledge he had made to himself five years before "as a blind cripple in the hospital not to pause or rest until the November criminals are cast down and until, from the ruins of the wretched Germany of today, a new nation shall arise—a Germany of greatness, freedom and glory. Amen!" The reaction was tumultuous. The audience stood up and burst into a roaring chorus of *Deutschland, Deutschland über alles*—"The most impressive singing of the national hymn I ever heard," said Putzi Hanfstaengl. Many were so moved they were unable to sing. Many more wept.

"What a magnificent thing, Germany will be united again!" breathed Dr. Fritz Michael Gerlich, the well-known editor, as he rushed off to write a glowing account of the night's events for tomorrow's edition of his newspaper, the *Münchener Neueste Nachrichten*. But the story Dr. Gerlich wrote that night was fated to lose much of its glow by the time it came from the presses next morning. Not for the first time, and not for the last, the combination of German beer and German patriotism had generated emotions that, however deep and genuine, had scant foundation in reality.

As the crowd streamed out into the starless Munich night, the leaders of the *Putsch* gathered in a little group to discuss the immediate program of the new government. The talk was animated, but Kahr was gnawing his mustache thoughtfully and saying little. Hitler was still in the euphoric state he had exhibited on the podium when he announced that the triumvirate was with him, and the great Ludendorff as well. Everything seemed to be progressing swimmingly. He did not become unduly alarmed when word came that there had been a hitch in the plan to take over the barracks of an Engineer Battalion and that some similar difficulty was developing at the 19th Infantry Regiment. Instead of dispatching a deputy to the scene, Hitler decided to deal with the affair himself. He left the hall.

This turned out to be a serious mistake.

After he left, the talk flagged. The evening had been a strain on everyone, and the hour was getting late. Ludendorff did not object when the suggestion was made that perhaps it was time to be leaving. Everyone was tired and there would be much to do on the morrow.

Kahr, Lossow and Seisser left the hall. When Hitler returned about a half hour later, he was appalled to learn of their departure, but Ludendorff was indignant that any suspicions should be expressed. He cut off further discussion with a sharp: "I forbid you to doubt the word of honor of a German officer!"

Ludendorff's trust in the word of honor of a German officer turned out to be another serious mistake.

Hitler's mission, moreover, had been fruitless.

At the engineer barracks an attempt by 250 Oberlanders to occupy the place and seize its weapons had been frustrated. An energetic *Reichswehr* captain rallied a handful of his men, out-maneuvered the insurgents, trapped them in the drill hall and locked the doors on them. An attempt by Storm Troopers to overpower the infantry barracks encountered similar resistance, and was beaten off. Without orders from above, *Reichswehr* officers were not yet ready to turn over their weapons and quarters to upstart semi-civilians.

When Hitler saw that two of the most important military installations in the city, with all their supplies of arms and equipment, remained firmly in the hands of the *Reichswehr,* his impulse was to wheel up cannon and blow the barracks to pieces. On second thought, he decided to wait until morning when General von Lossow, as local Army commander and supporter of the *Putsch,* would give the necessary orders to straighten out the situation.

It must have been heartening when an entire *Reichswehr* unit, about 1,000 strong and fully armed, came marching smartly up to the Bürgerbräu with a band playing and swastika banners flying—the first formation of the German Regular Army to march openly under the flag of National Socialism. These were elite troops, cadets from the Infantry Officers' Training School, young enthusiasts thoroughly impregnated with the nationalist idea, eager to support the *Putsch.* They comprised a kind of Free Corps inside the *Reichswehr,* and were not led to the Bürgerbräu by their own commanding officer. He had been put under room arrest because he opposed the *Putsch.* Their leader was Lieutenant Gerhard Rossbach, a notorious swashbuckler and freebooter for whom Berlin had issued warrants as an enemy of the Republic. Rossbach was, like Roehm, a homosexual, and, like Ehrhardt, a veteran of battles in the Baltic, of Free Corps actions everywhere and of the Kapp venture. In Munich, where he was given immunity from arrest and freedom of movement, he had formed his own battalion of Storm Troops and taken the cadets of the Infantry School as his special charges. Promising to make them the nucleus of a crack "Ludendorff Regiment" in the new National Army, he had convinced them that the true way of soldierly honor was to break their oath of allegiance to the Republic and, instead, march against it.

Now they stood at ramrod attention as the legendary Quartermaster General reviewed them. It must have seemed that they, not the Berlin government, were the legitimate representatives of Germany. Here was undoubted authority—Ludendorff and, as they had heard, their own general, von Lossow, and the head of the Bavarian government as well, supporting Hitler in his insurgency against the Republic. If this was a *Putsch,* it must have looked to many—as somebody said—like "a *Putsch* with police permission."

No opposition appeared as units of the Fighting Union continued to pour into the city from the suburbs and surrounding towns, from Ingoldstadt, Garmisch, Tölz, Weilheim. Trucks with Storm Troops and arms rumbled through the darkened streets, and units afoot marched and countermarched, most of them unsure of where they were going, or why. Oberland passed S.A. in the dark, exchanging the *"Heil!"* greeting as they went. A light, wet snow began to fall.

For Karl Kessler, the combat veteran, it all recalled the Army in wartime, with marching that seemed to go nowhere followed by pointless standing around. He, like many of his fellows, was puzzled that there were so few civilians on the street, aside from little groups of revelers squandering their inflation money. If a *Putsch* was really afoot, the people of Munich seemed unaware of it. At the telegraph office, Kessler was jarred to see not S.A. men but security police standing guard. But he was reassured when the Schupos, the police, waved at his unit and shouted *"Heil!"*

To Ludwig Hofmann, marching with the 3rd Company of the Munich S.A. Regiment, the night seemed wonderfully adventurous and warlike. He had joined the Storm Troops only a few months before and been trained in rifle marksmanship and the handling of machine guns. He was young and idealistic, eager for action. The *esprit* of his unit, he thought, was like that of soldiers at the front and he felt he was participating in the opening assault of an offensive that would purge Germany of the plagues that were afflicting her. For Ludwig Hofmann this was war.

At about 11 P.M. his company, unarmed, was marched from its assembly point east toward the river and halted at a square named for the church that stood upon it, St. Anna's. Its façade was neo-Romanesque topped by two delicate spires, and a Franciscan monastery was attached to it. Orders were given to block off the square, and Ludwig Hofmann's men formed a line across the north side. He was puzzled about being there at all. "What are we doing at a church, of all places, on a night like this?" he asked himself. Things became more puzzling when the men who were not on guard duty began to disappear, one by one, through a narrow door that led into the cloister. Then, after a time, the men came out again, each one with a rifle.

"I was astounded," said Ludwig Hofmann.

When his turn came to enter the cloister, he found a scene that he described as being "like something out of Karl May." He went through a narrow stone corridor to an arched cellar dimly illuminated by flickering candles. He was directed to a sealed vault whose walls, he noted, had recently been broken through with sledges, crowbars and picks. The vault was filled with rifles, thousands of them, and monks were handing them up to the Storm Troopers as they filed by. The rifles, Hofmann noted, were of the kind known as Model 98. They had formerly equipped units of the Free Corps and Citizens Defense and, when such units were forbidden, the arms were hidden to prevent seizure by the Allied Control Commission.

All through the night, guns were handed out by the monks to the insurgents. Sometimes a truck pulled up before the cloister, and a relay line was established from the cellar to the street, with the guns passing hand-to-hand from vault to truck. The monks served tea and rum as the work went on, and women from neighboring houses passed out coffee, cigarettes and candy. The loaded trucks drove off to the Bürgerbräu, now military headquarters of the *Putsch*. The marchers often arrived there in the highest spirits, and singing, as word spread from company to company that the uprising had succeeded and the shame of that

other November ninth was being wiped out at last. The beer
hall, inside and out, took on the look of an armed camp, but
with overtones of a party. Sentinels walked their posts. Arms
were stacked in readiness, machine guns emplaced. But an air of
exhilaration lasted all night as comrades congratulated each
other, new units constantly arrived, and free beer was passed
around, two liters to a man.

For all the mobilizing, arming and marching, the *Putsch*
had so far succeeded in occupying only one strong point in the
city's administrative and military complex. The man who took it
was not Adolf Hitler but Ernst Roehm, and, this being Munich,
his stroke was also launched from a beer hall.

Early that evening Captain Roehm had presided over a
gathering of his own at the Löwenbräu, another of the town's
more prominent "cellars." The guests were members of a troop
known as the Reich War Flag; Roehm was the commander. There
were S.A. and Oberland men there, too, as well as a number of
Reichswehr soldiers who, contrary to orders, involved themselves
in the politics of the paramilitary organizations. The meeting was
beery and relaxed, it having been announced as a fraternal evening such as all the units periodically staged. Hermann Esser, who
knew better, had left his sick bed to come to the Löwenbräu
and make a routine propaganda speech to fill in the time. While
he was speaking, a two-word message came for Roehm by telephone: *"Glücklich entbunden."*

"Successfully delivered" (of a child) was the code to convey
that Hitler's coup at the Bürgerbräu had succeeded. Now Esser's
speech, like Kahr's previously, was unceremoniously interrupted
as Roehm took the podium to announce that the Bavarian government had been deposed and that the nationalist revolution
under Adolf Hitler had been proclaimed.

The announcement touched off an explosion of joy. Men
leaped from their chairs, shouting and embracing each other,
some sobbing with emotion. The *Reichswehr* soldiers tore the
red-black-gold cockade of the Republic from their caps, threw
them on the floor, and stamped on them. The band struck up the

national anthem, but was scarcely audible above the uproar. It was minutes before Captain Roehm could induce the men to quiet down sufficiently to hear his instructions. He ordered them to fall in on the square outside, and march to the Bürgerbräu in support of the new regime.

As the column moved off, it was overtaken by a motorcycle courier with orders to change direction, march on the Military District Headquarters, occupy and hold it. In the van of the formation, and carrying the unit's flag, was a young man who peered shortsightedly into the night through thick glasses, and who, again, had less chin than a soldierly look required. He had only recently received a diploma in agriculture and taken a job in the office of a fertilizer plant. Though he was a fervent nationalist and loved to wear a uniform, he had not joined the Storm Troops or enrolled in the Nazi Party. He had picked Ernst Roehm, not Adolf Hitler, as the coming man, and his allegiance was not to the swastika but to the colors of the monarchy. His name was Heinrich Himmler, and he was twenty-three years old.*

The Military District Headquarters was seized without a struggle. The *Reichswehr* officer in charge had insufficient troops to defend it, and he was not eager to fire on a comrade-in-arms of the regular army like Captain Roehm. Roehm moved in with his 400 War Flag men, posted guards, set up machine guns aimed out the windows, strung barbed wire around the building, and stood ready to beat off any attack that might come.

He did not know for many hours afterward that his uncon-

---

* Only a few years would pass until Heinrich Himmler changed his mind and allegiance. In 1925 he joined the National Socialist Party and served Adolf Hitler so devotedly thereafter that he became the third most powerful man (after Goering) in the Third Reich. He was Hitler's chief terrorist and executioner as commander of the SS and head of the Gestapo, the Secret Police. He was in charge of all Nazi concentration camps and hence responsible for the extermination of millions in the gas ovens and torture chambers of Dachau, Buchenwald, Belsen, Auschwitz and the others. In World War II he commanded the Elite Guard Armies, known as the *Waffen-SS*. In May of 1945, at the hour of Germany's defeat, he was captured by the British as he sought to disguise himself as an enlisted man among the German prisoners of war. During his interrogation he bit on a poison capsule concealed in his mouth and committed suicide.

tested seizure of the District Headquarters was the lone military success of the entire *Putsch*.

Hitler arrived shortly afterward and made a little speech of congratulations and thanks to Captain Roehm and his men. At about 1 A.M., Ludendorff and Colonel Kriebel appeared with several other leaders of the insurgency, including Dr. Frederick Weber, a tall, gawky veterinarian who was the head of the Bund Oberland. For several hours the captured District Headquarters became the CP, the Command Post, of the *Putsch,* as all concerned tried to sort out what was happening and what was likely to happen.

An immediate difficulty appeared, and grew increasingly ominous. All efforts to get in touch with General von Lossow and Colonel von Seisser to discuss the next military and security measures proved fruitless. Roehm had tried earlier without success, and he began to wonder. There came a report, also, that a battalion of *Reichswehr* troops stationed at Passau, 100 miles away, had received marching orders for Munich.

There was speculation that perhaps Lossow and Seisser had been placed under arrest by Army elements opposed to the *Putsch* and were being held incommunicado. There had been no word from Kahr, either, since he left the beer hall, an additionally disturbing development. It was still too early, however, for anyone in the leadership of the *Putsch* to believe in an all-out betrayal. To Erich Ludendorff it seemed impossible that any German officer would go back on his word, especially a word given him, Ludendorff. And to everybody it seemed unlikely that Kahr would have the courage for such a betrayal or the initiative to act on it.

Lossow, it developed, had establishd himself in the Intelligence Section of the 19th Infantry Barracks and set up a Command Post of his own. He chose this place because it was securely in the hands of his own troops, and he could not be sure of the safety of his usual quarters. On his arrival from the beer hall, he had been confronted at once by his second-in-command, a Lieutenant General von Danner. "Excellency," said von Danner to his chief, "that was surely all bluff?" Danner was commander of the local garrison; he could muster two divisions of regular troops and was to be reckoned with no matter how the situation might develop. He and his fellow officers were against the *Putsch,* and offered Lossow a way out of his commitment at the Bürgerbräu. Lossow promptly agreed that it had all been bluff—"putting on act"—and began taking steps to suppress the insurgency he had publicly pledged to support. The Munich garrison was alerted. Outlying *Reichswehr* units were ordered into Munich by telephone and telegraph. A general military alarm was issued.

At District Headquarters Hitler and his group were unaware of these moves and were still trying to ascertain how things stood with their *Putsch;* it had ground to a halt for reasons nobody yet wanted to admit. They now knew where General von Lossow was, but several emissaries sent to summon him to a conference had not returned. It was after 2 A.M. when, in near desperation, they dispatched a retired major named Alexander Siry to the Infantry Barracks in the hope that a man of his rank would get through to Lossow and return with some useful information. Siry was in civilian clothes, but he went home, put on his uniform, and hastened to the Infantry Barracks. He was appalled to learn from the first officer he spoke to that the *Putsch* was being opposed by the Army.

"*Putsch!*" said Major Siry. "More than a *Putsch* is at stake. A great nationalist movement is at stake!" It seemed incredible to him that the Army should, even for a moment, consider using force against Hitler and his followers who were, after all, German patriots on the same side as the *Reichswehr.* Weren't they all struggling for the same goal?

It was a dilemma of divided loyalties that afflicted many a German as the polarization of attitudes intensified that night. Many officers and men of the *Reichswehr* sympathized wholeheartedly with the Nazis, but owed their first allegiance to the Army. They could not allow outsiders to invade their barracks, seize their installations, and thereby affront military dignity. Members of the S.A. and the Fighting Union, on the other hand, admired and respected the *Reichswehr,* and felt almost part of it.

To be opposed by it, or to fight against it, seemed an insanity, like warfare within their own ranks.

Major Siry was confident that some temporary misunderstanding had occurred, that once he had conveyed Erich Ludendorff's personal invitation to General von Lossow, the "great nationalist movement" would sweep onward. The Major was mistaken. He was coldly received by the triumvirate, Kahr and Seisser by now having joined Lossow in the Infantry Barracks. They listened stonily as Siry explained his mission, and the reply was: "*Herr Major,* there will be no negotiations with rebels." He was then placed under arrest.

Before he was led off, Siry noted that Kahr, hunched on a kind of settee, had said little and seemed to be brooding. He was, perhaps, struggling with his conscience, aware that now there was no way he could emerge from the affair with credit. Kahr's actions on the night of November eighth would be long debated and discussed. His behavior is not easily explained. If, as he afterward maintained, he had acted only under duress, why had he insisted on representing the monarchy in the new government? That would not have been necessary if he were only pretending. If he did not intend to take a leading post in the insurgent government, and strongly opposed it, he could have denounced the *Putsch* from the podium of the Bürgerbräu. No matter how threatening Hitler acted, he would not have dared to shoot the Commissioner General of Bavaria in sight of 3,000 witnesses. Nobody, or very few, who saw Gustav von Kahr on that platform doubted his sincerity as he gave his hand to Adolf Hitler and pledged his cooperation.

Even after he left the beer hall, he gave several associates the impression that he meant what he said there. But some time after midnight an emissary reached him from the Crown Prince with an urgent communication. Rupprecht let it be known that he would have nothing to do with a *Putsch* whose leaders included the notorious anti-Catholic, Erich Ludendorff, who was Prussian as well. The Prince was further outraged that his personal adviser and cabinet chief, Count von Soden, had been arrested without warrant by the Nazis at the Bürgerbräu. Further,

Michael Cardinal Faulhaber, the Archbishop of Munich, joined the Prince in condemning the Hitler coup. "Crush this movement at any cost," said the Prince's message. "Use troops if necessary."

For a monarchist, and a Bavarian patriot, it was perhaps unthinkable to act contrary to such a message from such a source, pledge or no pledge. Did Dr. Gustav Ritter von Kahr, on thinking it over, persuade himself that he, too, had only been play-acting in the Bürgerbräu? *

At 2:55 A.M. General von Lossow ordered the following message to be sent "to all German wireless stations":

State Commissioner General v. Kahr, Col. v. Seisser and Gen. v. Lossow repudiate the Hitler *Putsch*. Expressions of support extracted by gunpoint invalid. Caution is urged against misuse of the above names.

v. Lossow

That was curt and spare as military language required, but Kahr set about composing a proclamation that would speak on posters to the people of Munich. He had some difficulty with the wording, but the final version began:

"Deception and breach of faith by certain ambitious characters turned a demonstration for Germany's reawakening into a scene of repulsive force and violence. Declarations extorted from me, General von Lossow and Colonel von Seisser by pistol threat are null and void. Had the senseless and purposeless attempt at revolt succeeded, Germany would have been plunged into the abyss and Bavaria with it . . ."

The abolition of the National Socialist Party was announced together with the dissolution of the Bund Overland and the Reich War Flag. Those responsible for the uprising would, the proclamation concluded, "ruthlessly be made to suffer the punishment they deserved."

In view of the emergency, the seat of the government was shifted from Munich to Regensburg. In the continuing turmoil of

* Some Nazis afterward alleged that Kahr changed his mind when a Munich Jew named Otto Bernheimer bribed him with seven Persian rugs!

postwar German politics, yet another government was forced to flee, as the Hoffmann regime had done during the *Räte* period and the Berlin government at the time of the Kapp coup. However this *Putsch* of Adolf Hitler's might turn out, it had already contributed its share to the instability and confusion that would one day bring the Republic down in ruins.

Dr. Franz Matt, the Bavarian Minister of Culture, was not at the Bürgerbräu that night, and so escaped arrest. When he phoned Kahr to find out what happened, Matt asked: "What does Hitler want, actually?"

"He wants the famous march on Berlin," Kahr replied.

In Berlin, Chancellor Gustav Stresemann was having a late supper at the Hotel Continental when news of the *Putsch* reached him at 11:30. He broke off his conversation with Dr. Hjalmar Schacht, the financial expert and future president of the Reich Bank, and hurried to the Chancellery to call a Cabinet session. On the way to the meeting by motorcar, Colonel General Hans von Seeckt discussed the situation with his aide.

"Ha!" he said. "Comical happenings in Munich this evening. I am no longer head of the Armed Forces. Lossow is. Hitler is Reich Chancellor, Ludendorff Defense Minister. There is revolution in Munich."

His aide kept silent. "The words came so icily and bitingly, so sarcastically and cynically," he said afterward, "that I could only keep my mouth shut."

Friedrich Ebert, President of the Republic, presided at the midnight meeting in the Chancellor's study. As so often before in Germany, the crucial question was what the attitude of the Army would be.

"Tell us, please," said the President to the General, "whom does the *Reichswehr* obey? Does it obey the government or the mutineers?"

Trim, almost dainty, in his beautifully tailored uniform molded to his slight physique, Hans von Seeckt looked around the table coolly through his monocle. Then he addressed himself to Friedrich Ebert.

"Herr Reich President," he said, "the Army obeys *me.*" The matter was settled.

Colonel General von Seeckt was given extraordinary powers that made him virtual dictator of the Republic and the Army the supreme authority in the land. A proclamation was issued, warning the people of Germany that anyone supporting "this mad attempt in Munich" would be guilty of high treason. The proclamation concluded: "All necessary measures for the crushing of this attempt and the restoration of order have been taken . . ."

The most effective measure was a message by telegraph from General von Seeckt in Berlin ordering General von Lossow in Munich to suppress the Nazi uprising at once. It said in effect: "You do it—or I will."

What was happening in Berlin, and much of what was happening in Munich, remained either unknown or obscure to the *Putsch* leadership, still fuming and baffled at their Command Post. Ludendorff was increasingly grim as his faith in the pledged word of German officers dwindled. When, afterward, it vanished entirely, he would vow never to trust a German officer again and never again to don his uniform.

Scheubner-Richter occupied the time composing a proclamation for distribution next day. In it anyone opposing the new regime was threatened with instant punishment by National Socialist tribunals. He signed the proclamation *Dr. v. Kahr* and sent it to the Police Directory, where all posters had to be approved. There it was promptly recognized as a forgery, and torn up. Another poster was submitted separately to the police censors at the same time by two National Socialist officers who were also unaware of how matters stood. It announced fourteen mass meetings to be held at halls throughout the city the next day, November ninth. Adolf Hitler was advertised as the speaker at all fourteen meetings.

The group at District Headquarters seemed far more isolated from the reality of their situation than the facts warranted. Their information was incomplete, but they had learned enough to suspect with some degree of certainty that almost nothing necessary to the success of their venture was materializing. Yet they all seemed to block from their minds the implications of what they knew was happening.

Hitler, as in his worst moments at the Bürgerbräu, was far from the cool and decisive leader. He wavered between displays of pointless energy and fits of gloom: "If it comes out all right, well and good," he said more than once. "If not, we'll hang ourselves."

Among those at District Headquarters was Ernst Poehner, the former Police President who had done so much to foster and protect the NSDAP from its earliest days on. Poehner was designated as Minister President in the insurgent government, and it struck Hitler that Poehner should do something to demonstrate his authority. "We've given you the power, Herr Minister President," he said, "let us use it. We must seize the initiative, or the others will." He ordered Poehner to take a troop of Oberland men, march with them to the Police Directory and occupy it. Poehner, believing that force would not be required, went confidently to police headquarters on his own. He was ushered at once into the office of the Police Major in charge—and put under arrest. "It came like a blow from a club," he said afterward. He was informed that his colleague and collaborator in protecting the Nazis from the police, Dr. Wilhelm Frick, had been in custody for hours.

At about 5 A.M. unequivocal word came that the three men essential to the success of the *Putsch* had repudiated it. An officer from the Infantry Training School, a Colonel Leupold, came to pay his respects to Erich Ludendorff. He asked to speak to him privately with Herr Hitler, away from the others. Colonel Leupold had always been sympathetic with the Nazi movement, but now it was his painful duty to report that neither Lossow nor Seisser nor Kahr felt bound by the promises made at the beer hall. Not only that, said the Colonel, but the 7th (*Reichswehr*) Division was not supporting the new revolutionary government, either. It was standing ready to restore order in Munich by force if necessary.

Even now Hitler and Ludendorff were unwilling to concede that their *Putsch* was hopeless. The Quartermaster General clung to the idea that he could still, somehow, make contact with elements in the *Reichswehr* that would acknowledge his leadership. Hitler clung to the conviction that matters could be set right by a propaganda stroke of some kind. If he could reach the people of Munich, as he hoped to do in the fourteen scheduled mass meetings, he might yet turn the situation around, as he had done with his speech in the beer hall. "Propaganda!" he said, as so many times before. "Everything depends on propaganda!"

Beyond that he had no plan, and his subsequent behavior disappointed many of his followers, who had hoped to see him perform with the dash and decisiveness of a Mussolini that night. Munich was swarming with his men, all of them eager to be ordered into action, and there were more of them at that point than there were troops at Lossow's disposal. Yet no co-ordinated effort was launched to seize key public buildings like the telegraph office, the railroad station, the telephone exchange, or the main government offices. The mobilization of Storm Troops and their affiliated units had been efficiently carried out, and the affair at the Bürgerbräu had been swiftly and smoothly managed; but the uprising had, at that late hour, achieved little beyond the seizure of a beer hall and the room Hitler and Ludendorff were sitting in.

It was to the beer hall that the leaders of the *Putsch* repaired. After Colonel Leupold's report, the Military District Headquarters no longer seemed a prudent place to be. Captain Roehm and his troop were left behind to hold the place, like a fort in enemy territory, while Hitler and his staff made a strategic withdrawal across the river and into the haven of the Bürgerbräu.

The *Putsch* was back where it started.

A line of trucks with 150 Storm Troopers from the town of Landshut came rolling toward the Bürgerbräu on the morning of November ninth, at about six o'clock. An S.A. man named Paul

Goebel was sitting in the cab of the lead truck, and he did not like the look of things in Munich.

"What kind of a revolution do you call this?" he said to the driver. "People are going to work as usual. Something's wrong."

Like other outlying units, the Landshut battalion had been alerted the day before under a pretext of routine Party activity. Goebel and his comrades thought at first they were going to guard a meeting where the *Führer* would appear. They were told to bring "erasers and matches," which was S.A. code for rubber truncheons and pistols. But the *Führer* did not come to Landshut that night. Instead they heard a speech by their own commander, the local druggist, whose name was Gregor Strasser.* As they were all nursing the obligatory stein of beer before going home, two couriers arrived to announce that the *Putsch* was on; the troop was needed in Munich. Some of the men wrote hurried notes to their families in case they should fail to return. Others set about compiling a list of townspeople who were to be arrested and jailed under the new government. Then Paul Goebel, whose birthday it happened to be, waited with his commander for the arrival of the truck on which they would ride to the city. The truck was loaded with the troop's weapons.

While they were waiting a passenger car in obvious distress came down the road, and Goebel courteously volunteered to help fix it. The engine was overheated, and when that was set right, the car went on its way. Afterward Goebel learned that in the car were Minister Matt and his party, on their way to Regensburg to set up the legitimate government there and take counter-action against the *Putsch* that Goebel and his comrades were about to join.

The look and feel of Munich as he drove through it that Friday morning bothered Gregor Strasser, too. At the Bürgerbräu he immediately consulted with the Storm Troop commander, Captain Goering, who informed him that something was indeed

---

* Gregor Strasser of Landshut became one of the most influential men in the National Socialist movement. He was a regional leader in Bavaria, organized the Party in North Germany, and represented it in the Reichstag. His strong advocacy of Socialism alienated Hitler, who accused him of treachery and had him shot in the Roehm purge of 1934.

wrong. "Those fellows," said Captain Goering, "didn't come over to our side after all. They broke their word to the *Führer*, but the people are with us. We're going to try the whole thing over again."

Very few of the hundreds assembled at the Bürgerbräu were that sure of the situation. A beer hall was a better place than most for a bivouac, and with the coming of daylight, coffee, bread and cheese were served. But the night had been mostly sleepless, and the exhilarating tension produced by the first phase of the *Putsch* was going slack. The morning brought symptoms of anxiety and doubt. Telephone calls began to come in from worried women inquiring about husbands and sons who had gone off in uniform the evening before and had not come back. What was happening to them? When would they be back?

Nobody could answer, because nobody knew. There were no announcements from the leadership, no orders from unit commanders. There were only rumors. Most of them were to the effect that something had gone wrong, but nobody knew what. Ammunition and guns, some of them wrapped in wax paper, were distributed to those who had none, indicating that an action was still being planned, but nobody had any idea of what it might be.

The 3rd Company of the Munich S.A. Regiment held arms inspection, conducted by a noncom named Franz Wiechmann, a veteran of the Coburg and May first operations. Wiechmann was appalled to discover something that his men had evidently not noticed: more than half of the rifles they had been given at St. Anna's Church lacked firing pins. Wiechmann reported this privately to his unit commander, who told him to keep it quiet. It would only cause confusion, and perhaps panic, in case of a real emergency. Other rifles were clearly in working order, for isolated shots rang out here and there in the hall because of careless or clumsy handling of a firearm.

As the Kapp attempt had shown in Berlin, German troops expected pay even during a *Putsch*. Unlike Kapp's men, the troops in the Hitler *Putsch* got it. The Berliners had had compunctions about stealing money. Hitler's men had none. A detachment of Storm Troopers invaded the publishing plant of the Parcus brothers, who were Jewish, and "in the name of the nationalist regime," confiscated several stacks of freshly printed inflation money. It amounted to 14,605 trillion marks, for which the brothers Parcus demanded a receipt, and got it. The money was hauled to the beer hall and distributed at the rate of 2,000,000,000,000 (trillion) marks, which in normal times would have amounted to about eight marks, or two dollars. The distribution was supervised by Lieutenant Heinz Pernet who, besides being Erich Ludendorff's stepson, was a Nazi activist and Rossbach's adjutant in subverting the cadets of the Infantry School. Lieutenant Pernet's brief stint as paymaster at the Bürgerbräu that morning constituted the one official act carried to completion by Adolf Hitler's nationalist government.

Hitler did not address his Storm Troops, either to explain what was happening or to fire them up for what might be coming. Instead, a fierce, ugly, totally bald little man delivered several harangues intended to generate morale. He was Julius Streicher, who had hurried down to join the *Putsch* from Nuremberg, where he was an elementary schoolteacher. He was also a ferocious anti-Semite and the leading local Nazi. Once he had headed his own movement, the DSP, or German Socialist Party, which in political outlook and aim was indistinguishable from the NSDAP. Hopelessly outstripped by Hitler in mass appeal, Streicher gave up the competition and went over to the Nazis, bringing his party with him. He was a blustering street-corner agitator whose raucous obscenities sometimes repelled even hardened Nazis. Like his *Führer*, he habitually carried a whip.*

Streicher's oratory was not notably effective. Franz Wiechmann found it *"reichlich dunkel,"* or rather obscure. Others were puzzled because Streicher demanded loyalty to the Leader, even if it meant marching against the *Reichswehr* and the police; after

---

* Streicher was editor of *Der Stürmer*, The Stormer, which featured blatant pornography involving sexual relations between Jews and "Aryans." It advocated mass extermination of the Jews in issue after issue. *Der Stürmer* was the only paper Hitler read from cover to cover. Streicher became a *Gauleiter*, or Nazi regional chief, a member of the Reichstag, and an honorary S.A. general. He was hanged by the Nuremberg Tribunal for crimes against humanity.

all, they had all been given to believe that both Army and police were behind the *Putsch*.

Things became more confusing as the morning wore on.

Georg Zacherl, who had left his bed to join the uprising, found no chance to sleep since. He spent the night at the Bürgerbräu, which, he said, looked to him like Count von Wallenstein's camp, a rather unfortunate allusion. Wallenstein was the ambiguous generalissimo in the Thirty Years War about whom Schiller wrote a three-part play (the first called *Wallenstein's Camp*.) After some initial successes, Wallenstein was defeated, deposed and murdered.

Zacherl had little opportunity to brood over historical parallels, his unit being assigned to act as street sentinels in the headquarters area. As he left the beer hall to walk his post, he may have wondered about one of the orders he had been given: anyone caught tearing down proclamations of the new regime was to be shot. Who would be tearing down the announcement of the new regime?

It was being done by squads of the police.

The poster addressed "to the German people" proclaimed the end of the rule of the November criminals in Berlin and the establishment of a "provisional government consisting of General Ludendorff, Adolf Hitler, General von Lossow, Colonel von Seisser." While this was being pasted up—and then torn down by the police—Gustav von Kahr's proclamation repudiating the *Putsch* and dissolving the Nazi Party was also being pasted up —and then torn down by supporters of the *Putsch*. Sometimes the opposing posters managed to survive side by side on the same kiosks and billboards. When, toward noon, the morning newspapers appeared, the situation became even more clouded. Dr. Gerlich's enthusiastic story of Hitler's triumph at the Bürgerbräu duly appeared. But another paper flatly contradicted the story of Hitler's success by printing the Kahr statement denouncing the whole enterprise.

Most of the men in the beer hall, now 1,500 or more, saw neither the contradictory proclamations nor the contradictory newspapers. They mostly took for granted that the *Putsch* was still on and the *Führer* triumphant. The hole in the ceiling of the main hall where Hitler had fired his shot was pointed out to newcomers, who reacted with the awe due an historical sight (as visitors to the Bürgerbräu would do for years to come). Marc Sesselmann, a staunch adherent of the NSDAP, as he had been of the Thule Society, had lovingly gathered up the scattered shards of a beer glass the *Führer* flung away some time during the evening of the eighth. Sesselmann intended to preserve them as "souvenirs of a great experience," and was especially pleased that the handle of the glass was practically intact.

Long afterward Sesselmann recalled that, having had some difficulty recovering his overcoat, he was the last to leave the hall when the audience filed out that night. Only three "blue" policemen remained at the entrance, and they were about to leave, too.

Sesselmann joined them, and remarked jovially: "Well, gentlemen, after tonight there's going to be a different wind blowing hereabouts!"

For a moment there was no response to this sally. Then, Sesselmann remembered, one of the policemen said: "We'll just wait and see about that."

Neither the policeman nor Marc Sesselmann had long to wait. Here it was only the next day, and not even the *Führer* was sure how the wind was blowing.

Adolf Hitler was neither seen nor heard by most of the men encamped in the beer hall. He had temporarily abandoned his role of *Trommler,* or drum-beater; he had a different kind of talking to do. He had closeted himself with his staff in a second-floor room to discuss what the next step, if any, was to be. Many an uprising has sagged disastrously after the stimulation of the initial lunge wore off, and the leader was unable to solve the difficulty of what to do next. With Hitler's *Putsch* there was the additional problem of the blurring of the battle line. Despite what he had heard from Colonel Leupold, Hitler clung to a wisp of possibility that Lossow and Seisser were under outside restraint, that they might still find a way to redeem their pledges of the previous night.

Hitler had even dispatched an emissary to the Crown Prince, soliciting his support on the basis that only he, Rupprecht, could avoid a possible clash between the insurgent nationalists and the *Reichswehr,* an unthinkable eventuality— blood brothers at gunpoint. Perhaps the Crown Prince, with his great prestige among *Reichswehr* officers, could work out a compromise. Since Hitler's emissary, unable to find an available automobile, went by train to Berchtesgaden, where the Prince resided, the *Putsch* was over before the mission was completed.

It was a measure of Hitler's loss of nerve that he should turn to the Crown Prince to bolster his collapsing bid for power. From the start, the success of the *Putsch* was predicated on the cooperation of the authorities. Now its extinction seemed imminent because the authorities, contrary to expectations, were showing disapproval. "The *Putsch* with police permission" was paralyzed because permission had suddenly been withdrawn.

Ludendorff was stonily hostile to the appeal to Rupprecht, and the discussions in the upstairs room evidently made little progress. Hitler withdrew for a time to be by himself, and one of his S.A. men remembered seeing him pacing back and forth on a terrace, brooding.

He had much to brood about.

"Morning will find either a nationalist regime in Germany or us dead," he had trumpeted the night before. Now it was morning and there was no nationalist regime in Germany. He was still alive, and intended to remain so, but the prospect of failure, and the public humiliation that would come with it, was not pretty. "You have mighty things to do!" had been the message from the shrine at Bayreuth, but he was bogged down in his beer hall and could think of nothing decisive to do, whether mighty or expedient. The dream of turning Munich into another Ankara, a provincial city that could defy a capital and topple a government, was clearly not materializing. Not even the local government gave any sign of toppling, to say nothing of Berlin.

"This crazy mutiny" his *Putsch* was being called in Berlin, but the report of it had been enough for the capital to take precautions. Every highway leading into the city was being heavily guarded. A police cordon had been thrown around the government section of the Wilhelmstrasse. Unter den Linden was closed to traffic. Troops were being massed for the defense of the capital.

But the government gave no sign of falling.

Pacing back and forth on his terrace, Hitler was unaware that the world press was in less doubt about his situation than he was, and already had him on the march. "Adolf Hitler's troops have begun an offensive movement toward Berlin," said *The New York Times* that morning in an Associated Press dispatch datelined Paris. In another front-page report, his name was spelled Hittler. But the top headlines did not mention him at all, giving Ludendorff pride of place and assigning the general the role of dictator in the insurgent government. In a subsidiary story, Hitler was identified only as "the Fascist chief."

The *New York Tribune* had promoted him to "Lieutenant" Hitler, but it was the general, again, who dominated the headlines: LUDENDORFF LEADS ROYALIST ARMY AGAINST BERLIN. France, the next scare head said, was reacting by threatening war . . .

No one outside Bavaria was calling it the *Hitler Putsch*. Few, if any, sensed that the real menace to the world was the wavering demagogue pacing up and down at his beer hall. And when it actually did come to a march, the one who gave the orders was Erich Ludendorff and not Adolf Hitler.

For a man only two years short of sixty, Ludendorff had had a strenuous night, and no sleep. It reminded him, he said, of some of the nights he experienced during the Great War, especially that one in August of 1914 on the heights above Liège, before the triumphant march into the city. Actually, this morning had more of the atmosphere of defeat at Spa five years ago. More and more certain now that two German officers had indeed broken their word to him, and less and less sanguine of the prospects of the *Putsch* to which he had lent his name, Erich Ludendorff's mood was frankly depressed—*"wehmütig"* was the word he used, melancholy.

A new poster, torn from a kiosk, was brought in for everyone's inspection. It referred to "the Prussian Ludendorff" and called upon all good Bavarians to repudiate him. It also used, in fat, black letters, the words "High Treason." The various posters now plastered all over Munich were denouncing him as a Prussian, calling him an "ambitious character," branding him a traitor—a strong dose for a man accustomed to universal adulation.

His mood was not lifted when the Friday morning edition of the *Völkischer Beobachter* arrived, priced at 8,000,000,000 marks a copy and with ecstatic stories of Hitler triumphant all over the front page. The General was especially dispirited to read an article of his own. It was headed "Freedom and Bread," and began:

"The terrible misery, the hunger cry of the people, force me to speak. The smell of decay lies over Germany . . ."

There was the smell of something decaying in the Bürgerbräu that morning, and the gung-ho exuberance of the front page must have been painful to all present. Joyously hailing the new national regime (in *these* headlines Hitler's name came first), the paper described the events of the night before in terms of a Zarathustrian struggle between the forces of light and the powers of darkness, and light had, at last, triumphed. Kahr was praised as the "representative of all that is best in German officialdom," a true servant of the people. A beginning would be made to "clean up the Augean stable left behind by the November criminals." The slogan, said the paper, was: *"Nun auf zum Marsch nach Berlin...!* Now for the march on the capital, where the swastika would soon be waving.

But at Bürgerbräu the talk was of retreating, not marching forward. With Army and police mobilizing, the most prudent course, it was argued, would be to withdraw and fight another day. Captain Goering was in favor of pulling back to the town of Rosenheim, on the Austrian border. Rosenheim was strongly pro-Nazi (and, incidentally, Goering's home town.) There reinforcements could be assembled, the present troops regrouped, and another thrust for power made under better circumstances. Hitler agreed. His spirits had been sinking ever since he discovered that oratory and handshakes were not going to be enough to bring him into power. It was one thing to defy the Berlin politicians with the Army at one's back; it was something else to shake one's fist at authority and find the Army rolling up its sleeves to defend it.

Already he was beginning to feel the iron ring of authority tightening around him. During the night the *Reichswehr* had swiftly suppressed uprisings in his support in Augsburg, Nuremberg and Regensburg. New Army units were continually arriving in Munich, and there were reports of armored cars and mortars being set into position at key squares and crossings. Closer at hand, the "green" (State) Police were occupying bridgeheads just across the Isar, and his own troops were countering with the emplacement of heavy machine guns and even artillery. His men on the right bank of the river were referring to the armed police on the other side as *"der Feind,"* the enemy. His *Putsch* was beginning to look like civil war.

Though the situation in the city was turning increasingly serious, not everybody was taking it seriously. At the Museum Bridge, where a young trooper of the Fighting League named Hans Frank was laboring with his comrades to put a heavy machine gun in place, a knot of workers stood around jeering and asking what they thought they were doing. "Does your Mommy know you're playing with such dangerous things right on the open street?" one onlooker asked. Frank recalled the scene years later as "really grotesquely humorous." *

In the beer hall itself some units were so ill-equipped that their officers sent out details to confiscate windbreakers, boots

---

* He wrote the words in his cell at Nuremberg, where he was sentenced to hang for war crimes and crimes against humanity. He had been Hitler's "Governor-General" in occupied Poland, where he was responsible for mass atrocities against Poles, Jews and slave laborers.

and ski caps in an effort to achieve a halfway military look. One Storm Trooper had to leave his mates and hurry home to bring back a belt of machine-gun ammunition from his personal hoard. Such leaders as showed themselves while hurrying past on mysterious errands looked worried, which did nothing to arrest the sag in morale. Information was so scant and contradictory that even Dr. Weber, the head of the Oberlanders, claimed afterward he knew nothing of Kahr's defection all morning long. With signs of disorganization and disintegration multiplying among the men at the Bürgerbräu, Hitler's inclination to pull them back was understandable.

But in the presence of the Quartermaster General, the decision was not the Pfc.'s to make. Ludendorff flatly rejected the withdrawal to Rosenheim. It would, he said, lead to civil war, and the *völkisch* movement would probably perish in what he called "the filth of the streets." It was equally out of the question to stay where they were and be encircled and captured, or to disperse and go meekly home. Another ignominious ending, such as he had experienced in the Kapp affair, was not to be thought of. Perhaps the memory of Liège, which the preceding night had brought to his mind, prompted him to resume his old posture of warlord. In the high voice that came so oddly from his formidable façade, he said: *"Wir marschieren!"*

They would march.

It was a thoroughly German response to a difficult situation, and it accorded perfectly with Storm Troop doctrine. Marching was the sovereign recipe for creating enthusiasm and esprit, for producing a sense of power in the marcher and respect in the onlooker. "The sight of a marching column," in the words of the Storm Troop leader Franz Pfeffer von Salomon, "makes the deepest possible impression on a German and speaks to his heart a more convincing and compelling language than writing or talk of logic can ever do."

In the Quartermaster's proposal there was a flicker of logic as well. The idea behind the march was not simply to stage a display of martial power but to stir the city into a show of support for the *Putsch*. "We would go to the city," as Hitler later put it, "to win the people to our side, to see how public opinion would react, and then to see how Kahr, Lossow and Seisser would react to public opinion. After all, those gentlemen would hardly be foolish enough to use machine guns against a general uprising of the people [in our behalf]. That's how the march into the city was decided on. . . ."

It was to be, in essence, a propaganda march. As such it was an idea that might have been expected to come from Hitler. It conformed to his concept of propaganda as the decisive factor in situations involving public reaction and support. The night before, he had, in fact, suggested essentially the same maneuver. When it became clear that the official support he counted on was evaporating, he had proposed sending out armed patrols to shout, "Put out your flags!" as they went, meaning swastika flags.

"Do that," Hitler had said, "and you'll see the enthusiasm we'll get." It had not been done then; now, on the initiative of the Quartermaster General, the manpower of the *Putsch* was to be mustered to test the idea. It would, at the least, shake the *Putsch* out of the paralysis that had afflicted it ever since the Kahr defection. It might—who could tell?—be the start of that long-heralded, long-vaunted, long-awaited *Marsch auf Berlin* and a duplicate of Mussolini's *A Roma! A Roma!*

There were misgivings.

Scheubner-Richter had a foreboding, and confided to Hitler that he felt this would be their last walk together. Dr. Weber took Hitler aside and suggested he point out to Ludendorff the possibility that they might be shot at if they marched. Hitler did so, but the General's only reply was to repeat:

"Wir marschieren."

It was getting on toward noon when Colonel Kriebel gave the first orders for units to form up in front of the beer hall. There had been a band earlier in the morning, but, having been given neither breakfast nor pay, it disappeared after a half-hearted rendition of the *Badenweiler* march, Hitler's favorite tune. The column would have to create its own music as it went.

The order of march was more or less improvised, nobody having worked out a detailed plan of procession. Some units were not officially notified of the march at all, and scrambled into line wherever there was an opening when they heard about it. The November weather was miserably inappropriate for a parade—gloomy, cold and with flurries of wet snow.

A Watch Company was detailed to stay behind and guard the Bürgerbräu, where a number of city officials were being held hostage and Jews picked up at random were imprisoned. There had been no slackening in the terror tactics begun the night before, and the list of those still to be arrested included the names of Bertolt Brecht and Lion Feuchtwanger. "Whoever makes the slightest difficulty must be shot," was the principle on which Captain Goering was proceeding. He regarded "the sharpest terror" as the only basis for effective action, and wanted to insert his hostages into the line of march.

"The first dead man in our ranks means the immediate death of all the hostages," he announced. At the last minute, Hitler ordered the captives out of the column. "I wanted no martyrs," he said afterward.

Not all the marchers were in uniform. Conspicuous among the civilians was a tall, reserved gentleman named Theodor von der Pfordten. He was a high official of the Bavarian judiciary and an "idealist" of the movement. Von der Pfordten was one of the few members of the Party who came from a cultured background and had distinguished himself in a profession. He spoke and wrote in cultivated phrases and drew his allusions from Plato and the Bible, but his attitude was vehemently *völkisch*, anti-Semitic and nationalist. What brought him to the Bürgerbräu, and then into the march, was his feeling of solidarity for his friend Ernst Poehner, who was still under arrest. Von der Pfordten seemed broken and distraught as he took his place in the van. In his pocket was the draft of a new constitution for Germany, which Hitler had asked him to draw up. It was a revision of the law to eliminate its Roman elements and create a "Germanic" code.

There was a motley look about many of the formations as

they lined up and waited for the command that would set them
marching. Many of the uniforms were improvised, with wrap-
around leggings, scraps of leftover army gear, and homemade
brassards the sole means of distinguishing a member of an organized unit from an ordinary civilian. Sometimes the swastika on
the left sleeve was the only insignia that betrayed a marcher's affiliation. Some of the men were self-conscious about the appearance they made, but defiant about it, too. "People looked at us
askance," the Storm Trooper Ludwig Hofmann remembered.
"Some of them were on our side, but others glared at us with disapproval. To tell the truth, we didn't exactly inspire confidence in
our old, weathered, field-gray uniforms patched up with civilian
odds and ends. What did we care? We knew what was at stake."
The old jeer about "Hitler's Foreign Legion" still applied to
some of the units. To Hans Frank, who was part of it, the column looked like "a defeated army that hadn't fought anybody."
But the procession gave an impression of formidable strength as
well. Some segments looked more like army formations equipped
and ready for battle than like political demonstrators.

Well to the fore was the *Stosstrupp Hitler,* the Shock Troop
of seventy or eighty men all dressed and armed like soldiers
about to storm an enemy stronghold. Their uniforms were the
field greenish-gray of the regular army, and they wore steel helmets and bandoliers. Each man had two "potato masher" grenades in his belt and carried a carbine for which he was issued
seventy-one rounds of ammunition. The Shock Troop was never
far behind the leaders of the procession, and no one who saw
them could have had much confidence that their intentions were
wholly peaceful.

The formation directly behind Hitler and Ludendorff was
the crack 6th S.A. Company, the oldest Storm Troop unit and
the best equipped and disciplined. It had been seasoned at major
rallies, demonstrations, street fights and beer-hall brawls, and
consisted largely of veterans of Coburg and the German Day at
Nuremberg. The Company Sergeant-Major was Karl Eggers,
who had won nine decorations in the Great War, including the
Iron Cross I and II. Sergeant-Major Eggers and his 6th Com-

pany were known as *Draufgänger*, or reckless commando types, and they made no effort to persuade onlookers that they were anything but combat-ready soldiers. One of them carried the lead swastika flag, which would go down in Party history as the "blood banner" of the movement.

Most of the marchers had rifles, usually carbines, some of recent make. Often they were carried across their backs by the slings. Many had fixed bayonets, a feature not customary at purely political demonstrations. Many of the S.A. carried pistols, either at their belts or in their hands. The slapdash impression made by the variations in weapons and uniforms was partly off-set by the military smartness of the Infantry School cadets. Bringing up the rear of the column was a heavy machine gun mounted on a truck and manned by members of the Shock Troop.

The column had a menacing, martial air, but before the marching order was issued, a command came that all guns were to be unloaded. The step was evidently taken because of Hitler's anxiety that no open clash occur between his followers and the *Reichswehr*. A pitched battle would, he knew, mean the virtual annihilation of his own troops, and at this point he wished to do nothing to antagonize the Army further. Ludendorff concurred, and so the order to unload was issued. But, the disorganization of command at the beer hall being what it was, the order may not have reached everyone who carried a loaded weapon. And supervision was not strict enough to insure that everyone who heard the order necessarily obeyed it. At any rate, as events were shortly to prove, not all the guns carried in the column were un-loaded.

While the units were lining up in their more or less haphaz-ard order, the leaders of the *Putsch*—and of the parade—stood in a loosely formed group and talked among themselves. It was about noon. Just before the order to march was given, Alfred Rosenberg drove up. On his way he had passed through the spa-cious Odeon Platz with its Hall of the Field Marshals, the *Feld-herrnhalle*, and he was disturbed by what he saw there. The place was swarming with police armed with automatic weapons. In the center of the square, into which five streets converged, stood a camouflaged armored car, manned and ready for action. Rosenberg said nothing of what he had seen, and took his place next to Scheubner-Richter, who shook hands with him and said: "The situation stinks."

Rosenberg noticed that Hitler was grave and pale. The *Führer* had put on his trench coat over his egregious cutaway, and was holding his battered slouch hat in his hand. He wore a swastika brassard on his left sleeve. It is probable that the pistol of the night before was still in the pocket of his trench coat. Whether he actually drew it and flourished it in the course of the march became a matter of dispute. As he stood in the street in front of his beer hall waiting for the march to begin, it is unlikely that he had a weapon in his hand, but he had much on his mind.

Afterward he said that he grew dizzy when he looked back on this moment that marked "the most desperately daring decision of my life." If the march failed, the *Putsch* failed—or so it must have seemed to him then. If the *Putsch* failed, his career could well be over. This was, as he must have reminded himself, November ninth, the date when the Republic had been proclaimed from the balcony of the Reichstag in Berlin five years ago—the fatal climax of the *Dolchstoss*, the stab in the back. The all too obvious parallel must have weighed oppressively on him and his entourage, for what was the defection of Kahr, Lossow and Seisser but another *Dolchstoss?*

Still, the perfidy of that other revolution had begun in Munich, and perhaps the renewal of Germany could begin here also, and begin today. Not long ago, another march—a march through these same streets—had toppled a 1,000-year monarchy and destroyed Bavaria's traditional way of life. What Kurt Eisner and a handful of Bohemians could do must surely be possible for Adolf Hitler and his Storm Troopers. He had already won many a battle in the beer halls and on the streets of Munich. Now he was taking to the streets again in a straw-grasping effort to save face and salvage his *Putsch.*

It was noon when the march began.

First came a color guard with the swastika banner of National Socialism, the black-white-red of Imperial Germany and the flag of the Bund Oberland. The main column marched eight abreast, with all the leaders of the *Putsch* in the van. Hitler and Ludendorff were in the center of the first rank, which also included Captain Goering, Colonel Kriebel, Scheubner-Richter, Dr. Weber, Ulrich Graf, Hitler's bodyguard, and First Lieutenant Wilhelm Brueckner, commander of the Munich Storm Troop Regiment. Scheubner-Richter was on Hitler's left, Ludendorff on his right.

The command "Forward march!" had its anticipated uplifting effect on the spirits of the troops. They again felt, in Hitler's phrase, like "revolutionaries against the revolution," and something of the *élan* that had been withering away inside the Bürgerbräu returned with the march-step on the open street. They had not advanced more than a few hundred yards when, at the Ludwig Bridge over the Isar, they demonstrated that they were still in earnest with their uprising and were not carrying weapons for exhibition only.

The Ludwig Bridge led over the river to the center of the city, the goal of the march. It was being guarded by a small detachment of General von Seisser's State Police force, known as the Green Police. They wore steel helmets, they were armed, and their orders were "to prevent the crossing of this bridge by National Socialist units bearing arms."

As the column approached the bridge, there was confusion on both sides. The marching men were confident that there would be no opposition—"Why, Seisser's on our side, and so are his police!" In the Green ranks there was no clarity about what was happening in Munich or what role they were supposed to be playing. They had been rushed from Landshut as reinforcements during the night. Some of them thought that a Kahr-Ludendorff-Hitler dictatorship had been established, and that possibly they were being called on to defend it. Things were hardly clarified when they recognized a Landshut townsman or two in the approaching column and exchanged "Heil!" greetings with them.

In subsequent court testimony, and in Nazi mythology, the Green Police were pictured as being so overcome with patriotic emotion at the sight of the column that they stepped aside to let it pass. "They were deeply moved," Hitler himself would testify, "and there were some among them whose eyes overflowed." It is possible that the unarmed notables in the first ranks were allowed to proceed unmolested, but the passage of the main column was disputed. The commander of the Green Police, a lieutenant, ordered the march to halt. When it did not, he threatened to shoot, and ordered his men to load with live ammunition. Now the column did pause, and from the ranks came a cry of: "Don't shoot at your comrades!" Then, from somewhere, a trumpet blast suddenly sounded.

At this signal, men from the column rushed at the Green Police and menaced them with fixed bayonets, drawn pistols, and aimed rifles. The outnumbered police were struck with rifle butts, jostled and pummeled, choked and disarmed. There were shouts of "You dogs, you've betrayed your Fatherland! You've got it coming!" and "Put the bastards against the wall!" Nobody was shot, but the Green Police were taken back to the beer hall as prisoners, being jeered at and spat upon as they were led away.

The incident lasted less than ten minutes, but it afforded another lightning-flash revelation of what a National Socialist regime would be like. The unhesitating physical assault on the police also damaged whatever was left of the concept of Bavaria as the *Ordnungszelle,* the enclave of law and order, in the Reich.

Invigorated by the triumph at the bridgehead, the column crossed the river and moved west and north toward the center of the city, singing as it went. In lieu of band music, the singing was almost continuous—deep-throated bellowing of *Deutschland über alles,** Swastika on Steel Helmet* and Dietrich Eckart's *Storm Song.* Eckart himself was standing on the curb watching

* Though beloved by all enemies of the Weimar Republic, this "song of the Germans" was written by a liberal (Hoffmann von Fallersleben) and was adopted as the national hymn of the Republic in 1922. It puts Germany *über alles,* "above everything," but it is probably the only patriotic anthem that includes lines in praise of wine, women and song.

the parade. Hitler turned his head and looked at him. He seemed to look coldly, Eckart thought, as if to say: "The rest of us are here. Why aren't *you?*" Stricken, Eckart stopped an automobile that was accompanying the marchers, explained who he was, and asked if he could ride along. He was promptly taken aboard and so joined the parade.

About 2,000 men had started marching from the beer hall, but along the way spectators and supporters continually fell into step with the marchers, joined the singing and became part of the procession. Students, clerks and a scattering of workingmen walked shoulder to shoulder with the Storm Troopers as the column threaded through the Isar Gate and debouched into the broad and ancient thoroughfare called the Tal. Whenever the width of a street allowed, the column marched twelve and sixteen abreast, instead of eight, to present a more formidable front to onlookers as well as possible opposition. Another police cordon was broken through and swept aside by the sheer mass of the procession.

From the Tal the procession entered St. Mary's Plaza, the *Marienplatz,* middle point and heart of the city. The square was packed with people. From the lovely Gothic *Rathaus,* the Town Hall, the swastika flag was flying, and next to it the black-white-red. Storm Troopers, in advance of the parade, had invaded the Town Hall, and taken it over. They held the City Council captive, tore down the flag of the Republic, and hoisted the banner of the insurgency.

Relays of speakers had been haranguing clumps of listeners in different parts of the square, and to many the scene suggested the wild revolutionary days of 1918. At the foot of the graceful St. Mary's Pillar, in the middle of the square, one feverish Nazi alternated nationalist oratory with renditions of *Deutschland über alles* until his voice gave out. Julius Streicher, who had assumed the role of roving agitator for the *Putsch,* was attracting the largest audience in the square with the incendiary outbursts that were his speciality. The place was in a tumult of enthusiasm when the column arrived, and there could be no doubt that here the objective of the march—"to bring the people to our side, to see how public opinion would react"—was being bountifully achieved. But it was the crush of supporters and *Heil*-shouters that, ironically, caused a turn of events fatal to the procession and to the *Putsch*.

Unable to proceed because of the crowds, the march came to a halt and a certain amount of confused milling about ensued. The confusion, it developed, was as prevalent in the leadership of the column as among the men.

No one knew exactly where the march was going, and no one had known from the start.

Colonel Kriebel, the military commander of the venture, was under the impression that everybody would turn around at the *Marienplatz* and march back to the beer hall. So was Dr. Weber, the leader of the Oberland contingent. Hitler's thoughts about the route of march are not on record. It appears he was so little in command of the situation that now he was not even consulted.

At any rate, the column could not go back even if that had been the agreed-upon procedure; the press of people was too great. The decision, when it came, was to continue in the same direction, northward. It was made on the spur of the moment by Ludendorff.

Colonel Kriebel was surprised when the column resumed marching forward instead of turning around, but said to himself: "If Ludendorff is marching that way, naturally we'll go with him." The marchers were joined by jubilant spectators from the square, many of whom were under the impression that they were celebrating the success of the *Putsch*.

Ludendorff's subsequent explanation of why he took the direction he did suggests how impulsively, not to say irrationally, historic decisions can be made, whether on the battlefield or in the political arena. "At certain moments in life," Ludendorff said, "one acts instinctively and doesn't know why. I fought the battle of Tannenberg. When I ask myself why I fought it the way I did, I don't know. The reasons given in those splendid history books I only thought of afterward. We just wanted to get to Roehm and bring him back . . ."

Captain Roehm and his men, it was known, had been surrounded by the *Reichswehr* and were now virtual prisoners in
the Military District Headquarters they had occupied the night
before. But, if rescuing them was supposed to be the objective of
the march, Kriebel, Weber and others in the van were unaware of
it.

In another explanation of his move at the *Marienplatz*, Ludendorff was even vaguer. *"Maybe* I wanted to fetch Roehm," *
he said, as if, even afterward, thinking it over, he couldn't be
sure of why he acted as he did. But his impulse, or caprice, had
the result of introducing tragedy into an event that, in retrospect
and in history, might otherwise have been forgotten. It was the
element of tragedy that would allow Adolf Hitler to make a politically powerful myth out of a disaster.

To reach Roehm and his encircled men, it was necessary to
pass through Odeon Square, a few blocks to the north. With the
Pied Piper figure of Ludendorff in his dark-brown overcoat and
felt hat leading the way, the procession moved out of the *Marienplatz* and into the Wein Strasse toward Odeon Square. Looking
ahead, Ludendorff thought he saw the way blocked by guards.
He turned right at the intersection of Perusa Strasse, about halfway to the square. A short march brought the procession to the
Residenz Strasse, where it turned left and proceeded north again,
parallel to its previous route.

There was a certain congestion, since the street was narrow
and the original ranks were swollen by the accretion of civilians
along the way. On the right was the *Residenz,* the Wittelsbach
Palace, with its Italianate façade acting as a stone wall. The
marchers were now approaching the Hall of the Field Marshals,
the *Feldherrnhalle,* from the rear. The street ran past the east
side of the Hall as it issued into the spacious square beyond. In
spite of the crowding, the halts and the jostling, the spirit of the
column was high. A thin police line was easily broken, and
shouted police orders to stop and go no farther—*"Halt! Nicht
weitergehen!"*—were ignored. In the narrow chasm of the street,

* *"Vielleicht wollte ich Röhm abholen."* Italics above added. R.H.

the lusty singing of the column reverberated thunderously. The song was *O Deutschland hoch in Ehren,* "O Germany, high in honor."

Karl Kessler's 2nd S.A. Company was marching about thirty meters behind the head of the column, and he remembered afterward that he was singing the song with gusto when it happened. He remembered how the song died away along the length of the column as the shot rang out.

A platoon of Green Police reinforcements had come on the run from the other side of the *Feldherrnhalle* and formed a cordon athwart the street where it debouched into the square. The platoon was armed with carbines, pistols and rubber truncheons, and set for the shock of hostile contact. Johann Aigner, who was Scheubner-Richter's orderly and a combat veteran, was marching in the second rank of the column. He took one look at the set of the Green platoon and told himself that this would be no repetition of the easy breakthrough at the Ludwig Bridge. These men, he saw, meant business.

As the distance between the column and the cordon closed to a few feet, Ulrich Graf, the hulking bodyguard, shouted: "No shooting! General Ludendorff is coming!" The column was eight abreast again, owing to the narrowness of the street, and Hitler, still in the van, had locked arms with Scheubner-Richter. It was a peculiarly dependent act for a leader, perhaps another symptom of the state of his nerves. Scheubner-Richter was hardly a tower of strength, being small, forty, bald and myopic, but Hitler's grip on his arm was intense. Ludendorff held on to nobody. It seemed inconceivable to him, and to those around him, that any German in uniform would raise a weapon against the Quartermaster General of the Imperial Army.

But the commander of the Green Platoon was a vigorous, no-nonsense First Lieutenant, a Baron Michel von Godin. He had orders to stop the *Putsch* march, and he intended to do it here. What he saw coming at him, as he later reported, was a "Hitler troop armed with war material of every kind—fixed bayonets, rifles with safety catches off, and drawn pistols." He and his men were in no position to sort out which of the oncoming guns might be loaded, and which not. The bayonets were all too obviously unsheathed. Lieutenant von Godin, armed only with a pistol, seized a carbine from one of his men and used it to knock aside two of the bayonets pointed at him. His men struck out with their rifle butts and truncheons. Storm Troopers and men of the Shock Troop struck back. It was 12:30.

Suddenly the crack of a single shot cut through the commotion of the clash and the sound of singing that still continued in the rear ranks, where the activity at the head of the column could not be seen. Who fired first has never been determined. Each side afterward blamed the other under oath, and each claimed the first victim as its own. Lieutenant von Godin insisted that the shot came from "one of Hitler's men" who was aiming at him. Missing Godin, it killed the police officer standing behind him.

For an instant a paralysis of astonishment and uncertainty gripped both sides. "Then," said Lieutenant von Godin, "before I could give any kind of a command, my people opened fire that had the effect of a volley. At the same time the Hitler troops began firing . . ."

Some of the Green Police leaped upon the platform of the *Feldherrnhalle* and fired on the column from there, and the marchers charged afterward that shots came also from the windows of the *Residenz* on their right. They were enfiladed. At the same time, Godin's men were being fired at point-blank by Hitler riflemen who took cover in buildings on the other side of the street, including a pastry shop.

In the column there was panic.

The front surged back, pressing on the people behind and crushing them. Many threw themselves to the ground. There was shouting and screaming. Some in the rear thought the column was being attacked by Reds and tried to unsling their rifles, which was often impossible in the crush. Karl Kessler thought he heard the *tack-tack-tack-tack* of a machine gun up front, while close to him two Shock Troopers were trying to set up their own machine gun. Somebody shouted, "Shoot back!" but there were no authoritative orders or commands from anybody. Men were throwing away their weapons and running wherever they found an opening in the pack. From the front of the column, a man came shouting: "Ludendorff and Hitler are dead!" and the news swept the length of the column. An alley on one side was a refuge thick with men huddling together, deathly white and still.

At the first fusillade Alfred Rosenberg, in the second rank, threw himself down, but landed on the body of a comrade, which gave him a slight elevation from which he could see something of what was happening around him. He saw Hermann Goering bleeding on the pavement with a bullet in his groin and crawling for protection under a stone Bavarian lion that stood before the *Residenz*. Behind Rosenberg somebody was firing a rifle that, if it ever was unloaded, was now discharging live ammunition at the Green Police. The rifleman was using Rosenberg and the body under him as cover. "For God's sake, stop it!" Rosenberg shouted. "It's doing no good." Rosenberg was not eager for the police to concentrate their attention on the marksman who was using him as a sandbag. He saw another marcher lying across the sidewalk with the top of his skull shot off and his brains gushing out, steaming. The man was still breathing.

Johann Aigner, flat on the pavement, thought he saw an armored car in the middle of the square open fire, but then stop, as if its machine gun had jammed. He himself had loaded his rifle and was firing steadily. After his fourth shot, he saw his best friend, Kurt Neubauer, writhing in the street. Neubauer had been the youngest volunteer in the World War and was Ludendorff's orderly. Aigner crawled to him, holding his friend's hand and wiping the foam from his mouth as he died of a stomach wound. A moment later Aigner thought he had been hit himself. Warm blood was running down the back of his neck, but it was coming from another comrade lying next to him who was spurting from his jugular. Marc Sesselmann, who thought that a new wind had begun to blow in Germany, was hit in the first volley, and badly wounded. As the column disintegrated, and men lay on the street wounded and dying, Dr. Weber, the chief of the Oberlanders, was seen leaning against a wall and weeping hysterically.

Theodor von der Pfordten—"one of the purest idealists of the movement"—was among those dead in the street. His draft of a new constitution for Germany was still in his pocket. It contained thirty-one provisions, and many would be put into effect in the Third Reich: they included forced labor, "collecting" camps that became concentration camps, and the death penalty for advocates of democratic government. When they took the proposed constitution from Theodor von der Pfordten's pocket, it was smeared with blood.

Hans Frank, who had marched without enthusiasm, took cover in the doorway of a coffee firm when the shooting started. He saw the bodies in the street, and he had heard the rumors. He was shattered.

"It's all over," he said to himself. "Hitler is dead. Germany is dead."

Hitler was not dead, though many had seen him go down. Among the first to be hit was Scheubner-Richter, whose arm was locked in Hitler's. As Scheubner-Richter crumpled, he pulled Hitler with him. Hitler, conditioned to gunfire at the front, may at the same time have thrown himself to the pavement instinctively. Between being pulled by his partner and hurling himself down, Hitler struck the ground with an impact that dislocated his left shoulder. The injury was extremely painful, and at first he thought he had been hit.

But Adolf Hitler had not been hit. He had been missed—again. As he was spared through five years of combat at the front while thousands around him fell, now in the narrow Residenz Street, where bullets came flying at the shortest range, and where one of them instantly found the heart of the man at his shoulder, Adolf Hitler was spared again. His bodyguard, Graf, flung himself on Hitler and was seriously wounded by a half dozen bullets that otherwise would have struck the recumbent *Führer*. Near him, in a pool of blood, was a large man in a dark overcoat. Hitler was sure the man was Ludendorff, dead. "All around me," said Hitler afterward, "I saw nothing but dead men."

He was still alive, but a fire-fight of thirty seconds or less had been enough to break his column, scatter his followers in panic, and destroy his *Putsch*. Dietrich Eckart saw him get up from the pavement, and move slowly away from the *Feldherrn-halle*. His coat was filthy, his hat was off. Strands of hair were falling in his face, and he was very pale. He moved slowly and spoke a few words with two or three men who approached him. From the Max Joseph Square, which adjoined the street, a little yellow Fiat pulled up and its door was flung open. The driver was Dr. Walther ("Bubi") Schultze, the Chief S.A. doctor. Hitler got in, and the Fiat raced off, out of the city and into the mountains.

Though Hitler was not the first to flee the scene of battle, as some chronicles have it, he did not exactly cover himself with glory at the *Feldherrnhalle*. He had plunged to the pavement at the first volley, stayed there until the shooting was over, and made off as soon as opportunity offered. At no point did he behave heroically or show any flair for leadership. It was therefore necessary to invent something to redeem the *Führer's* lackluster performance, and he contributed generously to the invention himself. The story was that as he threaded his way among the dead bodies, while the bullets were still flying, he saw a little boy who had somehow wandered into the line of fire. The *Führer*, without hesitation and despite the excruciating pain of his shoulder, picked up the lad and wrapped his arms around him protectively (not an easy thing to do with only one arm in working order.) He then carried the child to safety before he thought of his own. The legend may have been suggested by Hitler's cradling his own injured arm, and thereby giving the impression that he was carrying something, or somebody. At any rate, the myth was offset by another one; it said his car *ran over* a child and killed it in the haste of his flight.

There was no reason to invent stories about Erich Ludendorff's actions at the *Feldherrnhalle*. While every other person in the front ranks threw himself to the pavement, Ludendorff remained stiffly upright, walked straight ahead into the fire of the Green Police and through their ranks into the empty square beyond. One hand was thrust into his coat pocket, and he never wavered. At first nobody followed him. Then his adjutant, a Storm Troop commander named Hans Streck, who had also flung himself to the pavement, saw his chief advancing alone. Streck leaped up and hastened to follow. Among all of Hitler's fire-eaters and *Draufgänger,* he was the only one who did so.

The General crossed the square, passing the silenced armored car. On the other side he presented himself to a guard of the State Police.

"Excellency," said the guard. "I must take you into protective custody."

"You have your orders," said the General. "I'll follow you."

The lone march of the Quartermaster General has been called "the one almost redeeming feature of an otherwise thoroughly sordid and disreputable affair." The phrase is from John H. Wheeler-Bennett, the Oxford historian of German military mores, and he added: "It was the last gesture of the Old Imperial Army."

The rest of the column ended the march with less dignity. Johann Aigner was still firing when he heard a Storm Troop officer, evidently the only one still on the scene, call out: "Pull back, comrades, there's only a couple of us left."

Johann Aigner looked around, and what he saw continued to puzzle him for years. A moment before, there had been several thousand men behind him. Now there was nobody. "Where they all disappeared to in the short time the fight lasted is and remains a riddle," he said afterward.

The dead and wounded were still in the streets, and before the day was out the count would be: sixteen fatalities among the marchers, three among the police, and more than a hundred wounded. Aigner helped to carry away some of the wounded, and then made his way to the home of a friend, where he changed into a borrowed civilian suit. Anybody who could be identified as one of the *Putsch* marchers was now in trouble with the police.

A young S.A. man named Alois Winderl, with a group from

his company, were hastening away from the *Feldherrnhalle* and looking for a place to hide their weapons when they were overtaken by a truckful of Green Police. Winderl's group was disarmed on the open street, and what he remembered afterward was that two waitresses in a nearby coffee shop stood at the window watching—and laughing. "And among us," said Alois, "front soldiers were crying. We were all howling with rage inside. Then we went home, beaten."

Not far from the Odeon Square was a ladies' academy, which somehow was singled out as a refuge by fleeing marchers. They begged to be hidden under beds or in closets, terrified at the prospect of being caught and shot by the Green Police. Others ducked into any handy haven where ski cap, jacket and weapon could be hidden or discarded. The pastry shop on the Residenz Strasse, Rottenhöfer's *Konditorei,* was inundated by fugitives from the firing. They pressed up the stairs, to the bakery on the second floor, and hid pistols, bayonets, rifles under the ovens, in flour sacks, behind stoves, and in coffee machines. One man stashed away 2,000 rounds of heavy machine-gun ammunition. It was still there when he came back for it five days later.

Two or three units managed to reach the woods on the outskirts of the city, and bury their weapons. Some of the men were so enraged by what they felt was betrayal that they senselessly slammed their rifles against the tree trunks in rage and frustration. One battalion marched to the woods in good order and methodically buried 500 rifles before dispersing and going home.

At the Military District Headquarters, where Captain Roehm and his men were encircled, there was one casualty before the place was surrendered. Though the *Reichswehr* had wheeled up artillery and mortars, there was little inclination for a fight on either side. Roehm announced he intended to defend his stronghold to the last man, but when news of the calamity at the *Feldherrnhalle* came, it seemed prudent to negotiate. While that was going on, somebody in Roehm's troop, probably out of nervousness, fired a shot that slightly wounded a *Reichswehr* soldier. The fire was promptly returned, and one of Roehm's officers, a Lieutenant Theodor Casella, was killed. When word was received from Ludendorff that holding out would serve no further purpose, Roehm canceled his last-man resistance and gave up. He and his men, including Heinrich Himmler, were disarmed and taken into custody by the *Reichswehr*. The one military achievement of the *Putsch* had been nullified, and Captain Ernst Roehm's career in the Germany Army was over.

There was no resistance at the Bürgerbräu, either, when troops and police arrived to clear out the Hitlerites still stationed there. The Storm Troop contingents left behind from the march were so dispirited at what they had heard of its fate that when they were told to stack their weapons and go home, they did so without argument. Among them was Josef Richter, who went back to his shoemaker's shop so depressed he could not eat or sleep for days. Karl Heinlein, who had shared guard duty at the beer hall with his two sons, comforted himself with the thought that, anyway, *"unser geliebte Führer"*—"our dear Leader"— was still alive. Most of them felt like Carl Fischer of the 12th S.A. Company, who, when his unit was dispersed and he was making his way home, asked himself: "Is there any sense in living any more?"

At the Bürgerbräu the State Police confiscated a mass of arms and liberated the Jewish prisoners and the officials being held there as hostages. The place ceased to be an armed camp, a prison, and the center of a political explosion. It became a beer hall again.

At three o'clock in the afternoon of November 9, 1923, the Military District Commander, Lieutenant General Otto Hermann von Lossow, was able to report to the General State Commissioner, Dr. Gustav Ritter von Kahr:

"Excellency, the Ludendorff-Hitler *Putsch* has been broken."

16 THE END WAS
THE BEGINNING

"THAT THE ATTEMPT FAILED WAS PERHAPS THE GREATEST
GOOD FORTUNE OF MY LIFE . . ."
                                        —ADOLF HITLER

WHEN THE POLICE delivered Adolf Hitler to the fortress-prison of
Landsberg, about thirty-five miles west of Munich, he announced that he would go on a hunger strike. "A man doesn't
deserve to live," he said, "who is responsible for so great a fiasco
as I am." He vowed to refuse all food until he starved to death.

It was his second threat to commit suicide since the failure
of his *Putsch*. He was arrested in the mountain home of his
friend Putzi Hanfstaengl, at a place called Uffing, on the second
day after the debacle at the *Feldherrnhalle*. When the police came
to seize him in the attic-bedroom where he was hiding, he tried
to shoot himself. His dislocated arm was in a crude sling, and it
was not difficult to disarm him.

It was not difficult, either, to dissuade him from his hunger
strike, though his despair continued. Who, he asked a visitor,
would follow a man who had such a fiasco—he used the word
again—on his record? His day as a leader was over, his political
career had collapsed.

He found confirmation of his fears in the newspapers that
were brought to his cell. He read that he had "held Germany up
to the ridicule of the whole world," that his enterprise was "the
craziest farce pulled off in memory." It was a "miniature beer-
hall revolution" that "alternately provoked amusement and disgust." In Munich it was called an *Indianerstreich*—an Indian

raid—and a Punch and Judy show. Abroad, where the affair was misunderstood as a royalist uprising, he was being dismissed as "Ludendorff's noisy lieutenant." The *New York Tribune* said: "It is generally felt that he will be executed." The European correspondent of *The New York Times* wrote on its front page: "The Munich putsch definitely eliminates Hitler and his National Socialist followers."

Definitely. It was the general opinion.

Yet it took him only the thirty days of his trial to retrieve everything he had lost, and then add to it immeasurably. "Only a miracle could save him," wrote Truman Smith, the American military attaché, when it was over, "but a miracle happened."

Hitler went on trial at a so-called "People's Court" before a bench consisting of two professional judges and three lay judges —two insurance men and a dealer in stationery. He was one of ten defendants; the others were Ludendorff, Roehm, Weber, Kriebel, Frick, Poehner, and several lesser leaders of the *Putsch*. The charge was high treason, and one foreign correspondent covering the trial said he had never seen an indictment with so many references to beer halls, beer cellars and restaurants as this one. In Munich, the reporter wrote, conspiracy against the state seemed to be inseparable from beer-swilling.

In spite of the derision the *Putsch* had evoked in the press at home and abroad, the trial attracted enormous attention. One hundred reporters from around the world were at the press table, and the rush for seats was so great that police, mounted and afoot, were needed to control the crowds. The building was protected by helmeted guards and barbed-wire barriers. It was the same building that housed the Infantry Officers School, but the school itself had been evacuated from Munich as punishment for participating in the *Putsch*.

The trial began on February 26, 1924, and was dominated by Adolf Hitler from the start, despite the presence of Erich Ludendorff resplendent in uniform and covered with decorations. He had evidently forgotten, or thought better of, his vow never to don the uniform again. Hitler wore his cutaway, with the Iron Cross I pinned to the left breast.

There was something fundamentally preposterous about the trial, and liberal journalists did not fail to emphasize it. The chief prosecution witnesses—Kahr, Lossow, Seisser—were as guilty of conspiring against the state as the defendants, and everyone knew it, including the judges. From the witness stand General von Lossow accused Hitler of attempting to "march the authority of the state to death," which was true; but his own defiance of the state's authority was also notorious. More than once Hitler told the court that, in all justice, his accusers should be sitting in the dock with him.

What really turned the trial into a triumph for Hitler was his astonishing ability to convert the courtroom into a sounding board to send his voice reverberating across the nation. With the indulgence of the judges, and the approbation of the audience, he made the dock a platform for long, impassioned speeches in his tested demagogic style. In deference to the dignity of the court, he dropped his cruder beer-hall tactics and added some unwonted touches of eloquence and elegance, but the theme was the same, and so was the effect. He struck all the nationalist chords with the full diapason of voice and language that had so often whipped crowds at the Krone Circus to frenzy.

But now all Germany was listening.

He had fully recovered his self-assurance; his fiasco had not, after all, seriously damaged his prestige with his followers. With every day of the trial, his confidence grew until, at the end, he was so fully in charge of himself, and of the courtroom, that it hardly seemed a trial any longer. It was a propaganda festival for the *Führer* of the National Socialist movement.

Already he had convinced himself, and was convincing others, that the *Putsch* was a success. "The greatest gain of the eighth of November," he said at the trial, "is this: that it did not lead to depression and discouragement, but contributed to lifting the people to the greatest heights of enthusiasm. I believe that the hour will come when the masses in the streets who today stand under our banner, the hooked cross, will unite with those who shot at us on November ninth. I believe this: that blood will not separate us forever. . . . One day the hour will come when the *Reichswehr* will be standing at our side, officers and men."

He touched all the wounds that made patriots squirm and ache for vengeance. The stab in the back. The revolution. Hunger. Marxism. Inflation. The Ruhr. Traitorous Berlin. He rejected the role of defendant and assumed the status of prosecutor. "I accuse Ebert, Scheidemann and company of treason against the Fatherland and of high treason," he said. "I accuse them because they destroyed a people of seventy million . . ."

This, said the presiding judge, was going too far, but Hitler ignored the rebuke, and continued his indictment. He spoke for four hours. When the judge was asked why this was permitted, he said it was impossible to stem the flood of Hitler's oratory. And reporters saw the audience literally moved to tears by the conclusion of his final speech before the court:

"The army we have assembled is growing faster and faster, from day to day, from hour to hour. Now, just in these days, I harbor the proud hope that one day the time will come when these wild bands will swell into battalions, and the battalions into regiments, and the regiments into divisions. The old cockade will be retrieved from the dirt, and the old flags will lead the way again . . ."

He then made a lofty appeal to the judgment of history, which, he said, would pass the final verdict "on the Quartermaster General of the old Army, on his officers and soldiers, who only wanted the best for their folk and Fatherland . . ." Let the present court find him and his comrades guilty of high treason a thousand times, he said; it would make no difference. "With a smile, the goddess of the eternal court of history will tear up the indictment of the prosecutor and the verdict of the judges. For she acquits us."

To this tawdry rhetoric, the country, or much of it, listened with mounting excitement. Newspapers that had never mentioned Hitler and his Nazis before were printing front-page stories of the trial and what Hitler was saying. People who had never heard of him began to cock their ears to catch his words. "How that man Hitler spoke!" said one tradesman, who had been a volunteer in the war. "Those days of his trial became the first days of my faith in Hitler. From that day I had no thought of anyone but Hitler." Many were sure that, at last, a new leader had arisen. "I felt electrified," said a miner, remembering how the word went through the newspapers about a man in Munich who, "aided by a little band of followers," had marched to rid the nation of Red rule, and restore honor to the German people. *"Here was a man of action!"* they said. Impressed by Hitler's defiant stand at the trial, and inspired by his speeches, many made their first contact with the movement and joined the Party. "As though by an explosion," in Hitler's words, "our ideas were hurled over the whole of Germany."

On April 1, 1924, the verdict was handed down. All the accused were found guilty except Ludendorff, who protested that his acquittal was an affront to his uniform. Half daft with crochets and obsessions, Ludendorff faded from history after the trial, an embarrassment to everybody but fellow fanatics. The trial also ended the public careers of Lossow, Seisser and Kahr.*

The maximum penalty for high treason was life imprisonment. Adolf Hitler got the minimum: five years' fortress arrest, which was the most lenient and dignified form of detention. Through the indulgence of the authorities, he was put on probation and served only nine months of his sentence, or a total of thirteen months' imprisonment if the time from arrest to trial is reckoned in.

A curious historical linkage occurred when Hitler entered Landsberg prison. He was given the cell that was being occupied by Anton von Arco-Valley, who was shifted to another prison. It was Arco-Valley who, by murdering Kurt Eisner, began the series of assassinations in postwar Germany, and set off the chain of events that led to the rise of the extremist Right in Bavaria. Historians would one day say that Hitler owed Arco-Valley a debt he could never repay.†

* In 1934, during the so-called Roehm purge, Gustav Ritter von Kahr was found beaten to death in a ditch on the road to Dachau. He was seventy-two. His family was forbidden to wear mourning.

† Hitler was never aware of the debt. In 1933 he had Arco-Valley imprisoned for plotting against him. Arco-Valley survived the war to be run over by an American jeep.

Prison was no more than a comfortable interruption in the career of Adolf Hitler. "You could have opened a flower and fruit stand, and a wine shop, with all the gifts stacked in his cell," Putzi Hanfstaengel noted, and among the donors were Siegfried and Winifred Wagner. The pampered prisoner read voraciously, and afterward referred to jail as "my university at state expense." Right in his cell he dictated to the faithful *Fräulein* Hess the first volume of the astonishing book that would be called "a kind of satanic bible" and into which he poured the turgid torrent of his ideas, dreams, plans, threats and forecasts for Europe and the world. His title for it was: "A Four and One-Half Years Struggle Against Lies, Stupidity, and Cowardice: Settling Accounts With the Destroyers of the National Socialist Movement." His publisher renamed it *Mein Kampf,* and for all its jumble of style and organization, it was an unmistakable warning to the world. It was ignored.

Throughout his book, Hitler did not sound like a provincial agitator, jailed after a humiliating failure, but like a figure of world stature involved in epic achievements. His performance at the trial restored his confidence and inflated it to new proportions. "It was during this incarceration," he said afterward, "that I acquired that fearless faith, that optimism, that confidence in our destiny, which nothing could shake thereafter." In prison he made a drawing of an arch of triumph; and when *Simplicissimus* printed a jeering cartoon of him in knight's armor entering Berlin in triumph on a white horse, he said: "They can laugh, but I shall get there yet."

It was in that spirit that he left Landsberg on December 20, 1924, free again to resume his drive toward power. He was thirty-five years old.

There would not be another *Putsch.* Hitler had learned at the *Feldherrnhalle* that it was fatal to underestimate the power of the state while overestimating his own. Now he would be known, derisively but significantly, as *"Adolfe Légalité."* He would work within the system, using its procedures to gain power over it and then destroy it. He had no doubt in 1924—he was "mathematically certain"—that he could become master of Germany by applying the same methods of mass psychology and the same principles of propaganda he had tested in the Munich beer halls. When the *Putsch* that should have disposed of him for good propelled him, instead, upon his way, he was surer of it than ever.

"Before the march to the *Feldherrnhalle*," he said, "I had seventy or eighty thousand followers. After this march I had two million." Overnight he had won the base to become a national figure. Alfred Rosenberg's way of saying it was apt: "November ninth, 1923, gave birth to January thirtieth, 1933," which was the day Adolf Hitler became Chancellor.

Even after his wild bands had grown into battalions, and the battalions into regiments, and the regiments into divisions of the mightiest army the world had ever seen, he returned every year to Munich to observe the two great days: November eighth at the beer hall and November ninth at the *Feldherrnhalle*. Every year, at the Bürgerbräu, he made a speech to the "old fighters"—the Ludwig Hofmanns, the Karl Kesslers, the Johann Aigners, or those who survived. He told them, "Everything I am I owe to you," or: "This uprising of ours was a seeming failure, but from the victims who fell then came the salvation of Germany. . . . That was when National Socialism began its victory march." And every November ninth he would stage the march all over again, walking behind the holiest relic of the movement, the swastika flag that was stained with blood that day, the sacred *Blutfahne*. The *Putsch* was mystically transformed: it became a religious ceremony, a secular Passion Play. In 1923 it had been a shoddy charade. Now the Nazi bards chanted of "the holiness of the *Feldherrnhalle*," and the "blood of its martyrs" became "the baptismal water of the Third Reich."

The aborted march of 1923 did, after all, turn into the famous *Marsch auf Berlin* that Hitler's early followers had dreamed of. And it took him farther than any conqueror before him had ever gone, making him master from the English Channel to the Black Sea, from the Mediterranean to the Arctic.

What began in the Munich beer hall ended, finally, in an underground bunker in Berlin on April 30, 1945, when he killed himself as he had threatened to do over the failure of his *Putsch* more than twenty years before. Then he had had only nineteen dead on his conscience.

When he swallowed the cyanide in his underground bunker, there were 30,000,000.

THE END

BIBLIOGRAPHICAL NOTES

IN PLACE of the usual marathon listing of every source and reference, which only burdens the reader and seldom enlightens the scholar, I have thought it better to indicate briefly how the materials that go to make up this book were gathered. I went to Munich, examined the locale for myself, visited the Bürgerbräukeller where the *Putsch* began, and walked the route of the march to its end at the *Feldherrn-halle* in Odeon Square. I talked to people in Munich who were living there in 1923, and to eyewitnesses of the events described. For my treatment of the *Putsch,* I have chiefly drawn on participant reports recorded *at the time* or as soon thereafter as possible, memories being notoriously fallible with the passage of time.

The Nazi Party was tireless in assembling, cataloguing and filing away its own history in the minutest detail. Allowing for bias and mythologizing, much valuable on-the-scene and I-was-there material is therefore available to the industrious searcher. I cite the source material on the *Putsch* gathered from the participants themselves by the *Hauptarchiv der NSDAP* and available on microfilm at The Hoover Institution on War, Revolution, and Peace at Stanford, Cal. The Institution has an invaluable collection of source material on the whole period, and I have resorted to it freely.

I have gone elsewhere, as well, for direct reports on the *Putsch* and its period. For instance, Johann Aigner's vivid account of his participation, at the beer hall and on the march, is recorded in his *Als Ordonanz bei Hochverrätern,* an undated typewritten document in the F.J.M. Rehse collection (Box 431) at the Library of Congress.

400

Alfred Rosenberg, the "philosopher" of the Party, was in the front ranks at the *Feldherrnhalle* and tells his story in his *Blut und Ehre* (Zentralverlag der NSDAP, München, 1934) which also contains participant material about the early days of the movement. So do his *Memoirs,* with analytical comment by Serge Lang and Ernst von Schenk (Ziff-Davis, Chicago-New York, 1949.) Ernst Roehm's *Memoiren* (Uranus-Verlag, Saarbrücken, 1934) and *In Angesichts des Galgens* by Hans Frank (Friedrich Alfred Beck Verlag, München-Gräfelding, 1953) are also valuable for their first-person but differing approaches to the period. Books like *Das Buch der NSDAP* (G. Schoenfeld's Verlagsbuchhandlung, Berlin, 1934) and *Rotmord über München* by Rudolf Schricker (Verlag u. Vertriebs-Gesellschaft, Berlin, 1935), though clearly propagandistic and tendentious, are valuable for the speeches, proclamations, leaflets, placards, and period photographs they contain. Similarly, pamphlets and booklets like Manfred von Killinger's *Ernstes und Heiteres aus dem Putschleben* (Zentralverlag NSDAP, written in 1927) and *Deutschlands Erwachen in Bild und Wort* (Verlag Photobericht Hoffmann, München, undated, probably 1924) tell more about the time—its temper, feel and look—than scholarly dissertations.

There is, of course, no lack of scholarly dissertations and treatments, some of them of great interest. I cite Werner Maser's paper prepared for his doctorate at the Friedrich-Alexander University, Erlangen, *Die Organization der Führerlegende* (1954); Ulrich von Hasselbach's *Die Entstehung der NSDAP, 1919–1923,* University of Leipzig (1931); Georg Franz's *Munich: Birthplace and Center of the National Socialist German Workers' Party* in "The Journal of Modern History" (December 1957), and Carl Landauer's excellent two-part study in the same journal (June and September, 1944), *The Bavarian Problem in the Weimar Republic, 1918–1923.*

Ernst Deuerlein's *Hitlers Eintritt in die Politik und die Reichswehr* in "Vierteljahrshefte für Zeitgeschichte" (2. Heft/April 1959) contains riches of fact and information in a little room, but every student of the period is now, and every future student will be, in debt to Dr. Deuerlein for his monumental collection of documents, commentaries, analyses, and reports from police, state, city and private archives, many of them secret when first compiled, on every conceivable aspect of the *Putsch* and its background. The work is called *Der Hitler-Putsch* and was published in 1962 by the Deutsche Verlags-Anstalt, Stuttgart. Dr. Deuerlein has also issued a valuable supplementary volume (Karl Rauch Verlag, Düsseldorf, 1968) whose title explains itself, *Der Aufstieg der NSDAP 1919–1933 in Augenzeugenberichten* ("The Rise of the National Socialist German Workers' Party, 1919–1933, in Eye-Witness Reports.")

Scholarly and richly foot-noted (1006 of them!) is *Der Hitlerputsch* by Hanns Hubert Hofmann (Nymphenburger Verlagshandlung, München, 1961). Though his interpretations are sometimes dubious, Herr Hofmann's accumulation of fact and detail is impressive. So are the fact and detail in Werner Maser's *Die Frühgeschichte der NSDAP: Hitlers Weg bis 1924* (Athenäum Verlag, Frankfurt a/M, 1965) and *Die Hitlerbewegung: Der Ursprung 1919–1922* by Georg Franz-Willig (R. v. Decker's Verlag G. Schenk, Hamburg, 1962.)

The numerous Hitler quotations are taken, for the most part, from *Mein Kampf* and from his early speeches. They are largely my own translations. I consulted particularly the earliest collection of Hitler speeches, *Adolf Hitler: sein Leben, seine Reden,* edited with commentary by Adolf-Viktor Koerber (Deutscher Volksverlag, 1924.) *Es spricht der Führer* gives a number of significant speeches in their context and with commentary by Hildegard von Kotze, Helmut Krausnick and F. A. Krummacher (Sigbert Mohn Verlag, Gütersloh, 1966.) Two illuminating studies of Hitler's early activity as Party orator are Reginald H. Phelps' *Hitler and the Deutsche Arbeiterpartei* in "The American Historical Review" (#68, 1963) and *Hitler als Parteiredner im Jahre 1920* (Vierteljahrhefte für Zeitgeschichte, II, 1962.)

For my picture of Hitler as a person, and in action, I have drawn chiefly on reports of men who were associated with him in the early stages of his life and career: *The Young Hitler I Knew* by August Kubizek (Houghton Mifflin, Boston, 1955); *Unheard Witness* by Ernst Hanfstaengl (Lippincott, Philadelphia, 1957); *I Knew Hitler* by Kurt G. W. Ludecke (Scribner's, New York, 1937); *Hitler and I* by Otto Strasser (Houghton Mifflin, Boston, 1940.); *Hitler Was My Friend* by Heinrich Hoffman (Burke Publishing Co., London, 1955.) Since Konrad Heiden's pioneering *Der Führer* (Lexington Press, New York, 1944) Hitler biographies have proliferated, and so have specialized treatments of various phases of his career, some of which I have used: *Hitler's Youth* by Franz Jetzinger (Hutchinson of London, 1958); *Vienna and the Young Hitler* by William A. Jenks (Columbia University Press, New York, 1960); *Der Mann, der Hitler die*

402

Ideen gab by Wilfried Daim (Isar Verlag, München, 1958). An interesting treatment of the myth-building and cult-making in the Nazi movement is *Der braune Kult* by Hans-Jochen Gamm (Rütten & Loening Verlag, Hamburg, 1962.)

I must express my appreciation to Mrs. Agnes F. Peterson of The Hoover Institution for her intelligent help in unearthing and transmitting valuable material for me, and I owe thanks to the Wiener Library in London for use of its exhaustive collection of materials on the Nazi era. Thanks are also due the Institut für Zeitgeschichte in Munich whose facilities I also used. I express my appreciation to Col. Truman Smith, of Fairfield, Conn., for allowing me to quote his reports and comments on the early Nazi movement prepared when he was attached to the United States embassy in Berlin in the early 1920s. His report is in the Yale University Library where I saw it through the courtesy of Howard B. Gottlieb, Librarian of Historical Manuscripts.

—R.H.

INDEX